THE PRACTICE OF HUMAN I

Human rights are now the dominant appro:
how do human rights work? What do they
studies of human rights work from around the world, this book ......
human rights in practice. It shows how groups and organizations mobilize
human rights language in a variety of local settings, often differently from
those imagined by human rights law itself. The case studies reveal the contradictions and ambiguities of human rights approaches to various forms of
violence. They show that this openness is not a failure of universal human
rights as a coherent legal or ethical framework but an essential element in the
development of living and organic ideas of human rights in context. Studying
human rights in practice means examining the channels of communication
and institutional structures that mediate between global ideas and local
situations.

MARK GOODALE is Assistant Professor of Conflict Analysis and Anthropology
at George Mason University.

SALLY ENGLE MERRY is Professor of Anthropology and Law and Society at
New York University.

THE PRACTICE OF HUMAN RIGHTS

Tracking Law Between the Global and the Local

Editors:
Mark Goodale

and

Sally Engle Merry

CAMBRIDGE
UNIVERSITY PRESS

CAMBRIDGE UNIVERSITY PRESS
Cambridge, New York, Melbourne, Madrid, Cape Town, Singapore,
São Paulo, Delhi, Dubai, Tokyo, Mexico City

Cambridge University Press
The Edinburgh Building, Cambridge CB2 8RU, UK

Published in the United States of America by Cambridge University Press, New York

www.cambridge.org
Information on this title: www.cambridge.org/9780521683784

First published 2007
Reprinted 2008

A catalogue record for this publication is available from the British Library

ISBN 978-0-521-86517-3 Hardback
ISBN 978-0-521-68378-4 Paperback

Contents

Contributors

John G. Dale is Assistant Professor of Sociology at George Mason University where he teaches in the Department of Sociology and Anthropology and Conflict Analysis and Resolution Program. In 2005 he was a National Endowment for the Humanities visiting scholar at Columbia University. He is the author of the forthcoming *Transnational Legal Action: Global Business, Human Rights, and the Free Burma Movement*.

Daniel M. Goldstein is Assistant Professor of Anthropology at Rutgers University. His research focuses on violence, human rights, and popular politics in urban Bolivia, where he is currently studying the competing discourses and practices of security, rights, and democracy with the financial support of the National Science Foundation. With funding from the MacArthur Foundation, he researched and wrote *The Spectacular City: Violence and Performance in Urban Bolivia* (Duke University Press, 2004).

Mark Goodale is Assistant Professor of Conflict Analysis and Anthropology at George Mason University. He is the author of two forthcoming books – *The Anthropology of Human Rights: Critical Explorations in Ethical Theory and Social Practice*, and *Dilemmas of Modernity: Bolivian Encounters with Law and Liberalism*, and coeditor of *Practicing Ethnography in Law: New Dialogues, Enduring Methods*. He was the guest editor of the 2006 special issue of the journal *American Anthropologist* entitled "Anthropology and Human Rights in a New Key."

Jean E. Jackson is Professor of Anthropology at the Massachusetts Institute of Technology. She is the author of *The Fish People: Linguistic Exogamy and Tukanoan Identity in Northwest Amazonia* and coeditor of *Indigenous Movements, Self-Representation and the State in Latin America*. Besides her research and writing on different aspects of Latin American politics, law, and culture, she has also conducted research in medical anthropology, work that led to her book *"Camp Pain": Conversations with Chronic Pain Patients*.

Lauren Leve is Assistant Professor of Religious Studies at the University of North Carolina-Chapel Hill. An anthropologist by training, her research focuses on the intersections between religion, gender, development, law, postcolonial subjectivity and the cultural dynamics of neoliberal globalization, including the current "ethical turn." She is currently completing a book on Theravada Buddhism in Nepal entitled *"Seeing Things as They Are": Ethical Practice, Religious Reform and the Buddhist Art of Living in Transnational Nepal*.

Sally Engle Merry is Professor of Anthropology and Law and Society at New York University. The author of over one hundred articles and reviews on law, anthropology, race and class, conflict resolution, and gender violence, she is past-president of the Law and Society Association and the Association for Political and Legal Anthropology. Her most recent book is *Human Rights and Gender Violence: Translating International Law Into Local Justice* (University of Chicago Press, 2006).

Laura Nader is Professor of Anthropology at the University of California at Berkeley. A member of the American Academy of Arts and Sciences and a recipient of the Kalven Prize from the Law and Society Association for distinguished research on law and society, Professor Nader is the author, most recently, of *The Life of the Law: Anthropological Projects*, and coauthor of the forthcoming *Plunder: The Dark Side of the Rule of Law*.

Balakrishnan Rajagopal is the Ford International Associate Professor of Law and Development and Director of the Program on Human Rights and Justice at the Massachusetts Institute of Technology. He served for many years with the United Nations High Commissioner for Human Rights in Cambodia, and has consulted with UN agencies, international organizations and leading nongovernmental organizations (NGOs) on human rights and international legal issues. He is the author of *International Law from Below: Development, Social Movements and Third World Resistance* (Cambridge: Cambridge University Press, 2003).

Shannon Speed is Assistant Professor of Anthropology at the University of Texas at Austin. Her research interests include human rights, indigenous rights, globalization, gender, social justice and resistance movements, and activist research methods. She is the author of the forthcoming *Global Discourse on the Local Terrain: Human Rights and Indian Resistance* and coeditor of *Dissident Women: Gender and Cultural Politics in Chiapas*.

Kay Warren served on the senior faculties of Princeton University and Harvard University before coming to Brown University, where she is currently the Charles B. Tillinghast Jr. '62 Professor in International Studies and Professor of Anthropology. At Brown she also directs the Politics, Culture, and Identity Program at the Watson Institute for International Studies. Her new work involves a multisited examination of major foreign aid donors and their production of knowledge about the developing world. She is currently working on two books: *Remaking Transnationalism: Japan, Foreign Aid, and the Search for Global Solutions*, coedited with David Leheny, and *Human Trafficking and Transnationalism: Global Solutions, Local Realities*.

Sari Wastell is Lecturer in Anthropology at Goldsmiths College, University of London. She has done research in Swaziland since 1997 on the legal, political, and social dimensions of divine kingship. She is the author of *Kingship and Custom: Law, Knowledge, and Sovereignty in an African Polity*, and one of the editors of *Thinking Through Things*.

Richard A. Wilson is the Gladstein Distinguished Chair of Human Rights and Professor of Anthropology and Director of the Human Rights Institute at the University of Connecticut. He is the author of *Maya Resurgence in Guatemala* (1995) and *The Politics of Truth and Reconciliation in South Africa* (2001). He has edited or coedited five books, including *Human Rights, Culture and Context* (1997), *Culture and Rights* (2001), *Human Rights in Global Perspective* (2003) and, most recently, *Human Rights in the "War on Terror"* (2005).

Acknowledgments

This book is in many ways a collaborative project. It began as a panel at the 2005 American Anthropological Association (AAA) meetings and continued through a second conference and ongoing conversations among the authors and editors. We have all learned from each other as we have worked to define and develop a critical study of human rights practices. In this process, we benefited from the insights of two scholars whose work did not, for various reasons, ultimately appear in the volume. David Nugent gave a paper and Ulf Hannerz a commentary at the AAA meetings. The second phase of the project was a wonderful conference and retreat that offered an opportunity for extended discussion and commentary on most of the papers included in the final volume. Again, Ulf Hannerz was an important contributor at this second meeting.

We would like to thank the Margaret MacVicar Faculty Fellows Program at the Massachusetts Institute of Technology, whose appointment of Jean Jackson as a Fellow provided the funding for the book's contributors to meet for three very congenial days in Chatham, Cape Cod in June 2005. We were able to discuss ideas, refine the book's internal structure and goals, and enjoy some beautiful weather and good cheer. We are very grateful to Jean Jackson for proposing this second meeting and for her generous support of the project.

We are appreciative of all we have learned from both anthropologists and other scholars, and activists in the field of human rights. Sally is grateful for a year as a Fellow at the Carr Center for Human Rights Policy at the Kennedy School at Harvard and for her ongoing contact with the Center for Human Rights and Global Justice at New York University School of Law. Her research on human rights has been generously supported by two grants from the Law and Social Sciences Program of the National Science Foundation. Mark would like to acknowledge the support of the National Science Foundation, the Organization of American States, and different internal grant programs at George Mason University, which have supported his research in Bolivia. Funding for his broader research and theorizing on human rights has been made possible by a Fulbright scholarship and the Irmgard Coninx Foundation.

For Sally, working with Mark Goodale has been intellectually rewarding and stimulating. He has been a terrific coeditor, helping her to think through new problems and keeping on top of deadlines. Sally appreciates the perspective he brings to the field of human rights, both philosophical and anthropological, and his leadership in promoting an anthropological approach to the practice of human rights. Mark would like to thank Sally for her deep wisdom and patience as this book project took shape and evolved through its different stages. As always, Sally was as much a guide and source of inspiration as she was a collaborator.

Finally, Mark wishes to acknowledge the sustaining presence of his family – Romana, Dara, and Isaiah. Sally is grateful for the continuing support of her husband Paul and daughter Sarah.

LOCATING RIGHTS, ENVISIONING LAW BETWEEN THE GLOBAL AND THE LOCAL

Mark Goodale

In January 2002 Fiji presented its first ever country report to the United Nations committee charged with monitoring compliance with the Convention on the Elimination of All Forms of Discrimination Against Women (CEDAW). One of the most controversial sections of the report addressed the use of the practice of *bulubulu*, or village reconciliation, in cases of rape. During the public presentation of the report in New York City by Fiji's Assistant Minister for Women, the nuances of *bulubulu* as a sociolegal practice in postcolonial Fiji were obscured within what quickly became complicated layers of political miscommunication, the imperatives of a surging Fijian nationalism, and, as always, the politicization of culture. On the one hand, the CEDAW committee, though staffed by members from a range of different countries, was required by its UN mandate to fulfill a fairly simple task: to decide whether individual countries were taking the requirements of CEDAW seriously, as measured by national self-assessments of violence against women and official responses to this violence. But, on the other hand, because CEDAW expresses both the conceptual and practical constraints of universal human rights discourse, the UN committee was prevented from considering the social contexts within which *bulubulu* functions in Fiji. To open up the possibility that CEDAW's requirements for defining, preventing, and redressing violence against women were contingent upon their correspondence with circumstance, tradition, or instrumental efficacy would be to deracinate CEDAW, to destroy its potential as one key component in a still-emergent international human rights system. As Sally Engle

1

Merry explains, in her multinational study of CEDAW practices, "it is of course impossible to understand the complexities of the operation of a particular custom when a committee is dealing with eight different countries in two weeks. One cannot expect committee members to spend a month reading the anthropological literature and two weeks interviewing Fijians in order to determine the meaning of a custom" (2006: 118).

Similarly, Maya Unnithan-Kumar (2003) has written about the ways in which national discourses of women's health and development in India have been transformed over the last fifteen years by human rights activism, which has led to a shift in the way issues of fertility control and health planning are articulated and understood. After the 1994 UN International Conference on Population and Development, family planning programs in India, which had been directed toward reducing or controlling childbirths as part of earlier health and economic policies, were deemphasized in favor of a policy of contraceptive choice, which reflected the fact that "the enjoyment of sexuality" (2003: 187) had been singled out as a human right at the 1994 UN meeting in Cairo. Yet even though Indian feminists were successful in shifting the terms of the debate over reproductive health and sexuality from the "problem of childbirth" to reproductive choice as a human right, the Indian government was faced with the challenge of reconciling preexisting material, political, and cultural realities with the new discourse of "consumer choice," as Unnithan-Kumar (2003: 188) revealingly describes the way human rights language reinscribed the question of women's sexuality through the metaphor of the market.

And finally, since 1999 Bolivia has been shaken by a series of social movements that have toppled two elected presidents and have put the entire foundation of Bolivia's neoliberal restructuring in jeopardy. A key dimension to these waves of social upheavals has been the reframing of a set of very old social grievances by the nation's indigenous majority as rights claims within one of several human rights frameworks. The opposition political party with the most support by the loose coalition of indigenous groups has been the *Movimimento al Socialismo* (MAS) party (Movement Towards Socialist Party), led by Evo Morales, the leading voice of Bolivia's coca growers. Although Morales is typically described as leftist or left-leaning by the international media, in fact his party employs a hybrid rhetoric that combines old-line Marxist (or neo-Marxist) categories and imagery with an entirely different – and much more recent – language of human rights in order to locate Bolivian struggles over natural resources, land, and political representation within broader regional and transnational indigenous rights movements (Goodale 2006c, 2008). This normative hybridity creates awkward moments for MAS: the vision of a more equal and just Bolivia, in which indigenous people control – by force, if necessary – a greater share of the nation's wealth, coexists uneasily with a vision of Bolivia as a nation of human rights-bearing modern subjects, who demand legal and political institutions that will enforce the different international human rights provisions that have been adopted within national law.

What makes these three vignettes from the recent research on human rights practices so revealing is both what they tell us, and don't tell us. They demonstrate that the human rights regimes that have emerged over the last fifteen years increasingly coexist with alternative, and at times competing, normative frameworks that have also been given new impetus since the end of the Cold War. Eleanor Roosevelt, the chair of the inaugural United Nations Commission on Human Rights, had hoped that a "curious grapevine" would eventually carry the idea of human rights into every corner of the world, so that the dizzying – and regressive – diversity of rule-systems would be replaced by the exalted normative framework expressed through the 1948 Universal Declaration of Human Rights. In fact, the curious grapevine of non-state and transnational actors did emerge in the way Roosevelt anticipated, but the resulting networks have been conduits for normativities in addition to human rights. Ideas, institutional practices, and policies justified through a range of distinct frameworks and assumptions – social justice, economic redistribution, human capabilities, citizen security, religious law, neo-laissez faire economics, and so on – come together at the same time within the transnational spaces through which the endemic social problems of our times are increasingly addressed. Yet even though the humanitarian goals of different international or transnational actors – the eradication of poverty, the elimination of discrimination against women, the protection of indigenous populations against exploitation by multinational corporations – might be fairly straightforward in principle, the emergence of different means through which these goals are met has created a transnational normative pluralism whose full effects and meanings are still unclear. Even so, there has been at least one effect that is clear: human rights have become decentered and their status remains as "unsettled" as ever, as Sarat and Kearns (2002) have rightly argued.

These excerpts from the recent study of human rights also show that the *practice* of human rights is more complicated than previously thought. This complexity is partly the result of the challenges associated with conducting empirical research on dynamic and, at times, illusive transnational processes. But, even more important, the study of human rights suggests that the "practice" that is being documented and analyzed has the potential to transform the framework through which the idea of human rights itself is understood. This is because the recent research on human rights, much of it carried out by anthropologists and others committed to the techniques of ethnography, suggests an alternative to the dominant modes of inquiry within which human rights has been conceptualized over the last fifty years. To study the practice of human rights is, in part, to make an argument for a different philosophy of human rights, what we can loosely describe as an *anthropological* philosophy of human rights.

And, perhaps most consequentially, these three windows into contemporary human rights practices illustrate the poverty of theory through which transnational processes have been conceptualized, explained, and located in time and space. The emergence of contemporary human rights regimes over the last fifteen years quickly strained the capacity of existing social theoretical frameworks to explain different problems: how human rights relate to other transnational normativities; the relationship between the epistemology of human rights practices and the social ontologies in which they are necessarily embedded; the disjuncture between the universalism which anchors the idea of human rights conceptually, and the more modest scales in which social actors across the range envision human rights as part of preexisting legal and ethical configurations; the relationship between human rights regimes and other transnational assemblages that structure relations of – especially economic – production; the impact of human rights discourse on alignments of political, economic, and other forms of power, alignments which predated the rise of the international human rights system in 1948 and which are motivated by an entirely different set of ideological and practical imperatives; and so on. The social theoretical literature that has emerged over the last fifteen years as a response to problems that are related to these has proven to be, while not exactly an orrery of errors (with apologies to E. P. Thompson), at the very least a problematic source of analytical guidance for those interested in making conceptual sense out of human rights practice and drawing out the broader implications for the study of transnational processes more generally. The mountain of writings that examines the nuances of "globalization," the relationship between the global and the local, the emergence of new world orders or new sovereignties, the withering away of culture and the rise of global ethnoscapes, even the more promising move to envision transnational processes through network analysis, all fail, in one way or another, to capture the social and conceptual complexities documented by the recent study of human rights practices.

This volume represents a different response to this social and conceptual complexity. Through the eight chapters and four critical commentaries, the volume is intended to speak innovatively to key problems in both human rights studies and the broader study of transnational processes. Although each of the authors, in one form or another, draws from anthropological forms of knowledge in order to develop one or more of book's main themes, the volume is not directed toward theoretical debates within any one academic discipline. The book is essentially interdisciplinary and expresses what I have described elsewhere (Goodale 2006a) as an ecumenical approach to the meanings and practices associated with human rights. Besides anthropology (Goldstein, Jackson, Merry, Nader, Speed, Wastell, Wilson), the authors come to the project from professional bases in conflict studies (Goodale), religious studies (Leve), sociology (Dale), international studies (Warren), and international law (Rajagopal). This ecumenism is critical for the study and analysis of human rights, whose claims are projected across the broadest of analytical and phenomenological boundaries, but whose meanings are constituted most importantly by a range of social actors – cosmopolitan elites, government bureaucrats, peasant and other organic intellectuals, transnational nongovernmental organizations (NGOs) and their national collaborators – within the disarticulated practices of everyday life.

THE DIFFERENT MEANINGS OF HUMAN RIGHTS

Before moving on to describe the book's main themes in more detail, it is necessary to consider the question of what human rights are and to locate this volume in relation to the different approaches to this question, which entail, as will be seen, much more than semantic or academic distinctions.[1] These different orientations to the problem of human rights as a normative category can be usefully placed on a spectrum of degrees of expansiveness. At one end of the spectrum, the restricted one, are the different variations of the view that "human rights" refers to the body of international law that emerged in the wake of the 1948 Universal Declaration of Human Rights and follow-on instruments. These different variations all express a broadly *legal* understanding of human rights. Although the legal approach to human rights is itself fragmentary and internally diverse – for example, some argue that human rights must be enforceable in order to be considered human rights, while others avoid the problem of enforceability – there are some important commonalities: the idea of human rights must be legislated, legally recognized, and codified before it can be taken seriously as part of the law of nations. The political scientist Alison Brysk, in the introduction to her edited volume *Globalization and Human Rights*, expresses the legal approach to human rights:

> Human rights are a set of universal claims to safeguard human dignity from illegitimate coercion, typically enacted by state agents. These norms are codified in a widely endorsed set of international undertakings: the "International Bill of Human Rights" (Universal Declaration of Human Rights, International Covenant on Civil and Political Rights, and International Covenant on Social and Economic Rights); phenomenon-specific treaties on war crimes (Geneva Conventions), genocide, and torture; and protections for vulnerable groups such as the UN Convention on the Rights of the Child and the Convention on the Elimination of Discrimination against Women [sic].[2]
>
> (Brysk 2002: 3).

---

[1] It is actually quite surprising how rarely studies of human rights take the time to explain how, in fact, "human rights" is being used. Within the voluminous human rights literature it is much more common that the intended meaning of human rights is kept implicit, or allowed to emerge in context without formally addressing this issue analytically. While a contextual strategy has much to recommend it – in particular, it suggests that the answer to the question "what is human rights?" is itself contextual – it is also possible that in taking the meaning of human rights for granted, when it is in fact highly contested, a certain opacity has crept into the literature. Different analyses or arguments come to be marked by the disciplinary orientations from which they emerge, when what is desired is an approach to this most encompassing of topics that transcends (or unifies) the many different academic and political traditions.

[2] Both the 1979 UN Convention on the Elimination of All Forms of Discrimination Against Women, and the Committee on the Elimination of Discrimination Against Women, which is authorized in Article 17 of the Convention to monitor compliance by "States parties," are at various times referred to with the acronym CEDAW, even though this usage was originally meant to refer to the Convention.

A somewhat more expansive orientation to the problem of what human rights are moves away from international legal instruments and texts to consider the ways in which the *concept* of human rights – which is also expressed through instruments like the Universal Declaration, but not, on this view, circumscribed by them – is itself normative. This is very much an analytical normativity, one that describes the ways in which the concept of human rights in itself establishes particular rules for behavior and prohibits others. Jack Donnelley, for example, who is a ubiquitous presence in human rights studies, occupies this middle location on the spectrum of degrees of expansiveness. As he explains (2003: 10), "[h]uman rights are, literally, the rights that one has simply because one is a human being" (i.e., completely apart from any recognition of these rights in positive international law). Having articulated the concept of human rights as clearly and axiomatically as possibly, Donnelly then goes on to deduce what are, in effect, logical corollaries to this first principle:

> Human rights are *equal* rights: one either is or is not a human being, and therefore has the same human rights as everyone else (or none at all). They are also *inalienable* rights: one cannot stop being human, no matter how badly one behaves nor how barbarously one is treated. And they are *universal* rights, in the sense that today we consider all members of the species *Homo sapiens* "human beings," and thus holders of human rights.
>
> (2003: 10; emphases in original)

This approach to the question of what human rights are, which, as Donnelly acknowledges, could be described as "conceptual, analytic, or formal" (2003: 16),[3] is also concerned with the ways in which the normativity of the human rights concept configures or shapes – again analytically, not empirically – the *concept* of the individual (not particular individuals in any one place or time). Through human rights, "individuals [are constituted] as a particular kind of political subject" (2003: 16). By making the constitution – even in the abstract – of the political (and legal) subject a basic part of the definition of human rights, this midpoint approach moves well beyond the legal positivism of human rights instrumentalists and, at least theoretically, broadens the normative category "human rights" to include both the norms themselves and the subjects through which they are expressed.

---

[3] Elsewhere (2003: 17) Donnelly describes his approach to the question of human rights as "substantively thin" and argues that the "emptiness" of his conceptual orientation is "one of its greatest attractions."

At the other end of the spectrum, the question of what human rights are is answered by treating human rights as one among several consequential transnational discourses.[4] Upendra Baxi expresses this mode well when he begins his important and wide-ranging critique of human rights by describing the object of this study as those "protean forms of social action assembled, by convention, under a portal named 'human rights.'" (2002: v). As can be imagined, the *discursive approach* to human rights is itself internally diverse. But, despite this diversity, there are several features that mark this orientation as the most expansive framework within which "human rights" is conceptualized, studied, and understood. First, the discursive approach to human rights radically decenters international human rights law. Legal instruments like the Universal Declaration, or legal arenas like the International Criminal Court (ICC), are seen as simply different nodes within the power/knowledge nexus through which human rights emerges in social practice. Second, the discursive orientation makes human rights normativity itself a key category for analysis. This does not mean that human rights is simply studied or analyzed *as* norms; rather, normativity is understood as the means through which the idea of human rights becomes discursive, the process that renders human rights into social knowledge that shapes social action. Third, the study of human rights as discourse reveals the ways in which actors embrace the idea of human rights in part because of its visionary capacity, the way it expresses both the normative and the aspirational. Finally, to conceptualize human rights as one among several key transnational discourses is to elevate social practice as both an analytical and methodological category. Despite the nod that the several strands of social or critical theory make toward practice, praxis, or agency within their broader studies of discourse, in fact the actual consideration of social practices more likely than not remains prospective, or merely categorical. In contrast, discursive approaches to human rights assume that social practice is, in part, constitutive of the idea of human rights itself, rather than simply the testing ground on which the idea of universal human

---

[4] "Discourse" is employed at this end of the spectrum with vaguely poststructuralist resonances to refer to the institutional, historical, political, and social formations through which knowledge (and power) is constituted in practice. The many dimensions of language are of course key parts of human rights discourse, especially since the *word* – as embodied most clearly by the text of the Universal Declaration – plays an essential role in expressing the idea of human rights; but the notion of human rights discourse goes well beyond language to include the full range of social knowledge regimes through which human rights emerges in social practice.

encounters actual ethical or legal systems. As we will see, this assumption has far-reaching implications for the way the practice of human rights is studied and conceptualized.

Although the chapters and critical commentaries here do not express a unified response to the question of what human rights are,[5] it is accurate enough to say that the volume would fit quite comfortably somewhere on the expansiveness spectrum between the conceptual approach of Donnelly and the broadly discursive orientation of Baxi. Even though many international lawyers and human rights activists – in particular – would consider the open and critical discursive approach to human rights either hopelessly vague, or ethically questionable (or both),[6] there is no doubt that scholars of human rights practices have demonstrated the usefulness in understanding "human rights" beyond the narrow confines of international law. As will be seen throughout the chapters, perhaps the most important consequence to reconceptualizing human rights as discourse is the fact that the *idea* of human rights

---

[5] A perhaps minor point within human rights studies is the problem of whether one uses human rights in the singular or plural. The plural is much more common, at least for US-based writers and analysts, and for international agencies like the United Nations. This last is not surprising given the fact that the plural is most appropriate for those for whom "human rights" refers to the rights enumerated in international law (the legal approach), or those who argue that human rights are rights that all humans have simply by being human (the conceptual approach). But if by "human rights" one is referring to a consequential transnational *discourse*, then it is more grammatically correct to use the singular: "human rights is . . ." Thus controlling for grammatically slippage or error, one signals one's orientation to the question of what human rights are/is through the form of the verb "to be." The matter – to give this point, as I have said, perhaps more importance than it deserves – becomes more complicated in English as between the American and British idioms, because British scholars adopt the singular form of "to be" much more frequently, so it is difficult to know (without context) whether a British writer on human rights is signaling allegiance to the discursive approach, or merely respecting British language usage, when she writes "human rights is . . ."

[6] I was reminded recently just how unethical the discursive or critical approach to human rights is considered during a graduate seminar on "human rights in comparative perspective." One graduate student – from a former Soviet bloc country – finally lost all patience with the ongoing discussion of problems within contemporary human rights. The student chastised me for subjecting any part of human rights to critical scrutiny and accused me of possibly weakening a normative framework that was clearly fragile to begin with. In the student's quite emotional reaction, one detected a peculiar – if perfectly understandable – ethical syllogism at work. If the official ontology expressed through the Universal Declaration is accepted – and people do, in fact, *have* human rights in that way – then critical scrutiny that calls this ontology into question can only be a modern kind of scholasticism: the pursuit of abstract analysis for its own sake. But here's the difference: to engage in intellectual casuistry in the area of human rights is to potentially damage or confuse the only transcendent moral fact – that we all have human rights by virtue of a common human nature or humanness – and thus to indirectly play a role in ongoing or future violations of these human rights. This is why many human rights activists – in particular – have reacted with more than simple incredulity at the emergence of a critical human rights literature over the last fifteen years, the same period that has provided an opening for greater human rights protection and enforcement.

is reinscribed back into all the many social practices in which it emerges. This inverts the dominant understanding, in which the idea of human rights refers to certain facts about human nature, and the normative implications of these facts, in a way that makes the practice of human rights of either secondary importance, or irrelevant. There are troubling implications to deriving the idea – or ideas – of human rights from human rights practice, including implications for the legitimacy of human rights, the epistemology through which they are known (and knowable), and their putative universality.[7] But, despite these complications, it makes no sense either to conceptually divide the idea (or philosophy) of human rights from the practice of human rights (and then exclude the latter from the category "human rights"), or to argue that one should only be concerned with the expression of the idea of human rights through international law, especially since at present international human rights law plays such a demonstrably small part in the total normative universe within which human rights is expressed and encountered.[8]

HUMAN RIGHTS BETWEEN THE GLOBAL AND THE LOCAL

The idea of human rights in its dominant register – the one expressed through instruments like the Universal Declaration – *assumes* the most global of facts: that all human beings are essentially the same, and that this essential sameness entails a set of rights, rights which might (or might not) be correctly enumerated in the main body of international human rights law. I underscore "assumes" because as a matter of philosophy – or perhaps logic – there is no question that to articulate the idea of human rights in

[7] I draw a distinction here between *universality* and *universalism*. The first refers to an assertion about – in this case – human rights ontology: that human rights are, in fact, universal, meaning coextensive with the fact of humanness itself. (Obviously universality in this sense does not only apply to human rights.) Universalism, however, is quite different. This *should be* used to refer to the range of social practices, legalities, political systems, and so on, that emerge *in relation to* universality. Universalism can be understood, in part, as the ideology of universality. Thus, as I have argued recently in a collection of essays on the anthropology of human rights (Goodale 2006b, 2007), the study of human rights practices is, in part, the study of *universalism*.

[8] To describe international human rights law in this way is to evaluate what can be said empirically: that human rights exerts a normative influence, provokes shifts in identity and consciousness, operates instrumentally by altering political configurations or calculations, and so on, apart from any connection to actual legal codes or instruments. Nevertheless, when present, human rights expressed through, or as, law assumes a different – and more specific – kind of influence (or power, see my chapter this volume) that can be as consequential as it is (so far) uncommon.

this way is to assert a first principle, one which is formally unproven, and which is, most likely, unprovable, if by proof we insist on empirical evidence. What follows from this first principle is the list of human rights themselves, which are also not discovered or justified inductively, but are rather "proven" through a process that is in large part deductive.

In other words, I am arguing here that the contemporary idea of human rights was – and continues to be – articulated through a form of reasoning that is both rational and essentially deductive: part Descartes and part Thomas Aquinas. Social scientists with empiricists like Francis Bacon or Jeremy Bentham for intellectual ancestors would not recognize the form of proof that justifies human rights. Bentham rejected the possibility of natural law (and, *a fortiori*, natural rights) for precisely this reason. Nevertheless, it is important to note that deductive proof was for centuries – and continues to be, by mathematicians, theologians, and others – considered the best kind of proof for something, if it was available. The trick for deductivists, in human rights philosophy as elsewhere, is in finding a basis of legitimacy for the first unproven principle, the linchpin upon which every other part of the system is based. In human rights there are several unproven first principles actually: common humanness as a moral quality (rather than simply a biological fact); the assertion that this essential humanness entails a particular normative framework; and that this normative framework is expressed through rights.

But to say that the idea of human rights is global from a conceptual or philosophical perspective is both to state the obvious and to make a point that is of only marginal importance for anthropologists and others who study human rights as a key contemporary transnational discourse. And, even more, the fact that the idea of human rights is global in the abstract has misled some into assuming that human rights practices do – or should – unfold at a much broader scale than they in fact do. In other words, there is a significant difference in this case between the conceptual scale within which the idea of human rights in its major form must be understood – the global, or universal, these are essentially the same for our purposes – and the scale within which human rights is encountered in practice. This difference has made it a difficult theoretical task, among other things, to account for the different dimensions of contemporary human rights discourse in a way that does not spiral into the regress of particularism that often characterizes accounts of human rights practice. Moreover, to speak of scale is to adopt a spatial metaphor in order to locate human rights discourse as a set of complicated social and ethical knowledge practices that appear in discrete places at discrete time with enough autonomy that they can be isolated analytically and studied in what is often described as their "local context."

Yet it is not at all clear, as the chapters in this volume show, that spatial metaphors are the best ordering principles for these analytical tasks. Some, like Annelise Riles (2000, 2004), have suggested that the virtuality and disembodiedness of human rights networks mean that the pursuit of human rights ontologies is futile; rather, the networks themselves are no more – but no less – than the sum total of all the legal and technocratic knowledge practices that constitute them. Others, especially those who adopt a non-discursive or legal approach to human rights (e.g., Alston 2000, 2006; Likosky 2005; Provost 2005), pursue what could be understood as a hyper-spatial framework: certain key locations and artifacts take on added significance as the places where human rights are expressed, all of which, added together, constitute the human rights system. Meetings of human rights activists, international legal forums, headquarters of transnational human rights NGOs, are all semi-sacred places where human rights norms are generated; but this hyper-spatiality is also reflected in the way major human rights documents are understood. The four corners of a foundational text like the Universal Declaration circumscribe an actual normative space, where the particular words used, the internal statutory architecture, and the language the document is written in are reified and invested with a kind of norm-generating autonomy.

The approach to the problem of how and where to locate contemporary human rights discourse that we develop in this volume attempts to strike something of a balance between the non-spatial (i.e., epistemological) and hyper-spatial extremes. Given the fact that human rights discourse has become increasingly transnational over the last fifteen years through the efforts of a range of actors whose work interconnects horizontally beyond the territorial boundaries of nation-states, there is no question that to reify these interconnections through spatial models is to impose an analytical structure that cannot account for the actual dynamism and temporality of human rights practice. Yet the notion of scale, as several chapters here show, is embedded in the idea of human rights itself (universality) and a feature of human rights that serves as an ordering principle in practice (universalism). Conversely, the virtuality, temporality, and transnationalism of human rights discourse suggest that the technocratic, legal, and other forms of knowledge through which the idea of human rights is translated or vernacularized, as Sally Engle Merry has recently shown (Merry 2005),[9] *are* constitutive, yet constitutive not of a discrete system or permanent network, but only the continually emergent collection of knowledge practices themselves. But to treat the study of human rights practices as merely a problem of comparative epistemology, as an example of competing knowledge practices that come together within complicated "global assemblages" (Ong and Collier 2005) of power, culture, and politics, is to ignore a key fact about human rights discourse: that the sites where human rights unfold in practice do matter, and that these sites are not simply nodes in a virtual network, but actual *places* in social space, places which can become law-like and coercive. How to characterize these sites, and where these places are in social space, are questions which this volume, in part, seeks to answer. But for now it is enough to recognize that the study and understanding of human rights require a reconceptualization of *both* the role of knowledge practices and the related problems of scale and location.

Global/local and other binaries

To recognize that the study of contemporary human rights practice requires a reframing of these ontological and epistemological problems through empirical research is to bring us only so far.[10] This is because

---

[9] In both her recent work and in an article that is part of a collection of essays on different problems in the anthropology of human rights (Merry 2006), Merry offers what is perhaps the most nuanced theoretical framework for understanding what actually happens when the idea (or ideas) of human rights is translated into the terms through which the idea becomes meaningful in different cultural, political, and legal contexts. It was not enough, as Merry soon discovered, to describe these processes through one or two different distinctions (vernacularization, appropriation, etc.). Instead, she found that her ethnographic data suggested a number of different categories of social practice and that these categories could explain the range of *possible* encounters with transnational human rights discourse, which means that she has developed a theory of human rights practice that is, to a certain extent, predictive.

[10] Indeed, this recognition is far from academic, although scholars do play an important role in pursuing new orientations to all of the different problems in contemporary human rights theory and practice. Recently, for example, the chief prosecutor of the ICC has enlisted the assistance of academics in developing the conceptual framework within which the ICC can carry out its responsibilities under a very general legal mandate. At a recent workshop at George Mason University's Institute for Conflict Analysis and Resolution, Chief Prosecutor Luis Moreno-Ocampo asked a diverse group of faculty and students to consider the relationship between human rights and the Court's mandate to undertake prosecutions in the interests of justice, the relationship between peace, justice, and human rights, and the problems of culture and traditional justice and their impact on international legal proceedings, among other issues that required critical and practical attention. Moreover, I recently attended a series of international conferences in Germany (October 2005, April 2006) entitled "reframing human rights," which brought together human rights activists from around the world with mostly European and American academics. The activists were, by and large, even more insistent than the academics that human rights – understood broadly – were ripe for conceptual reframing.

there are no obvious sources of theoretical guidance which can respond to the need to reframe these problems that are not problematic in yet different and, in some cases, much more serious ways. The most obvious difficulties are created when we consider the usefulness of the broad and interdisciplinary body of social theory that frames problems of space and social knowledge as more specific instances of the general problem of the relation between the global and its antithesis, the local. It is perhaps impossible to say when the global/local dichotomy emerged as the most common theoretical framing device for describing social processes that span multiple boundaries, but it is likely that this model emerged over the last fifteen years as a way of conceptualizing processes that were first included within the category "globalization." The global/local social theoretical literature is indeed voluminous, with endless debates revolving around different arguments for how these two levels relate to each other in terms of power, economic importance, ontological priority, and so on. But regardless of the approach, the global/local model for understanding widespread social processes has certain features in common.

First, and most obviously, it assumes that there are only two levels at which these social processes emerge or unfold, despite the many different arguments – which can be either empirical or normative – about how these levels relate to each other. Second, the global/local model is based on an entirely vertical spatial metaphor, with the local level at the bottom and the global at the top. This verticality is present in every analysis that describes particular processes "from below" or "from above." An exception to this scalar verticality is when the invocation of "below" or "above" is clearly not meant to be a spatial metaphor, but represents a critique of existing political or legal paradigms. A good example of this usage is Balakrishnan Rajagopal's *International Law from Below*, in which his use of "below" alludes to excluded and marginalized voices within dominant international law frameworks. And there is also a methodological argument in Rajagopal's rereading of international law from below: because the structure of dominant international law discourses – like human rights – masks certain forms of what he calls "economic violence" (2003: 231), it is necessary to expose this violence by studying actual social practices through ethnographic and other form of close engagement.

Third, the global/local framework is dialectical in the most formal of senses. Regardless of how a particular analysis describes the relation between the global and local levels, it is always locked in a Hegelian embrace in which the global and the local interact conceptually through the dynamic movement of people, cultural trends, economic goods and services, and so on, all tending toward some "new world order" (Slaughter 2004) or period of "global/local times" (Wilson and Dissanayake 1996). In other words, the global/local model is – perhaps unintentionally in many cases – teleological (and perhaps utopian). Moreover, the dialecticism of the global/local model is actually considered one of its chief advantages by scholars who employ it, in that it serves to clear up confusion and provide a window into deeper social forces. As Cvetkovich and Keller explain:

> [d]ichotomies, such as those between the global and the local, express contradictions and tensions between crucial constitutive forces of the present moment; consequently, it is a mistake to overlook focus [sic] on one side in favor of exclusive concern with the other (rejecting the local and particularity, for instance, in favor of exclusive concern with the global, or rejecting the global and all macrostructures for exclusive concern with the local). Our challenge is to think through the relationship between the global and the local by observing how global forces influence and even structure even more local situations and even more strikingly.
>
> (1997: 1–2)

Fourth, to explain transboundary social processes like human rights discourse in part by "articulating the global and the local" (Cvetkovich and Kellner 1997) is to both reify and then anthropomorphize what are at best social-theoretical categories of questionable utility. The mountain of literature within the global/local cottage industry – irrespective of perspective or points of emphasis – treats these levels (1) as if they had an independent empirical existence apart from their invocation by scholars and others, and (2) describes them in a such a way that they appear almost as social actors in their own right, moving through real political and social time and space.

And finally (this is not an exhaustive list), most studies that adopt the global/local framework are internally contradictory or, at best, analytically confusing. This confusion is particularly acute for social scientists and others whose analyses are based on – or at least associated with – actual social processes that unfold across different boundaries but which cannot be easily fitted into one of the two sides in the global/local binary. The contradictoriness of this approach is perhaps most marked in the cultural studies literature, so that authors like Wilson and Dissanayake (1996: 6) can rail against the "'binary machine' logic sustaining the dominant discourses of social science or political economy" and the "by-now-tired modernist binary of the universal (global) sublating the particular (local)," while at the same time not only adopting the global/local binary themselves, but, even more, giving it a kind of theoretical normativity indicated by the Foucauldian forward slash. This widely-cited work on the relationship between the global and the local is also analytically disoriented in the way it reinscribes transnationalism – which *is* a useful ordering principle – as just another "spatial dialectic." And confusion is further produced by a prevailing and theoretically precious cultural studies idiom, when what is needed (at least by social scientists) is social analysis that adheres to some semblance of analytical rigor and which is embedded in actual research data on social practice.[11]

All of this – and more – means that most of the theorizing within the global/local framework is simply irrelevant for helping us to understand the spatial and epistemological dimensions of transnational human rights practices. This is also true of much of the equally voluminous globalization literature, which suffers from many of the same problems, but which adds to them by overprivileging the "global" as a socio-political frame reference at the expense of the "local," which, no matter how misleadingly conceived within global/local studies, at least has the advantage of gesturing toward sites of social practice whenever it is invoked. But as a recent study of the "globalization of human rights" (Coicaud, Doyle, and Gardner 2003), shows, there is an unfortunate tendency for analyses of *conceptually* global categories like human rights to devolve into an analytical globalism, in which "global justice," "global institutions," "global accountability," and so on, are treated as if they were empirical descriptions rather than political goals, or moral ideals of particular institutions or individuals, or categorical or theoretical possibilities. And actual human rights practices which, as the chapters in this book demonstrate, unfold transnationally through concrete encounters in particular places and times, are elided as what is described as the "local" in global/local studies is replaced by

---

[11] A typical example of this preciousness: "[w]hat we would variously track as the 'transnational imaginary' comprises the *as-yet-unfigured* horizon of contemporary cultural production by which national spaces/identities of political allegiance and economic regulation are being undone and imagined communities of modernity are being reshaped at the macropolitical (global) and micropolitical (cultural) levels of everyday existence" (Wilson and Dissanayake 1996: 6; emphasis in original).

the "construction of human rights at the domestic level" (Coicaud, Doyle, and Gardner 2003: 22).[12]

A variation on the globalization approach to what are complicated transnational social processes can be seen in studies of human rights that reframe the global/local dichotomy in terms of relations between the international and domestic (or national) levels of norms and political action. This is a common framework for international lawyers and political scientists, for whom the relationship between states within the Westphalian system (international), and the relationships within states (domestic or national), more or less structure the way questions can be asked and answered. The relationships within and between these two levels – the international and domestic – are most often analyzed in terms of different and shifting power dynamics, which leads to studies of human rights that simply refract the binary approach through a realist prism. The results are useful in their own terms and represent a certain advance, if one is interested in what is actually a quite limited corner of the total universe of human rights discourse – that is, the relationship between "international human rights norms and domestic change" (Risse, Ropp, and Sikkink 1999) – but studies of the "socialization of international human rights norms into domestic practices" (Risse and Sikkink 1999) (again, where "domestic" means "national") cannot begin to shed light on the full range of human rights practices, nor help us understand exactly where and why human rights practices emerge in the ways they do.[13]

From structures of power to utopia – the emergence of human rights networks

Much more promising for our purposes are studies of transboundary social processes that drop the global/local: international/national dichotomy in favor of some version of network analysis. Network analyses emerged in large part to describe the changes in information technology and communications over the last fifteen years, the same period when transnational human rights discourses have become more

---

[12] "Domestic" is taken to mean here the national level, not the individual domestic unit, or home, which would actually come closer spatially to the places where transnational human rights discourse takes root and is in part constituted.

[13] Even if we grant the realist approach to human rights some legitimacy, it is clear that human rights discourse is most often effective – or at least instrumental – in social spaces that are neither international nor national, which is a fact that partly explains why adopting the transnational as an ordering principle opens up so many fruitful lines for research and analysis.

17

prevalent and consequential. Networks describe the spaces that provide the "material organization of time-sharing social practices" (Castells 2000: 442), practices which are determined by the imperative "not just to communicate, but also to gain position, to outcommunicate" (2000: 71; quoting from Mulgan 1991: 21). Within network analysis space is emptied of its usual ontological significance and given what is at best a supporting function: what is described as the "local" within global/local studies becomes in network analysis a node of articulation, a "location of strategically important functions that build a series of locality-based activities and organizations around a key function in the network," to draw again from Castells's important study of the contemporary network society (2000: 443).

The usefulness of network analysis, which overcomes many of the problems produced through the "binary machine logic" that dominates much social theory, has been noticed by human rights scholars, particularly those who study the groups of transnational activists and others whose activities form the "key functions" in what Keck and Sikkink (1998) describe as "transnational activist networks." The particular nodes of articulation within transnational activist networks are not described in the first instance *as* social movements, political institutions, international agencies, and so on, but rather through the different assemblages of epistemic communities which share certain characteristics: "the centrality of values or principled ideas, the belief that individuals can make a difference, the creative use of information, and the employment of nongovernmental actors of sophisticated political strategies" in furthering the cause of human rights transnationally (Keck and Sikkink 1998: 1–2). Keck and Sikkink also offer what they understand to be a solution to the problem of the relation between space and knowledge practices within transnational human rights networks, in that the networks are both structured and structuring – adapting Anthony Giddens' theory of structuration – and seem to "embody elements of agent and structure simultaneously" (1998: 5).

In other words, the spaces of transnational human rights discourse and the social practices of human rights are mutually constitutive.[14] Moreover, Keck and Sikkink's application of network analysis to transnational human rights advocacy is not merely – or entirely – an analytical

---

[14] As Castells explains on this same point, "the space of [transnational] flows is constituted by its nodes and hubs. The space of [transnational] flows is not placeless, although its structural logic is" (2000: 443).

move, one calculated to avoid the fallacies of the global/local binary: particularly in regions like Latin America, the "network" has become a ubiquitous social, political, and legal category within which ordinary social actors pursue human rights, public health, economic development, and other strategies. As they say, "over the last two decades, individuals and organizations have consciously formed and named transnational networks, developed and shared networking strategies and techniques, and assessed the advantages and limits of this kind of activity. Scholars have come late to the party" (1998: 4).

This is an important point and one that will find echoes in our discussion of the role of practice in helping to shape the meanings and possibilities of human rights discourse. In Bolivia, for example, the *red*, or network, is really the only organizational model within which initiatives focused on human rights, economic reform, maternal health, greater political participation, and so on, are organized. But despite what Keck and Sikkink say, the development of network models by human rights activists – in Bolivia and elsewhere (see Merry 2005; Riles 2000; Speed 2006) – has not been an isolated, country by country process, in which "a thousand flowers bloom, a hundred schools of [network advocacy] contend." Indeed, in light of what Keck and Sikkink describe about the rise of transnational advocacy networks, it would be surprising if the emergence of *justifications* for the network as the preferred advocacy model did not go hand in hand with the rise of the (networked) epistemic communities themselves. Moreover, it is also not possible to say that particular "actors" developed networks – and the accompanying networkism – before the participation or awareness of "scholars." Not only are scholars important social actors whose writing and presence shape transnational human rights advocacy, but, even more specifically, in many countries like Bolivia prominent human rights advocates are themselves full-time teachers or academics.

But even though network analysis does provide some suggestive possibilities for conceptualizing the study of human rights practices, problems remain. It is somewhat ironic, given the way critical political scientists like Keck and Sikkink have rushed to apply the insights of network analysis to transnational human rights, that the consideration of power as a variable shaping the transnationalization of human rights discourse becomes obscured by what appears as an ideological faith in the democratizing possibilities of networks, including human rights networks. Despite recognizing that "many third world activists ... [argue that] the focus on 'rights talk' ... begs the question of structural inequality" (Keck and Sikkink 1998: 215), they nevertheless go on to assert categorically that "networks are voluntary and horizontal, [and] actors participate in them to the degree that they anticipate mutual learning, respect, and benefits" (1998: 214). As several of the chapters in this volume demonstrate, it is, in fact, a continually open question – to be answered through the close ethnographic engagement with particular human rights practices – whether or not human rights networks should be characterized as "vehicles for communicative and political exchange, with the potential for mutual transformation of participants" (Keck and Sikkink 1998: 214), or whether the emphasis should not be placed on structural or other types of systemic constraints, all of which limit the emanicaptory potential of human rights discourse.

There is also a problem with using a network model in order to describe the spaces of transnational human rights practice in that the horizontality that does seem to characterize connections between different network nodes cannot account for the ways in which social actors often experience human rights "vertically," meaning as part of hierarchical social, political, and legal alignments of interests. In other words, in developing an analytical framework that will allow us to locate the practice of human rights in time and place, we must be careful to give equal weight to what the social theorist's eye sees *and* what participants in human rights networks themselves tell us about the meanings and experiences of human rights as it relates to other forms of social practice. This means that, from the perspective of the analytical observer, it might be quite clear that the webs of relations that form human rights networks span multiple boundaries without any obvious levels or formal hierarchy; indeed, even the idea of human rights implies a kind of ethical flatness, something that is built into the Universal Declaration itself in that its different articles are coequal and thus normatively undifferentiated. But since human rights discourse always emerges – as the chapters here show – as part of broader social structures through which meanings are constituted, the multiple experiences of human rights can be actually quite constrained or locked within what Ulf Hannerz has described as the "unfree flows" of meaning that remain despite the breakdown of cultural boundaries and the corresponding increase in cultural complexity over the last fifteen years (Hannerz 1992: 100). This problem with the social and political depthlessness implied by network analysis is one that also characterizes much of the related globalization literature, which likewise assumes the breakdown of traditional vertical relationships and the emergence of a kind of inherently emancipatory set of global relations of communication and production which resist the concentration or exercise of power.

A good example of this is the most recent book by the globalization guru Thomas Friedman (2005), which argues that the world is becoming increasing flat and that this flatness – the result of the breakdown of established hierarchies – is the key geopolitical force behind the empowerment of workers and industries outside the traditional centers of global economic power. In his critique of Friedman's book – mischievously entitled "The World is Round" (Gray 2005) – the British political theorist John Gray effectively flattens Friedman's flatness hypothesis, not only showing that its horizontality is more ideological than empirical, but that it is actually a kind of neo-Marxism! Nevertheless, as with Friedman's other globalization books, the utopianism of his perspectives on contemporary economic and political relations remains extremely popular, even soothing, to the vast swaths of the Euro-American bourgeoisie that have rushed to jump on the globalization bandwagon.[15]

And finally, in moving away from the global/local dichotomy in order to conceptualize the relationship between structure and agency within transnational human rights discourse through network analysis, we must be cautious not to overprivilege the role of cosmopolitan elites, those "activists without borders" whose very movements across both cultural and territorial boundaries seem to symbolize the normative transnationalism they advocate. The ethnographic study of human rights practice over the last fifteen years has shown that "transnationalism" has different meanings and should not be simply understood as a more accurate or revealing "ontological choice" (Orenstein and Schmitz 2006). In other words, transnationalism should not *only* be taken literally to refer to networks that open up – physically or discursively – beyond the boundaries of nation-states, as important as this meaning of transnationalism is – among other things – for moving the focus of attention away from both the state and international institutions. To take transnationalism too literally is naturally to concentrate on the range of social actors whose activities are most symbolic of the trans-boundary and horizontal interconnections that define (for example) contemporary human rights networks. But many of the most important actors whose encounters with human rights discourse

---

[15] As of April 2006, *The World is Flat* remained in the top five on the *New York Times* nonfiction bestseller list and number two among all books at Amazon.com – right after *The Da Vinci Code*.

contribute to its transnationalism never physically leave their villages, or towns, or countries. Instead, in order to encounter or appropriate the idea of human rights many social actors must *envision* the legal and ethical frameworks that it implies, which requires the projection of the moral imagination in ways that not only contribute to how we can (and should) understand the meaning of human rights, but also, at a more basic level, suggest that the emergence of transnational networks takes places "in our minds, as much as in our actions," a fact that Boaventura de Sousa Santos describes – in another, but related, context – as "interlegality" (1995: 473).

Betweenness and the human rights imaginary

The chapters in this volume suggest yet a different framework for locating the practice of human rights. By describing the locations in which human rights discourse emerges in practice as "between" the global and the local, we do not intend to replace one spatial metaphor with another. Indeed, it is partly our argument here that "ontological [or epistemological] choices" have the effect of severely limiting the ability of researchers to capture both the patterns across transnational human rights practice, and the ways in which such practices are non-generalizable and contingent upon the entire range of legal, political, and social variables that shape them. Instead, betweenness is meant to express the ways in which human rights discourse unfolds ambiguously, without a clear spatial referent, in part through transnational networks, but also, equally important, through the projection of the moral and legal imagination by social actors whose precise locations – *pace* Keck and Sikkink – within these networks are (for them) practically irrelevant. So, although Eleanor Roosevelt, the chair of the commission that was responsible for drafting what became the Universal Declaration of Human Rights (1948), hoped that a "curious grapevine" would carry the idea of human rights across state boundaries (she didn't describe this grapevine as a "network," but that is close to what she meant), the recent study of human rights practice has shown that actors (including academics) contribute to this grapevine in ways that are more complicated than simple network analysis assumes.

Yet even though betweenness is employed here as an analytical device meant to both emphasize the nonuniversality of human rights practice, and create an intentionally open conceptual space which can account for the way actors encounter the idea of human rights through the projection of the legal and moral imagination, we nevertheless retain "global" and "local" as referents. There are three reasons for this. First, despite the fact that global and local are highly problematic ways of framing the ontology of transnational human rights discourse, the binary global/local remains an important part of human rights discourse itself. Human rights activists talk in terms of global movements and the globalization of human rights; international institutions denounce the resistance of local institutions or cultures to the realization of a global human rights culture; the use of metaphors of the ultra-local – such as *grassroots*, which implies a kind of localism that actually burrows into the earth itself – takes on political meaning for human rights organizations; and, as I have already argued above, "the global" continues to be used teleologically, as a gesture toward the goal of transnational human rights discourse, the creation of a global moral community.[16]

Second, while we reject the reification of the global and local as points in an imaginary discursive hierarchy, we nevertheless believe that maintaining them in a different form allows us to emphasize the power asymmetries that have framed the transnationalization of human rights discourse over the last fifteen years. In other words, describing the practice of human rights *between* the "global" and the "local" evokes a self-consciously artificial verticality which serves a specific analytical purpose, one that should not be taken to imply an actual "top down" (or "bottom up") relationship between the different nodes within transnational human rights networks. Finally, if retaining the global and local within our study of human rights practices provides a way of illustrating the empirical dimensions of power within transnational human rights networks, it also recognizes an equally important side to the way power is mobilized through human rights discourse: the fact that human rights actors often experience human rights discourse betwixt and between, as a kind of legal or ethical liminality that can both empower the relatively powerless and place them at a greater risk of further violence at

---

[16] This emphasis on the global is reinforced by the academic human rights studies literature, which analyzes the global dimensions of human rights from every possible angle: the way human rights are an essential feature of globalization (Coicaud, Doyle and Gardner 2003); the fact that neoliberal globalization is incompatible with the protection of human rights (George 2003); the ways in which human rights form the foundation of an emerging global order based on news forms of sovereignty (K. Mills 1998); the relationship between human rights and an "ethic of global responsibility" (Midgley 1999); the ways in which human rights give voice to the oppressed within an emerging "global society" (Shaw 1999); the fact that the ethnographic study of human rights should be undertaken from a global perspective and framed in relation to the emergence of other global discourses, such as "global justice" (Wilson and Mitchell 2003); the role that human rights has played in creating a "global village" of rights-bearing citizens (Brysk 2000); and so on.

the same time. As activist-scholars like Shannon Speed have recently shown (2006), the use of human rights discourse within ongoing political and social movements has the effect of radically shifting the framework within which apparently "local" struggles are waged. But, at the same time, the liminality that is created by the introduction of human rights discourse exposes actors to greater scrutiny by dramatically expanding what might be in fact quite modest claims. The social and political implications of human rights between the global and the local are unpredictable.

THE PRACTICE OF HUMAN RIGHTS

The chapters in this volume suggest the diversity and ambiguity among the multiple meanings of human rights; they also point to a different way of conceptualizing the discursive spaces in which transnational human rights networks are constituted. Both of these contributions – among others – are based on the close and critical engagement with the practice of human rights in different regional and cultural contexts. But what exactly do we mean by the practice of human rights? At a basic level, the practice of human rights describes all of the many ways in which social actors across the range talk about, advocate for, criticize, study, legally enact, vernacularize, and so on, the idea of human rights in its different forms. By social actors we mean all of the different individuals, institutions, states, international agencies, and so on, who practice human rights within any number of different social contexts, without privileging any one type of human rights actor: the peasant intellectual in Bolivia who agitates on behalf of *derechos humanos* is analytically equal to the executive director of Human Rights Watch. In defining the practice of human rights in this way we draw attention to both the diversity of ways and places in which the idea of human rights – again, in its legal, conceptual, and discursive forms – emerges in practice, and the fact that the practice of human rights is always embedded in preexisting relations of meaning and production. The practice of human rights, defined in this way, is obviously a major part of transnational human rights discourse. Nevertheless, the idea of human rights discourse implies a set of structural relationships that mediate the practice of human rights, so that one cannot simply treat human rights practice and human rights discourse as different descriptions of the same thing; in other words, human rights discourse is the more encompassing category.

There are several important implications to the way we define the practice of human rights. First, to adopt such a broad definition of human rights practice is necessarily to reject all of the traditional analytical divisions that have been used to artificially parse the different types of engagement with human rights: between the philosophy of human rights and human rights practice; between human rights law and the politics of human rights; between the abstract idea of human rights and its messy and contradictory emergence within situated normativities; between universal human rights and the culturally-specific legal or ethical forms in which they are expressed; and so on.[17] This has been one of the most important contributions of the ethnographic study of human rights over the last ten years. This research, which has been documented in a series of edited volumes (Borneman 2004; Wilson 1997; Cowan, Dembour, and Wilson 2001; Wilson and Mitchell, 2003), and in more traditional monographs (Malkki 1995; Merry 2005; Povinelli 2002; Riles 2000; Slyomovics 2005), has demonstrated the following (among other things): that the idea of human rights is developed further, or transformed, or culturally translated, for political, economic, and other formally nonphilosophical reasons; that the notion of transcultural universal human rights is itself a product of particular histories and cultural imperatives, so that it is simply not possible to consider the idea of human rights "in the abstract;" that the different ways of *describing* the expression of human rights – in law, in politics, within economic relations – are at best temporary analytical expedients, whereas these in fact refer to fundamentally interconnected processes; and, perhaps most importantly, that non-elites – peasant intellectuals, villages activists, government workers, rural politicians, neighborhood council members – are very often important human rights theorists, so that the idea of human rights is perhaps most consequentially shaped and conceptualized outside the centers of elite discourse, even if what can be understood as the organic philosophy of human rights is often mistakenly described as "practice" (i.e., in false opposition to "theory").

And if the way we define the practice of human rights here is, in part, an argument for a different approach to human rights theory, then we must recognize that there are consequences to acknowledging that the

---

[17] It is not surprising that the traditional analytical divisions in the human rights literature are framed as dichotomies given the prevalence of related binaries that I describe in Part Two of this book. One detects, in the orthodox study of human rights, specific expressions of all the typical oppositions: theory and practice; structure and agency; pure and practical reason; tradition and modernity; communicative and subject-centered rationality; and so on.

idea of human rights is subject to – or the product of – open source theorizing: the meanings of human rights will remain contextual and relative (what I describe above as "universalism"); all truth claims on behalf of a particular approach to the idea of human rights are rein-scribed within the particular intellectual and political histories that produced them; and because the idea of human rights is essentially contingent and dynamic, its future is far from assured. If the idea of human rights is constituted through all the different forms of practice that anthropologists and others have so richly documented, then there is no reason why circumstances in certain places and times (or, indeed, more broadly) might not cause the practice of human rights – and thus the idea – to end, at least in its current transnational forms.

Finally, there are political or institutional implications to conceptua-lizing the practice of human rights in the way we do in this volume. If the ethnographic study of human rights has shown that the practice of human rights is characterized by contradictions, uncertainties, and a kind of normative incompleteness, these should not be taken to repre-sent a failure of universal human rights as a coherent legal or ethical framework, or, on a more practical level, a failure by different institu-tions to properly translate the idea of human rights in context. Rather, the openness and incompleteness within the practice of human rights are essential to the development of what are different – but living and organic – *ideas* of human rights, which can be expressed politically and institutionally precisely *because* their legitimacy does not depend on assumptions or aspirations of universality.[18] The argument here follows from my earlier discussion of universalism, which I described as social and legal practices that emerge *in relation to* the putative universality of human rights. Even if discourses of universalism obviously gesture toward the supposed universality of human rights, in practice this connection is often weakened because the ontological framework expressed through human rights must be reconstituted in terms that resonate culturally and politically. And to reconstitute the idea of universal human rights is, in part, to find grounds on which a formally transcultural ethical and legal framework can be *made* legitimate. This means that legitimacy – which is a key problem for human rights activists and lawyers in particular – is also anchored in social practice.

---

[18] One of the best examples of the way universalism transforms universal human rights claims into legitimate categories of legal, political, and social action, is Richard Wilson's study of the debates over human rights and justice in post-apartheid South Africa (Wilson 2001).

This is a problem – to be sure – from a certain legal and philosophical perspective, but it seems unavoidable and is yet another important implication of the study of human rights practices.

FOUR THEMES IN THE PRACTICE OF HUMAN RIGHTS

Although we intend this volume to contribute to new ways of conceptualizing the practice of human rights as a key transnational discourse, we are also aware that it represents only the beginning of what we hope will be an interdisciplinary dialogue on the meanings and possibilities of human rights within the orientations we develop here. As should be abundantly clear from the way I have described the volume's major claims, the volume itself is thematic rather than disciplinary. There is a certain risk in reframing human rights studies in this way, not the least of which is the fact that particular disciplinary perspectives have had a larger stake than others in defining both the terms of analysis, and the ways in which ideas about human rights have been translated into political and social action. But in drawing out themes in the practice of human rights we hope to create a space for collaborative dialogue and critique that is not dependent on the range of entrenched theoretical or institutional paradigms. To do this we have brought together scholars whose contributions coalesce around four openings or themes in the practice of human rights: violence, power, vulnerability, and ambivalence. In making the argument that these four themes reveal, among other things, the potential and limitations of universal legal or ethical frameworks, certain insights into how transnational discourses are to be understood and where they are to be located, and the persistence of structural inequalities and forms of pressure within human rights networks, we recognize that there might be other points of entry into the practice of human rights, other ways of organizing a thematic approach to human rights problems. In other words, although these four themes emerge from the study of human rights practice itself, as the chapters here demonstrate, we expect that other windows into the practice of human rights will emerge as more scholars and activists recognize its implications.

States of violence

The problems of violence have become epistemic within the practice of human rights. These include the relationship between violence as a complicated and historically specific social process and universal human rights, and the ways in which "violence" itself becomes problema-tized in certain ways – which exclude others – within transnational rights discourse (Rajagopal 2003). There is also a phenomenological dimension to violence within the practice of human rights: social actors experience violations and abuses at different levels of directness and remove, from the literal acts of physical and psychological trauma, to the vicarious forms of experience that lead to what Richard Rorty has described as "sentimental education" (Rorty 1993). The study of these different experiences of violence within the practice of human rights by anthro-pologists and others has shown that the effects and implications of violence are both empirically and ethically ambiguous.

Daniel Goldstein's chapter explores the way the problem of violence in Bolivia is understood in different ways depending on which transna-tional discourse is mobilized to address it. During the rise of neoliberalism in Bolivia, human rights discourses were deployed by political and social movements as part of various national campaigns against poverty, domestic abuse, the neglect of children, and so on. But in certain parts of Bolivia, like the peri-urban *barrios* of Cochabamba, the most serious problems from the perspective of particular communities – property theft, financial fraud, corruption among public officials, and (more recently) the sexual abuse of children – could not be managed through legal frameworks provided by the Bolivian state, which were increasingly linked to human rights. So an alternative discourse was developed by residents, one which wrapped the dominant concern with "citizen secur-ity" within the language of human rights to create what Goldstein describes as a "right to security." This is a complicated "human right" indeed, one which embeds a demand for a more robust and even vengeful police presence within the social ontology of rights. And if the police are not able – or willing – to enforce this right to security, community vigilantes take over this role. Goldstein's chapter demonstrates that certain human rights practices that might appear contradictory from the perspective of the international human rights community can be shown to express a set of logics from the perspective of the social actors for whom "human rights" becomes just one, unstable, part of a larger discursive approach to endemic social and economic problems.

Lauren Leve's chapter reveals violence to be an important theme in the practice of human rights in yet a different way. She describes the way a liberal human rights rhetoric emerged in Nepal as part of ongoing struggles against the violence and capriciousness of the Nepali state. Yet for Nepali Buddhists, this use of human rights discourse constituted a kind of categorical violence, since human rights assumes a form of identity – possessive individualist – that is at odds with basic Buddhist philosophy and theology. In other words, in order to use human rights discourse to support claims for Buddhist autonomy and religious freedom, Buddhists were forced to advance claims that undermined Buddhism itself. Leve describes this kind of violence as a "double-bind." As she puts it, these are the "double-binds Nepali Buddhists confront when they call on normative values associated with liberal democratic citizenship to protect a form of religious selfhood that denies the very logic of identity that human rights implies."

Registers of power

Despite the fact that human rights activists and scholars have persistently argued that transnational networks are inherently empowering and counterhegemonic frameworks for organizing the expansion of human rights discourse in its different forms, the close ethnographic engagement with the practice of human rights over the last fifteen years has revealed a more complicated picture. The ways in which power is expressed through – and within – human rights networks demonstrate that generalizations are problematic: for example, economic and other related pressures are clearly behind debates over human rights compliance within the European Union's so-called eastern enlargement, which has unleashed a kind of "moral imperialism" (Hernández-Truyol 2002) directed toward countries like Romania (see Goodale 2005);[19] but at the same time, a wide range of studies has shown that transnational human rights discourse *does* provide at times a radically transformative framework within which the different expressions of power can be resisted, from rights-based sex worker organizations in the Dominican Republic (Cabezas 2002), to the use of arguments for religious rights to resist the Chinese state in Tibet (M. Mills 2003), to the many examples of collectivities of different types (indigenous peoples, linguistic minorities, and so on) harnessing the power of human rights discourse as part of wider political and legal struggles (Cowan 2001; Jackson, chapter 5 in this volume).[20]

---

[19] On this point, see also Laura Nader's analysis of power within human rights networks (Nader 1999), in which she critiques the way international institutions and dominant nation-states address human rights issues based on self-interest and other ethically unsustainable grounds.

[20] Although it should be pointed out that in Cowan's study of the use of human rights discourse by the Macedonian minority in Greece, the relationship between human rights language and claims and political emancipation is far from unambiguous.

The two chapters in this section that focus on power as a theme within the practice of human rights likewise demonstrate the complicated meanings and implications of human rights discourse for actors engaged in movements for social change. My own chapter examines distinct but related processes in contemporary Bolivia. The first is the emergence of transnational configurations I call "empires of law," and Bolivia's location within these empires. Since the end of the Cold War, human rights discourse has increasingly acted as a conduit for specific – and much older – forms of transnational legal, economic, and political power. But social actors in Bolivia have picked apart and appropriated only some aspects of human rights discourse, a process that Sally Merry has described as "vernacularization" (2005, 2006), in order to construct discursive frameworks for contesting the same neoliberal policies through which human rights emerged in Bolivia. I call this the Pandora's box of neoliberalism: when the power of one part of neoliberalism (human rights discourse) is used to resist other parts (privatization of utility concerns, the rationalization of land tenure, democratization, the capitalization of property, and so on).

Shannon Speed's chapter explores the relationship between human rights, social movements, and power in another part of Latin America. Her study of the Zapatista *Juntas de Buen Gobierno*, or Good Governance Councils, in Mexico's Chiapas region, captures another way in which human rights discourse at times generates a set of unpredictable logics – of rule, of the market, of law. In the case of the Zapatista *Juntas de Buen Gobierno*, the very idea of human rights itself has been reconfigured through the practice of the dominant version of human rights recognized by both the neoliberal Mexican state, and the transnational actors who intervened on behalf on Mexico's indigenous peoples. As Speed explains, Zapatista leaders have developed an alternative human rights ontology in which rights "exist" only in their exercise. This is an organic theory of human rights, one in which Zapatista human rights practice is invested with both cultural and politico-legal legitimacy by the Zapatistas themselves.

Conditions of vulnerability

Vulnerability is another opening into the practice of human rights, another key theme that emerges from the ethnographic and critical engagement with human rights discourse in its different expressions. The international human rights system, though founded on statements of largely individual rights, was nevertheless created in order to protect vulnerable populations against the kind of large-scale outrages that had plagued Europe – and, to a lesser extent, other parts of the world, such as east Asia – for much of the first half of the twentieth century.[21] It is therefore axiomatic that the international human rights system is mobilized to protect populations in jeopardy, and, indeed, states of vulnerability have come to form the rationale for a permanent set of international (and transnational) interventions in the form of the ICC, postconflict truth and reconciliation commissions, International Labor Organization activism on behalf of indigenous and "tribal" peoples, and so on.

But the problem of vulnerability as a distinct category of meaning within human rights regimes has not been adequately examined. How, for example, does the employment of human rights as a normative framework actually affect the ongoing set of causes of vulnerability, regardless of how this is defined? If the opposite of vulnerability (stability) – if, in fact, we agree that stability is the opposite of vulnerability – is the real goal toward which interventions are directed, then is human rights discourse the best, or even most appropriate, framework for such interventions? Finally, what can the practice of human rights tell us about the usefulness of describing vulnerability in this way, as a transcultural ordering principle which justifies the range of international and transnational interventions?

Jean Jackson's chapter on the complicated intersections of human rights, law, and indigenousness in Colombia reveals the ways in which vulnerability takes on different meanings for different social actors within wider political and legal struggles. As she has done in her earlier work on the political and conceptual elasticity of "culture," here Jackson examines a series of legal cases in Colombia in order to show that vulnerability has been largely misconceived within conventional transnational human rights discourse. This is, in part, due to the fact that the rise of human rights in Colombia must be seen against a backdrop of ongoing violence, which shapes the way human rights are used in particular political and legal contexts. As she explains, "Vulnerable indigenous populations in rural Colombia, in their effort to find and maintain stability in a situation of tremendous violence and government neglect, enlist particular traditions and authorize

---

[21] As the intellectual historian Isaiah Berlin once said, "I have lived through most of the twentieth century without, I must add, suffering personal hardship. I remember it only as the most terrible century in Western history."

particular actors to carry out actions that without doubt challenge the transcultural scaffolding of the human rights regime."

In her critical analysis of the 2000 UN anti-trafficking protocol, Kay Warren examines the problem of vulnerability within human rights from yet another perspective. The study of the way human rights documents are produced is a well-established means through which the contradictions and contingencies of human rights practice are revealed, since human rights are so clearly shaped by the technocratic knowledge regimes that underpin the contemporary international legal human rights system. In exploring the way the problem of human trafficking is both understood and constructed within the international human rights community, Warren shows how vulnerability acts as a mediating framework that establishes discursive (and, in this case, legal) boundaries around what is in fact a complicated set of political, legal, sexual, and moral processes. As she found, the machinery of intentional human rights law was mobilized in an "attempt to tame this heterogeneous reality so it could be comprehended as an entity appropriate for a certain set of interventions." The discourse of vulnerability, in other words, works both to simplify different slices of "heterogeneous reality" and to reinterpret them in ways that bring them within the ambit of (new) categories of international human rights law.

Encountering ambivalence

Finally, the study of the practice of human rights is also necessarily the study of the donors and institutions whose support – financial, political, ethical – is a key variable that shapes the impact and meanings of human rights in context. The role of transnational human rights institutions is marked by several forms of profound ambivalence. For example, transnational donors are often caught between the demands of their own articles of incorporation or policy objectives – which typically define the institutional mission in terms of some normative good, like fostering a respect for human rights – and the demands of *realpolitk*, which force transnational actors to make choices, compromise, and redirect finite resources, for reasons that have nothing to do with fostering or protecting human rights. And if human rights has become a key transnational normativity over the last fifteen years, it is not the only one. It is not uncommon for transnational donors to work under a mandate that prescribes what are actually – at least conceptually – competing normative agendas, or at least agendas that coexist uneasily, so that an institution might work for human rights, social justice, environmental protection, and economic development (or justice), at the same time.[22] In practice this transnational normative pluralism can create confusion – and, at times, cynicism – for both transnational actors and their intended beneficiaries. Confusion (or cynicism) can lead to ambivalence about the efficacy or value of any one of these competing agendas, but what has become – in light of the amounts of money involved – a marketplace of transnational normativity can also create openings for social action by providing a kind of menu of options for individuals or groups enmeshed in ongoing struggles of different kinds.

John Dale explores the problem of ambivalence through an analysis of the use of the Alien Tort Claims Act (ATCA) by activists involved in the transnational Free Burma movement. Dale shows how the threat of a novel legal strategy against a transnational corporation by victims of human rights abuses in Burma altered the transnational legal landscape in subtle ways. Yet, as Dale's description of the different legal proceedings, negotiation, and aftermath makes clear, much of this alternation was unintended. In other words, the case against Unocal might, or might not, serve as a precedent for future claimants seeking to find legal arenas for human rights claims. Dale's chapter, which begins as a story of optimism by transnational human rights activists, ends on a note of multifaceted ambivalence: on the part of "foreign policy conservatives who have appropriated the language of international human rights for their own purposes"; on the part of transnational corporations who must look to the Unocal case as either a cautionary tale, or an example of how human rights claims become just another cost of doing business; and, finally, on the part of victims of human rights abuses, who desperately want – and need – ways to put teeth into international human rights, but who end up suffering anew when their efforts fizzle out in the Dickensian world of legal procedure and institutional compromise.

The theme of ambivalence within the practice of human rights is approached quite differently by Sari Wastell, in her analysis of the

---

[22] Many examples of this could be given. Catholic Relief Services undertakes projects around the world to promote the capacity for economic development, food security, gender equality, social justice, and human rights (www.catholicrelief.org). The Aga Khan Development Network advances the causes of "health, education, culture, rural development, institution-building and the promotion of economic development" (www.akdn.org/about.html). World Vision International is concerned with child labor, debt relief, the use of child soldiers in armed conflicts, the advancement of human rights, and the "hope of renewal, restoration, and reconciliation" that is offered by "God, in the person of Jesus Christ" (www.wvi.org).

political, legal, and cultural processes surrounding the struggles over a new constitution for the African kingdom of Swaziland. Here transnational legal experts were surprised to find the narrative of constitutionalism in Swaziland unfolding in completely unpredictable and ambiguous ways. Although some Swazi subjects had pressed for multiparty democracy and human rights in Swaziland for at least a decade, other large swaths of Swazi society resisted the constitutional process. As Wastell explains, "[a]nticipating that the very constituencies who had long pressed for multi-party democracy, the observance of the rule of law and the recognition of human rights in the country would welcome the constitution's passage into law, many were surprised by the vehemence with which the document was roundly rejected." This ambivalence was the result of different and cross-cutting political and cultural factors, but the most important was the fact that human rights discourse, as understood by ordinary Swazis, seemed to express a value system that was opposed to Swazi custom. As Wastell shows, Swazi custom emphasizes responsibilities to community, responsibilities which are centered on Swazi family and social relations more generally. It is through custom that one *becomes* Swazi. Human rights, however, place the highest value on one's humanness, which is invested with normative significance. So, for many Swazis, the adoption of human rights within the new constitution would have meant the adoption of a legal framework that rejected the structure of Swaziness, and thus the essence of the Swazi nation itself.

The volume is brought to a close with a concluding chapter by Richard Wilson. Wilson has played an important role in making the ethnography of human rights a robust area for debate and scholarship within anthropology over the last ten years. Through a series of edited volumes (Wilson 1997, 2001; Wilson and Mitchell 2003) and his study of the politics of truth and reconciliation in South Africa (2001), among other works, Wilson has helped to make the practice of human rights a legitimate and compelling object for empirical research. More recently, he has broadened his range of interests as the director of an interdisciplinary human rights institute. This position has given him the chance to reflect on both the radical potential, and limitations, of anthropological approaches to human rights theory and practice.

He titles his contribution "Tyrannosaurus Lex" as a way to signal a note of pragmatic caution for scholars and others who might lose sight of the fact that the international human rights system is, at least formally, a *legal* system. And over the last fifteen years, human rights have emerged within what can be understood as a transnational legal regime, comprised of human rights activists, international institutions acting across the boundaries of nation-states, and human rights victims themselves, who increasingly look for ways to press claims outside the boundaries of *both* national and international legal frameworks (see Dale, chapter 7 in this volume). Although the nature and scope of this transnational human rights law could not have been entirely anticipated, some scholars – like Merry (1992), who Wilson aptly quotes at some length in his chapter – had a sense relatively early on that human rights practice would emerge as a important transnational legal space, and that anthropologists would have a key role to play in tracking this emergence. This volume represents the maturing fruits of these efforts.

REFERENCES

Alston, Philip, ed. 2000. *Promoting Human Rights through Bills of Rights: Comparative Perspectives*. Oxford: Oxford University Press.

Alston, Philip, ed. 2006. *The United Nations and Human Rights: A Critical Appraisal*. Oxford: Oxford University Press.

Baxi, Upendra. 2002. *The Future of Human Rights*. Oxford: Oxford University Press.

Borneman, John, ed. 2004. *The Case of Ariel Sharon and the Fate of Universal Jurisdiction*. Princeton: Princeton University Press.

Brysk, Alison. 2000. *From Tribal Village to Global Village: Indian Rights and International Relations in Latin America*. Stanford: Stanford University Press.

Brysk, Alison. 2002. "Introduction: Transnational Threats and Opportunities." In Alison Brysk, ed. *Globalization and Human Rights*. Berkeley: University of California Press.

Cabezas, Amalia Lucia. 2002. "Tourism, Sex Work, and Women's Rights in the Dominican Republic." In Alison Brysk, ed. *Globalization and Human Rights*. Berkeley: University of California Press.

Castells, Manuel. 2000. *The Rise of the Network Society*. Oxford: Blackwell.

Coicaud, Jean-Marc, Michael Doyle, and Anne-Marie Gardner, eds. 2003. *The Globalization of Human Rights*. Tokyo: United Nations University Press.

Cowan, Jane K. 2001. "Ambiguities of an Emancipatory Discourse: The Making of a Macedonia Minority in Greece." In Cowan, Jane K., Marie-Bénédicte Dembour, and Richard A. Wilson, eds. *Culture and Rights: Anthropological Perspectives*. Cambridge: Cambridge University Press.

Cowan, Jane K., Marie-Bénédicte Dembour, and Richard A. Wilson, eds. 2001. *Culture and Rights: Anthropological Perspectives*. Cambridge: Cambridge University Press.

Cvetkovich, Ann, and Douglas Kellner, eds. 1997. *Articulating the Global and the Local: Globalization and Cultural Studies.* Boulder: Westview Press.

Donnelly, Jack. 2003. *University Human Rights in Theory and Practice.* Ithaca: Cornell University Press.

Friedman, Thomas. 2005. *The World is Flat: A Brief History of the Twenty-First Century.* New York: Farrar, Straus and Giroux.

George, Susan. 2003. "Globalizing Rights?" In Matthew Gibney, ed. *Globalizing Rights: The Oxford Amnesty Lectures 1999.* Oxford: Oxford University Press.

Goodale, Mark. 2005. "Empires of Law: Discipline and Resistance within the Transnational System." *Social & Legal Studies* 14(4): 553–583.

Goodale, Mark. 2006a. "Introduction to 'Anthropology and Human Rights in a New Key'." *American Anthropologist* 108(1): 1–8.

Goodale, Mark. 2006b. "Ethical Theory as Social Practice." *American Anthropologist* 108(1): 25–37.

Goodale, Mark. 2006c. "Reclaiming Modernity: Indigenous Cosmopolitanism and the Coming of the Second Revolution in Bolivia." *American Ethnologist* (33)4: 634–649.

Goodale, Mark. 2008. *The Anthropology of Human Rights: Critical Explorations in Ethical Theory and Social Practice.* Philadelphia: University of Pennsylvania Press.

Goodale, Mark. 2008. *Dilemmas of Modernity: Bolivian Encounters with Law and Liberalism* (forthcoming).

Gray, John. 2005. "The World is Round." *New York Review of Books,* August 11.

Hannerz, Ulf. 1992. *Cultural Complexity: Studies in the Social Organization of Meaning.* New York: Columbia University Press.

Hernández-Truyol, Berta Esperanza, ed. 2002. *Moral Imperialism: A Critical Anthology.* New York: New York University Press.

Keck, Margaret, and Kathryn Sikkink, eds. 1998. *Activists Beyond Borders: Advocacy Networks in International Politics.* Ithaca: Cornell University Press.

Likosky, Michael. 2005. *Privatising Development: Transnational Law, Infrastructure and Human Rights.* Leiden: Martinus Nijhoff.

Malkki, Liisa. 1995. *Purity and Exile: Violence, Memory, and National Cosmology among Hutu Refugees in Tanzania.* Chicago: University of Chicago Press.

Merry, Sally Engle. 1992. "Anthropology, Law, and Transnational Processes." *Annual Review of Anthropology.* 21: 357–379.

Merry, Sally Engle. 2005. *Human Rights and Gender Violence: Translating International Law into Local Justice.* Chicago: University of Chicago Press.

Merry, Sally Engle. 2006. "Transnational Human Rights and Local Activism: Mapping the Middle." *American Anthropologist* 108(1): 38–51.

Midgley, Mary. 1999. "Towards an Ethic of Global Responsibility." In Tim Dunne and Nicholas Wheeler, eds. *Human Rights in Global Politics.* Cambridge: Cambridge University Press.

Mills, Kurt. 1998. *Human Rights in the Emerging Global Order: A New Sovereignty?* New York: Palgrave/St. Martin's Press.

Mills, Martin. 2003. "This Turbulent Priest: Contesting Religious Rights and the State in the Tibetan Shugden Controversy." In Richard Wilson, and Jon P. Mitchell, eds. *Human Rights in Global Perspective: Anthropological Studies of Rights, Claims, and Entitlements.* London: Routledge.

Mulgan, Geoff. 1991. *Communication and Control Networks and the New Economies of Communication.* New York and London: Guilford Press.

Nader, Laura. 1999. "In a Women's Looking Glass: Normative Blindness and Unresolved Human Rights Issues." *Horizontes Antropológicos* (5)10: 61–82.

Ong, Aihwa, and Stephen Collier, eds. 2005. *Global Assemblages: Technology, Politics, and Ethics as Anthropological Problems.* Oxford: Blackwell.

Orenstein, Mitchell, and Hans Peter Schmitz. 2006. "The New Transnationalism and Comparative Politics." *Comparative Politics* 38(4): 479–500.

Povinelli, Elizabeth. 2002. *The Cunning of Recognition: Indigenous Alterities and the Making of Australian Multiculturalism.* Durham: Duke University Press.

Provost, René. 2005. *International Human Rights and Humanitarian Law.* Cambridge: Cambridge University Press.

Rajagopal, Balakrishnan. 2003. *International Law from Below: Development, Social Movements, and Third World Resistance.* Cambridge: Cambridge University Press.

Riles, Annelise. 2000. *The Network Inside Out.* Ann Arbor: University of Michigan Press.

Riles, Annelise. 2004. "Collateral Knowledge". Paper given at the 2004 Law and Society Association meeting, Chicago, IL.

Risse, Thomas, Stephen Ropp, and Kathryn Sikkink, eds. 1999. *The Power of Human Rights: International Norms and Domestic Change.* Cambridge: Cambridge University Press.

Risse, Thomas, and Kathryn Sikkink. 1999. "The Socialization of International Human Rights Norms into Domestic Practice: Introduction." In Risse, Thomas, Stephen Ropp, and Kathryn Sikkink, eds. *The Power of Human Rights: International Norms and Domestic Change.* Cambridge: Cambridge University Press.

Rorty, Richard. 1993. "Human Rights, Rationality, and Sentimentality." In Stephen Shute and Susan Hurley, eds. *On Human Rights: The Oxford Amnesty Lectures 1993.* New York: Basic Books.

Santos, Boaventura de Sousa. 1995. *Toward a New Common Sense: Law, Science and Politics in the Paradigmatic Transition.* New York: Routledge.

Sarat, Austin, and Thomas Kearns, eds. 2002. *Human Rights: Concepts, Contests, Contingencies.* Ann Arbor: University of Michigan Press.

Shaw, Martin. 1999. "Global Voices: Civil Society and the Media in Global Crises." In Time Dunnes and Nicholas Wheeler, eds., *Human Rights in Global Politics*. Cambridge: Cambridge University Press.

Slaughter, Anne-Marie. 2004. *A New World Order*. Princeton: Princeton University Press.

Slyomovics, Susan. 2005. *The Performance of Human Rights in Morocco*. Philadelphia: University of Pennsylvania Press.

Speed, Shannon. 2006. "At the Crossroads of Human Rights and Anthropology: Toward a Critically-Engaged Activist Research." *American Anthropologist* 108(1): 66–76.

Unnithan-Kumar, Maya. 2003. "Reproductions, Health, Rights: Connections and Disconnections." In Richard Wilson, and Jon P. Mitchell, eds. *Human Rights in Global Perspective: Anthropological Studies of Rights, Claims, and Entitlements*. London: Routledge.

Wilson, Richard. 2001. *The Politics and Truth and Reconciliation in South Africa: Legitimizing the Post-Apartheid State*. Cambridge: Cambridge University Press.

Wilson, Richard, ed. 1997. *Human Rights, Culture and Context: Anthropological Approaches*. London Pluto.

Wilson, Richard, and Jon P. Mitchell, eds. 2003. *Human Rights in Global Perspective: Anthropological Studies of Rights, Claims, and Entitlements*. London: Routledge.

Wilson, Rob, and Wimal Dissanayake, eds. 1996. *Global/Local: Cultural Production and the Transnational Imaginary*. Durham: Duke University Press.

PART ONE

STATES OF VIOLENCE

INTRODUCTION: STATES OF VIOLENCE

Sally Engle Merry

How does the human rights framework deal with violence? Asking this question from the perspective of human rights practice rather than human rights principles means focusing on how principles are translated in everyday situations. The argument of the book is that understanding the practice of human rights requires attention to the people who translate documents into social situations and situations into human rights violations. The people in the middle are activists, movement leaders, academics, and those who speak for victims, including some victims themselves. These are the people who construct human rights cases, transform them in ways that will increase their appeal, and try to mobilize pressure behind the principles. A key dimension of this process is defining and naming problems as human rights violations.

As they define problems as human rights issues and generate support for them, these intermediaries confront the question of what constitutes violence. Violence is a fundamental aspect of many human rights violations, yet only some kinds of violence are considered human rights offenses. Physical injury and death are often viewed as violations, but other forms of violence are not, such as economic violence, environmental degradation, or the violence of development. Moreover, on closer examination even the violence of injury and death is very ambiguous. The meaning of injury or death depends on cultural assumptions about how and why it occurred, whether it was justified, whether it was the product of malice or accident, and whether it served the good of the country. Killing a person can be murder, success in a duel, a patriotic duty, or punishment for a capital offense. In practice, there are many meanings of violence just as there are of human rights. The definition of violence and its designation as a human rights violation cannot be achieved in the abstract. Instead, it is the product of particular situations, experiences, and histories.

Much human rights doctrine is directed toward protecting individuals from injury and death. Some of the key provisions of the human rights system are the United Nations Convention against Torture and the United Nations Convention against Genocide, both of which prohibit physical harm or murder. Gender violence has taken center stage as a woman's human rights violation, in part because it focuses on protecting women's bodies from harm. Although the human rights system often confronts complicated questions of imposing one set of cultural standards on a group with different standards, as in the condemnation of child marriage, for example, violence appears to be a substratum beneath culture, a kind of violation that cannot be defended as cultural practice.

Yet, despite its apparent transparency, violence is deceivingly simple. It appears to refer to physical pain and suffering, but clearly has emotional, psychological, and financial dimensions as well. It is not only an injury inflicted by one person on another but also part of systemic violations and humiliations that a person experiences based on racism, social class hierarchies, military occupation and armed conflict, among many others. In their overview of anthropological work on violence, Nancy Scheper-Hughes and Philippe Bourgois emphasize that violence is a slippery concept that cannot be understood only in physical terms. It also includes assaults on personhood, dignity and the sense of worth and value of a person (2004: 1). Violence is fundamentally a culturally construct. As they say, "The social and cultural dimensions of violence are what gives violence its power and meaning" (Scheper-Hughes and Bourgois 2004: 1). They argue that there is not simple "brute" force, but that violence has a human face and is rarely "senseless." Instead, it often has meanings that render it heroic, justified, reasonable, or at least acceptable. From an anthropological perspective, violence as an act of injury cannot be understood outside of the social and cultural systems which give it meaning.

Nor are the meanings of violence stable, since they depend on the social position of the observer and the social context of the event. Some violence is interpreted as legitimate, such as the actions of state police controlling unruly mobs, while other violence is defined as illegitimate, such as that of the protesting mobs themselves. Police violence against criminals is authorized to some extent while the violence of criminals is not. One person's heroic revolutionary act is another's terrorist assault. These differences are often murky. When a community lynches an offender because the police fail to act, as has occurred in rural Bolivia, is this legitimate or illegitimate violence? (Goldstein 2004).

Nor are systemic dimensions of violence, called structural violence, usually included in the analysis of violence. Structural violence causes injuries that impact the everyday lives of people yet remains invisible and normalized. It includes poverty, racism, pollution, displacement, and hunger. Structural violence is usually concealed within the hegemony of ordinariness, hidden in the mundane details of normal life like gender performances in football games or the celebration of machismo. It sometimes erupts into public view in events such as the American military abuse of prisoners in Iraq but is more often part of taken-for-granted social practices, justified by ideas of racial inferiority, threats to security, or the need to control irresponsible people. Violence is sometimes highly visible, as revolutionary violence or state repression, but it is often hidden in the everyday violence of infant mortality, slow starvation, disease, destitution, and humiliation (Scheper-Hughes and Bourgois 2004: 2). Colonialism can be understood as a form of structural violence that shaped the modern world. The initial conquest of territories in Latin America, Africa, and Asia by European and North American powers was usually done by force, while the subsequent regimes of resource extraction and labor control were legitimated by ideologies of racial inferiority and cultural difference. Out of this violence, anti-colonial movements emerged that themselves insisted on the need for violence to achieve liberation of the spirit as well as the land (Fanon 1963). In the current period, development can be a violent process that disrupts livelihoods, moves people for dam construction, and forces peasants into the cash economy and off their lands (see Kapadia 2002; Rajagopal 2003).

Structural violence is intimately connected to more interpersonal forms of violence. For example, upper caste men in parts of India use the rape of lower caste women to maintain their dominance (e.g., Srivastava 2002: 272–275). Bourgois' work on crack dealers in East Harlem, New York reveals links between self-destructive substance abuse, the gendered violence of family life, adolescent gang rape, and the structural violence of US urban apartheid (Scheper-Hughes and Bourgois 2004: 3). Scheper-Hughes argues that the family is a violent institution, but sees its violence as responsive to larger socioeconomic conditions which make violence the only option (2004: 3). In post-colonial societies, such as Papua New Guinea, violence is embedded in systems of power such as colonialism, family institutions such as bride-price, development projects and their large-scale environmental degradation, and the poverty and social exclusion experienced by poor rural migrants to the city who face unemployment and residence in squatter settlements without adequate drainage and sewage systems or clean water. They confront high levels of violent crime as well as disease (see Dinnen and Ley: 2000: 2–3). Violence here includes the violence of police and security forces as well as the fear of sorcery.

Activists working in the field of domestic violence have long empha-sized the importance of the psychological, emotional, and financial dimensions of violence. Many forms of violence do not involve physical harm, such as beating children in front of their mothers, torturing pets, hurling insults, withholding funds, or refusing to speak to a person. In my own research on victims of battering, some said that the emotional pressures were worse than the physical violence. Narratives of violence evoke terror even in the absence of physical harm, such as stories of past assaults. In David Valentine's study of violence against transgendered people in New York, he points out the importance of the way violence is represented and discussed (2003). After describing the high level of violence and murder experienced by transgendered people, he notes that there is considerable discussion about this pervasive violence within the transgendered community. In some ways, these narratives of pervasive threat contribute to the constitution of the category of transgender itself (2003: 32).

To live with the perpetual threat of violence and death is to enter a world of terror and fear that Michael Taussig calls the "space of death" (1984). In Taussig's study of the treatment of rubber tappers in Columbia in the early twentieth century, he shows how the pervasive violence on this frontier is narrated as a space of death. These narra-tives talk of the danger and violence of the Indian savage in the forest. The managers, who brutally forced the indigenous people to gather rubber, also lived in a world of terror populated by angry and vengeful spirits and fierce people. Their narratives of savage and violent Indians contributed to their sense of anxiety and fear and justified their vio-lence toward the Indians. For transgendered people, as for many victims of gender violence and the indigenous Indians of Columbia, the "space of death" is a familiar location.

In sum, violence cannot be understood in the abstract, apart from its social and cultural meanings. Moreover, it cannot be restricted to physical injury: the experience of violence is a culturally mediated event, wrapped in threats, emotional loss, fear, and anxieties of various kinds. Representations of violence and narratives about violent groups and spaces serve to construct fear and anxiety, even in the absence of blows.

Given these complexities, how does the human rights system, for which protection from violence is a core principle, deal with violence? Does it seek to restrict its meaning to physical harm, or does it incorporate larger issues of context and meaning? Does it include structural violence, or focus only on individual harm? And how does the narration of violence shape human rights practice? Such narratives are fundamental to the politics of human rights and frequently the stuff from which social movements are made. How is violence theorized in these narratives? Many of the chapters in this book tackle this question, as do the two in this section.

Lauren Leve's fascinating study of the efforts by Buddhists in Nepal to claim secularism as a human right in order to create a space for their religious practice shows the importance of an expansive conception of violence. She argues that Buddhist activists are caught in a double-bind, having to assert that secularism is a human right and that they possess human rights to freedom of religion even though the very notion of self-embedded in Buddhism is fundamentally different from the rights-bearing individual. In order to make this political claim, they are forced to adopt the possessive individualist assumptions underlying the human rights framework, one which sees the self as a kind of property owned by the person. Buddhists focus on the non-self, the shifting sensations and experiences of existence. Yet, political efficacy depends on taking on the human rights self, given its intimate linkage to discourses of development and democracy. Leve calls this juncture "epistemic violence," a situation in which radically divergent ideas must be joined together without any possibility of resolution.

As her analysis indicates, the difficulty of the conjunction is not simply one of cognitive dissonance, but of unequal power. The Buddhists are confronted with only one discourse in which to make their claims: that of human rights, with its embedded notions of the person as a stable and possessing entity. The regimes of power within which the Buddhists in Nepal can make political claims is defined by development discourse, the priorities of international agencies, and the benefits of democracy. Taken together, they represent a form of modernity. As Leve notes, this is also an attractive set of ideas for Nepali Buddhists, who seek to be modern. Yet, such a framework provides no space to make claims in their own religious terms. They must choose between remaining voiceless or adopting a framework which in subtle ways does violence to their religious sensibilities. Leve recognizes this choice as a kind of violence, but a very subtle one forced by the global hegemony of modernity and its associated notions of secularism, human rights, and possessive selves.

What does it mean to include this kind of violence within the overarching rubric of human rights? Does an expansive definition of violence beyond that of physical harm better represent the experience of victims? In the field of domestic violence, reference to non-physical forms of abuse such as intimidation, harassment of children and pets, humiliation, financial losses, and isolation is necessary to describe a battered woman's experience of violence. Does stretching the idea of violence far outside the domain of physical wounds mean that it loses its specificity, its anchor in the realms of pain, injury, and death? Jean Jackson has argued recently that pain crosses the border between medical and psychological understandings of the body and cannot be separated into physical and psychological dimensions (2005). Is it realistic to circumscribe the violence of human rights violations to pain and injury? It seems that there are many other forms of violence that would be neglected by this definition.

Daniel Goldstein reveals the ambiguity of violence in his analysis of the tension between a discourse of human rights and that of security in urban slums in Bolivia. He argues that these are competing, often contradictory, discourses. Bolivian politics are shaped by a focus on human rights, defined as social and economic rights, but rising rates of crime put the lives and property of poor people at risk, inspiring them to turn against those human rights workers seeking to protect the rights of the accused. Thus, poor barrio residents come to see human rights as contributing to the problem of crime. Goldstein's analysis of the current crime situation in Cochabamba, Bolivia, reveals the slippage between violence and security, and shows that securing protection often requires violence, even by the very police forces that have oppressed urban poor residents in the past.

The idea of an emergency puts a new twist on the intersection of rights and security. When situations are defined as emergencies, rights are put aside in the name of security. Even human rights conventions acknowledge that under conditions of crisis, some rights can be ignored. But the documents do not define what constitutes an emergency or who decides, although states are clearly the decision makers. States determine whether the violent crime suffered by the urban poor is an emergency, or whether it is the practice of lynching with which they attempt to deal with this crime. Security readily becomes the basis for declaring a state of emergency.

In Bolivia, a new concept of "citizen security" is emerging. This concept shows the slippage between rights talk and security talk. Security discourse under these conditions is mobilized to deny human rights, but security can be a human right itself. However, in the pursuit of security, barrio residents sometimes resort to collective lynching, even though they recognize that this is also a denial of human rights. Bereft of adequate police protection because of the violence of neoliberal downsizing, they use collective violence to counter the violence of crime. The hostility toward the foreign import of neoliberalism slides over to the foreign import of human rights, leading to skepticism and opposition to both. Some oppose both as potentially alien while others adopt both as possibly modern. Similarly, for some the state is a form of protection, while for others it is a source of violence.

How the class position of a person shapes his or her orientation within these overlapping and intersecting discourses of security and human rights is a critical question. Barrio residents clearly feel more pressured by crime and hostile to human rights than the general electorate, yet even in these communities, those with adolescent children worry more about rights than security. Young barrio men resist the language of security while older people and women seek it out. This example shows the importance of examining who mobilizes rights language and who uses security language and in what contexts. Goldstein's rich ethnography suggests new ways to trace how human rights get made in the context of particular political and economic struggles and practices of violence and highlights who makes these rights.

Both of these articles reveal the deeply specific and historical nature of rights concepts. They emerge as ways of handling particular crises. The local evocation of rights has a distant and sometimes incoherent relationship with the sources of these concepts in UN documents and deliberations (see Goodale, chapter 3 in this volume). The common practice is a broad adoption of an overall human rights framework and a recognition that there are international sources for these ideas. There seems to be no consistency in the mobilization of or resistance to human rights, any more than there is consistency in the security discourse. Moreover, the human rights regime has no control over these various mobilizations of rights talk.

Taken together, these chapters underscore the volatility of concepts of rights and the ambiguity of violence, even though violence is the apparently stable core of human rights concepts. They point to the way particular histories construct human rights ideas and mobilize them in different situations. They show the malleability of these ideas in practice. And finally, they show that violence remains resistant to definition, even as it is omnipresent in what are understood to be human rights violations.

REFERENCES

Dinnen, Sinclair, and Allison Ley, eds. 2000. *Reflections on Violence in Melanesia*. Annandale, NSW, Australia: Hawkins Press/Asia Pacific Press.

Fanon, Frantz. 1963. *The Wretched of the Earth*. New York: Grove Press.

Goldstein, Daniel. 2004. *Spectacular City: Violence and Performance in Urban Bolivia*. Durham, NC: Duke University Press.

Jackson, Jean. 2005. "Stigma, Liminality, and Chronic Pain: *Mind-body Borderlands.*" *American Ethnologist* 32: 332–353.

Kapadia, Karin, ed. 2002. *The Violence of Development: The Politics of Identity, Gender and Social Inequalities in India*. London: Zed Books.

Rajagopal, Balakrishnan. 2003. *International Law from Below: Development, Social Movements, and Third World Resistance*. Cambridge: Cambridge University Press.

Scheper-Hughes, Nancy, and Philippe Bourgois. 2004. "Introduction: Making Sense of Violence." In Nancy, Scheper-Hughes, and Philippe Bourgois, eds. *Violence in War and Peace*, pp. 1–33. Malden, MA and Oxford, UK: Blackwell.

Srivastava, Nisha. 2002. "Multiple Dimensions of Violence Against Rural Women in Uttar Pradesh: Macro and Micro Realitites." In Karin Kapadia, ed. *The Violence of Development: The Politics of Identity, Gender and Social Inequalities in India*, pp. 235–295. London: Zed Books.

Taussig, Michael. 1984. "Culture of Terror – Space of Death: Roger Casement"s Putumayo Report and the Explanation of Torture." *Comparative Studies in Society and History* 26 (1): 467–497.

Valentine, David. 2003. "'The Calculus of Pain': Violence, Anthropological Ethics, and the Category Transgender." *Ethnos* 68 (1): 27–48.

1

HUMAN RIGHTS AS CULPRIT, HUMAN RIGHTS AS VICTIM: RIGHTS AND SECURITY IN THE STATE OF EXCEPTION

*Daniel M. Goldstein**

In some respects, the recent and unprecedented election to the Bolivian presidency of Evo Morales (widely hailed as the first indige-nous person to be elected president of a Latin American nation) can be attributed to his command of the transnational discourse of human rights. In the last several years Bolivia has seen the emergence of powerful social movements demanding greater political inclusion and representation for indigenous peoples, and against the privatization and/or expropriation of natural resources (particularly water and gas), all expressed, in various ways, using the transnational language of human rights. As leader of the Bolivian coca-growers' union and head of the *Movimento al Socialismo* MAS party (Movement Towards Socialism party), Morales articulated the protest against state and transnational programs of neoliberal political economy as struggles for human and citizens' rights in a context of centuries of indigenous exclusion and exploitation by foreign powers (Goodale, chapter 3 in this volume). Violent state repression of civil protest was critiqued in the same idiom. Like other indigenous activists around the hemi-sphere, Morales and other leaders and participants in Bolivian social

* Earlier versions of this chapter were presented at the 104th annual meeting of the American Anthropological Association, November 30–December 4, 2005, Washington, DC; and at the Department of Anthropology, Northwestern University, Evanston, IL. Thanks to Mary Weismantel, Gilberto Rosas, Mark Goodale, and Sally Merry for these opportunities, and for comments on this paper. Research was supported by a grant (no. 0452350) from the National Science Foundation, Cultural Anthropology Program and Law and Social Sciences Program. The author wishes to acknowledge the contributions of Rose Marie Achá, Eric Hinojosa, and Theo Roncken of *Acción Andina* to this research.

movements have deployed the language of human rights (elaborating their own takes on "indigenous" and "cultural" rights in the process; see Albro 2005) to reframe their struggles for political recognition, social inclusion, and access to land and other natural resources in terms of democratic citizenship, and the right to participate in shaping the future of the Bolivian nation. Morales' notoreity as a progessive, populist figure defending the rights of Bolivia's poor and marginalized was further underscored by his explicit denunciation of neoliberalism, and his pledge to reverse decades of free market economic policies that have further impoverished South America's poorest nation. This rhet-oric translated to electoral success in December 2005, as he carried more than 50 percent of the popular vote – a landslide by Bolivian standards – defeating the rightist candidate Jorge "Tuto" Quiroga, widely regarded as representing the status quo on neoliberal economic policy and continued elite domination of national politics.

As the Bolivian social movements illustrate, "human rights" has achieved a kind of global ascendancy as the discourse of political and moral accountability, in the process becoming "the language of progressive politics in the Third World" today (Rajagopal 2003: 168). But as the urban security crisis in Bolivia also reveals – in a contra-diction which this chapter explores – in parts of the same developing world human rights is being demonized, fueling a violent reactionary politics as well. Since September 11, 2001, "security" has become a global sociopolitical watchword, and what might be called "security talk" now stands prominently alongside "rights talk" in contemporary geopolitics (see Cowan, Dembour, and Wilson 2001; Merry 2003). The quest for security has come to dominate the agendas of government policymakers, international lenders, and social service nongovern-mental organizations (NGOs) worldwide but especially in the Americas, where rising crime rates and social uncertainty are seen as threatening the democratic achievements of the last decade (UNDP 2004). At the local level as well, "security" has emerged in recent years as a powerful discourse coloring the perceptions and daily practices of ordinary citizens. As the Bolivian state has configured the nation's economy according to the dictates of the Washington Consensus, adopting a strict neoliberal line of privatization, flexibility, and the decentralization and diminution of the state, poverty, income inequal-ity, and quotidian social violence have mounted. The general eco-nomic insecurity is compounded by a pervasive sense of physical insecurity, as crime rates rise and "talk of crime" and its accompanying fear intensify, particularly in the poor urban communities (*barrios*) that ring Bolivia's cities. The neoliberal Bolivian state, lacking the resources and the will to provide honest and reliable police protection and judicial services to these communities, has lost credibility in the eyes of barrio residents, who do not regard it as a source of either economic or physical security. In the absence of official provision of security and "justice," many barrio residents have turned to violence, taking the law into their own hands by lynching suspected criminals, as both a means for controlling crime and as a demonstration to both prospective criminals and the Bolivian state that they are willing and able to provide their own security by any means necessary (see Goldstein 2004). Despite this lack of confidence in the state, however, many people continue to agitate for more, and more violent, police protection, creating a contradiction whereby people fear and hate the police and other judicial authorities, but at the same time many call for greater discretionary powers for police personnel to control crime and other security threats.

In the barrios of Cochabamba city, then, two transnational discourses find contradictory expression. The intense preoccupation with security encounters the question of human rights as barrio residents, concerned with defending their own "rights" to security, property, and freedom from fear violate the rights of others by arbitrarily depriving them of life without benefit of due process, and by embracing state practices that seem to promise greater security in exchange for greater police latitude in using violence to control crime (Smulovitz 2003; Tulchin, Frühling, and Golding 2003). This emphasis on security, precipitated by the scarcities and perceived dangers of life under neoliberal democracy, serves to introduce a new kind of "right" into the debate over the meaning of human rights (in this case, "the right to security"), shifting local understandings of human rights in ways that are increasingly violent and at odds with normative transnational human rights ideals. At the same time, by embracing the discourse of security, barrio residents position themselves as antagonistic to the discourse of human rights: Even as they claim to be defending their own rights through violence, barrio residents view the rights of criminal suspects as forfeit, obstacles to be overcome on the way to achieving security, and regard with suspicion those NGOs and their representatives who espouse the transnational discourse of "human rights" in defense of the accused. Ironically, this move could ultimately drive a wedge between the social movements and their calls for indigenous, citizen, and human rights, and the urban residents for whom they advocate, who instead are coming to view human rights as an arbitrary limitation on the state's capacity to provide "security."

As Goodale points out in the introduction to this volume, the practice of human rights in what are typically defined as "local" contexts is much more complex than international human rights law and its theorists might presume.[1] As with all cultural phenomena, the meanings of human rights shift and change over time, as local actors redefine them in response to current material conditions and socio-political configurations. The consolidation of neoliberal political economy in Bolivia over the last twenty years has created such profound economic and social "insecurity" for the urban poor that political and civil rights, originally intended to protect the poor from state violence and abuse, are now seen by those same people as "rights for criminals," and hence as challenges to their own security that must be overcome, by violence if necessary. Human rights, then, in the course of this history, have shifted from a guarantor of protections for the poor and vulnerable to an obstacle to their protection, in the minds of many (though not all) of the poor themselves. As this chapter shows, human rights discourse in urban Bolivia thus represents a transnational normativity that is adapted, rearticulated, challenged, and redeployed, both by state actors and poor barrio residents, in ways that even local human rights advocates could never have imagined, and which challenge basic assumptions about the inherent liberatory potential of human rights discourse itself. In Bolivia, as elsewhere throughout the Americas, "human rights" as an emancipatory discourse encounters a competing transnational ontology of "security," which not only has the power to defeat "rights" in the daily social practice of ordinary Bolivians, but seems able to rework and redefine "rights" itself, to recast it as a foreign idea inappropriately imposed on local reality, while at the same time appropriating it to the struggle for "security." This redefinition emerges, I suggest, from the unexamined ideology that informs both "security" and "human rights," what Giorgio Agamben (2005) has identified as "the state of exception" that both discourses contain, and which circumvents the limits on state power and abuse that these

---

[1] To speak of local and global contexts or "levels" here is not to rank them hierarchically, but rather, as Goodale suggests (chapter 3 in this volume), to acknowledge and operationalize them as distinct domains of discourse and practice, which may be profitably explored ethnographically.

discourses supposedly entail. Within the state of exception, violence becomes an unending normativity in itself, a practice not antagonistic to rights but, bizarrely, a means of securing them; meanwhile, "human rights" and its advocates become demonized as enemies of security and well being for the poor. This resistance to and redefinition of "rights" at the local level threatens to undermine the political and legal gains that the transnational discourse has globally attained, and must be taken very seriously by those concerned for the emancipatory potential of "human rights" in the new world order.

RIGHTS, SECURITY, AND THE STATE OF EXCEPTION

The exception, according to Italian political philosopher Giorgio Agamben, has become the rule in contemporary states. At the heart of every democratic state operating under a declared rule of law, there exists the "state of exception," a provision whereby the state (in times identified as "crisis moments" that threaten the very continuity of the state itself) is empowered to act outside the constraints of law, permitting the state to adopt extreme measures (including violence against its own citizens) in its own defense. The question of what constitutes such a crisis is of course up to the state to decide, and is therefore inherently conservative: revolutionary movements intending to transform the political status quo necessarily fall under the category of "emergencies," their existence justifying the declaration of an at least temporary suspension of the normative legal order and the state's invocation of emergency powers. In Agamben's terms (2005: 38–39), the state of exception is an anomic space in which the *force de loi* ("force of law") becomes detached from the law itself, emerging as a kind of naked power that the state (or, potentially, revolutionary groups) can seize and wield without accountability to ordinary legal norms. The state of exception is thus a space without law, a "juridical void" in which violence in the name of "national defense" (for example) becomes possible and, ironically, necessary for the maintenance of the juridical order.

Agamben's singular contribution is to identify the state of exception (analyzed previously by several European theorists, most notably Carl Schmitt [1931]) as a general condition of modern democratic society. That is to say, rather than an exceptional moment, the state of exception today has in fact become the norm, a permanent condition in which the abrogation of rights and personal protections is justified by a more or less permanent "war" that "requires" the sovereign's unrestrained response. Operative here is the subjective but potent doxa of "necessity," by which violence and limitations placed on personal freedoms and basic rights are justified: in a crisis like war, it is implied (and sometimes stated outright), rights become a luxury that society can ill afford.[2] Thus we have the US "War on Terror" waged by the Bush administration since September 11, 2001, which has witnessed the suspension of rights of Guantanamo detainees, effectively stripping them of their very legal identities (Butler 2004); the humiliation and torture of prisoners at Abu Ghraib (Hersch 2004); and the implementation of new systems of mass surveillance and other encroachments on civil liberties, in an effort to create a heightened sense of "security" in the face of an unspecified but ever-present "threat."[3]

As it has become the norm, then, the state of exception has given way to a more generalized and pervasive "paradigm of security" (Agamben 2002), in which security provision becomes the singular activity of the state, its key discourse and preoccupation, and principal source of legitimation. Implicit in this expansion of "security talk" and security-making activity is the notion that rights may have to be sacrificed for security, that civil and human rights cannot be respected in the context of "emergency," in which threats to national and personal security arise. Curiously, though, the ease with which human rights may be abrogated is not merely a product of the security paradigm's hegemony but a problem internal to human rights law itself. At the core of international human rights law lies the very state of exception that Agamben has identified, a "doctrine of emergency" whereby states are free to commit atrocities against their own citizens should threats to national security and stability be perceived as imminent. As Rajagopal (2003) has pointed out, this emergency doctrine derives from British colonial efforts to regulate an ever-menacing colonized population, justifying violence against nationalist anti-colonial movements as efforts to maintain "law and order" in the streets. This colonial exemption has

---

[2] The metaphor of war is thus a powerful instrument for states to deploy in characterizing a variety of political undertakings, including the US "War on Drugs," which has justified the suspension of a host of basic rights of accused drug offenders, both in Latin America and the United States; see Farthing 1997; Reinarman and Levine 1997.

[3] The hegemony of an emerging discourse of (in)security as a condition of life under modern democracy is indicated by the apparent willingness of the majority of US citizens to accept new limits on their freedom in exchange for a perceived heightening of security (Davis and Silver 2004), a finding that correlates well with my argument in this chapter.

been maintained by postcolonial regimes and incorporated into the cannon of international human rights law, such that "the culture of emergency" has become an unquestioned principle within the human rights framework, one that allows states to suspend the guarantee of human rights to citizens, if the protection of these rights can be represented as posing a threat to security.[4] Pragmatically, of course, the incorporation of such provisions into the human rights framework was a necessary step to gaining international approval of human rights doctrines. But, given this exception at the core of human rights principles: "One must then ask if the present human-rights corpus, which incorporates the concept of emergency, is fatally flawed because it perpetuates the same fear, contempt, and loathing of the masses, the same legal void that enables governments to take extreme measures without sanction" (Rajagopal 2003: 182).

The discourses of security and human rights, in many ways perceived as inherently at odds with one another, thus share a fundamental principle in the state of exception. At the heart of both of these paradigms – each in a sense seeking to define the permissible at the conjuncture of state and civil society – we find not the rule of law but an exception to the rule, a back door through which limitless state violence and the abrogation of basic rights re-enter supposedly demo-cratic society uncontested. And while "human rights" has received considerably more anthropological attention than "security," both paradigms constitute a set of practices and discourses that – in an era of global terrorism, preventive war, and the consolidation of neoliberal democracy – are distinctly transnational in scope and effect, transcend-ing the territorial and discursive space of the nation-state and jointly serving to define the landscape of political domination and resistance within and across nation-states today. But, as the ethnographic discus-sion below suggests, the discourse of rights is vulnerable to critique from the security paradigm: given the state's practical failures to defend rights equitably across social groups and classes, and the fear and insecurity generated by the permanent state of exception found

---

[4] Strictly speaking, international human rights law requires that in a state of emergency, states operate under a differently configured legal framework in recognition of the exceptional nature of the emergency. In this sense, the legal void within human rights is not entirely empty, as it does contain law, albeit modified by circumstance. Nevertheless, within this context human rights protections are contingent, rather than guaranteed under the law. The special tribunals before which Guantanamo prisoners are to be secretly tried are examples of this kind of exceptional law, which privileges security over rights in the state of emergency.

within neoliberal democracy, rights themselves come under scrutiny, and in the quest for "security" the ability of "human rights" to serve as a platform for resistance against state violence becomes debilitated.

"SECURITY TALK": SECURITY AS TRANSNATIONAL DISCOURSE AND PRACTICE

To speak of a transnational security discourse is to connect with a rich Pan-American conversation ongoing since at least the 1970s, when authoritarian regimes invoked a "national security doctrine" to combat threats to the regime in a context of Cold War anxiety and anti-communism. Deployed by military governments throughout the region, this doctrine emphasized a definition of security predicated on defense of the nation from "internal enemies" bent on creating social disorder and threatening national stability (Dammert 2004). In the name of maintaining "public order," institutional violence was the order of the day: the armed forces played a central role in daily policing functions, and special security units were created, specifically charged with the maintenance of order by any means necessary (including violence and torture), while enjoying immunity from prosecution. With the transition to democracy in the 1990s, the role of the military in civilian life was significantly curtailed, but state and police violence against citizens continued and in some cases intensified, while the general climate of suspicion, impending danger, and police impunity persisted (Neild 1999). The state of exception introduced with the doctrine of national security continues into the post-authoritarian period, with its target remaining the "enemy within," only shifting now from communists to criminals: The focus of security campaigns remains on members of the "dangerous classes" who threaten social order and who must be controlled, by violence if necessary, permitting the abrogation of human rights in the name of state security and protection from crime (Chevigny 1997; Pinheiro 1999).

In point of fact, measures of "criminality" have shown a steady increase throughout Latin America since the 1980s, intensifying in recent years. Despite the inadequacy of data in most countries (police often fail to record accurate crime statistics, and underreporting due to mistrust of the police is rampant), by all existing measures crimes against property and persons are on the rise across the region (Ungar 2003), and the incidence of violent crime has gotten worse (Carranza 2004). Latin America has a homicide rate that is virtually off the charts: whereas the global average for homicides is 5 per 100,000 people, with a rate of over 10 considered to be "dangerously high," the average for middle- to low-income countries in Latin America is 27.5, the highest regional average in the world (Moser, Winton, and Moser 2003; WHO 2002). Within Latin America, the majority of violent crimes are committed in large cities, and the Andean region reports the highest incidence of violent crimes in both rural and urban areas (Arriagada 2001). Furthermore, while in the last few years crime rates have fallen somewhat in the region's wealthier countries they have worsened in the poorer countries, a function of income disparity that many observers attribute to the inequities that have intensified under globalization (Carranza 2004). It is these inequities, more than absolute poverty, that social scientists have correlated most closely with violence, suggesting that violence is most likely to be found in contexts of extreme inequality and social exclusion. Fear of crime, meanwhile, has mounted exponentially and without necessary correlation with crime statistics, spurred on by daily conversation, rumor, and gossip (Caldeira 2000), and by the contributions of the media, which sensationalize the most horrific incidents of violent crime for their own commercial purposes (Briceño-Leon and Zubilaga 2002). Personal fear and what has become identified as *inseguridad* ("insecurity") is further exacerbated by the loud and furious debate in all Latin American countries (as in the US and Europe) over "public security," amid efforts to prepare and protect the public from criminal and terrorist violence. The result is a pervasive climate of dread and insecurity, such that the *habitus* of daily life, particularly in urban areas, is one of overwhelming anxiety, uncertainty, and despair (Garland 2001; Giddens 1990; Merry 2001).[5]

Adding to this pervasive sense of insecurity is the absence of a reliable authority, operating according to a rule of law, to which people can turn to report crimes, resolve conflicts, or seek redress of grievances. As I have described elsewhere (Goldstein 2003; 2005), corruption is widespread in the Bolivian police force (as it is in other Latin American police institutions), and people reporting crimes to the authorities are likely to be revictimized by extortionist police practices, with demands for money to initiate routine police procedures

---

[5] So while violence may have become "normalized" or "routinized" as part of everyday social existence for the urban poor, as many observers claim (e.g., Scheper-Hughes 1992), this should in no way imply an acceptance by the poor of this condition, in the classic sense of false consciousness.

being commonly reported. "This sense of the law as worse than crime, the ultimate injustice" (Taussig 2003: 30) is widely held, and contributes to the sense of powerlessness that crime victims typically experience. Additionally, the court system is beyond the reach or comprehension of most poor urban residents, who have an incomplete knowledge of the workings of the system and lack the financial or cultural capital to access it (Domingo and Seider 2001). The spaces of policing and justice-making vacated by the state are increasingly occupied by private security firms, often staffed by ex-police officers and ex-convicts alike, who know the workings of the official system and who now profit from this knowledge by selling security services to those who can afford them. These private security firms are increasingly coming to operate like paramilitaries or mafias, dividing the city into turfs under their control and pressuring all local residents to pay for protection, or else become the next victims of crime in the neighborhood.[6]

Despite the many problems with the formal justice system, many poor urban residents nevertheless advocate for a stronger and more violent police presence in their neighborhoods, contending that crime would be reduced and "security" enhanced were the authorities to take *la mano dura* ("heavy hand" approach) to crime in the streets. Throughout Latin America, political candidates are being elected on "get tough on crime" platforms that promise to circumvent the due process rights of the accused; the election of ex-dictator Hugo Banzer in Bolivia in 2001 was in part due to his strong anticrime pledge (Prillaman 2003). Some states are adopting a "zero tolerance" approach to crime, a philosophy derived from the Giuliani administration in New York City now gone transnational. Exported throughout the hemisphere by luminaries like William Bratton, former NYPD chief and proponent of the "broken windows" philosophy of crime prevention, zero tolerance justifies a strong police response to relatively minor crimes in order to deter the evolution of greater ones (Escobar, Muniz, Sanseviero et al. 2004).[7] Though studies have shown that "zero tolerance" is not a realistic approach to crime control (indeed, no city, in

---

[6] The "privatization of justice" (Caldeira and Holston 1999) that this implies also motivates the lynch mob, the perfect expression of neoliberal logic (see Goldstein 2005).

[7] According to this model, the presence of one broken window in a building communicates neglect to other would-be vandals, encouraging further vandalism which leads to crimes of greater magnitude. "Broken windows" literally and symbolically identify high-crime urban areas (Wilson and Kelling 1982).

the US or elsewhere, has actually instituted all of its principles: Petrulla and Vanderschueren 2003), the discourse of zero tolerance has become a powerful instrument for states attempting to project an image of efficacy in the fight against crime (Prillaman 2003). It also appeals to many citizens within these societies, who are willing to accept harsh penalties and violent police practice in exchange for enhanced security.

A new and apparently more progressive variety of the security discourse has emerged in recent years, in the transnational conversation about what is now called *seguridad ciudadana* ("citizen security"). Across the hemisphere, governmental policy makers, international development organizations, academic analysts, and average citizens have adopted the language of "(in)seguridad ciudadana" to characterize the struggle for greater personal and social security guaranteed by a democratic rule of law. By one definition of this new security paradigm, seguridad ciudadana refers to "the protection of the normal functioning of democratic institutions, the defense of the citizenry from criminality in all of its facets and typologies, [and] the defense of citizens against corruption and other asocial acts that impede or problematize the normal development and enjoyment of the fundamental rights of persons" (Delgado Aguado and Guardia Maduell 1994: 20). Implicit in this definition is the right of citizens to a safe and secure life, and to demand that the state respect and guarantee this right (del Olmo 2000). This new wrinkle in the transnational discourse of security is clearly distinct from earlier meanings of "security" in Latin America: Rather than pitting rights against security, seguridad ciudadana acknowledges security to be a right, guaranteed by the state to its citizens.[8] In an expanded sense, citizen security has become a platform for the realization of other rights, the attainment of security facilitating equal opportunity and the expansion of economic, political, and social rights for the poor and marginalized (Bobea 2003). As such, improving "seguridad ciudadana" in the region has become a major goal of transnational development activity in the last few years. Since September 11, 2001, "security" has become extraordinarily fundable, and many international development organizations (including the United Nations Development Programme, the World Bank, and United States Agency for International Development [USAID])

---

[8] The United Nations Development Program acknowledged this "right to security" more explicitly in a recent statement of its human rights priorities in Bolivia; see UNDP 2005.

have recently made grants to Latin American states with the aim of heightening citizen security.[9] The United States now regards "security" in Latin American nations as critical to its own national security: In the words of a USAID report (in which the agency quotes its own congressional budget justification for USAID 2005):

> Establishing the rule of law also helps to fight crime more effectively, and in the process improve security in those countries and throughout the region. In the new environment of security concerns and the War on Terror, the stability of the hemisphere is a high priority for the United States, especially as it recognizes that, in the post-Cold War environment, "the greatest threats to U.S. interests at home and abroad stem not from conquering states, but from failing ones."

> (USAID 2007)

Similarly, at a 2003 conference on Security in Latin America and the Caribbean sponsored by the Inter-American Development Bank, a representative of that organization noted: "The effects of the terrorist attacks of September 11 have radically modified the security agenda, and new threats have deepened the consciousness of the Western Hemisphere on the interdependence in facing this problem;" he stressed that security should be "the political axis of international cooperation" in the Americas (IDB 2003). Not surprisingly, on the heels of this transnational funding impetus, concepts of citizen security have recently been written into some Latin American constitutions, and the language of "seguridad ciudadana" has been incorporated into a number of hemispheric pacts and programs of transnational cooperation (Gabaldón 2004).

Citizen security as a transnational discourse of rights encounters problems, however, in the daily practice of security in Latin America. Given the high incidence of crime and violence, the profound mistrust in and ineffectiveness of police and judicial systems, and the generalized climate of fear and suspicion that clouds everyday life, talk of security experiences a slippage away from this progressive language and back into the inherited meanings of the authoritarian past. Old equations of "security" with public order reassert themselves, and violence targeting the enemy within reemerges (if indeed it ever went away) as a publicly acceptable method of dealing with social

---

[9] For example, USAID has pledged grants of nearly $50,000,000 over the next five years to strengthening democratic institutions and improving "access to justice" in Bolivia; USAID 2005.

disorder. The idea of citizen security as a human right, and as a portal to other rights, again falls victim to the state of exception that lies at the heart of both security and human rights; citizen security in its progressive sense is framed within a logic that postpones the realization of such rights until such time as "delinquency" can be controlled and threats to social order permanently quelled. From the vantage point of the security paradigm, "security" can only be attained if the forces of "insecurity" and "delinquency" are opposed by the superior force of state repression, and "rights" become obstacles that have to be circumvented so that "law and order" in the streets may prevail. For the state, this equation creates a space of exemption that allows for the remilitarization of policing, reversing human rights groups' hard-won gains in excluding the armed forces from the daily work of internal security (Machillanda 2005); the expansion of police latitude in the use of violence in criminal investigation; the adoption of harsher criminal penalties, including the death penalty (now making a resurgence in Latin America: Dammert and Malone 2003); and the prosecution and penalization of minors as adults. And for citizens concerned with their own "security" but lacking the confidence in the state to provide it, the idea of "the right to security" emerges as a justification for extra-legal violence, permitting the adoption of local forms of violent revenge (including lynching: see below) as instruments of crime control and security promotion. The right to security takes its place as the paramount right, the right that trumps all other rights, and violence – either state, collective, or private – is justified on the road to its attainment.

It bears repetition here, however, that the quest for security and the conjuncture of official and popular support for *la mano dura* contradict other forms of political activity in Bolivian society. While increased measures of "security" enjoy broad, cross-class support in Bolivia, at the same time suspicion of the state remains extremely high, and popular responses to state violence not apparently connected to crime control are swift and severe. The full reemergence of the old authoritarian "national security" paradigm is limited by the progressive politics of social movements in Bolivia today, even as many in Bolivian society share the goal of greater "security" from crime. Thus the state's effort to recast the Gas War (a 2003 uprising in which thousands of Bolivians took to the streets to protest the role of foreign corporations in the extraction and sale of natural gas, an event which resulted in the deaths of nearly a hundred protestors and the resignation of the Bolivian president) as a threat to national security was firmly rejected by people across Bolivian civil society, who denounced state killings of protestors as a violation of their human rights.[10] This discrepancy points to the contradictions inherent in the security paradigm, under-scoring the rich and likewise contradictory sociopolitical field in which discourses of rights and security emerge and are deployed. It is also important to point out that while *la mano dura* does enjoy widespread support as a response to crime control, this view is not universally held among the urban poor, a point to which I will return below.

DEFENDING SECURITY IN COCHABAMBA: VIOLENCE AND RIGHTS

There are a number of reasons why Bolivians might distrust the transnational discourse of human rights, even as Bolivian social move-ments and their spokespeople publicly deploy rights talk in advancing their own programs for democratic inclusion. For one, as Rajagopal (2003: 196) points out, human rights law and language, while highly critical of various forms of physical violence, are virtually silent when it comes to economic violence – that is, violence caused by development, market forces, or transnational economic policy regimes. The violence brought on by neoliberal economic policy, felt widely throughout Bolivian society and motivating the recent uprisings and political confrontations within Bolivia, do not fall under the rubric of human rights, and are not typically addressed as such by international or domestic rights NGOs. This lacuna is recognized by social movements, as they recast the language of rights to characterize their struggles against market violence of privatization, debt repayment schemes, and the War on Drugs, but rarely by rights NGOs themselves. Additionally, human rights, while expressing a profound mistrust of the state, at the same time is predicated on "a total reliance on the moral possibilities of the state" (Rajagopal 2003: 189); human rights incorporates an implicit model of an expansionary state as the only means for the realization of a just society. Contrary to what is

---

[10] The Bolivian state's audience for this claim was more likely the international community (and particularly the United States) rather than its own citizens. In other areas as well, the Bolivian state has invoked an authoritarian discourse of security to characterize its own recent policy-making. For example, the national Law of Citizen Security, passed in 2003, contains strong penalties for groups that blockade roads (a common tactic in subaltern political protest in Bolivia), but no provisions for augmenting police presence in marginal communities.

commonly assumed, many states actually embrace human rights as the sanctioned language of resistance, welcoming the advocacy by human rights discourse for a strong and expanding state, a position that accords well with the desires of the ruling class who controls it (Rajagopal 2003: 191). In Bolivia, the creation of state agencies like the *Defensoria del Pueblo*, the human rights ombudsperson intended to serve a watchdog role over state activities and yet clearly a political entity of the state itself, are regarded by many Bolivians as evidence of the collaboration between "human rights" and the state, and thus a further source of skepticism of the discourse.

Furthermore, and perhaps in contradiction to the above, for many Bolivians human rights as discourse and ideology retains an association with the non-local sources from which it originated. Having arrived in Bolivia as part and parcel of a larger globalizing movement toward democratization and neoliberal political and economic transformation, human rights, like these other projects, is regarded by many as a foreign imposition that reduces national sovereignty and illegitimately shapes local realities. To use Santos' (1997: 3) terms, human rights in Bolivia remains a kind of "globalized localism," a form of "globalization from above" that clearly bears the label of its foreign manufacture. As such, human rights, though powerful as a global discourse of resistance, does not automatically enjoy local legitimacy, nor does it necessarily serve a counter-hegemonic function in local struggles. To the contrary, as evidenced by the local condemnation of "human rights" described below, ordinary Bolivians are more likely to reject human rights precisely because of its global character, as though recognizing and rejecting the power relations implicit in the impositions "from above" (see the discussion of the politics of global/local verticality in Goodale's introduction to this volume). Thus even as they fear and loathe the state, many Bolivians, confronting problems of insecurity, also denounce the state's diminution and loss of sovereignty vis-à-vis foreign nations (especially the United States) and international economic institutions like the International Monetary Fund and the World Bank. Suspicion of human rights discourse accompanies the mistrust of other transnational interventions into Bolivian national economic and political life, which are perceived as having contributed to the nation's enduring poverty and social insecurity.

In the arena of personal security from crime, human rights discourse and those national and international NGOs that deploy it are frequently regarded by residents of poor barrios as antagonistic to local security (see Caldeira 2000).[11] Human rights defenders and activists, long critical of state violence in Bolivia and so historically threatened and persecuted by the state, are now being demonized by average citizens, who regard activists' defense of the rights of criminal suspects as another kind of antisocial act, something akin to police corruption. In Cochabamba, much of this animosity is directed against the *Asamblea Permanente de Derechos Humanos* (Permanent Human Rights Assembly), or Derechos Humanos for short, whose offices collect citizen complaints of human rights abuses by the state, and whose representatives sometimes hold workshops in the barrios to train citizens in human rights language and tolerance. But many barrio residents regard representatives of Derechos Humanos, like the police, as accomplices of thieves, owing to their insistence on the rights of individuals facing arbitrary incarceration and punishment. Thus, a focus group interview with female artisans that I conducted in 2004 produced this remarkable exchange:[12]

ARTISAN 1: Last week a *señor*, my neighbor, took his car out of the garage to wash it, he left it out for five minutes and it was stolen. And this señor worked for Derechos Humanos, those who defend the delinquents! They robbed him, in five minutes they robbed him.

ARTISAN 2: He deserved it, no?

It is widely believed in the barrios of Cochabamba that human rights advocates defend the delinquents, positioning them as enemies of law-abiding citizens. This sentiment comes through clearly in interviews I have conducted (with the help of colleagues in *Acción Andina*, a Bolivian research NGO) with residents of marginal barrios throughout Cochabamba's southern zone. Some, like the speaker quoted below, point to Bolivian law and its defense of basic human rights principles as the cause of local insecurity, suggesting that "human rights" represent unfair advantages for criminals, while the innocent victims receive no protection: "I believe that we have to reform our laws ... I don't know if Derechos Humanos, who they want to defend, but ... There are more advantages for the delinquent than there are for the citizen. Everybody knows it, they know how it is. That's especially the case in the peri-urban barrios. Now we are impotent."

---

[11] For a detailed historical and ethnographic account of urban life in Cochabamba, see Goldstein 2005.

[12] All translations from the Spanish are my own.

Others describe human rights and social service NGOs, even those who devote service to the poor, as creating social imbalances that favor the criminal class of society. Such evaluations rely on a Manichean moral calculus, a familiar staple of the security paradigm, which divides the world into good and evil, the deserving and the undeserving, and arranges these categories in an oppositional and exclusionary relationship to one another.[13] In the security discourse of Cochabamba, the "evil" group is identified as *delincuentes* ("delinquents") or *antisociales* (anti-social elements), those who turn to crime to support themselves, taking unfair advantage of the good, hardworking barrio residents. In the interview text below, the "antisocials" referred to are *cleferitos*, glue-sniffing street children who live by petty crime, often robbing market vendors in *la Cancha* the city's large outdoor market, and who are frequently the targets of police and resident reprisals. Though they are often beaten, harassed, and sometimes executed in extra-judicial killings (either by lynch mobs or in covert police actions), the cleferitos are characterized in this informant's testimony as constituting a privileged class, who are rewarded by human rights defenders for their delinquency:

> This [privileging of the bad over the good] is one thing that has to change. A clear example: The *antisociales* that are in the street, there is an NGO ... where they provide these antisociales with food, they provide them with clothing, health care, they provide them with everything. Turns out that this NGO, to have 30 or 40 cleferitos, they go to the Cancha and recruit them. "Come on, I'm going to rehabilitate you." ... There has to be a total change. These kids that want to reform have to make their living by the sweat of their brow. If you want to eat you have to work ...

Barrio leaders and intellectuals, articulating more sophisticated political ideologies, point to the evident link between human rights NGOs and the system of global capitalism to call into question the goals of Derechos Humanos and similar organizations. In the town of Vinto, a short distance outside of Cochabamba city, a group of local leaders and MAS party affiliates explained that while Derechos Humanos representatives do advocate for the rights of working people in Bolivia, ultimately they must be seen as "accomplices of capitalism":

---

[13] This division of people into categories of good and evil, or just and unjust, is another component of the transnational security discourse, as watchers of the War on Terror will easily recognize. As mentioned earlier, in Latin America this language also has its roots in the authoritarian past: see Dammert 2004.

Derechos Humanos too is part of the system, that is to say, they try to humanize the capitalist system but they don't try to destroy it ... Take the Communist Party as an ideal, as an example, no? The Communist Party tried to educate or raise the consciousness of the people so that they could take power. Has Derechos Humanos, as defender of human rights, ever thought of doing that? ... Or have they stuck only with providing welfare services (*asistencialismo*)? Because what Derechos Humanos does is welfare ... Think for a moment of [the former national director of Derechos Humanos, who recently became Defensor del Pueblo] ... He made a political decision to try and involve himself in the system through the Defensoría del Pueblo. And the Defensoría del Pueblo, what is that? It is a state institution that precisely tries to "humanize capitalism," in quotes. And what does that mean? To be an accomplice.

This speaker points to the Defensoria del Pueblo, the state's human rights ombudsperson's office, as evidence of the incorporation to the state of human rights law and language intended to protect citizens from the state. It is interesting to note from this testimony, offered by populist party members and activists in Bolivian social movements, that the condemnation of a transnational human rights, regarded here as a collaborator with the state and transnational capital, even as these individuals are liable to use human rights language in their protests against political exclusion and state policy on natural resources.

Human rights defenders like the representatives of Derechos Humanos are demonized by both state officials and ordinary citizens for their efforts to ensure that suspected criminals are prosecuted according to the dictates of the Bolivian legal code. The Bolivian state's New Criminal Procedural Code (*El Nuevo Código de Procedimiento Penal*), introduced in 2001, is in many ways a landmark effort in the country, the first real attempt at judicial reform in the democratic era. The New Code was intended to replace the former "inquisitorial" system, by which judicial authorities could, among other things, arrest and detain criminal suspects indefinitely and without leveling formal charges. The New Code introduced a set of procedures for police investigations, ensuring that *habeas corpus* and the presumption of innocence would be respected, and severely restricting the measures (including, typically, violence and torture, or their threat) that police could use to extract confessions from detainees. Based on fundamental values of transparency, equity, and enforcement of constitutional guarantees, the New Code represents an attempt to bring the judicial system under a rule of law. However, given the low budget, lack of training, and widespread corruption within the Bolivian National Police force, as well as the relatively small number of police officers on the streets in Cochabamba, the requirements for detention imposed under the New Code are difficult to satisfy, and criminal suspects are frequently released (it is said) for lack of evidence.[14] Thus, the Code itself has become a scapegoat for all manner of social ills: the New Code is the target of much official and popular criticism in Cochabamba, and the rights it guarantees to accused criminals are widely regarded as obstacles to security in the marginal barrios. For example, asked to identify when the incidence of crime in Cochabamba began to worsen, one informant related: "Since they began to implement the New Criminal Procedural Code, it began to grow. Why? One, you can't detain him [the suspect] for very long. Two, we don't have definitive proof [of guilt]. So it is on this basis that delinquency is growing and growing with greater intensity."

In particular, many regard the elimination of "preventive detention" from Bolivian law as a serious obstacle to keeping delinquents off the streets. Human rights activists in Cochabamba have been forceful campaigners for this aspect of the New Code, and often take it upon themselves to ensure that police respect the eight-hour limit on detention, after which time they must file charges or release the suspect. But many barrio residents complain that, even if they turn a criminal suspect over to the police for prosecution, all too often these individuals are quickly back on the street, owing either to police corruption (e.g., an officer accepts a bribe to free the prisoner) or to the law itself, which requires the presentation of evidence to continue a detention. Judicial authorities make similar complaints, encouraging the perception that requiring proof of culpability limits police effectiveness and compromises citizen security. Another interview subject, himself a police officer and barrio resident, condemns the New Code for limiting the investigative powers of the police and hence jeopardizing the security of the populace. At the same time, he reiterates the belief

---

[14] There is much official hostility to the Nuevo Código de Procedimiento Penal, given that it places limits on the police's ability to act arbitrarily and with violence. Human rights advocates in Cochabamba claim that police will accept a bribe to release a prisoner from custody, and then tell victims that they had no choice but to release him under the terms of the New Code. Such disinformation contributes to public misunderstanding of the law, and resentment against the "rights of criminals" it is believed to protect.

that delinquents receive more services and protections than do ordinary citizens, in this case in terms of their rights to legal counsel:

> The policeman is a common citizen like us, the only difference being that he wears a uniform and complies with what the law says, nothing more. Because beyond that he can do no more, because he doesn't have power like before. Before at least with a stick, or with kicks, the policeman could make the delinquent talk, and later he recovered. But now, no, even the worst delinquent we can't touch a hair on his head, so says the law. These are exactly the reasons given by Derechos Humanos, the Defensor del Pueblo, *Defensa Pública* [the public defender's office]. For the delinquent, I tell you honestly, I think they bring four or five professionals, but for the common citizen not even one professional do they provide. So there are circumstances in which the citizen has to be prepared, he has to know the law.

Curiously, although it obviously limits the abuses that police and other state officers can commit against detainees, some barrio residents also interpret the New Code as allowing for the use of lynching to secure justice in criminal cases. Many barrio residents regard lynching as an expression of "community justice" (*justicia comunitaria*), an autochthonous practice that supposedly precedes the modern state and derives its justification from its purported antiquity. Making this assertion grants a powerful legitimacy to vigilante violence, rendering it "traditional" and thus beyond criticism by modern law. It also provides a powerful counterpoint to the law, which many regard as illegitimate by virtue of the blatant corruption of its practitioners; lynching, by comparison, is represented as a collective response, based on historical precedent, in defense of the community. While the historical precedence of lynching in Bolivia is highly debatable,[15] the fact remains that the New Code does sanction the use of "*justicia comunitaria*" in situations where it has traditionally been practiced. In the absence of an effective police and judicial presence, barrio residents contend that the New Code permits the reactivation of rural community justice practices (including lynching), that supposedly have been lying dormant in the urban community.

The New Code is thus read by barrio people to contain an exemption for violence, a state of exception whereby rights violations creep

---

[15] Indeed, in most ways urban lynchings do not approximate rural community justice procedures: see Colloredo-Mansfeld 2002.

back into the system of justice administration.[16] This is underscored by the tacit approval given to lynching by state authorities, who consistently fail to investigate and prosecute lynching cases. It also highlights the exception at the heart of the security discourse, wherein the perils of daily urban life are invoked to justify extreme measures in pursuit of security. Again, human rights is conjured as an antagonist, an obstacle to justice that not only contributes to delinquency, but remarkably is described as driving extra-judicial violence itself. For example, the young man quoted below attributes the violence of lynching to the actions of human rights defenders:

> The police are always on the side of the thief. And so is Derechos Humanos. Derechos Humanos is always involved, when a thief is caught, we lock him up, in less than eight hours there is Derechos Humanos. Derechos Humanos arrives, they investigate, for what, for what reason is he there, if there is no plaintiff then no one can accuse him, they take him out and right away the offender is back on the street. So for that reason I believe, more than anything else I say, we poor people, we want to make justice with our own hands.

The complex combination of police inaction and corruption, and people's perceptions of the law is evident in these quotations, as informants conflate deliberate police abuse (i.e., corruption, failure to investigate criminal complaints, etc.) with the legal limits placed on police procedure and use of force. Here again, violence is viewed as the only recourse for those whom the state, the law, and the NGOs have abandoned:

> If we go to the Police, in two, three days he [the delinquent] will be out on the street and will come back to kill us. Better to hang him in a tree, like they did in Sacaba, like they did in Vinto. The citizen is looking to make justice, as they say, by his own hands. They are forming these kind of clans[17] that are going to settle the score ... Those who have to do it are those who understand the problem, and who are they? They are the

---

[16] While the New Code does recognize the validity of "*Derecho Consuetudinario Indígena*" (indigenous customary law), it only sanctions its expression in mediating conflicts internal to indigenous communities, and requires that fundamental rights and guarantees be respected, as stipulated by the Bolivian constitution. According to the terms of the Code, then, lynching would not under any circumstances represent a sanctioned form of customary law. Nevertheless, barrio residents often refer to the Code's recognition of *derecho consuetudinario* in defending lynching practice.

[17] The use of the word "clans" (*clanes*) is unusual here, and seems to reference lynchings from the southern US context. The term *linchamiento* ("lynching") in Bolivia is a cognate from English, though when it entered common usage is uncertain.

citizens themselves, the leaders, the residents, these should be our representatives [*diputados*]. Because some punk at a desk sitting there in his tie, who never goes out, who never sees nothing, who's in Parliament, what's he going to change? Nothing, because he doesn't understand our problems.

The preceding quote expresses a strong statement about the importance of the local in confronting problems of insecurity in the barrios today. Echoing the testimony of others quoted in this chapter, the speaker critiques all those non-local entities (imagined here as the tie-wearing bureaucrat) whose failures are responsible for the insecurity of life in the barrios. The bureaucrat, like the NGOs who are perceived as defending the rights of criminals against barrio residents, and whose practice is so clearly informed by transnational discourse, lacks the legitimacy of local actors to defend themselves and their interests. At the same time, local discourse reveals itself to be a hybrid, a complex interweaving of traditionalist rhetoric (the defense of lynching as "*justicia comunitaria*," for example) and the transnational discourse of human rights. Below, the testimony of another barrio resident reveals the hybrid nature of the rights discourse in this context. On the one hand, the very idea of "rights" is stigmatized, an avowal of the commonly held belief that "human rights" equal "rights for criminals." While this belief is clearly operative here, at the same time the speaker reveals the penetration and local appropriation of the rights discourse, deployed here to characterize the difficulties facing poor rural and urban Bolivians, who are neglected and abandoned by the neoliberal state and its allies, the transnational and domestic NGOs. When asked to explain who is responsible for this state of affairs, this speaker points to the international NGOs at work in Bolivia, invoking a rights discourse to argue, in a backhanded way, against certain basic human rights assumptions:

> In some respects it's the NGOs (that are at fault). For example, the *Defensor del Pueblo*,[18] or rather the officers of DNI (*Defensa de los Niños Internacional*, or Defense of the Children International), for example, it's an NGO, isn't it? It isn't administered by the state. It happens that some clefero is mistreated, and the DNI automatically is

---

[18] As mentioned above, the *Defensoría del Pueblo* is the office of the national human rights ombudsperson. Officially a government office, the Defensoría is officially charged to be a watchdog agency, to which citizens can appeal to level charges of human rights violations against the state. Here, the speaker tellingly conflates this state agency with the international NGO, Defense of the Children International.

called, right? ... Yes, the Defensor, DNI, for example, always protects the rights of the clefero. And the children of peasants that are without food, don't they have the same rights as the clefero? *We all have the same rights.* The DNI for example, if they want to protect the rights of the child they have to protect all children equally, not only those who sniff glue, who do harm to the population ... In other words there is not a fair administration of justice in this respect, it is more on the side of the wrongdoer in this case. (Emphasis added)

The hybrid discourse that conjoins security and rights, often in contradictory ways, combines with the insecurity of life on the margins to create strong contradictions for barrio residents. This is particularly evident in regard to lynchings, whose violence is interpreted through the optics of both security and rights. Lynching obviously represents an assault on the rights of individuals living in a supposedly free and democratic society – a point not lost on many residents of Cochabamba. For many poor cochabambinos, the fact that lynching and harsh police practice disproportionately impacts the poor is cause for mistrust of the state, the police, one's neighbors and acquaintances. Even as they reproduce the security discourse in interviews and private conversations, many barrio residents also express strong reservations about the ends to which security practice seems to be leading, and the means that people (themselves incuded) are willing to employ. Indeed, many people express grave misgivings about lynching violence, even as they sympathize with the conditions and the mindset that produce it.

> No, I don't think it's good to kill people to teach them a lesson, so that they won't come back [and commit further crimes], right? But in this case the authorities should support us, they should give us security, they should warn that person, for example, that has committed a crime, that he shouldn't come back and do it again. So the people look for their own vengeance, their own justice, by killing.

Young people in particular are frequently the targets of lynching violence and police repression, and express grave doubts about the pursuit of security in Cochabamba. Teenagers and young adults complained to me of the criminalization of youth that is occurring in the city: young people, by virtue of their age alone, are often assumed to be criminals, and even in ordinary circumstances may be watched and harassed by vigilant adults, be they police officials or ordinary barrio residents. The young adults I interviewed expressed a profound mistrust of the security discourse, which limits their freedom to move about the city and socialize, for fear of falling victim to a lynch mob. This skepticism of "security" is shared by some adults, mostly women, mothers of teenagers and post-adolescents who similarly fear that their children might be mistaken for criminals and lynched. But even for these people, this fear for personal safety seems to blend with the generalized fear of crime extant in Cochabamba, so that the two become indistinguishable, and concerns for safety, security, and rights become conflated. The result is a kind of contradictory consciousness, an ambivalence captured in one woman's testimony:

> So whom can you trust? Not the police, not private security, I don't know ... I don't know who I can trust ... I think that this then leads to something else, to lynchings, for example. That to me seems like a crime but, that is to say ... I don't know if it is justified or not but more or less it has a basis. Everybody is fed up, sick and tired of seeing their things taken that they have earned with so much effort, then the only thing that they can do is try to make justice with their own hands. But that also is a crime, and a grave one, too, because we are violating the rights of another person.

CONCLUSION

> In a world that prefers security to justice, there is loud applause when-ever justice is sacrificed on the altar of security. The rite takes place on the streets. Every time a criminal falls in a hail of bullets, society feels some relief from the disease that makes it tremble. The death of each lowlife has a pharmaceutical effect on those living the high life. The word "pharmacy" comes from pharmakos, the Greek name for humans sacrificed to the gods in times of crises.
>
> Eduardo Galeano (cited in Sundar 2004: 157)

My analysis in this chapter puts a finer point on Galeano's poignant observation. For, as I have shown, it is not only those "living the high life" who support state programs (formal and unofficial) of expanded violence, surveillance, and control, but also the poor and indigenous, those who typically find themselves on the receiving end of state violence. The familiar dichotomies break down in the climate of pervasive fear and insecurity that characterizes the state of exception. The poor line up with the rich to administer violence to the poor, or to advocate for its administration; men and women alike are capable of brutal force and acts of extreme vengeance; civil society does not restrain the state or provide a protection against its abuses, but spurs the state on to greater acts of violence, undermining the very limits put in place to moderate state excess. Meanwhile "human rights," the transnational discourse of resistance from the developing world, becomes demonized as antagonistic to the well being of the citizenry, its very transnationality being a further source of its delegitimation in the minds of those skeptical of any perceived threats to national sovereignty.

As I stated in the introduction to this chapter, a powerful irony inherent in this situation is that even as some kind of rights are being demonized, the discourse of rights itself continues to provide Bolivian social movements with a powerful platform from which to articulate demands of the state and to garner international attention and support. Struggles over control of natural resources (like gas), access to land, political representation, self-determination for indigenous communities, production of coca: all are framed within a discourse of human rights that is both transnational and deeply "local," deployed on the ground in very Bolivia-specific ways. But on issues of crime and social violence, as this chapter has suggested, it is the "right to security" which is paramount, and which justifies the suspension of the rights of the accused. The distinction here rests on the longstanding compartmentalization of rights within human rights law and language itself, which separates political and civil rights from social and economic rights. Whereas Bolivian social movements advocate for the social and economic rights of the poor, poor urban barrio residents regard the political and civil rights of accused criminals as compromising to their security harmful to the creation of "justice," and thus illegitimate and disposable. Imagined as oppositional rather than part and parcel of a single human rights regime, these two sets of rights confront one another in the struggle for security, justifying a stronger and more repressive state to foster their realization. This has been due, in large part, to the generalized insecurity that decades of neoliberalism has produced in Bolivia, creating a climate in which political and civil rights, once intended to protect the vulnerable from state violence and repression, are now imagined as unfair protections given to the guilty and the antisocial, and so are invoked as reasons to justify state violence and repression. In this, even the social movements are complicit: the MAS party's own electoral platform in the 2005 presidential campaign promised to "modify the penal laws, to guarantee the effective sanction of delinquents"; "to install [police] control posts in the barrios"; increase the police presence in the nation's principle cities; and "to utilize new technologies to combat crime" (MAS 2005).

For scholars of human rights in transnational perspective, what is perhaps most significant about the predicament of violence and insecurity described in this chapter is the way in which the discourses of security and rights are not merely oppositional, but are being reworked in the barrios of Cochabamba into a single hybrid discourse that accounts for and perpetuates violent practice. Much as the state invokes the emergency, with its accompanying discourse of necessity, to justify its own abrogation of citizens' rights, so do citizens claim the "right to security" to justify their own state of exception, one that allows them to take the law into their own hands in defense of this right, and to commit acts of violence that shock even themselves. Of course, the equation of security with the punitive not only leads to rights violations; it also is ineffective in achieving its end of creating greater security, contributing instead to an ever-expanding cycle of intensified violence and fear. The consequences for democratic societies of this rising authoritarianism bear watching, as the transnational "security crisis" continues to unfold.

REFERENCES

Agamben, Giorgio. 2002. "Security and Terror." *Theory and Event* 5(4). Available on-line at muse.jhu.edu/journals/theory_and_event/. Accessed February 6, 2007.

Agamben, Giorgio. 2005. *State of Exception*, trans. K. Attell. Chicago: University of Chicago Press.

Albro, Robert. 2006. "The Culture of Democracy and Bolivia's Indigenous Movements." *Critique of Anthropology* 26(3): 387–410.

Arriagada, Irma. 2001. "Seguridad Ciudadana y Violencia en América Latina." Paper presented at the meeting of the Latin American Studies Association, September 6–8, 2001, Washington, DC.

Bobea, Lilian, ed. 2003. *Entre el Crimen y el Castigo: Seguridad Ciudadana y Control Democrático en América Latina y el Caribe.* Caracas: Editorial Nueva Sociedad.

Briceño-Leon, R., and V. Zubilaga. 2002. "Violence and Globalization in Latin America." *Current Sociology* 50(1): 19–37.

Butler, Judith. 2004. *Precarious Life: The Power of Mourning and Violence.* London: Verso.

Caldeira, Teresa P. R. 2000. *City of Walls: Crime, Segregation, and Citizenship in São Paulo.* Berkeley: University of California Press.

Caldeira, Teresa P.R., and James Holston. 1999. "Democracy and Violence in Brazil." *Comparative Studies in Society and History* 41(4): 691–729.

Carranza, Elías. 2004. "Políticas Públicas en Materia de Seguridad de los Habitantes ante el Delito en América Latina." *Nueva Sociedad* 191: 52–64.

Chevigny, Paul. 1997. *Edge of the Knife: Police Violence in the Americas.* New York: New Press.

Colloredo-Mansfeld, Rudi. 2002. "Don't be Lazy, don't Lie, don't Steal": Community Justice in the Neoliberal Andes. *American Ethnologist* 29(3): 637–662.

Cowan, Jane K., Marie-Bénédicte Dembour, and Richard A. Wilson, eds. 2001. *Culture and Rights: Anthropological Perspectives.* Cambridge: Cambridge University Press.

Dammert, Lucia. 2004. "De la Seguridad Pública a la Seguridad Ciudadana: Chile 1973–2003." Paper presented at the Seminario Internacional Política de Seguridad Ciudadana, Quito, Guayaquil y Cuenca, 24–26 March 2004.

Dammert, Lucia, and Mary Fran T. Malone. 2003. "Fear of Crime or Fear of Life? Public Insecurities in Chile." *Bulletin of Latin American Research* 22(1): 79–101.

Davis, Darren W., and Brian D. Silver. 2004. "Civil Liberties vs. Security: Public Opinion in the Context of the Terrorist Attacks on America." *American Journal of Political Science* 48(1): 28–46.

del Olmo, Rosa. 2000. "Ciudades Duras y Violencia Urbana." *Nueva Sociedad* 167: 74–86.

Delgado Aguado, J., and J. Guardia Maduell. 1994. *Seguridad Ciudadana y Función Policial: Una Aproximación al Análisis de Entornos Concretos.* Barcelona: Unión de Ciudades Capitales Iberoamericanas.

Domingo, Pilar, and Rachel Seider. 2001. *Rule of Law in Latin America: The International Promotion of Judicial Reform.* London: Institute of Latin American Studies.

Escobar, Santiago, Jackeline Muniz, Rafael Sanseviero, Marcelo F. Sain, and José M. Zacchi. 2004. *La Seguridad Ciudadana como Política de Estado.* Santiago de Chile: Prosur.

Farthing, Linda. 1997. "Social Impacts Associated with Antidrug Law 1008." In M. B. Léons, and H. Sanabria, eds. *Coca, Cocaine, and the Bolivian Reality.* Albany: SUNY Press, pp. 253–369.

Gabaldón, Luis Gerardo. 2004. "Seguridad Ciudadana y Control del Delito en América Latina." *Análisis y Propuestas: El Observatorio de Nueva Sociedad.* Caracas: Nueva Sociedad.

Garland, David. 2001. *The Culture of Control: Crime and Social Order in Contemporary Society.* Chicago: University of Chicago Press.

Giddens, Anthony. 1990. *The Consequences of Modernity.* Cambridge: Polity.

Goldstein, Daniel M. 2003. " 'In our Own Hands': Lynching, Justice and the Law in Bolivia." *American Ethnologist* 30(1): 22–43.

Goldstein, Daniel M. 2004. *The Spectacular City: Violence and Performance in Urban Bolivia.* Durham: Duke University Press.

Goldstein, Daniel M. 2005. "Flexible Justice: Neoliberal Violence and Self-help Security in Bolivia." *Critique of Anthropology* 25(4): 389–411.

Hersch, Seymour M. 2004. "The Gray Zone: How a Secret Pentagon Program Came to Abu Ghraib." *The New Yorker*, May 17.

Inter-American Development Bank (IDB). 2003. "Citizen Security: New Challenges for the Region," vol. 2005. Available on-line at www.iadb.org.

Machillanda, José. 2005. "La Remilitarización de la Seguridad en América Latina." *Nueva Sociedad* 198: 130–144.

Merry, Sally Engle. 2001. "Spatial Governmentality and the new Urban Social Order: Controlling Gender Violence through Law." *American Anthropologist* 103(1): 16–29.

Merry, Sally Engle. 2003. "Rights Talk and the Experience of Law: Implementing Women's Human Rights to Protection from Violence." *Human Rights Quarterly* 25(2): 343–381.

Moser, Caroline, Alisa Winton, and Annalise Moser. 2003. "Violence, Fear and Insecurity and the Urban Poor in Latin America." In *World Bank LAC Regional Study of Urban Poverty.* Washington, DC: World Bank.

Movimiento a Socialismo (MAS). 2005. "Ayuda Memoria MAS: Diez Medidas para Cambiar Bolivia. Comisión de Planificacíon y Estragies, MAS.

Neild, Rachel. 1999. "From National Security to Citizen Security: Civil Society and the Evolution of Public Order Debates." Paper presented to the International Center for Human Rights and Democratic Development, Montreal, Canada.

Petrella, Laura, and Franz Vanderschueren. 2003. "Ciudad y Violencia: Seguridad y Ciudad." In M. Balbo, R. Jordan, and D. Simioni, eds. *La Ciudad Inclusiva.* Santiago de Chile: CEPAL, pp. 215–235.

Pinheiro, Paulo Sérgio. 1999. "The Rule of Law and the Underprivileged in Latin America: Introduction." In J. E. Mendéz, G. O'Donnell, and P. S. Pinheiro, eds. *The (un)Rule of Law and the Underprivileged in Latin America*, pp. 1–15. Notre Dame: University Notre Dame Press.

Prillaman, William C. 2003. "Crime, Democracy, and Development in Latin America." *Policy Papers on the Americas* 14(6): 1–30.

Rajagopal, Balakrishnan. 2003. *International Law from Below: Development, Social Movements and Third World Resistance.* Cambridge: Cambridge University Press.

Reinarman, Craig, and Harry G. Levine, eds. 1997. *Crack in America: Demon Drugs and Social Justice.* Berkeley: University of California Press.

Santos, Boaventura de Sousa. 1997. "Toward a Multicultural Conception of Human Rights." *Zeitschrift Fuer Rechtssociologie* 18(1): 2–16.

Scheper-Hughes, Nancy. 1992. *Death without Weeping: The Violence of Everyday Life in Brazil.* Berkeley: University of California Press.

Schmitt, Carl. 1931. *Der Hüter der Verfassung.* Tübingen: Mohr.

Smulovitz, Claudia. 2003. "Citizen Insecurity and Fear: Public and Private Responses in Argentina." In H. Frühling, J. Tulchin, and H. A. Golding, eds. *Crime and Violence in Latin America: Citizen Security, Democracy, and the State*, pp. 125–152. Washington, DC: Woodrow Wilson Center Press.

Sundar, Nandini. 2004. "Toward an Anthropology of Culpability." *American Ethnologist* 31(2): 145–163.

Taussig, Michael. 2003. *Law in a Lawless Land.* New York: New Press.

Tulchin, Joseph S., Hugo Frühling, and Heather Golding, eds. 2003. *Crime and Violence in Latin America: Citizen Security, Democracy, and the State.* Washington, DC: Woodrow Wilson Center Press.

Ungar, Mark. 2003. "Prisons and politics in contemporary Latin America." *Human Rights Quarterly* 25: 909–934.

United Nations Development Programme (UNDP). 2004. *Democracy in Latin America: Towards a Citizens' Democracy.* New York: UNDP.

United Nations Development Programme (UNDP). 2005. Promoción y Defensa de los Derechos Humanos, Proyecto BOL/97/01/05. Available on-line at ddhh.pnud.bo/DDHH.html.

United States Agency for International Development (USAID). 2005. "USAID Bolivia mission". Data sheet. Washington, DC: USAID. Available on-line at www.usaid.gov/policy/budget/cbj2006/lac/pdf/bo511-007.pdf. Accessed on February 6, 2007.

United States Agency for International Development (USAID). 2007. "USAID Promotes the Rule of Law in Latin America and Caribbean Democracies." Washington, DC: USAID. Available on-line at www.usaid.gov/locations/latin_america_caribbean/democracy/rule/index.html. Accessed on February 6, 2007.

Wilson, James Q., and George Kelling. 1982. "Broken windows." In *Atlantic Monthly*, 211, pp. 29–37.

World Health Organization (WHO). 2002. *World Report on Violence and Health.* Geneva: WHO.

2

"SECULARISM IS A HUMAN RIGHT!": DOUBLE-BINDS OF BUDDHISM, DEMOCRACY, AND IDENTITY IN NEPAL

*Lauren Leve**

A colorful photograph on the cover of the May/June 1994 issue of *The Dharmakirti*, a Kathmandu-based Buddhist monthly magazine, shows a field of Theravada Buddhist monks marching down a main street in downtown Kathmandu waving flags and carrying banners. Marking the cover of a special issue devoted to the topic of secularism, the scene was readily recognizable to the magazine's Buddhist readers, many of whom had themselves attended the rally where the picture was taken. It was, at that time, the largest political gathering yet seen in Nepal: over 100,000 people reclaimed the streets of the capital to march for the constitutional redefinition of Nepal as a secular state. Clad in their characteristic yellow robes and shaven heads, the stream of monks in the picture stretches as far down the road as the eye can see. A large red banner proclaims their message to the state and the world: "Secularism is a human right!" (*Dharmanirapekshanā mānab adhikār ho*).

This picture, and the events surrounding it, raise a number of questions for students of transnational politics, religion, and human rights.

* Research for this paper was funded by the Fulbright Foreign Scholarship Board; the joint committee of the ACLS and the SSRC; the Council on Regional Studies and the Center of International Studies, Princeton University (Daiwa Fund); the Mildred McAfee Horton Fund and a Faculty Research Grant from Wellesley College. I would like to thank Mark Goodale, Sally Merry, and the other contributors to this volume for collegiality and feedback on earlier drafts of the paper, as well as Ilana Gershon, David Graeber, and Lamia Karim. Thanks also to Anna Bigelow, Julie Flowerday, Sandria Freitag, David Gilmartin, Matthew Hull, Yasmin Saikia, Meenu Tiwari, and other members of Triangle South Asia Consortium for their queries, insights and suggestions.

Why would Buddhist monks – quintessential religious subjects – lead a march in support of secularism? And, given that human rights conventions guarantee freedom of *religion*, how and why do they make the claim that *secularism* is a human right?

This chapter tracks the intersection of three transnational institutions (Theravada Buddhism, liberal democracy, and human rights discourse), one constitutional debate (over the legal status of Hinduism in Nepal), and the innumerable double-binds Nepali Buddhists confront when they call on normative values associated with liberal democratic citizenship to protect a form of religious selfhood that denies the very logic of identity that human rights implies.

My conception of the double-bind in this context is inspired by Kim Fortun's analysis of the challenge of environmental activism in the wake of the Union Carbide gas leak in Bhopal (2001). She writes that a "double bind situation is not simply a situation of difficult choice, resolvable through reference to available explanatory narratives." Rather, " 'double bind' denotes a situation in which individuals are confronted with dual or multiple obligations that are related and equally valued, but incongruent" (2001: 13). For Fortun, such binds come into being when pursuing justice for Bhopal gas victims demands, on the one hand, that the trial of Union Carbide be held in the United States (to establish that multinational corporations are responsible for the actions of their foreign subsidiaries) but also, on the other hand, that the trial should be held in India (to show that Indian courts can successfully exert sovereignty in cases affecting Indian citizens on Indian land) (2001: 12). Both claims are equally logical and desirable, but they entail incompatible demands.

Fortun's ethnographic example parallels the logical contradiction that emerges when Theravada Buddhists deploy human rights claims against the Nepal state – the representational stage and stakes are somewhat different, but the dilemma and its violence are strikingly the same. In order to defend themselves as Buddhists against the Hindu state, Buddhists have been compelled to call on human rights and to represent themselves according to the ontologies of identity that inhere in liberal law. However, it is precisely by disavowing key aspects of this liberal way of understanding the person that Buddhism distinguishes itself and constitutes its adherents as Buddhist. There is, therefore, an irreconcilable tension between what Buddhists do and the subjectivities they inhabit when they call on human rights, and the acts and identities those rights are supposed to guarantee.

In Nepal in the early 1990s, the incongruous imperatives of this double-bind called on Buddhists to perform a number of unexpected interpretive moves. These moves shed light on characteristic dilemmas of the practice of human rights "between the global and the local," where positioned participants draw on transnational languages and forms of authority to conceptualize, advance, and support their own locally-determined ends. In arguing, as we will see, that a Hindu nation-state can never be fully democratic, and that political secularism is a human right, Theravada Buddhists invoked understandings of themselves as selves that are simultaneously global, national, ethnic, and intimately localized. They are also based on notions of the self that to be Theravada Buddhist is, by definition, to deny. Tracking these claims in practice highlights the ways that human actors inhabit and negotiate demands associated with different, and often conflicting, scales and ontologies of identity – and the ways that these identities are bound up in transnational, and vernacular, understandings of democracy.

The contradictions that Nepali Buddhists live, between the nature of the "human" that is assumed by liberal law and the nature of the "human" as revealed in Buddhist experience, offers a window onto two centuries of shifts in religion's role in defining law in Nepal, and vice versa. They also reveal the extent to which the expansion of international human rights participates in a globalizing socio-political grammar that I have come to think of as a transnational "identity machine" – a global cultural imaginary that compels people to represent themselves in certain terms and make their claims in certain ways (Leve 2003). In this case, in ways that remake the very forms of personhood that Buddhists are trying to protect by invoking human rights!

To observe this is not to dismiss the critical role that human rights discourse plays in upholding democratic ideals and supporting national minorities. However, it does entail recognizing the ways that a certain type of discursive imperialism may be carried in rights-talk and its associated institutional formations.[1] This, then, is the double-bind that faces Theravada Buddhists and others who would call on human rights (and, by implication, the liberal democratic guarantees that they metonymically connote) to protect non-liberal identities: that the ethico-juridical double-binds that the rhetoric and practice

---

[1] See also Goodale, chapter 3, and Speed, chapter 4, this volume.

of human rights brings into existence may themselves constitute a subtle, epistemic form of violence.[2]

TRANSNATIONAL NEOLIBERALISM AND NEPALI DEMOCRACY

The massive secularism rally depicted on *The Dharmakiriti*'s cover took place in July 1990. But the events that led to the demonstration must be understood in the context of a global post-Cold War democratic transition, a process that, in Nepal, began with a popular revolution the previous spring and brought Buddhists and ethnic activists together in calls for secular democracy. Then, as now, Nepal was the world's only extant Hindu kingdom. But since 1990–91, it has also been a constitutional monarchy with a Westminster-style parliamentary structure – the outcome of what Nepalis speak of as the *jana andolan*, or popular democracy movement, that overthrew the reigning political structure in the spring of 1990. Between the late 1950s and February 1990, when leaders of the banned political parties brought their hopes for liberal democracy to the streets, the country was governed according to a partyless political regime known as the Panchayat system. Promulgated in 1962 as a uniquely Nepali structure, this system institutionalized elections to a series of local and regional assemblies, called panchayats, but reserved effective political power for the Monarchy. When, after months of street struggle, King Birendra capitulated to popular demands in May 1990, he dissolved the Panchayat system, transferred national sovereignty from himself to "the people," established an interim government headed by one of the leaders of the revolution, and appointed a constitutional drafting committee to draw up the formal architecture of the new democracy. It would be almost a year before the new government was elected and installed. But the movement had succeeded, and a carnival atmosphere prevailed throughout much of the country as Nepalis looked forward to the coming democracy.

---

[2] Let me stress at the outset that I'm not arguing against the conception or practice of human rights – without with many actors might end up suffering much more. I would, however, caution against an analytical innocence which is blind to the subtle forms of violence that the translations required by global justice often entail. As Merry observes in her review of recent literature on the anthropology of law and transnational processes, law is itself "a form of violence endowed with the legitimacy of a constituted authority"(1992: 360).

In the midst of the generalized celebration, however, a hitherto unanticipated problem appeared: the rise of ethnic-based political identities. The interim government had only been in place a few weeks when organizations claiming to represent Nepal's diverse ethnic groups and religious minorities began to appear on the public stage and to demand structural changes in the constitutional framework that would guarantee ethnic and linguistic minority rights.[3] The demands – for official recognition and protection for ethnic languages, scripts, and cultural symbols – made sense according to the conventional norms of liberal democracy, which guarantee liberty, equality and opportunity to all citizens equally. They also made sense as a response to the repressions of panchayat nationalism, which had aggressively promoted (and vigorously reinforced) a vision of the nation that repressed and denied ethnic, linguistic and religious diversity. With the end of the Panchayat system and the ushering in of democratic freedoms, however, minority citizens sought to contest this nationalism and its claims.[4]

To their disappointment, however, their requests were greeted with surprise and distrust – and not just by the old guard but also by the former leaders of the democracy movement. The street protests had been ethnically diverse and had mobilized youth. However, the leaders of the *jana andolan* and the political parties that organized it came disproportionately from the kinds of high-caste Nepali speaking social backgrounds that panchayat nationalism had long privileged, a class that Lawoti characterizes as CHHE, the caste-hill-Hindu elite (2005). Moreover, they were typically older men who had spent most of their lives fighting the Monarchy. As a result, most espoused a relatively narrow vision of democracy that conceived of it in terms of political parties, competitive elections, and popular sovereignty. Few of the new leaders seemed to have considered that the Panchayat government had suppressed both political and cultural freedoms. And few seemed prepared to rethink the national-cultural status quo. Indeed, many public figures interpreted the previously-suppressed groups' multicultural claims as a dangerous threat to national unity and thus, to the very survival of the new democracy. In contrast, ethnic

---

[3] When the constitutional drafting committee turned to the public to solicit input on what kinds of institutions people wanted to create, they were reportedly amazed that most of the feedback concerned what they understood as social demands, rather than political or economic structures. See Hutt (1994).
[4] See Gellner (2001) for a complementary account of the rise of cultural politics and their reflection of international legal discourses, including rights-talk, after the *jana andolan*.

activists drew on transnational discourses of self-determination and autonomy to claim that recognizing cultural differences and protecting minority rights were requisite legal guarantees in any "full and free" democracy.

In theory, the rise of ethnic activism in Nepal in the early 1990s should not have been surprising. The timing of the *jana andolan* had, according to its leaders, been inspired by the fall of the Berlin Wall and the democratic transitions taking place across Central and Eastern Europe. Post-Cold War ideology depended on an understanding of liberation that associated freedom of the market with individual empowerment. And the new Nepali government adopted these economic principles along with its avowal of multiparty democracy, opening Nepal's markets, privatizing state enterprises, and enacting far-reaching banking and finance sector reforms. They were supported in this effort by hundreds of thousands of development dollars directed at encouraging individual entrepreneurship, "deepening" civil society and empowering royal subjects to act as liberal citizens. One effect of this massive effort, which in fact has been going on – albeit less explicitly – for two decades or more, was that Nepalis of all classes, castes, genders, and geographical locales have been exposed to a litany of liberal and neoliberal ideas that have come to shape their understandings of self, modernity, and democracy.

Given this connection, and a global scene that would soon witness the bloody dissolution of a number of multiethnic states, the dawning of ethnic consciousness in Nepal in the early 1990s is hardly remarkable. One need not posit the presence of long-smoldering primordial identities to imagine that the combination of the Hindu state's historical neglect and exploitation of its ethnic peoples and an international discourse on self-determination might inspire a similar politics of identity and ethnicity.[5] Furthermore, an often-remarked characteristic of neoliberal governance in the post-Cold War era has been the "globalization of the rule of law" – and particularly of constitutionalism (Klug 2002: 277). When considered against this broader backdrop,

---

[5] Nancy Fraser has observed that a "shift in the grammar of political claims-making" from equality-based claims to identity-based ones is a "defining feature of the post-socialist condition" (Fraser 1997: 2 quoted in Cowan, Dembour, and Wilson 2001b: 2). Similarly, neoliberalization has been linked to a range of challenges to homogenizing nationalisms and the proliferation of subnational rights and identity claims in places as far apart as Latin America and Australia (see Hale 2005; Postero 2005; Povinelli 2002; Rata 2003; Speed 2005; Speed and Sierra 2005).

the proliferation of ethnic and religious minority organizations in the early 1990s in Nepal, and their vociferous demands for constitutional recognition, is almost, perhaps, to be expected.

What is more surprising is that, for so many people, these ethnic concerns came to be articulated in terms of religion.[6] As the next section will discuss, the form that the struggle took – and particularly the ways that secularism became a rallying call for multicultural democracy – was conditioned by political and historical conditions that were specific to Nepal.

NATION AND RELIGION IN A MODERN HINDU KINGDOM

What brought ethnic activists into alliance with Buddhist monks? To fully understand the politics of nationalism and identity in Nepal, it is helpful to know something about the history of relations between national Hinduism and the Nepal state. Religious domination and ethnic suppression were closely associated for many of Nepal's ethnic minorities, the majority of whom were historically Buddhist groups who had long been familiar with various cultural strategies that the state used to integrate its ethnically non-Hindu subjects on unequal terms.[7] According to the latest census figures, Nepal is 80 percent Hindu, 11 percent Buddhist, 4 percent Muslim and 5 percent "Other" – a highly conservative count that serves state interests by treating many Buddhists as Hindus, many activists say (Gurung 2002). Despite this, the Panchayat constitution defined Nepal as a Hindu kingdom (*Hindu Adiraj*) and enacted laws against proselytization (*dharma pharkaunu*), and even converting oneself (*dharma pharknu*). By thus inscribing the religion onto all Nepali citizens and outlawing any challenges to this identity, these laws attempted to assure that all Nepalis called themselves – or at least, were called – Hindu.

---

[6] Gellner has acutely observed the "salience of religion, rather than culture, or religion *as* culture, as a principle of identity" at that time (2001: 178).

[7] The role of a caste-based national legal system, land grants to Brahmans throughout the country, Hindu symbolism, and Hindu festival practice in integrating an ethnically, religiously and linguistically diverse population, brought together through conquest and only later conceived as common members of a modern nation-state, has been well documented by scholars who have shown how the Hindu state integrated its non-Hindu subjects on unequal terms (see Burghart 1984; Caplan 1970; Gellner, Pfaff-Czarnecka, and Whelpton 1997; Gellner and Quigley 1995; Hofer 1979; Holmberg 1989; Pfaff-Czarnecka 1993).

As this suggests, although it is common in some circles to interpret Nepal's contemporary Hindu identity as evidence of the country's anachronism, political underdevelopment, or marginality on the world stage, it is actually the outcome of a series of very modern, global processes that have transformed the practical and material meanings of religion over time. From Prithvi Narayan Shah, the so-called "founding father" of Nepal, who, on his deathbed in 1774, instructed his descendents to preserve the mountain kingdom as a "true (*asal*) Hindustan" in order to maintain independence (from the "insolent followers of Islam" and the "vile Feringis" on the plains);[8] to the country's first national legal code, promulgated in 1854, which drew on Hindu principles to incorporate all of Nepal's diverse subject peoples in a single caste system; to Maharaja Jang Bahadur Rana's late nineteenth-century protestations that he would like nothing better than to open the country to his British allies and friends but feared that if he did so he would be overthrown by a conservative Hindu populace (and hence he simply could not allow British soldiers or merchants onto Nepal's sacred soil);[9] Nepal's rulers have long styled themselves and their subjects as Hindu. Thus when the Panchayat constitution declared Nepal a Hindu Kingdom in 1962, it appeared only to be restating what was already the case – that the Nepali state had long drawn on Hindu symbolism, and on Hinduism as a symbol, to organize national belonging in accordance with political demand.

Yet, there is a difference between an eighteenth-century king's belief that he governed as a gift from the gods in return for upholding the moral order of society and the Panchayat promotion of a paternalistic *Rajdharma* that stressed a modern king's moral claim to the devotion of

---

[8] "When the banner of Hinduism dropped from the hands of the Mahrattas in 1817, they solemnly conjured the Nepalese to take it up and wave it proudly till it could again be unfurled in the plains by the expulsion of the vile Feringis [the British], and the subjection of the insolent followers of Islam (Hodgson 1857: 234 in Burghart 1996 #25: 234).

[9] On his return to Cambridge from Kathmandu where he resided for many years as the Residency Surgeon, Wright wrote:

> Great though his power is, there are still some matters in which Sir Jung Bahadur dares not interfere with the customs and prejudices of the people. Thus though he has restricted Sati, still he seems unable to abolish the custom entirely, as the priests, who are a much influential body, are of course strongly opposed to such a course. And as regards throwing open the country to Europeans, I believe that he himself would not be unwilling to do so; but the measure would be so unpopular among all grades of inhabitants, that to attempt it might endanger his position, if not his life. Bhimsena's unfortunate fate is often ascribed to the fact of his having been party to the admission of a European Resident into the country. (Wright 1877: 68)

his citizens in order to suppress social and political critique. Cultural policy during the Panchayat period was succinctly summed up in the schoolchildren's rhyme, *"ek bhasa, ek bhes, ek Dharma* (or *ek Raja), ek dhes"* ("one language, one national costume, one religion (or King), one country") – a discursive and material construction of national identity that was written into the Panchayat constitution in the laws mentioned above as well as others designating Nepali as the single national language, for instance. A staple metaphor of Panchayat nationalism represented Nepal as a harmonious flower garden of different ethnicities and castes ("four varna and thirty-six jāt"), artfully integrated into a single national whole by the synthetic qualities of Hinduism, and lovingly maintained by a caring King. By this way of thinking, Hindu monarchy and its associated symbolism, sentiments, and obligations ("Rajdharma") were what bound diverse groups of Nepalis together and made the nation unique.

When Buddhists and ethnic minorities found their political voices after the revolution, however, they raised them forcefully against these claims. In contrast to the one language, one King, one culture ideal, they observed that multiple mother-tongues were spoken and multiple religions practiced in Nepal – as many as fifty-four languages and six non-Hindu religions according to one demographer's recent count.[10] Rather than assuring a pluralist peace, they charged that official national Hinduism had been the cornerstone of an all-embracing inequality that privileged high caste Hindus and repressed everyone else.[11]

A past president of a Theravada organization that was deeply involved in the secularism drive and which continues to work closely with politically-active ethnocultural organizations characterized the problem as a history of dispossession and loss. According to him, two hundred-plus years of state Hinduism have resulted in a situation in

---

[10] According to the 2001 census, Nepal has forty-three official non-caste Hindu ethnic groups who make up 37.8 percent of the population. The same census further estimates that fifty-four languages are spoken across the country, and that the country is 80 percent Hindu, 11 percent Buddhist, 4 percent Muslim and 5 percent "Other," "Christian," "Kiranti," or Jain (Gurung 2002).

[11] Parodying Panchayat rhetoric, ethnic activist H. Tamu alleged rather that the Hindu garden model masked systematic oppression: "To conceal their partyless system, the partyless system's promoters lied to the people saying '[Nepal is] a garden of the four varna and thirty-six jaat' while in practice they instituted their evil policy of 'One language, one custom'. Whenever they may have shouted, except for a few plants, all others were pruned, cut with the razor of oppression, stripped of their leaves, the new shoots destroyed, and buried beneath the soil." (Des Chene 1996a: 139–140).

which high caste Nepali-speakers dominate the country politically and economically, and other caste and ethnic groups have lost their cultures and hence social identities.

"Take the case of [ethnic] Magars," he explained. "If we look at their history, they ... were Buddhists." It was the state, he said, that destroyed Magars' and other ethnic minorities' languages and cultures, turning them into "pure Hindu" subjects of the Nepali kingdom:

> Before, Magars used to have Buddhist Lamas as their priests ... But [Magars are known for serving in the Nepali military and] if they didn't use Brahmans as their priests they wouldn't get promoted in the army. And they needed promotion. So in order to get promotion they had to use Brahmins as their priests. The role of the Brahman was to convert them to Hinduism. Also, they were not allowed to speak their Magar language; if they spoke their language, they were charged a penalty of 3 paisa at that time ... As a result of not being able to speak their language, their history and literature were destroyed. And these were replaced with the Mahabharata, the Ramayana, and other Hindu religious literature ... This is how they became pure Hindu ... It was a state policy. According to [the Brahman] who established it, you have to abolish other people's religions, cultures, literatures and histories to make your own state and government strong ... If people have their own religions, literatures and cultures, they'll have a feeling of ownership and they'll resist the imposition of others.

In this way, he charged, non-Hindu ethnic peoples in Nepal had been subjected to a deliberate policy of religious and cultural suppression that converted cultures into castes, assigned each a place in a ranked rituo-political system, and aimed to make people who hailed from non-Brahmanical cultures and histories into loyal subjects of the Hindu nation-state. He understood this as a process of dispossession that perceived cultural identity itself as valuable property, and he saw the destruction of this identity as a type of social death.

But democracy, he believed, was bound to protect cultural difference. In this way, it required new categories of citizenship based on a rational commitment to democratic principles rather than symbolic encompassment by a divine king. And as a result, he argued, the Hindu identity and assimilationist cultural policy that had been imposed on religious and ethnic minorities throughout the Panchayat period were fundamentally incompatible with the promises of the new era. Ethnic activist Adhibhakta M. S. Thapa Magar, himself likely one of the people that this speaker had in mind when he offered this interpretation of Magar history, took this analysis to its logical political conclusion in the essay he contributed to the special secularism issue of *The Dharmakirti*: "Not to recognize Nepal's multi-religious composition," he wrote, "demands that everyone reconsider whether this is or isn't a *real* democracy" (Thapa Magar [1994 (2051)], emphasis added).[12]

CONTESTING THE CONSTITUTION

Despite this history and its seeming discrimination, it was only in the summer of 1990 that Nepali citizens, led in part by a group of Theravada Buddhist monks and laymen, began to openly criticize the *political* role that Hinduism played in maintaining social and economic inequalities. Together, religious leaders and ethnic minorities formed a movement to challenge clauses in the panchayat constitution that defined Nepal as a "Hindu kingdom" (*Hindu Adhirājya*) and laws that supported that the national Hindu identity. They demanded that the forthcoming constitution break with Hindu symbolism and monarchial authority by formally declaring the country a "secular state" (*dharma-nirapekshata rastra*).

Almost as soon as the constitution drafting committee was named, Buddhist leaders leapt into action. By the end of June, the Nepal Dharmodaya Sabha, the oldest Buddhist organization in Nepal, formed by exiled Theravada monks and nuns in 1943, had publicly called on the committee to declare the constitutional monarchy a secular state – and their call was soon endorsed by a host of other organizations. One of the first of these was the newly-formed Action Committee of Various Religions, Languages, and Nationalities[13] – an umbrella association devoted to advancing ethnic rights. Others followed, including representatives of the Newar, Tamang, Magar, and Tharu ethnic communities.

Over the summer of 1990, Buddhists and their allies organized a continuous stream of events in support of secularism and minority rights. These included a 10,000-strong silent demonstration in June; a petition drive that delivered a statement signed by 10,780 people into the hands of the Constitutional Recommendation Committee Chair; and, of course, and the massive march/rally in July memorialized on *The Dharmakirti* cover. An even larger event that was scheduled for August

---

[12] All quotes from *The Dharmakirti* are my translations from the original Nepali. Special thanks to Sarala Shrestha and Geeta Manandhar for their help with this.
[13] *Bibidh Dharma, Bhasha, Jati Tatha Janajati Sangharsha Samiti.*

was called off following the death of the charismatic Theravada monk who had been organizing it. Despite their stated aversion to politics, which I will discuss below, Theravada Buddhists were among the primary planners of all of these activities. In addition, they spearheaded a letter-writing campaign by individuals and lay Buddhist organizations, and organized international media coverage of their struggle in Buddhist countries like Thailand and Taiwan. Equally significant, if less immediately visible, Theravada religious leaders began offering Buddhism lessons to Mahayana Buddhist and other more Hindicized ethnic groups in an attempt to help them reclaim their putatively pre-Hindu religious practices and identities.[14]

In response, Hindu nationalists and Royalists launched their own counter-campaign which charged that secularism was anti-religion, that Hinduism was what bound the country together (as in the flower-garden model), and that without it, ethnic and religious violence would surely result. A Brahman minister in the interim government, Acchyut Raj Regmi, threatened a hunger-strike to the death on the steps on Pashupatinath, the country's holiest Hindu temple, if the call for secularism succeeded. Over the following months, rumors abounded: that the Communists would never compromise on the matter of secularism, that the Congress Party had struck a deal with the King, that the interim Prime Minister was being lobbied by an Indian cabinet minister who was also a top official of the World Hindu Congress. Tension mounted as delays beset the draft document's release.

When the constitution was finally made public in October, Nepal's transition to democracy was pronounced a success by the political party leaders and international constitutional consultants. Buddhists, however, were enraged. In form, the new constitution was a classically liberal document that guaranteed basic rights and granted official recognition and some cultural accommodations to ethnic and linguistic minorities. It rejected the call for official secularism, however, leading Theravada Buddhists and their allies to charge that the document failed to live up to its democratic promises and claims.

International observers and the Nepali political elite were most enthusiastic about the range of rights and freedoms that the 1990 constitution established. These included new guarantees of freedom of the press (new Article 13); the right against preventive detention

---

[14] See Hangen (2005) for an account of the movement to reject Hinduism led by the banned political party, the Mongol National Organization.

89

(Article 15); the right "to demand and receive information on any matter of public importance" (Article 16); the right to privacy (Article 22); a new prohibition on torture and other cruel, inhuman or degrading treatment (Article 14, clause 4) and, of course, the right to form political parties (Article 119) that did not exist under the Panchayat regime.[15]

The constitution also won praise for the recognition that it seemed to extend to minority communities. For instance, the 1990 constitution defines "the nation" as the following: "Having common aspirations and united by a bond of allegiance to national independence and integrity of Nepal, the Nepalese people irrespective of religion, race, caste, or tribe, collectively constitute the nation" (Article 2). To many people, this seemed to grant minority claims for formal recognition. Moreover, the phrase "united by a bond of allegiance to national independence and integrity of Nepal" represented a clear and important departure from the Panchayat declaration "united by the common bond of allegiance to the Crown" (Nepal 1962: Article 2). Moreover, all of this seemed to be reinforced by Article 11 and its fundamental guarantee of social equality:

> (1) All citizens shall be equal before law. No person shall be denied equal protection of the laws. (2) No discrimination shall be made against any citizen in the application of general laws on grounds of religion (*dharma*), race (*varya*), sex (*linga*), caste (*jāt*), tribe (*jaati*) or ideological conviction (*vaiārik*) or any of them. (3) The State shall not discriminate among citizens on grounds of religion, race, sex, caste, tribe, or ideological conviction or any of these.
>
> (Article 11/2)

In one of the first sustained English-language analyses of the 1990 constitution, anthropologist Ter Ellingson summed up the dominant sentiment among Nepal's political elite and foreign analysts: "All in all, the 1990 constitution provides for substantial gains in human rights over and above those guaranteed in the 1962 constitution" (1991: 9).

Others, however, disagreed. Those who had called for secularism were particularly enraged that Article 4 defined the country as a "multi-ethnic, multilingual, democratic, independent, indivisible, sovereign, *Hindu* and Constitutional Monarchial Kingdom," rather than as the

---

[15] See Ellingson (1991) for a detailed analysis of the constitution of Nepal 1990. An official English translation was published by the Ministry of Law, Justice and Parliamentary Affairs I 1992 (1992).

secular state they had lobbied for.[16] Some lamented that their supporters had been unable to insert a comma after "Hindu," which they felt at least might have modified the claim somewhat. Others felt that such a compromise wouldn't have been acceptable anyway, that the word "Hindu" needed to be removed and "secular" inserted there instead. But for all of the reasons mentioned above, secularism supporters criticized the constitution for betraying and subverting the popular will. A "Hindu ... Monarchial Kingdom" – constitutional or not – they declared, is fundamentally different from what the people had demanded: a modern liberal multicultural democracy.[17]

To substantiate their claims, they pointed to contradictions in the document. For instance, they observed that the religious freedoms that the constitution extended to communities were rendered impracticable by limitations on individual rights. Article 19/2 promised "every religious denomination ... the right to maintain its independent existence and for this purpose to manage and protect its religious places and trusts" – a key step that seemed to legitimate the existence of non-Hindu groups and to grant them at least limited self-determination. Yet, supporters of state secularism observed, the preceding line granted "every person the freedom to profess and practice his own religion as handed down to him from ancient times having due regard to traditional practices; provided that no person shall be entitled to convert another person from one religion to another" – which in fact negated freedom of religion by making it illegal to profess or practice a creed other than the one that the state deemed traditional. Ellingson reports that this last clause was inserted between when the draft was released in mid-October and November 9, when the constitution was formally promulgated (1991: 14). Buddhists noted that this phrase was carried over from the 1962 constitution and reproduced Panchayat laws against freedom of conversion and, hence, individual or collective religious expression.

Finally, critics alleged, the new constitution undermined the support it seemed to offer ethnic and linguistic minorities by reinscribing the

[16] All direct quotes from the constitution come from the official English translation released by the Ministry of Law, Justice and Parliamentary Affairs. See The Constitution of the Kingdom of Nepal 2047 (1990).
[17] "In a modernizing society," a *Dharmakirti* editorial proclaimed, "Brahmanical politics, philosophy and religion play a vital role in disrupting the process of development. Secularism was invented to overcome these obstacles ... [Secularism] is the political imperative of a true and full democratic system" ("Buddha's Birthplace Secular Nepal – Why?" [May–June 1994]).

symbolic centrality of the Hindu King. Defining the state as a Hindu Kingdom, they charged, negated any potential benefit of recognizing it as multiethnic and multilingual. On the one hand, they acknowledged, the constitution seemed to guarantee the cultural and educational rights of "every community residing within the Kingdom of Nepal" by granting every minority community the right "to preserve its language, script and culture." But, on the other hand, they asked what practical impact this recognition of difference could possibly have when the same document declared the King the "symbol of the Nepalese nationality and of the unity of the Nepalese people," and, furthermore, specified that the monarch be an "adherent of the Aryan culture and the Hindu religion."[18] Whatever its progressive pretensions may have been, they said, the continued legal imbrication of nation, state, and religion in the body of the King revealed the constitution's ultimately antidemocratic intent.

In the wake of this defeat, Buddhists moved their activities off of the streets. But they have continued to press their cause, first by sending a Theravada monk to the Upper House of Parliament to introduce the country's first constitutional amendment, to remove the word Hindu from the Preliminary (the monk, Bhikshu Ashvagosh, resigned when his proposal was defeated), and since then in publications like the special issue of *The Dharmakirti*, and in seminars, workshops and "Buddhist awareness" campaigns that seek to educate ethnic minorities about their putatively non-Hindu religious roots. One result of these efforts has been that over a million more people declared themselves Buddhists on the 2001 census than in 1991 (see Gurung 2002).

Notably, however, they have hesitated to revive their public movement in the last few years, even as the constitution has come under renewed criticism and as human rights discourse has become increasingly omnipresent in public debate. The main reason for this is that the

---

[18] They might also have asked about the long series of limitations that specified that nothing in any of the rights otherwise granted (including the freedom of opinion and expression, the freedom to assemble, the freedom to form unions and associations, etc.) "shall be deemed to prevent the making of laws to impose reasonable restrictions on any act which may undermine the sovereignty and integrity of the Kingdom of Nepal, or which may jeopardize the harmonious relations subsisting among the peoples of various castes, tribes or communities . . .; or on any act which may be contrary to decent public behaviour or morality." While some would-be ethnic parties did protest these limitations when they were denied registration to contest the 1991 election on the ground that their communal politics could cause dissent, less attention has been paid to the implications of giving an officially Hindu state the right to decide public morality. And the first part of that clause has been used to radically restrict civil liberties since the start of the Maoist rebellion in 1996.

political situation in Nepal has shifted as a result of the ongoing Maoist rebellion and resultant civil war. Popular understandings of human rights have been re-inflected in light of state security forces' and Maoists' atrocities, and, besides the fear that they would mistakenly be interpreted as Maoist sympathizers, most Buddhists feel that the most pressing problem now is, simply, peace.[19]

THE LEGAL LOGIC OF POLITICAL SECULARISM: DEMOCRACY, EQUALITY, AND HUMAN RIGHTS

This section will track the mechanics of the argument whereby secularism comes to be claimed as a human right and human rights becomes a signifier of modern, multicultural democracy. There are a number of steps to this argument, following which sheds light on the creative interpretive practices that translating local imperatives into universal frameworks (and vice versa) entails, and also onto the transformations in meaning that may take place in these processes.

Where the Panchayat system had extolled itself as a uniquely Nepali (i.e., local cultural) institution, Buddhists made the argument that secularism was (or should be) an inalienable aspect of democracy by drawing on an international discourse and insisting that their government conform to this putatively universal standard. The argument commonly advanced in the mobilizations of the early 1990s could be summarized as follows: (1) secularism is about equality and freedom of religion; (2) equality and freedom of religion are internationally-recognized human rights; (3) human rights are the essence of modern democracy; and (4) democracy is the only appropriate form government today. Let's observe what this look like in practice, using articles that appeared in the special secularism issue of *The Dharmakirti*.[20]

---

[19] In fact, Maoists and Theravada Buddhists share many of the same objections to the constitution. The Maoist ideologue and leader Baburam Bhattarai even contributed an article to *The Dharmakirti* before he launched the People's War and went underground. But the Maoist demand for Republicanism and a new constitution are offered as part of a more radical political restructuring than most Theravada Buddhists would publicly espouse today.

[20] While some of the essays were written especially for the journal, others were reprints of speeches or writings released at any point over the four years between the *jana andolan* and when the special issue was released. Most of the contributors were Theravada Buddhists (monks, nun, and laymen) or spokespeople for allied ethnic organizations, but the editors also reprinted statements by political leaders, both those supporting secularism and their opponents. As a result, the issue offers a representative sample of the arguments for and against secularism that were publicly articulated in the early 1990s.

The first step in the argument is an adamant rejection of the often-cited assumption that secularism represents a retreat from or rejection of religious subjectivity, and a corresponding redefinition of the concept as the institutional instantiation of freedom of religion and equality. Responding to the criticism that secularism is anti-religion, the Theravada Buddhist monk Bhikshu Ashvagosh invoked the dictionary definition of "*nirapeksha*" – the word that, when appended to "dharma," is used to translate "secular" in Nepali:

> Balchandra Sharma's dictionary defines *nirapeksha* in this way: (1) not to want anything, to be free of desire; (2) to be self-dependent; (3) freedom from hope/desire/expectation, apathy; (4) not to favor any one thing, indifferent, neutral. Thus it seems to me that secularism means that the state must be unbiased towards all religions. It does not mean that religion must be stopped. If a country is truly democratic, the state must be secular!
>
> (Ashvagosh 1994 (2051): 39)

What does this mean? Here, a senior Theravada Buddhist monk insists that secularism is not a religious commitment. To the contrary, he suggests, it is a political arrangement. It is the duty of a democratic state to recognize and patronize all religions equally because to privilege one religion formally by proclaiming it the national one creates a compulsory category of religious citizenship that discriminates against other traditions. In this quote, the monk denies accusations that a secular state would banish religion from public life and its associated institutions. Rather, he argues the illegitimacy of official state Hinduism. Declaring Hinduism the national religion of Nepal is anti-democratic, he implies, because it negates the principles of equality and freedom associated with democracy. "Whatever freedom there is said to be in our country, this is only an illusion in the case of religion," the end of the essay laments. "What kind of democracy is this?" (Ashvagosh 1994 [2051]: 41).

Once having established that secularism is about democratic practice and not religious belief, activists next appeal to the transcendent authority of international conventions to argue that equality and freedom of religion are human rights. Ex-Attorney General, member of the constitution reform advice committee and Theravada Buddhist ally Ramanand Prasad Singh articulated a common argument when he wrote that "without legal recognition of the freedom to religion, the idea that we have civil rights has no meaning" (Ashvagosh 1994 [2051]: 61). Elbis

Joshi too invokes the sacred status of freedom and equality, calling on the transcendent authority of United Nations covenants:

> In the preamble to the Universal Declaration of Human Rights, there is a worldwide guarantee of the freedom of religion. Article 2 establishes a human right prohibiting discrimination on the basis of religion. And the International Covenants on Civil and Political Rights and on Economic, Social and Cultural Rights, for example, testify to international accord on religious freedom ... Putting a putative all-Nepali ... veneration for an ancient Vedic religion above Nepalis of other religions in the name of Hinduism ... is certainly the death of human rights!
>
> (Joshi 1994 [2051]: 43)

From here, contributors quickly linked human rights with democracy. "It is now clear that there is no democracy in terms of religion," wrote Subarna Shakya: "Nepalis say religion is life and we are proud of it. But now this pride has become non-democratic and illegitimate because it violates democratic rights" (Subarna Shakya 1994 [2051]).

The argument is best summed up by Keshab Man Shakya, who concludes that secularism, democracy, and equality are the hallmarks of any modern, developed state:

> The meaning of secularism is not to establish any one religion as the national one (*Rajdharma*). Equal rights must be given to all religions. Religious equality is the backbone of democracy; this is stated in the International Declaration of Human Rights. All these things add up to one thing: Nepal's constitution is not yet fully democratic! Without religious equality, national development cannot take place ... "*Hindu Adhirājya*" (Hindu Kingdom) means domination.
>
> (Kehab Man Shakya 1994 [2051]: 10)

There are two points to make here. The first is that Nepali activists did not see themselves as calling on a foreign discourse when they invoked international and liberal ideals. By 1994, a powerful set of desires for development and democracy was deeply entrenched in middle-class urban consciousness and many Nepalis had come to evaluate their experiences in these terms (see Ahern 2001; Des Chene 1996b; Liechty 2003; Pigg 1992; Pigg 1993; Shrestha 1995).[21] Indeed, if Sagar Man Bajracharya exaggerates somewhat when he claims that

---

[21] This rhetoric had also been affirmed, at least formally, by the state. The 2046 Constitution echoes UN language in its very Preamble, which declares that its objectives include "securing to the Nepalese people social, political and economic justice" and guaranteeing "basic human rights to every citizen of Nepal."

"the main intention of the People's Movement was to give every Nepali the democratic experience of liberty and equality in keeping with the United Nation's Universal Declaration of Human Rights" (Bajracharya 1994 [2051]: 51), Vincanne Adams has demonstrated that it was the ideal of universal modernity in the form of political democracy that led the urban middle classes to support the *jana andolan* (Adams 1998). And, indeed, the extent to which the Nepali popular consciousness has come to take for granted transnational programs and bureaucratic ideas of "development" is evidenced by a group of middle-aged Buddhist nuns' decision to organize a public cleansing of the stupa in front of their temple not on the occasion of any Buddhist holiday, but in conjunction with a *Safa-Safai*, or Cleanliness Campaign, jointly sponsored by UNICEF and the Nepal Water Supply Corporation.[22] All of this testifies to the power – and presence – of ideas of rights and democracy in the Nepali political and social imaginary.[23]

The second point is that, as unexceptional as secularist activists' chain of associations may seem, the overall effect is an argument that reads religion through the lens of liberal democracy; indeed disciplines it according to these terms. Thus I must disagree with scholars who argue that "Indian secularism"[24] – as the definition that Bhikshu Ashvagosh presented is known – is best understood as the populist watering down of a universal principle that actually signifies the failure of liberal democracy to take root in South Asia (e.g., Chatterjee 1994: 1769). To the contrary, Bhikshu Ashvagosh's argument recasts religion according to liberalism's very ideals. By establishing secularism as a procedural principle empowered to adjudicate religious worldviews, Buddhist activists recast religion in a way that makes it democratically accountable. Secularism becomes a matter of equality, democracy, and rights.

HUMAN RIGHTS AND THE IDENTITY MACHINE

Such insights are singularly compatible with Talal Asad's analysis of the secular as a historical and political category of thought. For Asad,

---

[22] Notably, they also did this in conjunction with the Nepal Bhasa Women's Organization (*Nepal Bhasa Misa Khala*), an ethnic association organized around language-rights.

[23] Indeed, if modernity is better understood as a set of "promissory notes" than as a historical achievement, as Joel Robbins (2001) has proposed, the Buddhists I worked with were intensely concerned to see them actualized and they identified Hindu nationalism as a barrier to this progress!

[24] That is, the idea that secularism merely demands that the state patronize all religions equally, rather than a total separation of church and state.

secularism is by no means merely the post-Enlightenment, Weberian successor to a religious or a mythic worldview. Rather, it is "an enactment by which a *political medium* (representation of citizenship) redefines and transcends particular ... practices of the self" (Asad 2003: 5, emphasis in original). Summarizing an argument with which I think Bhikshu Ashvagosh would largely agree, he writes: "a secular state is not one that is characterized by religious indifference or rational ethics ... it is a complex arrangement of legal reasoning, moral practice and political authority" (2003: 255). Moreover – and again, most Buddhists I know would strongly agree – Asad associates secularism with the modern state and with liberal democracy.

The point at which Asad and Ashvagosh Bante[25] would probably part company, however, is when Asad defines secular modernity as an ideology based on a myth. I have already observed the degree to which modernity and development – and the teleological assumptions they contain – have become embedded in Nepali public consciousness. But for Asad, these values are historical contingencies that create the realities they describe. "Modernity is not primarily a matter of cognizing the real, but of living-in-the-world," he argues. "What is distinctive about modernity as a historical epoch includes modernity as a political-economic project" or rather, "a series of interlinked projects ... that aims at institutionalizing a number of (sometimes conflicting, often evolving) principles: constitutionalism, moral autonomy, democracy, human rights, civil equality, industry, consumerism, freedom of the market – and secularism." (2003: 13–14). For these purposes, he proposes, it employs "proliferating technologies ... that generate new experiences of space and time, of cruelty and health, of consumption and knowledge" (2003: 14) and, particularly, knowledge of the self.

Elsewhere, I have argued that a distinctive concomitant of the international extension of liberal democracy since the Cold War has been the emergence of what I have called a transnational "identity machine" – a particular global cultural imaginary, concretized in a constellation of institutions, ideologies, frameworks, structures, forms of knowledge and norms, that acts in such a way as to establish not only the categories of democratic social identities, but the very ontology that underlies these identifications itself (Leve 2003). The global

---

[25] "Bante" means "monk." A common, polite but informal way to refer to monks in Nepal is by their name, followed by "Bante", e.g. Ashvagosh Bante, Mahanama Bante, Amritandanda Bante, etc.

extension of liberal political structures and neoliberal economic ortho-
doxies around the globe in the name of democratization has played a
key role in propagating this identity machine, which creates new kinds
of subjects and subjectivities that are legible to, and governable within,
the structures of liberal and neoliberal democracy and law. Today,
human rights have become part of this discursive and institutional
apparatus, and rights-talk is a significant vector through which the
identity machine reproduces itself. What interests me here is that
when Buddhists insist that national Hinduism violates their human
right to religious equality, they represent themselves as particular
types of persons and political subjects. Yet, in other contexts – and
significantly, in this case, when they are practicing Buddhism – they
reject the very premises associated with these claims. In fact, for many,
the very essence of Buddhism lies in the recognition that these premises are illusory.

   This kind of dilemma has largely gone unrecognized in critical
discussions of human rights. Recent years have seen the rise of a rich
area of social science scholarship concerned with the ways that techniques of transnational neoliberal governmentality are encoded in ideologies, institutions, laws, and procedural norms.[26] A growing literature
recognizes human rights as part of this, and questions concerning the
Rights regime's cultural assumptions, transnational scope, actual practice and (intended or unintended) effects as governmental tools have
sparked important debates.[27] Cowan, Dembour, and Wilson have
observed how national and international legal regimes, including the
Rights regime, "dictate the conditions and content of claims and even
identities" and identified an "intriguing ... dialectic between the discourses and practices – one might say, the culture – of human rights,
and those of the groups that appeal to them" (2001: 11). Asad takes the
same problem and moves in a different direction, to explicitly engage
the historical and ontological assumptions "about 'the human' on
which human rights stand" (2003: 129). The genealogy of natural rights
that he derives from Richard Tuck (1979), suggests affinities between
key components of the human rights ideal, especially those related to the notion of individual sovereignty, and the philosophical

[26] See Cruikshank (1999); Dezalay and Garth (2003); Ferguson and Gupta (2002); Ong and
Collier (2005); Rose (1993, 1996). In Nepal, see Leve (2001); Rankin (2001, 2004).
[27] For just a sample of such discussions among anthropologists and those who have influenced
them, see Brown (1995); Gledhill (1997); Hannerz (1996); Preis (1996); Merry (2005);
Povinelli (2002); Speed (2005); Wilson (1997); Warren (1998); Warren and Jackson (2003).

assumptions about human nature and freedom that C. B. Macpherson (1962) has famously called "possessive individualism."

Put bluntly, the implications of Asad and Macpherson's arguments are that human rights are dependent on a conception of identity that sees identities as personal and/or collective possessions.[28] According to Macpherson, democracy as we know it is rooted in the particular historical circumstances of seventeenth century England, and it reflects a uniquely market-driven conception of human nature that sees individuals as the self-owning proprietors of their own bodies and labor capacities, such that people can legitimately contract to alienate themselves by selling their labor, making the wage labor system possible. He tracks this implicit mode of understanding through eighteenth and nineteenth century liberal political theory, and argues that its assumptions continue to underlie modern constitutional democracy. When possessive individualism becomes a practical and philosophical norm, he proposes, "the relation of ownership . . . is read back into the nature of the individual" and "political society becomes a calculated device for the protection of this property and for the maintenance of an orderly relation of exchange" (Macpherson 1962: 3).

Extending Macpherson's insights to liberal multiculturalism today, one could say that it is this way of thinking that allows "identities" to claim an independent status in modern democratic thought, that is, to be understood as *properties of* peoples and groups as opposed to *relations between* them.[29] Thus identity becomes a property of the person – specifically, the kind of personal property that a liberal state is compelled to protect. That the Nepal state can be called upon to protect and maintain the languages, practices, and beliefs of its citizens as concrete forms of cultural property is enduring evidence of modern democracy's possessive individualist legacy. Given the liberal state's commitment to property rights, and MacPherson's insight that liberal political philosophy transforms people into the owners of themselves as property, it becomes only logical for self-owning democratic subjects to argue that the repression or abuse of any part of the self, including one's cultural or religious identity, constitutes a strikingly literally human

---

[28] Rouse (1995) makes a similar point about possessive individualism and social identities. Here, I extend the argument to the particular operation of human rights. See also Gledhill (1997); Ree (1992); and Leve (2003).

[29] For instance, it would be meaningless to claim that one were English if France, Germany, Denmark, etc. didn't exist; likewise to be Newar in the absence of other Nepali ethnic groups and/or a national Nepali identity.

violation of rights. This is the understanding of religious identity that Buddhists implicitly invoke when they call for legal secularism.

From this perspective, it is easy to see the many ways that human rights partake of, and help to extend, the identity machine. Human rights have been part of the democracy/development enterprise from their formal beginning, originating as governmental tools in the 1940s, at which time a simple division of labor saw the newly-formed World Bank and the International Monetary Fund as instruments for global economic stability while the United Nations committed itself to the struggle for political stability by standardizing modes of governance internationally. But if rights emerged in this context as a discursive framing of suffering and a narrative genre for deprivation – i.e., to protect people from certain kinds of action by others – it is also true that they constitute a form of action as well; they contribute to extending liberal norms of personhood and governance into the postcolonial world.[30] Considering that the UN Convention on Human Rights posits the "right to culture" as a fundamental human right on the basis that one may be unable to live and thrive without it – as if "culture" were a lung or a leg – it becomes easy to see understand why Asad interprets the recent expansion of human rights law that I see as part of the identity machine as a "mode of converting and regulating people, making them at once freer and more governable in this world" (2003: 157). "The historical convergence between human rights and neoliberalism may not," Asad speculates, "be purely accidental" (2003: 157).

How do Buddhists participate in this? I have already noted the way that the meaning of religion is transformed when secularist rhetoric establishes it as a subject of modern democracy. The grammar of rights shapes the selves who use it by compelling them to represent themselves in certain (possessive individualist) terms and make their claims in certain ways (that conform to the regulatory structures of human rights law). The practice of human rights encourages petitioners to conceive of themselves in terms of a property-based ontology of the human self. As the Theravada Buddhist activists' above-cited assertion – "if people have their own religions, literatures and cultures, they'll have a feeling of ownership and they'll resist the imposition of others' [religions, literatures and cultures]" – suggests, the rhetorical forms of

---

[30] Here, I am describing the kind of rights that political philosophers identify as "negative rights." "Positive rights" – such as the right to work, as opposed to the right of freedom from involuntary enslavement – are slightly different and raise somewhat different questions.

subjectivity Buddhists occupy when they argue for state secularism reflect both possessive individualist assumptions and a liberal governmental frame.

When Buddhists challenge the democratic legality of constitutionally-imposed national Hinduism in the language of human rights, they cast localized issues in a way that makes them internationally legible and actionable – actionable because they are able to claim they have been wronged in globally normative political terms, and legible because they represent themselves as possessors of a social identity – Buddhism – that a democratic state is committed to preserve. On one level, there is nothing surprising in this – after all, people all over the world do it, and for obvious and understandable reasons, every day. What is interesting in this case, however, is that the ontology of identity that they draw on when they make these claims directly contradicts the very commitments and ways of knowing that the same Buddhists declare are precisely the most meaningful in constituting them as Buddhists. The final section of this chapter will explore this double-bind.

SELVES, NOT-SELVES AND SECULAR DOUBLE-BINDS

Even as Theravada Buddhists have organized to contest the cultural politics of the democratic, Hindu state, they have faced a unique and interesting problem: although they present themselves politically as an identity group, their religious practice conceives of identity in terms that radically undermine that claim. Specifically, one of the core Buddhist teachings – and perhaps the one that most definitively distinguishes Buddhist beliefs from Hindu theologies – is the principle of *anatta* or not-self.[31] This teaching says that despite that mode of subjective experience that is called self-consciousness, there is, in truth, no such thing as a self. "We" – that which Buddhist texts say that all people by everywhere in the world instinctively think of as our "selves" – are merely the composite products of an ongoing series of physical and mental perceptions. There is no enduring, experiencing subject that is ontologically distinguishable from the experience itself. In other words, Buddhism believes, the whole experience of identity is an illusion, and many Nepali Buddhists dedicate their religious lives to cultivating this insight, most directly through vipassana – or "insight" – meditation.

---

[31] This is the translation offered by Collins (1982) in his classic study of the concept in Theravada thought.

Unlike the Judeo-Christian heaven, Nirvana is not a place, they say. It is the state – Enlightenment – that reflects the most perfect comprehension of this truth. The consequence of this freedom from self-attachment is the cessation of the kinds of acts that generate *karma* and thus, liberation from worldly suffering and the cycle of rebirth.

For many of the most committed Theravada Buddhists I worked with, this was the essential truth that the Buddha taught. Historically, such other-worldly aspirations had tended to be considered the exclusive province of monks. However, a dramatic consequence of modernization and education has been the emergence of a powerful lay meditation movement, particularly among the Buddhist middle class. Over the past two decades in Nepal, vipassana meditation has become standard practice for Theravada Buddhists, many of whom say they were drawn to Theravada by its doctrinal orthodoxy and the fact that its preference for rationalism over ritual seemed compatible with the scientific logic that they associated with modern life. In other words – and this will become important later – Theravada Buddhism as it is understood and practiced in Nepal is the product of a modern, modernizing mentality.

Early on in my fieldwork I discovered that seemingly every time I asked someone the reason for practicing Theravada Buddhism or what that individual, personally, felt that Buddhism was really about, I was met with the same answer: "go meditate." "It's the only way to understand," my interlocutors insisted. While they were perfectly happy to talk with me about any and all aspects of their secularism strategizing and what was wrong with the Hindu state (as also the details of everyday life, hopes, etc.), when I asked about the content or meaning of the religion itself as they understood it, I was summarily referred to the meditation center. "Take a ten-day vipassana course," my friends would command. "Then you'll understand" (and implicitly, "only then will we talk to you").

Faced with such an imperative, I did. And I was taught that Buddhism is about achieving and living the knowledge of the principle of eternal change (*anicca*), and that that vipassana meditation is the practice by which a superficial, cognitive understanding of that supposedly natural reality is transformed into deep experiential knowledge. Through meditation, practitioners aim to develop an awareness of self as nothing more than a substance-less confluence of physical-mental sensations, a constant and overlapping collection of physical and emotional feelings that are continuously arising and passing away.

A pamphlet available to beginners at the foremost vipassana center in Kathmandu explains the process in this way:

> As one proceeds on [the Buddhist] path, one's awareness becomes sharper. One is no longer oblivious to what is happening inside. One now observes sensations in all parts of his body: heat, cold, throbbing, pulsation, lightness, heaviness, itching, burning, pain, etc. One observes that these sensations arise and pass away. One understands their impermanent character, their ephemeral nature, at the experiential level. A proper grasp of this natural process is indeed a breakthrough. One observes these sensations objectivity without an identification of "I," "me," or "mine". The student is just an observer of the constantly changing mental and bodily phenomena. Continued and proper practice of Vipassana brings about even the elimination of the concept of an observer. Only observation remains.
>
> (from *Vipassana Meditation: An Introduction*)[32]

"Upon fully grasping that there is no 'I,' 'me,' or experiencing agent" – only experience itself – another text explains, one loses the craving for future rebirths, and "approaches closer and closer to the goal of nibbana – of liberation" from the cycle of suffering in the phenomenal world (Goenka 1992 [1987]: 79). Or, as S. N. Goenka, the teacher, himself puts it in the recorded sermon that plays on Day 3 of the meditation course, "when one experiences personally the reality of one's own impermanence, only then does one start to come out of misery."

The identity-implication of the "not-self" idea is clearly illustrated in an interview which was one of the most frustrating moments of my fieldwork in Nepal. I had gone to the home of a senior Nepali meditation teacher, whom I will call Acaryaji, for a prearranged interview. Yet, although he had agreed to the meeting, he dismissed all of my questions – "How long have you been meditating? Under what circumstances did you first come to take a vipassana course? What made you decide that you wanted to become a teacher?" – responding only: "that doesn't matter." We spoke about his daughter's M. A. thesis, my own recent experience at a vipassana class, the weekly group sittings he hosted at his house, and so on. But he systematically refused to tell me about any personal experiences that were significant in his own development, or to provide any kind of narrative that would help me to organize an account of how or why he had become the

---

[32] *Vipassana Meditation: An Introduction.* Pamphlet published by the Vipassana Research Institute, Igatpuri, India.

person he was. I left two hours later with no more information than I had arrived with (or so I thought), and feeling thoroughly frustrated and confused.

It was only later that I began to understand what had happened that afternoon as a product of the ontological dissonance between our conceptual projects. What had happened in that interview was that I had been trying to collect a "life history" from someone who understood life as nothing more than a succession of sensations, arising alternately from desire or repulsion, and just as quickly passing away. Moreover, for him any other perspective was a normal but overcome-able illusion that he, for my own happiness and liberation, hoped I would learn to dispel. My questions sought narratives of inner experience. He rejected the notion of an interior truth. I wanted to learn about the effects of religion on political personhood. He meditated to experience the a-cultural, trans-historical non-truth of any sort of a subject-self. I thought only later about the epistemological differences underlying the ethnographic enterprise and the way in which he understood himself and the world. And it was only *much* later that I realized the differences in our respective ontological assumptions about self and identity.

As an inheritor of the possessive individualist ontology, at the time of the interview I assumed that everyone has – and sees themselves as having – an identity: as we own ourselves, we own our personal histories, which are what make us the unique individuals that each of us are, and what we identify as our "identities." What I had wanted to elicit in the interview was a personal history that would tell me about "his" development as an individual and as a social role-holder (i.e., meditation teacher). My intention was to connect this to developments at other levels of collectivity – for example, changes in the Theravada community, changes among ethnic Newars, and/or changes at the level of the nation-state. But Acaryaji believes that the impression of continuity of self over time is an illusion that masks the deeper reality of constant change. In fact, he thinks it is *the* illusion that binds humanity to the cycle of rebirth and suffering and, as a teacher, he has devoted himself to helping others to realize the truth:

> As the understanding of *anicca* develops within oneself, another aspect of wisdom arises: *anatta*, no "I", no "mine". Within the physical and mental structure, there is nothing that lasts more than a moment, nothing that one can identify as an unchanging self or soul. If something

is indeed "mine", then one must be able to possess it, to control it, but in fact one has no mastery even over one's body: it keeps changing, decaying, regardless of one's wishes.

(S. N. Goenka, Day 3 of the Ten Day Discourses [Goenka 1992])

Being a senior meditator and instructor, Acaryaji is widely recognized as an exceptionally attained Theravada Buddhist and he spends far too much time at the vipassana center to get deeply involved in identity politics. Yet, he belongs to the YMBA (Young Men's Buddhist Association), one of the organizations that was active in demanding secularism and recognition of Buddhist identity as an essential human right. One of closer relatives – an avid meditator and community leader who begins meetings at his home with twenty minutes of group meditation – was the YMBA president in 1990, and also led another campaign to preserve local Buddhist culture and architecture. And he told me he presumed that other relatives, including his nephews, cousins, students, and son, had joined in at least some of the marches and protests. Intriguingly, at least on the practical level, neither he nor his many students seemed to have any problem combining an anti-essentialist understanding of the self with the call for secular human rights and its implied identity.

CONCLUSION: THE DOUBLE-BINDS OF SECULAR BUDDHIST SUBJECTHOOD

How can a person reconcile this understanding – that there is no such thing as "me" or "mine"; that an individual doesn't possess or even have mastery over her body; that there's not even any such thing as a self to possess – with political action that relies on a possessive individualist ontology where one not only is presumed to have an identity, but it is seen as so integral to one's humanity itself that (1) it can legitimately mediate relations between subjects and their states and (2) one is thought to own it and to be entitled to state protection of it based on a democratic government's responsibility to guarantee property rights?

Such contradictions, I have come to believe, are characteristic features of citizenship that is at once global *and* local in the age of universal human rights and the neoliberal identity machine. If Charles Taylor is correct in arguing that the politics of liberal democracy are the politics of recognition (1994), there can only be a profound if subtle violence in the fact that Buddhists are compelled to represent themselves in ways that directly contradict the values and truths they say they are fighting to protect in order to defend themselves against another form of representational violence, perpetrated by the state. But what is the nature of this violence? Cowan, Dembour, and Wilson have commented on the ethical complexities inherent in situations like this one, and suggested that "they ways in which rights discourses can be both enabling and constraining" represents a paradox – "the paradox of rights" (2001b: 11). But what, we may ask, is at stake in this paradox? Are Theravada Buddhists simply deploying a form of strategic essentialism when they represent themselves as possessive individualists and their religion as a particular social identity, assumptions which are deeply embedded in democracy's public framework, but which on a personal level they know is not really the case? Do they perceive anything lost in the process of subjecting their Buddhism to the secular logic of the identity machine in order to win protection by the modern state? Appiah and others have commented on the implicit violence in the ways that the construction and deployment of essentialized identities may exclude or erase more heterodox ways of being (Appiah 1994; Cowan 2001; Gledhill, 1997; van Beek 2001; Warren 1998). How do Buddhists *feel* this double-bind?

In part, this is an empirical question: are Buddhist activists themselves disturbed by the personal and cultural translations that the discursive practice of human rights entails? As far as I can tell, the answer to this question is no. I have never heard anyone explicitly lament the disjuncture between the ethnicized religious identity that they are claiming to embody and the profoundly non-foundational notion of personhood that Buddhist teachings propose. Nor should this be particularly surprising: students of social behavior, not to mention legal pluralism, have long recognized that people apply different logics and standards in different domains of life. Moreover, Buddhists may be especially comfortable with the theoretical idea of coexisting levels of truth; it is said that the Buddha himself adjusted his teachings according to his listeners' capacities to understand. Mahayana Buddhism has even elevated this to a principle, the doctrine of "skillful means" (*upaya*).[33]

Yet, the fact that Buddhists themselves don't articulate their double-bind situation as a problem does not mean that it has nothing to teach.

---

[33] David Gellner has also suggested that Newars – the ethnic group to which most Theravada Buddhists in Nepal belong – are used to occupying and negotiating different levels of identity. See Gellner (1986, 1991, 2001).

Fortun, from whom I borrowed the term, has commented on the socio-historical circumstances that give rise to double-binds. She observes that they emerge "as entrenched signifying systems are being challenged and displaced [and] subjects are drawn into new realities and fields of reference," and they act, she writes, "as a social register of profound change" (2001: 13).

Certainly this is the case in Nepal, where the idea that laypeople would practice meditation at all is no less novel than the establishment of democracy as a popular political norm. The growth of the lay Theravada Buddhist meditation movement has taken place at the same time and alongside the expansion of democratic ideals in Nepal.[34] As over-determined as the instinct to represent it otherwise may be, the double-bind I am pointing to is in no way a conflict between "local culture" and "universal rights," still less "tradition" and "modernity." Modern forces are equally responsible for both the expectation that laypeople should pursue Nirvana and the liberal logic that packages religion as a personal property.[35] Thus, the violence of the double-bind is *not* that Nepali Buddhists are losing an "authentic" culture or religiosity in the process of protecting it; the problem is that the dual demands of the moment pull in equally important but mutually exclusive ways.[36]

I said above that the logical contradictions of the double-bind I identified do not seem to manifest as a form of existential pain at the level of conscience for individual activists. Yet, this does not mean that this kind of epistemic violence is without material consequences. Rather, the conflict has found expression at the level of community. By 1995, it was impossible not to note that many Theravada Buddhists who had enthusiastically supported the secularism movement in 1990–91 were now overtly critical of the same leaders and organizations. Specifically, critics accused monks and lay leaders of betraying "Buddhism" – conceived as a set of other-worldly oriented practices and

[34] The vipassana center where Acharyji teaches was founded in the late 1980s, opened to a broader public in the early 1990s, and has been growing exponentially since.
[35] Theravada's very presence in contemporary Nepal is tied to the legacy of British colonialism and the Christian missionary/Theosophical Society's presence in Sri Lanka in the late nineteenth century. See Gombrich and Obeyesekere (1988 [1990]) for descriptions of the transformation of Theravada Buddhism in Sri Lanka at that time.
[36] Even Derrida's concern about "the violence of an injustice" when people are required to represent themselves in "an idiom they do not understand very well or at all" seems inappropriate here, applied to people whose aspirations have been shaped by what they firmly hold to be democratic principles, vernacularized as those understandings of democracy may appear to be from other perspectives (Derrida 1990: 951, quoted in Fortun 2001: 598).

aspirations – by becoming too "political," that is, involved in secular, this-worldly affairs. The most immediate effect of this shift in public sensibilities was that some of the lay leaders who had been most visible in the movement found themselves marginalized and a few monks became the object of gossip and a more or less subtle censorship. I read this dischord – which split the Theravada Buddhist community and was certainly painful for many of the actors involved – as the practical outcome of the dual imperatives of the contradictory cultural forces associated with neoliberal modernity that, one the one hand, compelled Buddhists to represent themselves as a sociopolitical identity group while, on the other, encouraging them to conceive of what it meant to be Buddhist in almost the opposite terms, ones that stressed meditation and soteriologically-focused action and devalued social and political life.

Of course, many will say that this is a negligible price to pay for the critical protections that human rights tools offer vulnerable groups. And, especially now, I'm sure that most of people I've been writing about would agree. As I noted above, one of the most commonly-cited reasons that Buddhists abandoned their calls for a new, secular constitution and backed away from aggressive identity-based claims is simply that the political landscape has changed radically with the rise of the armed Maoist rebellion and the state's equally brutal and absolutist response. Indeed, the spectacular scale of abductions, killings, rapes, disappearances, and population displacement – as well as the King's apparent dismissal of constitutional democracy – have dramatically transformed the everyday meanings of the struggle for democracy, political violence, and human rights, replacing the epistemic violence of (mis)representation with the literal violence of bodily injury and death. Against this new backdrop, activists' priorities have shifted. And, recently, there have been signs that Theravada Buddhists may again cultivate a public presence to advance their goals, this time identified with a nascent peace movement. An energetic young monk has lately been cultivating alliances with civil society groups, arguing that as vowed and bound supporters of nonviolence, Buddhists are uniquely positioned to act as emissaries of peace. And there are signs that this new representation of Buddhist identity may prove broadly compelling. In the future, I would not be surprised to see Buddhists take to the streets again, this time defining and acting out a new set of relations between human rights, religious identity, democracy, and the state.

REFERENCES

Adams, Vincanne. 1998. *Doctors for Democracy: Health Professionals in the Nepalese Revolution.* Cambridge: Cambridge University Press.

Ahern, Laura. 2001. *Invitations to Love: Literacy, Love Letters, and Social Change in Nepal.* Ann Arbor: University of Michigan Press.

Appiah, K. Anthony. 1994. "Identity, Authenticity, Survival: Multicultural Societies and Social Reproduction." In A. Gutmann, ed., *Multiculturalism.* Princeton: Princeton University Press.

Asad, Talal. 2003. *Formations of the Secular: Christianity, Islam, Modernity.* Stanford: Stanford University Press.

Ashvagosh, Bhikshu Mahastavir. 1994 (2051). "Dharmanirpekshata ra Rajaniti" ("Secularism and Politics"). *The Dharmakirti* 12(1): 36–43.

Bajracharya, Sagar Man 1994 (2051). "Hindu Shabdale Rastriyataa Jogaaundaina." *The Dharmakirti* 12(2): 51–53.

Brown, Wendy. 1995. *States of Injury: Power and Freedom in Late Modernity.* Princeton: Princeton University Press.

Burghart, R. 1984. "The Formation of the Concept of Nation-State in Nepal." *Journal of Asian Studies* 44(1): 101–125.

Burghart, R. 1996. *The Conditions of Listening: Essays on Religion, History and Politics in South Asia.* Oxford: Oxford University Press.

Caplan, Lionel. 1970. *Land and Social Change in East Nepal: A Study of Hindu-tribal Relations.* Berkeley: University of California Press.

Collins, Steven. 1982. *Selfless Persons: Imagery and Thought in Theravada Buddhism.* Cambridge: Cambridge University Press.

Cowan, Jane 2001. "Ambiguities of an Emancipatory Discourse: The Making of a Macedonian Minority in Greece." In J. Cowan, M.-B. Dembour, and R. Wilson, eds., *Culture and Rights: Anthropological Perspectives.* Cambridge: Cambridge University Press.

Cowan, Jane, Marie-Benedicte Dembour, and Richard Wilson. 2001a. *Culture and Rights: Anthropological Perspectives.* Cambridge: Cambridge University Press.

Cowan, Jane, Marie-Benedicte Dembour, and Richard Wilson. 2001b. "Introduction." In J. Cowan, M.-B. Dembour, and R. Wilson, eds., *Culture and Rights: Anthropological Perspectives,* pp. 1–26. Cambridge: Cambridge University Press.

Cruikshank, Barbara. 1999. *The Will to Empower: Democratic Citizens and Other Subjects.* Ithaca and London: Cornell University Press.

Derrida, Jacques. 1990. "Force of Law: The Mystical Foundation of Authority." *Cardoza Law Review* 11(5–6).

Des Chene, Mary. 1996a. "Ethnography in the *Janajati-yug*: Lessons from Reading *Rodhi* and Other Tamu Writings." *Studies in Nepali History and Society* 1(1): 97–162.

Des Chene, Mary. 1996b. "In the Name of Bikas." *Studies in Nepali History and Society* 1(2): 259–270.

Dezalay, Yves and Bryant G. Garth. 2003. *Global Prescriptions: The Production, Exportation and Importation of a New Legal Orthodoxy.* Ann Arbor: University of Michigan Press.

Ellingson, Ter. 1991. "The Nepal Constitution of 1990: Preliminary Considerations." *Himalayan Research Bulletin* XI (1–3): 1–18.

Ferguson, James and Akhil Gupta. 2002. "Spatializing States: Toward an Ethnography of Neoliberal Governmentality." *American Ethnologist* 29(4): 981–1002.

Fortun, Kim. 2001. *Advocacy After Bhopal.* Chicago: University of Chicago Press.

Fraser, Nancy. 1997. *Justice Interruptus: Critical Reflections on the "Postsocialist" Condition.* London: Routledge.

Gellner, David. 1986. "Language, Caste, Religion and Territory: Newar Identity Ancient and Modern." *Archives of European Sociology* 27: 102–148.

Gellner, David. 1999. "From Cultural Hierarchies to a Hierarchy of Multiculturalism: The Case of the Newars of the Kathmandu Valley." In Sasakawa Peace Foundation USA, ed., *Multiculturalism: Modes of Coexistence in South and Southeast Asia.* Washington DC: Sasakawa Peace Foundation, USA.

Gellner, David. 2001. "From Group Rights to Individual Rights and Back: Nepalese Struggles over Culture and Equality." In J. Cowan, M.-B. Dembour, and R. Wilson, eds., *Culture and Rights: Anthropological Perspectives.* Cambridge: University of Cambridge Press, pp. 177–200.

Gellner, David, Joanna Pfaff-Czarnecka, and John Whelpton. 1997. *Nationalism and Ethnicity in a Hindu Kingdom: The Politics of Culture in Contemporary Nepal.* Amsterdam: Harwood Academic Publishers.

Gellner, David and Declan Quigley. 1995. *Contested Hierarchies: A Collaborative Ethnography of Caste among the Newars of the Kathmandu Valley, Nepal.* Oxford: Clarendon Press.

Gledhill, John. 1997. "Liberalism, Socio-Economic Rights and the Politics of Identity: From Moral Economy to Indigenous Rights." In R. Wilson, ed. *Human Rights, Culture and Context: Anthropological Perspectives.* London: Pluto Press.

Goenka, Satya Narayan. 1992 (1987). *The Discourse Summaries: Talks from a Ten-day Course in Vipassana Meditation* condensed by William Hart. Igatpuri, India: Vipashyana Vishodhan Vinyas.

Gombrich, Richard and Gananath Obeyesekere. 1988 (1990). *Buddhism Transformed: Religious Change in Sri Lanka.* Princeton (Delhi): Princeton University Press (Motilal Banarsidass Publishers).

Gurung, Harka. 2002. "Social Demography of Nepal: Census 2001." Talk sponsored by the Gurung Association of New York, Columbia University, 2002.

Hale, Charles. 2005. "Neoliberal Multiculturalism: The Remaking of Cultural Rights and Racial Dominance in Central America. *PoLAR: Political and Legal Anthropology Review* 28(1): 10–28.

Hangen, Susan. 2005. "Boycotting Dasain: History, Memory and Ethnic Politics in Nepal." *Studies in Nepali History and Society* 10(1): 105–133.

Hannerz, Ulf. 1996. *Transnational Connections: Culture, People, Places.* London: Routledge.

Hodgson, B.H. 1857. "Papers Relative to the Colonization, Commerce, Physical Geography, etc., of the Himalayan Mountains and Nepal." (Selections from the Records of the Government of Bengal No. 27). Calcutta: Calcutta Gazette Office.

Hofer, A. 1979. *The Caste Hierarchy and the State in Nepal: A Study of the Muluki Ain of 1854.* Innsbruck: Universitätsverlag Wagner.

Holmberg, David H. 1989. *Order in Paradox: Myth, Ritual and Exchange Among Nepal's Tamang.* Ithaca, NY: Cornell University Press.

Hutt, Michael. 1994. "Drafting the 1990 Constitution." In M. Hutt, ed. *Nepal in the Nineties*, pp. 28–47. Delhi: Oxford University Press.

Joshi, Elbis. 1994 (2051). "Sanvidhaanma Hinduadirajya ra Rajatantra" ("Hindu Kingdom and Monarchy in the the Constitution"). *The Dharmakirti* 12(1): 43–45.

Klug, Heinz. 2002. "Hybrid(ity) Rules: Creating Local Law in a Globalized World." In Y. Dezalay and B. G. Garth, eds. *Global Prescriptions: The Production, Exportation, and Importation of a New Legal Orthodoxy.* Ann Arbor: University of Michigan Press.

Lawoti, Mahendra. 2005. *Towards a Democratic Nepal: Inclusive Political Institutions for a Multicultural Society.* New Delhi, London, and Thousand Oaks: Sage Publications.

Leve, Lauren G. 2001. "Between Jesse Helms and Ram Bahadur: Women, NGOs, 'Participation,' and 'Empowerment' in Nepal." *PoLAR: Political and Legal Anthropology Review* 24(1): 108–128.

Leve, Lauren G. 2003. "Identity." Paper presented at the American Anthropological Association Meetings. Chicago, IL. Panel titled: The New Keywords: Unveiling the Terms of an Emerging Orthodoxy (organized and chaired by Lauren Leve and David Graeber).

Liechty, Mark. 2003. *Suitably Modern: Making Middle Class Culture in a New Consumer Society.* Princeton: Princeton University Press.

Macpherson, C. B. 1962. *The Political Theory of Possessive Individualism.* Oxford: Oxford University Press.

Merry, Sally. 1992. "Anthropology, Law and Transnational Processes." *Annual Review of Anthropology* 21: 357–379.

Merry, Sally. 2005. *Human Rights and Gender Violence: Translating International Law into Local Justice.* Chicago: University of Chicago Press.

Ong, Aiwa and Stephen Collier. 2005. *Global Assemblages: Technology, Politics, and Ethics as Anthropological Problems.* Oxford: Blackwell.

Pfaff-Czarnecka, Joanna. 1993. "The Nepalese Durga-Puja, or Shaping a State Ritual in Quest for Legitimacy." In C. Ramble and M. Brauen, eds. *Anthropology in Tibet and the Himalaya.* Zuriche: Volkerkunde Museum.

Pigg, Stacy Leigh. 1992. "Inventing Social Categories Through Place: Social Representations and Development in Nepal." *Comparative Studies in Society and History* 34(3 (July)): 491–513.

Pigg, Stacy Leigh. 1993. "Unintended Consequences: The Ideological Impact of Development in Nepal." *South Asia Bulletin* 8(1 & 2): 45–58.

Postero, Nancy. 2005. "Indigenous Responses to Neoliberalism: A Look at the Bolivian Uprising of 2003." *PoLAR: Political and Legal Anthropology Review* 28(1): 73–92.

Povinelli, Elizabeth. 2002. *The Cunning of Recognition: Indigenous Alterities and the Making of Australian Multiculturalism.* Durham: Duke University Press.

Preis, A-B. S. 1996. "Human Rights as Cultural Practice: An Anthropological Critique." *Human Rights Quarterly* 18: 514–540.

Rankin, Katherine N. 2001. "Governing Development: Neoliberalism, Microcredit, and Rational Economic Woman." *Economy and Society* 30(1): 18–37.

Rankin, Katherine N. 2004. *The Cultural Politics of Markets.* Toronto: University of Toronto Press.

Rata, Elizabeth. 2003. "Late Capitalism and Ethnic Revivalism, 'A New Middle Age'?" *Anthropological Theory* 3(1): 43–63.

Ree, Jonathan. 1992. "Internationality." *Radical Philosophy* 60 (Spring): 3–11.

Robbins, Joel. 2001. "God is Nothing but Talk: Modernity, Language, and Prayer in Papua New Guinea Society." *American Anthropologist* 103(4): 901–912.

Rose, Nikolas. 1993. "Government, Authority and Expertise in Advanced Liberalism." *Economy and Society* 22(3): 359–367.

Rose, Nikolas. 1996. "The Death of the Social? Re-figuring the Territory of Government." *Economy and Society* 25(3): 327–356.

Rouse, Roger. 1995. "Questions of Identity: Personhood and Collectivity in Transnational Migration to the United States." *Critique of Anthropology* 15(4): 351–380.

Shakya, Keshab Man. 1994 (2051). "Rastriya Sabhama Dharmanirpekshat" ("Secularism in the National Assembly"). *The Dharmakirti* 12(2): 9–10.

Shakya, Subarna. 1994. (2051). "Nepal Dharmanirpeksha rastra Nahunuko kāran ke sakcha?" (Why isn't a Nepal a Secular State?"). *The Dharmakirti* 12(2): 55.

Shrestha, Nanda. 1995. "Becoming a Development Category." In J. Crush, ed. *Power of Development.* London and New York: Routledge, pp. 266–277.

Speed, Shannon. 2005. "Dangerous Discourses: Human Rights and Multiculturalism in Neoliberal Mexico." PoLAR: *Political and Legal Anthropology Review* 28(1): 29–51.

Speed, Shannon and Maria Teresa Sierra. 2005. "Introduction to Symposium on 'Critical Perspectives on Human Rights and Multiculturalism in Neoliberal Latin America'." PoLAR: *Political and Legal Anthropology Review* 28(1): 1–9.

Taylor, Charles. 1994. "The Politics of Recognition." In A. Gutmann, ed. *Multiculturalism: Examining the Politics of Recognition*. Princeton: Princeton University Press.

Thapa Magar, M. S. (1994 [2051]) "Dharmanirpeksha Nepal – Aajako Aawashyakataa" ("Secular Nepal – Today's Necessity", written in Nepali). *The Dharmakirti* 12(2): 13–19.

Tuck, Richard. 1979. *Natural Rights Theories: Their Origin and Development*. Cambridge: Cambridge University Press.

van Beek, Martijn. 2001. "Beyond Identity Fetishism: 'Communal' Conflict in Ladakh and the Limits of Autonomy." *Cultural Anthropology* 15(4): 525–569.

Warren, Kay B. 1998. *Indigenous Movements and Their Critics: Pan-Maya Activism in Guatemala*. Princeton: Princeton University Press.

Warren, Kay B, and Jean Jackson. 2003. *Indigenous Movements, Self-Representation, and the State in Latin America*. Austin: University of Texas Press.

Wilson, Richard. 1997. *Human Rights: Culture and Context*. London: Pluto Press.

Wright, Daniel. 1877. *History of Nepal*. London: Cambridge University Press.

Legal document

1992 The Constitution of the Kingdom of Nepal 2047 (1990) [English translation]. Babar Mahahl, Kathmandu Nepal: Ministry of Law, Justice and Parliamentary Affairs Law Books Management Board.

PART TWO

REGISTERS OF POWER

INTRODUCTION: REGISTERS OF POWER

Laura Nader

In any discussion of human rights practice it is useful to return to the setting and contexts that preceded the 1948 Universal Declaration of Human Rights. Eleanor Roosevelt was Chair of the United Nations Human Rights Commission, a figure persistent in reminding her collaborators that they were charged with writing a declaration acceptable to all religions, ideologies, and cultures. The delegates from Western Europe, the Eastern Communist countries and Third World nations debated *in philosophical terms* the future of the declaration of human rights, each from their own particular view – the Chinese representatives insisting that Confucian philosophy be incorporated into the Declaration, the Catholics the teachings of St. Thomas Aquinas, the Liberals advocating the views of John Locke and Thomas Jefferson, and the Communists those of Karl Marx. There were no representatives from the places where indigenous peoples lived, nor from the peoples of Islam (Berger 1981). Eastern countries wanted to confine the charter to social and economic rights. Western countries wanted to inspire borrowings from the American Bill of Rights and the French Declaration of the Rights of Man.

Mrs Roosevelt, who was later nominated, but not awarded, the Nobel Prize had her own vision: "We hope its proclamation by the General Assembly will be an event comparable to the proclamation of the Declaration of the Rights of Man by the French people in 1789, the adoption of the Bill of Rights by the people of the United States, and the adoption of comparable declarations at different times in other countries (Berger 1981: 73). To her the world was one world. As she herself expressed it:

> Where after all, do universal human rights begin? In small pleces, close
> to home – so close and so small that they cannot be seen on any map of

the world. Yet, they are the world of the individual person: the neighborhood he lives in; the school or college he attends; the factory, farm or office where he works. Such are the places where every man, woman, and child seek equal justice, equal opportunity, equal dignity without discrimination. Unless these rights have meaning there, they have little meaning anywhere.

(Romany 1994: 90)

Eleanor Roosevelt and the New Deal women of that era were reformers or social welfare workers. *They knew what was best for others.* Today the issues are not so clear cut – individual rights or collective rights, national sovereignty or international human rights, a hegemonic human rights of western origin or a global movement?

At the start the issue of human rights as a part of a western and mainly American hegemonic movement was transparent. The movement to create a new international apparatus for the promotion of human rights was largely led by Americans with the US State Department working up early drafts and the crucial meetings taking place in the United States. Not surprisingly, the international "Bill of Rights" had an obvious American flavor – everyone had a right to life, liberty, security of person, freedom of thought and religion. No one shall be held in slavery, subjected to torture, arbitrary arrest, detention or exile, and all but two drafts were written in English. And from the start human rights have been those which Americans took to others.

But there were problems (Renteln 1990). The focus on individual rights at the expense of collective rights meant that indigenous people would be poorly served by the Universal Declaration. Group rights of native peoples are the most important and most endangered of all Native American Indian rights. Indian groups need their own land and water for group survival. Richard Falk (1992) argued that the neglect of indigenous peoples was a result of "normative blindness," which reflected assimilationist policies. In the name of development indigenous peoples have been and are still being destroyed and disappeared, their wealth taken. Not surprisingly, since indigenous peoples were excluded from the rights forming process, their issues were not part of the 1948 effort. In 1948 the concern was with the state, an orientation that excluded private domains. Since 1948, however, there have been volumes written on the non-state aspects of human rights, such as the concerns with domestic violence.

The emphasis on international human rights versus universal human rights touches on issues of national sovereignty and relativism.

Assertions of dominant cultural superiority (Said 1978) plus the American impetus for human rights efforts engenders cynicism about western self-righteousness. The other is not mute. Chinese prison human rights violations? As compared to the United States? The Abu Ghraib scandals led California prison watchers to call attention to human rights violations in US prisons. And, in spite of the 1978 American Indian Freedom Act in the 1980s and 1990s, the US Federal courts denied Native Americans religious freedom in over ten consecutive cases (see Nader and Ou 1998). Violent cases of rape in Pakistan capture the headlines in US newspapers, but, in spite of the crime rate moving downwards in the past year in the United States, the one area where crime has increased is rape. FBI statistics on incidents of rape in the United States might lead others to teach Americans something about themselves. In other words, human rights are not something that Americans can any longer take to others without allowing human rights advocates from other countries to intervene here.

Today, transportation technologies, travel and tourism, media attention, cross-cultural education and an increase in human interaction of all varieties has opened opportunities and presented obstacles for human rights interventions. For example, tourists have played a regulatory role in the Chiapas, Mexico uprising and in the defense of Tepoztecan villages of Morelos, Mexico from state violence. Since the conception of human rights transcends the citizenship of the individual, support for human rights can come from anyone, anywhere. "Insiders" and "outsiders" are often involved in human rights practices, sometimes making the story a difficult one to tell (Nader 1999).

One cannot envision how the law works *between* the global and the local without following the dynamics of power, up, down, and sideways (Nader 1969). As illustration, one would be forced to notice that the three examples opening the introduction to this volume were from Fiji, India, and Bolivia. As Mark Goodale notes in the Introduction, the vignettes both tell us and don't tell us things. One thing they do tell us is that, although a lot has happened in the intervening years since the 1948 Declaration, the selections indicate that human rights practices still involve "them" and not "us," whether the story is about women's rights in Fiji, or India, or the indigenous movement in Bolivia. There are continuities over the more than fifty years since the Declaration. Human rights regimes coexist with other competing rule systems.

To understand how power works in the contexts described in this volume one must have a sense of history. In Bolivia, for example,

June Nash (1993) has sketched the way in which exploitation works in the mining sectors, which involves the local, the state, and the international economic firms, the owners of the mines. William Taylor (1979), in writing about Mexico and violence against women, found that violence against women was prevalent while peaceful relations were common among male members of the same community. Violent conflict was restricted to that which did not get the community into trouble with state authorities, and did not spread to the community, the primary focus of allegiance. Many human rights abuses in Latin America stem from American foreign policies that support dictatorships. The Monroe Doctrine, which justified the exercise of US influence in the Latin sphere, is still with us. And the same can be said about World Bank policies that leave communities in dire circumstances – the humanitarian impulse is not always benign. Then, of course, there are the resource wars in which people get caught: the oil that may lie below the surface in Chiapas; the mining potential for gold and silver in Oaxaca; the extraction possibilities for timber throughout Central America. The context for human rights abuses must be recognized because, if they are not, human rights practices will be seen either as a band-aid, a cover for local corruption or a cover for broader upheavals in the world, some of which might be traced back to Euro-American expansions worldwide and include present day resource wars by multinational corporations. Thus, my comments on the following two essays will be framed by history, by comparisons, by methods that scrutinize the dynamics of power, especially in the context of grossly unequal relations.

In chapter 4 in this section, by Shannon Speed, we are deftly introduced to European philosophical underpinnings in relation to the reconfiguring of resistance in the Zapatista uprising in Chiapas, Mexico. In their efforts to reorganize, the Zapatistas are interested in human rights practices, not policies that do not translate into practice. The people in the Zapatista autonomous *municipios* use the familiar language of human rights and indigenous rights to challenge the logic of the neoliberal Mexican state. Concrete and effective policies, new forms of local governance, a collective right to autonomy: they are concerned not with philosophy but with a practice where rights are understood to exist prior to and regardless of their recognition by the state.

Speed documents the move from armed uprising to autonomous civilian government over the past ten years. She speaks of the failed San Andres' Accords on Indigenous Rights and Culture and of the failed peace talks. The thirty-eight "municipalities in rebellion" emerge as a space for organized resistance and as models of indigenous political participation. The keystone of good governance is one where authorities carry out consensually arrived at decisions.

The Mexican Constitution of 1917, Speed tells us, was one of the first in the world to establish social rights based on premises of social justice and human dignity, and during the following decades the Partido Revolucionario Institucional (PRI) (the International Revolutionary Party) drew support from indigenous communities. Restructuring along neoliberal lines began in the 1970s, accelerating to the present. By 1992 the state had radically changed land and labor in Articles 27 and 123, and relations between the state and indigenous peoples changed as a result. Her story is of a downhill move whereby the state has given up ensuring social rights and state enterprises are privatized. In this context, organizations defending rights have flourished while the primary responsibility of the state is to ensure law and order so that markets may operate freely. In this environment, indigenous rights movements emerge as resistance to the state and to neoliberal practices. But how?

Speed indicates that rights struggles may work to reinforce neoliberal government strategies if indigenous groups are forced to petition the state, and legalism may actually reinforce inequalities, feeding the illusion that organized power can only be exercised through the state. Speed is examining the Zapatista's *autonomy* process and the formation of the *Juntas de Buen Gobierno*. The Zapatista movement has from the start maintained an alternative project to that of negotiating with the state, their ideas of alternatives to state petitioning have been able to mature since 1994.

What appears to be going on here is a dance between neoliberal state hegemonies and counter-hegemonies that originates, not with the recent indigenous resistance, but goes back as far as the encounter with the Spanish conquerors, the colonists, and the Spanish Crown (Nader 1989). As Eric Wolf noted in 1959, the relationship that the Spanish Crown created between itself and its colonists, both Spanish and Indian, led to the semiautonomous village communities that Wolf found described in the colonial records as *la república de indios*. The Spanish Crown's policy of creating Indian communities resulted from maneuvers over the relative power of the Crown, the colonists and the Indians, in order to guard against the rise of powers that could rival the authority of the Crown. "Each Indian community was to be a

121

self-contained economic unit ... Communal officials were to administer the law through the instrumentality of their traditional custom, wherever that custom did not conflict with the demands of church and state ... The autonomy which the crown denied to the Indian sector of society as a whole, it willingly granted to the local social unit" (Wolf 1959: 214). For centuries this system allowed the indigenes a good deal of room to maneuver. The Indian community has been described as one where the group is more important than the individual. As I noted in 1989, these communities have had transformative elements and have never developed in a single direction. They oscillate, they fluctuate in change in fits and starts, never independent of the larger society to which they send their excess population and to which they are bound by a series of interlocking interests. So what is happening in Chiapas is not altogether new, although it is worth having Speed describe the way present-day control is working as a dynamic of power distribution or redistribution.

From the point of view of the neoliberal state and its maneuvers, a number of analysts have noted that human rights discourses are double-edged. From the point of view of the neoliberal state, strategies of inclusiveness have meant that collective indigenous rights may be recognized even if they are limited. Inclusive policies are processes of control that form the subject and strengthen the state's role as purveyor and protector of rights, both of which regulate the indigenes and give them the power to self-regulate. Such negotiation allows the state to give a little in order to expand its power. Thus, dissenting identities are "fixed" in legal regimes, which produces a self-regulating policing of identity.

Furthermore, according to examples from other parts of Latin America, indigenes would be put in a position of having to prove to law makers that they and their cultural practices really are indigenous. Thus, with the formation of all five of the *Juntas de Buen Gobierno*, the Zapatista's process of autonomy-making would serve not only to empower themselves, but to disempower the state by attacking the state's first site of legitimacy – the rule of law. For when the state failed not once but during successive attempts since 1994, the Zapatistas openly disregarded the state as the source of their rights and expressed their right to autonomy and self-determination, arguing that rights exist in their exercise, a philosophical position radically different from state power in the current neoliberal world scene whereby economic interests increasingly take over state functions in their own interest. The indigenes are not only reordering rule, they are reordering order.

122

Speed's description of the Juntas resembles much of what anthropologists have written about indigenous self-governing for some time – an emphasis on the collective process, consensus decision-making, rotating of citizens who serve as members of the councils of each autonomous township, the inversions of power relations with the intent to prevent corruption and abuse of powers. In the process of this revitalization effort the Zapatistas are manipulating the discourses of human and indigenous rights and using them to reinforce a project that has a long history in Mexican indigenous communities, one in which indigenous people have sought to reconfigure power relations in different ways since the sixteenth century.

But I want to return to Speed's observation that there is potential for "rights-based claims to be seduced into a system where legal process is an empty signifier for the resolution of immediate conflict, while leaving the architecture of power that created those conflicts unquestioned ... and the law's illusion that organized power can only be exercised through the state ..." There are indeed larger processes and structures of power in which such action is inscribed.

In a fascinating recent essay on indigenous peoples in Paraguay (Reed 2003), Richard Reed describes the larger process and structures of power determining the fate of the Ache and Guaraní peoples – the first hunters and gatherers, and the second also hunters, gatherers, and agriculturalists – before external changes entered to subvert their traditional subsistence strategies. The actors are the Paraguayan government. The Nature Conservancy, the World Bank, the concerned indigenous peoples, and the anthropologists. Reed describes the history of the creation of a national park or reserve in Paraguay where initially indigenous peoples were to have access – with land for subsistence and cultural purposes. At the same time they were to be involved in managing the parkland. The context was one of unequal power. By the time the park was created only the real indigenes were to have access to the park reserve, while those Indians who were acculturated were not allowed in. The Nature Conservancy was defining who was a real Indian and who was not. As Reed notes, from the point of view of the indigenes this was an old story with a long history. The Nature Conservancy was just another latifundista, people to be distrusted despite the brokering of well-intentioned anthropologists. The Guarani and the Ache were not the ecologically noble savages that the Nature Conservancy thought. Because the Nature Conservancy defined the terms of the debate, confrontations would be common occurrences, especially since the

Paraguayan government has been expropriating forest lands to satisfy agro-industrialists and a growing peasant population.

It is critical to note the role of corporate capitalists and the multi-national firms from Brazil, the United States, and Japan as actors determining the shape of state-indigenous relations in Paraguay, and influencing whether the law is used for legal or illegal purposes. At stake in this case and others is the paradigmatic use of the state as privileged sites of the political which Machiavelli should have abused us of centuries ago. In the case of Chiapas, most of the discussion has ignored the question of natural resources that may be in the long-term interest, not only of the Mexican state, but of its partners in plunder, the multinational corporations.

Mark Goodale's chapter on "Tracking Empires of Law and New Modes of Social Resistance in Bolivia (and elsewhere)" is complex in different ways from Shannon Speed's work. To track contemporary transnational configurations while grounding our understanding of how power works in descriptions of social practices, beyond techniques of observation or empirical study, is indeed a large task. Goodale is particularly interested in the way power shapes the emergence of human rights as a new category of sociolegal practice in Bolivia, and in particular the locale of his field site, one of the poorest regions of Bolivia, the *norte de Potosí*. The *norte de Potosí* is overwhelmingly a region of subsistence agriculture carried out by Aymara and Quechua speaking peoples in places outside of the various mining camps in the area. Goodale is interested in the possibilities for new forms of social resistance that have been developing over the past ten years in Bolivia at the same time that Bolivians are experiencing more alienation and socioeconomic exploitation that is accompanied by cultural poverties. Human rights expressions are found even in the most "local" of social practices, normative pluralism and universalist discourses.

Goodale distinguishes between the scientific development paradigm of the 1960s and 1970s and organizations which operated in Bolivia under a different umbrella beginning in the mid-1980s. The first is characterized by technical transnationalisms while the second by neo-liberalism, international and western financial institutions, privatizing land and resources, *and* an official commitment to human rights in the collective sense. Suddenly, international development agencies like the United Nations, pan-regional organizations like the Organization of American States, national Bolivian agencies such as the Ministry for Human Development, and community-based organizations, like the rural peasant unions, as well as the many transnational development nongovernmental organizations (NGOs), come together to constitute the new human rights configurations, both networked and transnational. According to Goodale, this human rights development was value-saturated and at the service of particular power vectors. Human rights was operating at registers different from other ideological frameworks in Bolivian life. In the vocabulary of controlling processes (Nader 1997), I would refer to this development as a form of mind colonization. For example, the director of a human rights legal services center in *norte de Potosí* introduced the *idea* of human rights – that locals share a common humanity with all humans, that they are entitled to respect and dignity, that they are equal. Important is Goodale's point that people's encounter with human rights is personal, as for example during marriage rituals. One NGO (PROCLADE) Goodale mentions is active throughout the region, but has headquarters in Spain and the European Union, which makes human rights encounters not only personal but trans-local and European.

In Bolivia, human rights discourse is closely associated with law and legality for Goodale. He introduces us to a rural-legal intellectual who received his training in human rights during trips to La Paz and other Bolivian cities. His focus on human rights for women works to expose mostly peasant agriculturalists to the idea of human rights and in this manner to transform existing or "traditional" ideas about the relationship between men and women, between individuals and their community, including the ethical commitment to the rightness of human rights, and the lack of same locally. This local intellectual is the only lawyer in the province. He officiates at weddings and in local courts.

In his conclusion, Goodale reconnects macro and micro and asks us to evaluate such human rights activities. Are human rights development schemes a project to mask increasingly inequalities? Or do they do some good? There is concern about the selection of which human rights one brings to Bolivia and how the protection of women's rights, for example, is associated with international systems of power. After all the NGOs he mentions are all of European origins; it is perhaps significant they do not come from Southeast Asia or from Africa or the Middle East.

Goodale argues that the rise of human rights discourse is inseparable from neoliberalism as a dominant frame of reference. Nevertheless, new forms of social resistance have developed along with the rise of human rights discourse, which he describes as a Pandora's box or perhaps an expression of capitalism's hypocrisy. At the very local level, the theory of human rights requires respect for diversity. So, although universal human rights are homogeneous in relation to a common human nature, they also allows people to organize themselves in ways that respect their inherent human dignity. Thus, Goodale notices that during conflict resolution processes, more indigenous traditions were supplanting formerly "legal" explanations for disputes over property, in conjunction with damage to crops by animals, in boundary disputes and so forth. As I said at the outset, this chapter was complex in its organization of the different levels of action or practices entailed in human rights development, needed to understand the very local changes in practice that might result.

The one unexplored dimension that might further enrich this analysis is the observation with which I began this commentary on registers of power. From the outset, the notion of human rights was European or Euro/American in its form and content. The work that is revealed in this volume is expressive of a larger movement of critical thought that brings to the fore the need to decolonize human rights discourse. In a recent analysis of "Rwanda's Gacaca and Postcoloniality" (Meyerstein 2005), the author calls attention to the tension between an elite human rights establishment and the views of their subaltern "clients," in their effort to secure human agency for all the world's inhabitants. The *gacaca* courts were instituted by the Rwandan government in 2001 to process prisoners in the aftermath of the 1994 genocide. Meyerstein writes of the criticisms of Amnesty International and others in the West who insist on holding *gacaca* up to international standards. He questions the basis for judging the *gacaca* on western expectations rather than on Rwandan norms and expectations, which require us to understand the role of prior colonial actors (Germans, Belgians, the French, and the international community through the "development enterprise"). Meyerstein despairs that "in yoking Rwandans to the international norms, as if there were no other norms by which to judge the *gacaca*, we risk repeating the conceptual violence of the 'civilizational' project that was colonization."

The anthropologist Thomas Barfield expressed the same warnings in a slightly more nuanced manner, in "Securing the Rule of Law in Post-Taliban Afghanistan." This is the way Barfield put it:

> I think one of the difficulties the international community is going to find in Afghanistan is that the Afghans have a very well-developed

structure of law, of morality and of justice, but it's following a different logic than our own . . . [W]hile state structures are very underdeveloped, the question of running a society without state structures is highly developed. And that is not something that people in the international community are used to dealing with . . .

(Barfield 2002 quoted in Ahmed 2005: 17)

Indeed international human rights discourses are fruitless endeavors unless achieved by indigenous actors comfortable in their own socio-legal contexts (Ahmed 2005: 20).

In a more sweeping articulation of some of the same issues, Issa Shivji (2003) speaks about future possibilities of "reconstructing a new civilization, a more universal, a more human, civilization . . . We cannot continue accepting Western civilization's claim to universality. Its universalization owes much to the argument of force rather than the force of argument." Shivji, a professor of law at the University of Dar es Salaam, argues for weaving a "new tapestry borrowing from different cultures and peoples."

As Goodale notes in his introduction to this volume, human rights have become decentered. Indeed the papers in this section are part of an argument for a different philosophy of human rights. That such an effort will be difficult is indicated by Goodale (p. 9, n. 6), in which he notes that human rights activists react strongly against the emergence of a critical human rights literature, although the study of human rights practices is sure to indicate the range of possible encounters with transnational human rights discourse (see p. 9, n. 6). Goodale observes that human rights activists may be more insistent than academics that human rights are ripe for reframing.

My concluding remarks on registers of power will underscore several points in the introduction and in the chapters in this section to which I alluded earlier. First is the importance of tracing networks both vertically and horizontally, in and out of the academic and activist world. The importance of so doing is heuristic, a device for locating hegemonies and counter-hegemonies, controlling processes or idea systems that make it possible to predict the direction of practice. Second, it is important to recognize what is surprising, or idiosyncratic events that do not fall into obvious hegemonic formations, because it is in such examples that new ideas might be found. The location of surprising events or practice means that we need to learn to listen better. Thirdly, I would underscore what Goodale mentions in the

127

Introduction: the importance of examining all the social actors – institutions, states, international agencies, and more, without privileging any one type of human rights actor; they are all sociologically of equal significance. And, finally, I would argue that it is not possible for anthropologists/ethnographers to consider the idea of human rights "in the abstract" although it is indeed possible to consider the Universal Declaration "in the abstract" and discuss how and where it has traveled, and how it has been affected by the current expressions of American Empire that run counter to the 1948 Declaration, which specifically mentions that no one shall be held in slavery, subjected to torture, or subjected to arbitrary arrest, detention, or exile. The scandals at Abu Ghraib, Guantanamo and elsewhere, are surely fueling the talk from places outside of Euro-American worlds about interrogating the very premises of Anglo-American law, while questioning the intent of universalist notions of rights that have a western origin. When practice and idea systems are in collision, hypocrisy provokes a challenge to the very integrity of Enlightenment ideas.

REFERENCES

Ahmed, Faiz. 2005. "Judicial Reform in Afghanistan: A Case Study in the New Criminal Procedure Code." *Hastings International and Comparative Law Review* 29(1): 93–124.

Barfield, Thomas. 2002. "On Local Justice and Culture in Post-Taliban Afghanistan," Ct Jr of Int'l Law 17: 437.

Berger, Jason. 1981. *A New Deal for the World: Eleanor Roosevelt and American Foreign Policy*. New York: Social Science Monographs. Columbia University Press.

Falk, Richard. 1992. "Cultural Foundations for the International Protection of Human Rights." In Abdullahi Ahmed An-Na'im, ed., *Human Rights in Cross-Cultural Perspectives – A Quest for Consensus*. Philadelphia University of Pennsylvania Press, pp. 44–64.

Meyerstein, Ariel. 2005. "Who's Afraid of Gacaca?: Decolonizing Human Rights Discourse." Paper presented at the annual meeting of the 2005 Law and Society Association meetings, Las Vegas, NV.

Nader, Laura. 1969. "Up the Anthropologist-perspectives Gained from Studying up." In D. Hymes, ed., *Reinventing Anthropology*: New York: Pantheon Press, pp. 285–311.

Nader, Laura. 1989. "The Crown, the Colonists, and the Course of Village Law." In June Starr and Jane Collier, eds., *History and Power in the Study of Law*. Ithaca: Cornell University Press, pp. 320–344.

Nader, Laura. 1997. "Controlling Processes – Tracing the Dynamic Components of Power," Mintz Lecture. *Current Anthropology* 38(5): 711–737.

Nader, Laura. 1999. "Em um Espelho de Mulher: Cegieira Normative e Questioes nas – Resolvidas de Direitos Humanos." *Horizonetes Antropologicos* (10): 61–82. Special Issue on Cidadania e Diversidade Cultural.

Nader, Laura and Jay Ou. 1998. "Idealization and Power: Legality and Tradition." *New Directions in Native American Law.* Special issue of *Oklahoma City University Law Review*, 23(82): 13–42.

Nash, June. 1993. *We Eat the Mines and the Mines Eat Us – Dependency and Exploitation in Bolivian Tin Mines.* New York: Columbian University Press.

Reed, Richard. 2003. "Two Rights Make a Wrong – Indigenous Peoples Versus Environmental Protection Agencies." In A. Podolefski and P. Brown, eds., *Applying Cultural Anthropology.* New York, McGraw Hill.

Renteln, Alison. 1990. *International Human Rights: Universalism Versus Relativism.* Newbury Park, California: Sage Publications.

Romany, Celino. 1994. "State Responsibility Goes Private." In R. J. Cook ed., *Human Rights of Women – National and International Perspectives.* Philadelphia: University of Pennsylvania Press.

Said, Edward. 1978. *Orientalism.* New York: Vintage Books.

Shivji, Issa. 2003. "Law's Empire and Empire's Lawlessness: Beyond Anglo-American Law." *Social Justice of Global Development Journal.* Available on-line at www2.warwick.ac.uk/fac/soc/law/elj/lgd/2003_1/shivji2/shivji2.rtf. Accessed February 9, 2007.

Taylor, William. 1979. *Drinking, Homicide, and Rebellion in Colonial Mexican Villages.* Stanford: Stanford University Press.

Wolf, Eric. 1959. *Sons of the Shaking Earth. The People of Mexico and Guatemala: Their Land, History and Culture.* Chicago: University of Chicago Press.

3

THE POWER OF RIGHT(S): TRACKING EMPIRES OF LAW AND NEW MODES OF SOCIAL RESISTANCE IN BOLIVIA (AND ELSEWHERE)

Mark Goodale

INTRODUCTION

At the end of Michael Hardt and Antonio Negri's dizzyingly suggestive but frustratingly vague book *Empire*, the authors take the leap that we all know is coming, but which, given the heights that have come before, we anticipate with a certain amount of dread. After having described what they understand to be a new global socio-political configuration, and having shrouded their analysis in a kind of ominousness, given the fact that Empire emerges through the self-disciplining of millions of individuals around the world, outside of the traditional institutions that can be resisted or even appropriated, they nevertheless go on to predict a revolution by the "multitude" against Empire. It is not the neo-Marxist epistemology that is so unsatisfying about this abrupt end to what is surely one of the most innovatively forethinking works of critical scholarship in recent years, one perfectly and organically embedded in its times. And nor must we necessarily object to the way in which its neo-Marxist social analysis reflects a peculiar transformation since 1989, in which the scientific trappings of dialectical materialism have been replaced by a giddy mysticism, so that the fall of the Soviet system should no longer dampen the "irrepressible lightness and joy of being communist" (2000: 413). Rather, the disappointment with their invocation of revolution is two-fold. First, it is entirely prefigured, rather than established; as I said, we know a prediction of massive system disrupture is coming because we know the theoretical trajectory in which the analysis of Empire is located. For those of us who have tracked the expressions of systemic inequality and disadvantage ethnographically, the intersubjectivity of the research experience itself is enough to produce acute empathy with those at the receiving end of structures of domination, even if there weren't ethical or political rationales for opposing what the ethnographer's eye sees. But nothing that ethnographers have documented, irrespective of theoretical orientation, or belief in the influence of structures large or small, can justify a forecast for system transformation that is anchored in what is merely a modern version of the ancient doctrine of historical inevitability.[1]

And second, and most important for purposes of this chapter, the different paths through which the multitude are supposed to realign the networks of power within Empire are not observed as emergent or actual, but are rather inferred through a process of sheer analytical imagining. Now as I will argue below, in order to understand the scope and meanings of contemporary transnational configurations, it is necessary to synthesize and envision the data of social practice in a way that requires the application of the critical imaginary; as I have argued elsewhere, in a call for a new anthropology of human rights, even if ethnography is a necessary methodological strategy, it is not enough (Goodale 2006). But even if the sustained empirical observation of social processes – no matter how skillful or multisited – cannot fully capture the ways in which current socio-political formations unfold across traditional geopolitical and even cultural boundaries, the role of ethnography has nevertheless become as indispensable as ever. This is because the scope and diffuseness of "Empire" lend themselves to an obfuscation of a different kind when our understanding of Empire is not grounded in descriptions of social practices, however fragmentary and contingent. It is one thing to agree that the transnationalization of social life – including, as this chapter will show, normative life – has made it difficult to rely exclusively on techniques

---

[1] Despite the fact that anyone concerned with the dignity and even meaning of the individual, of whatever culture, time, or place, should find the idea of historical inevitability inherently inimical, it has proved enduringly attractive, which can perhaps be attributed to the way analytical systems forged in its wake are, if nothing else, explanation-generating machines. Yet even if the idea of historical inevitability continues to structure thinking from evangelical religio-politics to law and economics, from the Panglossian bromides of Oprah-think to the mystical uprising by Hardt and Negri's multitude, we should continue to express the gravest skepticism about this tendency "to return to the ancient view that all that is, is ('objectively viewed') best; that to explain is ('in the last resort') to justify; or that to know is to forgive all; [all of which are] ringing fallacies (charitably described as half-truths) which have led to special pleading and, indeed, obfuscation . . . on a heroic scale." And this was Isaiah Berlin (1997: 119) taking stock of the persistence of the idea of historical inevitability in 1953!

of observation or empirical study in order to trace the contours of transnational networks. But it is quite another thing to deny the importance of observation and focused attention on particular places and times altogether, as if the practice of everyday life had either become so internalized as to be functionally invisible to the social scientist (an analytical trapdoor which awaits any anthropologist hewing too closely to the Foucauldian line), or so embedded in global structures that its "real" or "meaningful" features lie at too great a remove to be encountered empirically.

This chapter retains the spirit of Hardt and Negri's analysis of emerging transnational configurations, although in a much reduced and more theoretically modest form, but departs from (or expands) it so as to address the problems I've just described. By analyzing the rise of human rights discourse in Bolivia over the last ten years, I am able show how social research illuminates a key transnational network that features many of the characteristics ascribed to *the* Empire; as it turns out, it is not necessary (or empirically accurate) to work toward an understanding of emergent transnational configurations by adopting such a totalizing framework. As the case of human rights in Bolivia indicates, it would be more accurate to describe these networks as *empires*, with reference to the specific social or political or legal imperatives that they express, as in *empires of law*. Yet even if the empire framework must be reconceptualized and dramatically reduced in order for it to be useful as an interpretive model, its application to current Bolivia does create new spaces for analysis and future engagement, most obviously – as I will describe in detail below – in the way power is isolated as a distinct vector shaping the emergence of human rights as a new category of sociolegal practice. But, equally important, the study of empires of law in Bolivia reveals the possibilities for new forms of social resistance, forms that have been emerging in Bolivia over the last ten years. What is so intriguing as a matter of analysis is that these new forms of resistance have arisen as the result of the type of configurations that Hardt and Negri envision, but their structures and rationales are quite different than what Hardt and Negri predict. In other words, they are right to argue that the emergence of transnational networks of biopolitical power – their Empire, my *empires* (of law, for example) – create new conditions for social resistance at the same them they establish conditions that are engendering more alienation (individual and cultural), greater opportunities for socioeconomic exploitation, and a decrease in the potential for the realization of human capabilities.

But, as the analysis of human rights discourse in Bolivia indicates, the relationship between empires and social resistance unfolds in several ways that have not been anticipated by social theorists.

Given the transnational scope of contemporary human rights regimes, I think the kind of framework for understanding I develop here will resonate beyond the boundaries of Bolivia and, in light of this, I believe I am justified in framing my analysis of some aspects of these regimes in such a way that its claims are not explicitly restricted to current sociolegal developments in Bolivia. Nevertheless, this chapter is not the place for a comparative discussion of the merits of my approach to understanding human rights discourse in Bolivia, an approach which is also, in part, an argument for moving beyond current analytical frameworks that locate transnational social processes within an imaginary global/local ontology. Rather, given my concerns with the unfortunate abstractness and social disembeddedness of the source of this chapter's theoretical inspiration, I embed the chapter's different theoretical interventions in ongoing social research in Bolivia.

To this end, in the next section I describe an analytical framework for understanding the emergence and reproduction of human rights discourse in contemporary Bolivia (and, as I have just implied, elsewhere).[2] I think it is vitally important to try to capture the changes, if any, that have followed in the wake of the significant political and ideological realignments of the last fifteen years without (1) reproducing yet another simplistic or reductive macrotheoretical approach to social processes (something to which anthropologists, in particular, should be constitutionally adverse), or (2) ignoring, in a rush to

---

[2] By "human rights discourse" I am not referring primarily to the body of positive international law that forms the basis for recent efforts to advance legal and political claims in courts of international law (e.g., the International Criminal Court). This is an entirely reasonable way of understanding "human rights," one that limits the usage to the narrow confines of positive law *as informed by* an analysis of this law's actual ability to demonstrate that it is instrumentally efficacious. This way of defining and studying human rights is best left to international lawyers and others for whom the analysis of processes of justifiability and conflict of international law come within their special competencies.

I use "human rights" much more broadly: the phrase captures the constellation of philosophical, practical, and phenomenological dimensions through which universal rights, rights believed to be entailed by a common human nature, are enacted, debated, practiced, violated, envisioned, and experienced. When I describe "human rights discourse," I am referring to these coteries of concepts, practices, and experiences through which human rights have meaning at different levels, levels which are prior to, and go beyond, the merely instrumental or legal, important as these levels obviously are. My understanding of human rights is not quite as broad as Upendra Baxi's "protean forms of social action assembled, by convention, under a portal named 'human rights'" (2002: v), but conceiving of human rights as discourse does, obviously, broaden the referent beyond any one of its most consequential parts (e.g., international human rights law).

"discover" everything that is supposedly *sui generis* about the post-Cold War world, the deeply embedded structures – political, intellectual-historical, and, especially, economic – that give shape, and even prefigure to a certain extent, the emergent transnational configurations that are increasingly present in even the most "local" of social practices. In describing the study and analysis of human rights discourse in Bolivia as an expression of an "empire of law," I am attempting to make sense of the emergence of and, to a certain extent, triumph of human rights discourse in Bolivia over the last ten years while keeping these two points of caution in mind.

After developing a framework within which the social practice of human rights in Bolivia can be understood within broader transnational networks which unfold horizontally "between" the global and the local, yet in which the global/local dichotomy is as much a part of vernacular human rights discourse as anywhere else (this is only an *apparent* paradox, see below), I then narrow the focus to consider the ways in which power emerges as a distinct vector that shapes the way human rights enter and transform normative universes in Bolivia. An analysis of the power of human rights in Bolivia is simply another way of analyzing human rights in practice, an approach that respects both the instrumental nature of human rights discourse as well as its significance in relation to other normative and, indeed, social categories. To do this I distinguish between "right" and "rights," the first of which draws attention to what I call the *connotative* power of human rights; the second refers to what can be understood as their *denotative* power. And finally, the last section of this chapter draws what has come before together in order to move in a new direction, one which goes some way toward filling in the large gaps in existing visions for resistance to emergent transnational social-political configurations, at least as they revolve around legal or normative regimes like human rights.

In describing some of the ways in which current social and legal movements in Bolivia appropriate and transform human rights discourse, I am able to point to both actual and potential forms of social resistance to, and within the terms of, broader transnational networks. Indeed, there is a peculiar fact about the relationship between platforms for social resistance and human rights discourse in contemporary Bolivia: social resistance becomes hybridized in such a way that it is articulated within a rights framework at the same time it formally opposes a western or neoliberal "oppression" of the Bolivian people that is expressed through projects that are justified, in part, by human rights, whether the right to economic development or the right of companies or individuals to pursue their own (enlightened) self-interest. I will try in this section to show how this fact expresses a contradiction at the philosophical core of the (neo-)liberalism that structures the rise of human rights discourse in Bolivia. The fact of this contradiction both gives the lie to the totalizing picture of transnational networks offered by some social theorists, and shines a light on an intriguing aspect of current transnational legality: its production of normative pluralism – a potential new source of social resistance – *through* universalist (and thus homogenizing) discourses like human rights.

Finally, it should be acknowledged that my analysis of the complicated uses of human rights discourse within struggles for social change in Bolivia is somewhat different from the one offered by Daniel Goldstein in this volume. He places more emphasis on the traditional political-ideological roots of current social movements and raises certain questions about the emergence of human rights in Bolivia during the era of neoliberal consolidation. As he notes, this was also the period in which indigenous and other social movements surged in influence, a process that culminated in the recent election of Evo Morales as Bolivia's first self-identifying indigenous president. Yet, as I will show in the final section, the differences between us are perhaps not as stark as they might appear. We both agree that (neo-)liberalism and the rhetoric of resistance in Bolivia bring disparate ideological and even moral categories together. But whereas Goldstein explores the important effects of this clash of discursive regimes – such as the emergence of "citizen security" and other alternative frameworks for coping with social problems in Bolivia – I try to show in this chapter how the bringing together of these disparate regimes is essential to both the functioning of larger transnational configurations I call empires of law, and, even more important, the source of resistance to them.

EMPIRES OF LAW

The *norte de Potosí* is among the poorest and most iconic of regions in Bolivia. Potosí is one of nine departments in Bolivia. Its eponymous capital, Potosí, was the center of the Spanish Empire's silver mining operations until a century-long economic depression (1650–1750), from which the region never regained its former economic and cultural centrality. The north of the department, which has a distinct identity – people self-identify as *nortepotosinos* and there is a regional newspaper with the same name – is comprised of five provinces, some of which are leading Bolivian mining centers (of tin and other non-precious metals). Nevertheless, the region is regularly "ranked" among the poorest in the country by national and international development agencies on the basis of standard Human Development Index indicators like literacy, infant mortality, access to potable water, and so on. Outside of the bleak mining camps (see Nash 1993), the region is overwhelmingly subsistence agricultural, with Quechua or Aymara serving as first languages for the majority of both men and women throughout rural areas. The *norte de Potosí* occupies a special place in the national Bolivian imaginary, expressing as it does a peculiar blend of inhospitable and frigid landscapes, closed and equally inhospitable indigenous peoples (symbolized by their inexplicably barbarous, but nevertheless heroic, ritual combats called *tinkus*), and pre-modern land-holding patterns and lifeways, which have been seen as major obstacles to Bolivia's entry into modernity since the early republican era – that is, when they have not been successfully converted into folklore.

In this iconic and complicatedly rendered region of Bolivia, transnational human rights nongovernmental organizations (NGOs) are thick on the ground. To say that transnational NGOs are "human rights" organizations is not necessarily to say that their operations in rural Bolivia are focused exclusively on ensuring that the human rights of Bolivians are recognized or protected – as outlined in international human rights instruments, or the portions of Bolivian national law that incorporate these provisions – although, as we will see in the next section, there are many human rights NGOs in Bolivia who formalize their engagement with human rights in these ways. Rather, the distinction I want to draw here is between the international and (eventually) transnational organizations that first operated within the scientific development paradigm in Bolivia during the 1960s and 1970s, a period associated with the Green Revolution and the emergence of private transnational development philanthropy (see Cueto 1994, 1995; Escobar 1995), and the organizations which operated in Bolivia under a quite different paradigm beginning in the mid-1980s.

The scientific development model was distinguished by its inherent materialism and its supposed ideological neutrality. As part of the postwar march of progress, western governments, international agencies (typically linked to the United Nations), and private donors understood their goal to be the delivery of the fruits of modern (read: western) biotechnology to regions in need, but without any of the ideological baggage associated with the most recent period of western outreach (read: colonialism and/or wars of conquest). The lack of human development in Bolivia was not, under the scientific paradigm, a sign of any essential or intrinsic inequality or deficiency on the part of Bolivians; it was simply that the contingencies of history had led some nations or cultures to develop or acquire the scientific tools necessary to continue advancing, while others had been left behind. Scientific development, in other words, arose to meet the challenges of political-economic, and not cultural, inequality. Science would be the great equalizer, providing the means through which even subsistence agriculturalists in Bolivia could produce enough yield so that surpluses could be stored or sold for profit, thus freeing up peasants to devote time to all of those nonsubsistence activities that herald the advance of civilization.[3]

The idea of "progress" was often employed during this period in such a way that it acquired a kind of nonsubstantive normativity. By this I mean that if progress was both the driving force, and justification, for scientific development, it functioned as a kind of floating signifier that intersected with different political and economic interests without acquiring its own detailed or programmatic content. But "progress" was clearly normative in that the word was used not only to describe the supposed march of history, but to legitimate *this* way (or ways) of understanding the present and future. In this sense, "progress" functioned then much like "justice" functions today (as a non-substantive normativity), in contrast to "human rights," as this chapter makes clear. Compared with what came after, the era of scientific development represented a *technical transnationalism*, the creation of transnational networks in order to transfer technologies that had, at least formally, been detached from their political or intellectual-historical roots.

By contrast, beginning in the mid-1980s, and picking up a qualitatively different kind of momentum in the early 1990s, human rights development in Bolivia operated within quite a different framework.

---

[3] I'm obviously *representing* here the claims of scientific development in Bolivia in their own terms; I'm not positioning myself critically in relation to them, at least not yet. As Escobar (1995) and (by this point) many others have shown for other parts of Latin America, the first wave of postwar development was indeed wrapped in an ideological shell that was in many ways as rigid as those ideologies that supported earlier periods of interconnection. But what is important for my purposes here is the formal discursive position of scientific development (neutral and non-ideological) and the way it was expressed in practice in opposition to ideological – and thus normative – alternatives.

The emergence of human rights development as a full-blown transnational regime, which I will characterize below as an "empire of law,"
can be attributed to two factors, the first of which is characteristic of
Bolivia (though shared by other Latin American countries), and the
second of which is more global in scope. The early 1980s was the period
in which Bolivia made what has proven to be a lasting transition to
civilian and democratic rule; whether this represents a permanent
break with the traditional pattern in Bolivia of alternating between
civilian and military governments remains to be seen.[4] The reemergence of civilian rule coincided – and was partly facilitated – by the rise
of "neoliberalism," which meant, among other things, the following:
closer ties with international and western financial institutions; moves
to decentralize decision making and control over capital and other
resources to subnational levels of government; a renewed emphasis on
"rationalizing" land tenure (read: privatizing corporate holdings); and,
above all, an official commitment to human rights in both their orthodox and what can be understood as their "neoliberal" versions, which in
Bolivia (as elsewhere in Latin America) meant the recognition of collective human rights. There are several key examples of the importance
of neoliberal human rights in Bolivia during the 1990s, but perhaps the
most illustrative is the Law of Popular Participation (Law 1551, 1994),
which articulated a theory of decentralization of power and recognition
of indigenous political and legal organizations that mirrored portions of
International Labor Organization Convention 169, which describes the
rights of "Indigenous and Tribal Peoples" as human rights, and requires
nation-states to take these rights into account when formulating
national policy (see Goodale 2001; Van Cott 2000).

And second, the mid-1980s to mid-1990s was a time when transnational human rights networks emerged with new and, in certain
cases, efficacious urgency. There are different and contested reasons
for this, including the end of the Cold War and the symbolic and
human rights-infused end to apartheid in South Africa, the latter of
which could be said to have engendered as much as expressed a new
transnational focus on human rights (see Klug 2000; Wilson 2001). But
whatever the macro-political or social reasons, the fact remains that
networks of human rights discourse suddenly evolved into something

---

[4] For an overview of recent Bolivian history, the best treatment in English remains Herbert
Klein's 1982 Bolivia: The Evolution of a Multi-Ethnic Society, which was revised and reissued in
2003 as A Concise History of Bolivia.

approximating that "curious grapevine" that Eleanor Roosevelt predicted would serve as the conduit for nurturing and transmitting human rights consciousness around the world.[5] This curious grapevine took various forms, and interconnected (and continues to interconnect) organizations and individuals who represent different constituencies and political interests, including international development agencies (e.g., the units working under the auspices of the United Nations), pan-regional organizations (e.g., the Organization of American States), national agencies (in Bolivia, agencies like the Ministry for Human Development), community-based civil society organizations (in Bolivia, *sindicatos campesinos*, or rural peasant unions, for example), and, finally, all the different transnational development NGOs that emerged in the 1990s constituted – or reconstituted – within a human rights framework. The new human rights configurations were, despite their different constituencies and diversity in composition, both networked and transnational. Groupings of organizations came together through an underlying commitment to an idea (human rights) and region (Latin America, for example) in a way that was non-hierarchical and, as Annelise Riles (2000, 2006) and others have argued, without permanent ontological significance, in the sense that their association was expressed through a complementary set of knowledge practices without establishing enduring and observable structures (see also Keck and Sikkink 1998).

Moreover, human rights networks emerged beyond the nation-state, but not in any way that could be described as "global." Rather, whether the specific human rights issue was violence against women (Merry 2005), or the protection of indigenous lifeways through the use of indigenous knowledge (see Goodale 2001; Lowrey 2003; Turner 1997), the networks that emerged to address it included key national actors, but opened up across national boundaries. As Sally Merry explains in her recent ethnographic study of human rights networks organized around violence against women:

> Human rights processes such as CEDAW [Convention on the Elimination of All Forms of Discrimination Against Women]

[5] Eleanor Roosevelt, the chair of the United Nations committee that would eventually draft what would become the 1948 Universal Declaration of Human Rights, predicted that a nongovernmental "curious grapevine" would carry word of human rights to places where governments would not otherwise permit it to reach. For an overview of the role of NGOs in carrying the message of human rights "behind barbed wire and stone walls," see William Korey's useful, but uncritical, account (1998).

monitoring take place in the space of transnational modernity. This space incorporates postcolonial elites as well as elites from the global North. It is not an exclusively Western space but a transnational one within which people from all over the world participate to produce a social reformist, fundamentally neoliberal vision of modernity governed by concepts of human rights. Its participants – government representatives, NGO representatives, and staff – are, of course, products of particular localities, but within global human rights settings, they have developed a distinctive cultural repertoire of procedures … and [t]hey spend a considerable effort drafting and editing documents that express the norms of this culture.

(2006: 100)

Yet despite the fact that the idea of human rights has become perhaps the most consequential contemporary *universalism*,[6] human rights networks have not been, as a matter of practice, global or globalizing, but operate within more modest frames.

But the most important difference between human rights development and earlier, scientific development is the fact that human rights development is fundamentally normative, and, if we adopt a sufficiently broad enough definition, legal.[7] If the Green Revolution unfolded under the banner of science, which, as I have argued, was normatively neutral in relation to the political-economic conditions that led to technological inequalities between nations or cultures, human rights development represents quite a different orientation: because human rights are universal and entailed by the only normatively relevant trans-cultural fact (i.e., a common and irreducible human nature), any position in relation to human rights is, and must be, itself normative. To be normative, as human rights development is, is to be both value-saturated, meaning informed by particular values among a range of alternatives, and, equally important, "political," by which I mean embedded in – and at the service of – particular alignments of power. One could argue that to the extent to which, as Sally Merry has demonstrated, the emergence of transnational human

---

[6] For a discussion of the distinction between *universal* and *universalism*, which is, I argue, an important point of contrast for the anthropology of human rights in particular, see my recent article in *American Anthropologist* (Goodale 2006).

[7] For example, human rights development can be described as "legal" if we adopt an understanding of law that focuses on rules or norms backed by some legitimate enforcement mechanism, without having to specify in greater detail the kinds of rules, legitimacy, or enforcement mechanism (or some similar formulation) we have in mind. This is the understanding of "legal" I employ in this chapter.

rights networks over the last fifteen years must be seen as one important expression of a broader "fundamentally neoliberal vision of modernity," that it is neoliberalism (or liberalism)[8] itself (or even modernity) that is normative in this way (value-saturated and political).

Yet, as I will describe in more detail in the next two sections (on power and social resistance), this is a position I do not adopt here; indeed, the uniqueness of human rights within liberalism (and modernity), their *hyper-normativity*, their apparent self-evidence, place human rights in opposition to other key political and economic dimensions of the liberal project. So, rather than understanding human rights as just one among several co-equal expressions of (neo-)liberalism, I would argue that the anthropology of human rights in Bolivia demonstrates that human rights operate at registers – social, psychological, cultural – that are fundamentally distinct from other broad ideological frameworks that structure the practice of everyday in life in Bolivia. Moreover, the characteristics of human rights discourse in Bolivia that separates it in some ways from its economic and political cousins are precisely those that make it a potential source for resistance against and within the neoliberal project, which is another indication that human rights unfold in practice in more complicated ways than one is normally led to believe.

What, then, are these characteristics, and how do they make human rights discourse a driving force behind the emergence of new transnational configurations in Bolivia? The first, and most important for my purposes here, is the fact that as people encounter the idea of human rights, the discourse in which the idea is transmitted does not demand of people that they adopt a particular set of behaviors, or refrain from

---

[8] I insert liberalism in parentheses here in order to signal that I think any usage of "neoliberalism" must remain contested. There is no question that the discourse of neoliberalism has become dominant in Latin America, particularly as an ordering principle for social movements searching for "new" (i.e., non-marxist) paradigms under which they can successfully organize. This is not an unimportant meaning for neoliberalism. But there is quite another way in which neoliberalism is invoked, again, to take Latin America, and Bolivia, as an example. This is when neoliberalism is used to describe a set of intellectual, political, and economic developments within history, developments that differ from liberalism in important and "new" ways, but which retain at least historical links to the earlier constellation of political, economic, and legal ideology we call "liberalism." I have argued recently that when employed in this second sense, "neoliberalism" is misleading at best, inaccurate at worst. In writing about Bolivia's encounters with law (Goodale 2008), I have located current developments on an intellectual-historical trajectory that begins, more or less, at the beginning of the republican era in the early nineteenth century, one which continues to feature the most important characteristics of "liberalism." For more on debates over neoliberalism in Latin America, see the recent special issue of the *Political and Legal Anthropology Review* on this topic (Speed and Sierra 2005).

others; nor does it even represent human rights instrumentally, as a potentially effective framework within which to address specific social problems, analogous to all those proffered technological solutions to problems of resource use or scarcity associated with the Green Revolution. Rather, people's experiences of human rights are more intransitive: human rights reveal to people a fact about themselves that is beyond their control – as the fact of a person's humanness is beyond their control – and in the process *reposition* them in relation to other members of their community, the community itself, and, indeed, all other social categories in terms of which actors in Bolivia shape their identities. For example, when the director of a human rights legal services center in the *norte de Potosí* introduces people in his province to the *idea* of human rights – and at this point, it is very much human rights-as-idea that is important – he does so by *revealing* to community members certain facts about themselves that they had not known before: that they share a "common humanity" (*humanidad común*) with everyone else (not just in Bolivia, but everywhere); that by virtue of this common humanity they possess certain rights, which also entail certain duties;[9] and, finally, because they possess human rights like everyone else, they are essentially equal and are entitled to a kind of dignity and respect that is derived from this simple – but profound – fact of human equality.

To describe the experience of human rights discourse in Bolivia as intransitive is not, of course, to deny that there is a link between human rights discourse and specific social practices. But the main purpose of human rights development in Bolivia is to transform legal (and social) consciousness, one person at a time, so that, at some future point, the historic causes of Bolivia's social problems – ethnic and class discrimination, corruption, exploitation of key national resources by multinationals, etc. – will become moot as a new generation of human rights-bearing subjects are unable to either reproduce these problems, or even imagine them. The distinction I am trying to draw here between human rights development and earlier regimes of

---

[9] As I have written about elsewhere, this important rural-legal intellectual, Lucio Montesinos, who was also the director of a human rights legal services center that operated in the north of Potosí Department until 1998, has vernacularized human rights discourse in interesting ways. For example, during wedding ceremonies at which he officiates as the province's only titled lawyer (there are other, "unofficial" lawyers), he commonly tells young men that the human rights of their new brides create certain duties for them, like a duty to help carry equipment on the trail. See Goodale 2001, 2002.

interconnection can be illustrated by adapting the cliché about teaching people to fish: human rights discourse in Bolivia seeks to reveal to people their true selves, and the normative-legal implications that result from this revealed truth; it does not provide concrete guidelines for action, nor does it give people some normative good – like justice – directly.

The second characteristic of human rights discourse in contemporary Bolivia is its disciplinarity. Although I can be as impatient with this way of understanding the constitution of modern subjectivity as anyone (an analytical framework's sheer prevalence should give us pause), there are several lessons from this social theoretical tradition that help explain what I describe as *empires* (of law, for example): that they are, and are intended to be, self-unfolding; that the imperatives of (neo-)liberalism are not imposed on anyone anymore in the way dependent economic and political relations were imposed during the periods of imperialism and neocolonialism; and that a self-unfolding empire is not constituted by elites but by the "multitude" – those millions of people in the core, periphery, and everywhere in between, for whom the production and reproduction of empire becomes coextensive with the production (and reproduction) of self. This is the essence of the empire hypothesis: that its imperatives – to erect particular legal systems, to desire particular modes of production, to understand the relationship between the individual and the collective in a particular way – dissolve into individual (and collective) identity so that the production of empire is both naturalized and made invisible. When the *corregidor auxiliar* of Molino T'ikanoma, a community in the *norte de Potosí*, told me "human rights indicate the future to us," he was not talking about a future course of action, but a future that would unfold through new parameters of identity.[10]

And finally, human rights discourse is experienced by people in most cases outside of the traditional "institutional architectures" that we have come to associate with the rise of modern regimes of knowledge: the university, the mayor's office, the courts, and even culture itself. Rather, individuals encounter human rights in Bolivia in ways that are both *personal* (and thus non-institutional) and *trans-local*. The encounter with human rights discourse is personal – though obviously

---

[10] It has been my practice not to use the real name of this ambitious politico-legal authority, even though I have received permission by him to do so. A *corregidor auxiliar* is what is understood in rural Bolivia as a "state" authority position, one with historical links to a system of patronage and surveillance that dates to the early colonial period.

embedded in social relations – in a very specific sense. Because universal human rights, in their dominant register (i.e., the one expressed through instruments like the Universal Declaration of Human Rights [UDHR]), are above politics, before culture, and, quite literally, outside of history, the individual who encounters them for the first time does so inwardly; as I have already argued above, the encounter with human rights is the encounter with a more real, more exalted, and more consequential self. Although human rights can be protected, violated, enabled, etc., by the range of legal and political authorities or entities to which the individual is subject, they are prior to these external forces in the way that an individual's human nature is prior to them.[11]

And though the individual's encounter with human rights in Bolivia, especially in cases of "normative first contact," is personal in this very specific sense, it is also *trans-local*.[12] By this I mean two things, one quite empirically observable, the other more abstract and thus more difficult to track. In the first place, it is simply an ethnographic fact that the networks through which individuals come to engage with human rights discourse in Bolivia are obviously not limited to particular communities or regions or any other narrowly circumscribed spaces; although these networks differ in their scope, they are all trans-local and usually trans-*national*, though not global. It is important to emphasize that even if, as Sally Merry (2005a, 2006) and others have written about recently, human rights discourse is often "vernacularized," meaning (among other things) rendered into conceptual and cultural terms appropriate to the particular social context, the fact remains that the trans-local networks within which human rights discourse is embedded are not somehow reduced or compressed in the process, but maintain their trans-locality. So when a human rights-oriented NGO like PROCLADE (*Promoción Claretiana de Desarrollo*

---

[11] As with my discussion of scientific development, I am merely invoking here the dominant ontological understanding of universal human rights in order to draw certain conclusions about the social consequences of this understanding as it expresses itself in human rights discourse in Bolivia.

[12] I coin the phrase "normative first contact" only partly ironically. On the one hand, I am sympathetic to the now-canonical position within anthropology that sees the older descriptions of cultural first contact among dazed and confused natives as an expression of the Orientalist project *par excellence*. On the other hand, anyone who has been present (as I have) when the idea of human rights is suddenly introduced to people whose everyday normative universe is starkly different – non-universalist, non-individualist, non-atomistic, non-liberal – can't help but appreciate the sense of disorientation that results, even if the idea of human rights is eventually vernacularized and thus reinterpreted in ways that make sense to people.

Navarra), which happens to be active throughout the region of rural Bolivia I know best (the north of Potosí Department), reinterprets a potable water project in terms of human rights (see Goodale 2001), community members participate in such a way that a direct and open connection – of ideas, material resources, and communication – is created between the community, other PROCLADE centers in Bolivia, La Paz, PROCLADE's headquarters in Spain, and the European Union, with which PROCLADE often collaborates in their work in Bolivia. And in the second place, an individual's encounter with human rights is trans-local in that the terms of the discourse itself invite individuals to re-envision themselves beyond the boundaries of expected context, which otherwise structure the practice of everyday life. Again, to the extent to which human rights discourse on the ground accurately reflects the ontological assumptions of major human rights instruments like the UDHR, it interconnects people at the broadest possible scale. And even if social actors in rural Bolivia speak in universalist terms as a result of their encounters with human rights discourse (see Goodale 2001, 2002), it is obviously quite difficult to capture what is a complicated social-psychological dynamic, one which can only be approached ethnographically through its second-order effects. This is why, as I have argued elsewhere (Goodale 2005), the anthropology of human rights calls for the application of the ethnographic imagination in new, and not entirely empirical, ways.

Up to this point, I have described in relatively broad terms the ways in which human rights discourse in contemporary Bolivia both constitutes, and reflects the emergence of, transnational configurations that display many of the characteristics that social theorists have *deduced* about "Empire." Even if anthropologists of law, not to mention legal philosophers, might raise questions about whether one can describe the networks of biopolitical power within which human rights discourse in Bolivia expresses itself as empires of *law*, I would argue that this is in fact the most compelling description – assuming my appropriation of the empire hypothesis is compelling in the first place. This is in large part because human rights discourse in Bolivia is closely associated with law and legality more generally, despite the fact that if we restrict our frame of analysis to the workings of the positive law (through courts, the police, day-to-day activities of lawyers, etc.), the link between human rights discourse and the law becomes much more tenuous.

145

In the next sections, I build on this theoretical framework by examining in greater detail the mechanisms through which empires of law emerge – through human rights discourse – in Bolivia (and elsewhere); in other words, the relationship between empires of law and power.

THE POWER OF RIGHT(S)

Although power is a notoriously difficult, and highly contested, variable (effect? intention?) to isolate for purposes of either social or ethnographic analysis, there is no question that human rights discourse in Bolivia has the effect of displacing other normativities and quickly achieving a kind of low-grade hegemony in relation to what remains. It's not that human rights discourse in Bolivia suppresses other normative frameworks. But neither does its presence in any particular context simply lead to a greater multiplicity of normative or legal frameworks.[13] As I have already described above, there is something different about contemporary human rights discourse in relation to other possibilities, not the least of which is its association with the emergence of new transnational social-political configurations over the last fifteen years. In this section I will suggest several ways in which "power" can, and, given the relationship between human rights and political mobilization, *should* be described as it functions as something like an independent vector impelling the rise of human rights discourse in Bolivia.

Connotative and denotative power

There are two broad ways in which power functions within human rights discourse in Bolivia, and I have tried to capture this important distinction with the admittedly awkward parenthetical construction "right(s)." What I mean by this is that power infuses human rights practice in the way individuals (or groups) connote, or gesture toward,

---

[13] As I have already suggested above, my analysis of the presence, and effects, of power as an isolatable variable within contemporary human rights discourse differs here from the way scholars like Sally Merry have recently discussed the effects of human rights in context. Merry describes in convincing detail the ways in which the presence of human rights discourse has the effect of multiplying both normative options and subjectivities. For purposes of this chapter, I have placed the emphasis on something else: the ways in which human rights discourse, because of its peculiar characteristics and, even more important, close association with the emergence of new forms of what Laura Nader has described as "controlling processes" (Nader 1997), tends to supplant existing normativities by inviting social actors to re-envision themselves in fundamental ways.

certain essential aspects of human rights without actually invoking specific human rights themselves. And this connotative power of human rights discourse can itself be distinguished by two different forms of reference (more below). But power also infuses human rights practice in another way: when actors refer to, or, in certain cases, actually invoke, specific human rights. As we will see, through the denotative power of human rights, social actors reference specific human rights at a number of different levels, which range from the general (vague invocations of major human rights instruments, like the UDHR) to the quite specific (recourse to provisions of Bolivian law that represent what they call the *reglamentación* of international human rights).

I have already mentioned the work of an important rural-legal intellectual, Lucio Montesinos, but here I want to focus on him in more detail in order to illustrate the two ways in which power can be connotative within human right discourse in Bolivia. Montesinos is the only "titled" lawyer in the province Alonso de Ibañez, which is a province in the north of Potosí's Department that is interesting for a number of different ethnographic reasons that go beyond the scope of this chapter, one of which is the fact that Ibañez is not located near any major mining centers. Between 1995 and 1998 Montesinos served as the director of a human rights legal services center called the *Centro de Servicio Legal Integral* (SLI). Before taking over as Director of the SLI, which was located in the provincial capital, Montesinos had received training in human rights over a period of several months during trips to La Paz and other major Bolivia cities. The purpose of the SLI was to provide the means through which the human rights of women in the province could be protected by processing cases of spousal abuse, spousal abandonment, and other violations that had been reinterpreted as human rights violations within Bolivian law during the early to mid-1990s, which was a period of intense neoliberal reform.[14] Although the

---

[14] Law 1493 (September 17, 1993), a law passed through Bolivia's executive branch, created the Ministry of Human Development. Article 71, No. 5 of Supreme Decree 23660 (October 12, 1993) created the National Secretariat for Ethnic and Gender Issues. Articles 85, 86, and 87 of this same Supreme Decree created the Subsecretariat for Gender Issues responsible for all political matters related to women. The Ministry of Human Development, in Resolution 139/94 (September 21, 1994), adopted the National Plan for the Eradication, Prevention, and Punishment of Violence Against Women. Article 1 of this Resolution created the system of *Servicios Legales Integrales* to carry out the Resolution's objectives. Law 1674 (1995), passed by the Bolivian Congress, outlined the nature and function of the SLIs and authorized their establishment. For more on the legal and political details surrounding the SLI in Alonso de Ibañez, see Goodale 2001, and especially Chapter 5.

SLI closed involuntarily in 1998, its outreach in the region, and sustained attempts to bring human rights cases in the local court (a *juzgado de instrucción*, in most cases the lowest rung on the Bolivian judicial ladder), established an innovative normative beachhead, from which Montesinos launched a program of human rights education that continues to the present. The main goal of this unofficial program is to expose the mostly peasant agriculturalists in the province to the idea of human rights, and the vastly different worldview that it represents. Montesinos does this primarily at weddings – as the only titled lawyer in the province, he's the only one who can legally officiate civil weddings – and during court sessions at the *juzgado*, at which he invokes the idea of human rights and its strictures even though a particular case might revolve around what seems like completely unrelated provisions of, say, the Bolivian civil code. And his invocation of human rights has been taken up by local high school students, who, in a spontaneous display of human rights consciousness,[15] painted a multicultural mural on one of the walls in Alonso de Ibañez's capital that was titled "organizados por nuestros derechos" ("we are organized for our rights," i.e., human rights).

Now there are two ways in which Montesinos's activities illustrate the connotative power of rights. On the one hand, his work at the SLI, which included intake interviews, discussions with women about the role of human rights in relation to Bolivian law, and human rights "counseling," among other things, engaged with human rights largely as an idea that revealed a particular, previously unknown (to him and others in the province) truth about the age-old Aristotelian question of the place of "man in the universe." Montesinos was convinced about the self-evident truth of human rights, and the moral vision that it expressed and anticipated. But what gave his invocation of human rights its power, its ability to transform – or begin to transform – existing and "traditional" ideas about the relationship between men and women, the relationship between the individual and the community, and the ultimate contingency of all law not derived from universal rights (which includes much of Bolivia's national law), was the fact that it was based on an ethical commitment to the truth of human rights; this was the basic message Montesinos sought to impart to others. In other words, for Montesinos the power of human rights flowed from

---

[15] I say spontaneous because the mural was not prompted by any specific political or legal event in the province; it simply reflected a new and powerful collective self-awareness. This mural appeared at the end of 1999.

their rightness, from the fact that they were as self-evidently true as any other fact of nature (hence, the power of "right," as in "correct"). But, on the other hand, as Montesinos's program of human rights education outside of the SLI shows – especially his wedding regime, which is calculated to achieve maximum effect – there is another sense in which the power of human rights can be connotative. When Montesinos draws from human rights discourse during weddings, for example, he does so in a way that is explicitly comparative: he refers to existing ways of doing things and shows – in great descriptive detail – the ways in which they fall short of the newly revealed normative universe. For example, he might point out that men have traditionally beaten their wives (or children) when they don't work hard enough in the course of their daily duties. He then states categorically that this is no longer permissible because such actions violate the "dignity" of women (or children). He doesn't refer to a specific human rights provision, in Bolivian law or otherwise. He simply gestures toward the real, and thus obviously better, moral universe that is entailed by the fact of human rights (hence, the power of "right" in another sense, as in "best" or "superior").

In drawing this distinction between two senses of "right" – correctness and comparative superiority – I build on the distinction Jack Donnelly (and others) make between "being right" and "having a right" (see, e.g., Donnelly 2003: 7–13), but depart from it in important ways. As my research shows, it is not enough to describe the first sense of right, as Donnelly does, as referring to "rectitude." By this Donnelly is invoking a very old distinction in (western) philosophy between moral *right*, and legal (or positive) *rights*. But this way of explaining right is – given its intellectual history – itself normative! The distinction I draw here is based in what I have documented ethnographically and perhaps explains the power of rights in other contexts; but my framework does not claim universal applicability. Rectitude is a notoriously slippery descriptor, embodying as it does (or can) everything from simple correctness (a truth-value) to moral rightness. In order to avoid this potential confusion, I have simply rendered in the best way I know how the sense in which human rights constitute a source of power: through their self-evident truth (correspondent, not moral), and their comparative superiority in relation to other, less true (or even false) and thus inferior normative possibilities.

If the connotative power of human rights is a key factor in the recent rise of human rights discourse in Bolivia, and thus a key dynamic impelling the emergence of the broader transnational configurations

I call "empires of law," this is not the only, or even most overt, way in which human rights are expressed in social practice. The power of human rights is also, as I have said, *denotative*: social actors invoke specific human rights provisions – accurately or not, in Bolivian law or elsewhere, and for a variety of reasons – instrumentally, as a way of *using* human rights in a way that can be understood as "legal" in light of the broad, essentially legal-anthropological, way in which I have employed the idea of the legal throughout this chapter. But in describing this second form of power as denotative, I am *not* making a legal positivist argument, or arguing that the power of human rights in this second sense derives from their instrumental effectiveness.

Although much of the literature within human rights studies (especially from within international law and political science) focuses on problems of conflict of laws, justiciability, enforcement, and so on, this is not the kind of human rights instrumentalism I am describing here. The distinction I am making here is an ethnographic one: in Bolivia, there is clear difference between the allusive reference to the idea of human rights, the gesture toward the moral universe which the fact of human rights implies, and the attempt to anchor claims (legal and non-legal) in relation to specific human rights provisions, regardless of whether such claims are actually enforceable in these terms, or even whether such attempts are legally or philosophically plausible. So when actors invoke the right to culture, or a women's right to be free from domestic abuse, or the right to freedom of speech, they are drawing on the denotative power of human rights. To say that the denotative power of human rights does not necessarily mean the actual and correct framing of claims within an enforceable system of rights is not, of course, to say that in cases where such framing does exist, this is not also an example the denotative power of human rights. As the recent case of the International Criminal Court shows, social actors *can* invoke the denotative power of human rights when to do so means that their claims actually stand a chance of being actualized through international human rights law. But what interests me here is the *attempt* to link claims to specific human rights provisions. It is the attempt that has clear ethnographic and conceptual importance for me, and which distinguishes the denotative power of human rights from the other ways in which human rights exert themselves discursively within specific settings in Bolivia.[16]

[16] My analysis of denotative power roughly corresponds to Donnelly's second meaning of rights, which he describes as "having a right."

If it is indeed useful to distinguish between connotative and denotative forms of power in relation to human rights discourse in Bolivia (and elsewhere), there are at least two further points that must be made, one of which is a qualification (or caveat) to this analytical framework, the other which is an important implication that leads into the next, and final, section of this chapter. First, in delineating between connotative and denotative power I am not making the claim that social actors in Bolivia, or anywhere else, necessarily think of human rights in this way, or that there is something in the nature of contemporary human rights discourse itself that creates this distinction. Rather, this is simply an analytical framework that is derived from the observed ways in which actors invoke human rights discourse in Bolivia. Having said this, there is something to be said for looking to the broader social, political, and other factors that bear on the emergence of human rights discourse in practice, and it would be a worthwhile comparative question, one which could only be answered ethnographically, whether or not there are links between particular political and legal conditions and the different ways in which human rights can be referenced. One would imagine that connotative references would be more common in places in which human rights discourse is either new, or where the possibility of legalizing specific human rights provisions is remote, or both. (In Bolivia, the first condition obtains; less so the second.) And second, even if the distinction between connotative and denotative power is, in part, a heuristic device for making some sense out of the complicated reality of human rights practice in Bolivia, it is also true that both of these modes of power are potential or actual sources of social resistance, and we can observe human rights operating in these different registers within current movements for social change. In other words, if human rights discourse is invoked connotatively or denotatively in ways that, from one angle, seem to contribute to the increasing hegemony of transnational regimes like empires of law, from another angle it appears as if the power of human rights is being employed in order to resist these same transnational regimes, or at least certain aspects of them.

SOCIAL RESISTANCE WITHIN EMPIRES OF LAW

I would like to conclude this chapter by bringing it full circle. I began with a brief discussion of different dimensions of Hardt and Negri's Empire hypothesis as a theoretical jumping-off point. I argued that there is much that is hugely suggestive in their social analysis of the shape and meaning of emergent transnational configurations, which they designate as "Empire" as a way to distinguish current developments from the broad networks of political, economic, and legal power that characterized earlier eras of imperialism, colonialism, and neo-colonialism. I nevertheless indicated the different ways in which I have found their framework unconvincing. In particular, I was most concerned with their speculations about (1) whether "Empire" should or will be resisted, (2) if so, why, and (3) if so, how. They speculated that the "multitude" would begin to resist the consolidation of Empire, which, it will be recalled, represents a form of global power that unfolds outside of traditional institutional architectures and which insinuates itself at the level of individual consciousness by compelling social actors to internalize the imperatives of global power and then reproduce themselves in its terms. Hardt and Negri argue that the beginnings (or seeds) of resistance to this process can be gleaned in several current developments, including the rise of vibrant diasporic communities, the ability of social movements to turn the decline in mediating institutions of power to their advantage (i.e., power is closer to people, for both ill and, hopefully, for good), and the very contradictions of Empire itself, which engender corruption and signal its eventual decline and fall.

There are two things that must be said at this point. First, I agree that we should try and understand potential or actual resistance to Empire, or *empires* (of law, for example). Even so, if I have at least begun to account for the emergence of empires of law, which encompass contemporary Bolivia, and if empires of law unfold in large part through human rights discourse, a basic question should immediately arise: What's wrong with that? If human rights discourse plays a large part in establishing the conditions for new forms of global power, then shouldn't we put our intellectual and political efforts behind these new "empires"? Even my four-year-old daughter knows that not all witches are bad (see Glinda, the Good Witch of the North). Is it not true that empires of law, as I have described them, represent the emergence of precisely the kind of biopolitical power that is necessary to force authoritarian regimes to stop torturing people, engaging in secret surveillance of their own citizens for political purposes, and, most of all, maintaining extra-judicial human warehouses, where political enemies are humiliated, brainwashed, and otherwise subjected to all manner of physical and psychological indignities? (I'm of course alluding to the case of Myanmar, formerly known as Burma.) Yet the critique of empires of law is not necessarily a critique of some still unrealized global human rights culture, in which the vision of the UN Commission on Human Rights would finally be realized and individuals and communities around the world would thus be able to realize their capacities free from restraint and oppression. In other words, I have nothing to say about the island of Utopia, nor the role of international human rights in getting us there.

The analysis of the actual employment of human rights discourse in practice in Bolivia is an analysis of the political and economic imperatives – e.g., late global corporate capitalism – that harness the idea of human rights, not an analysis (theoretical, empirical, or otherwise) of the idea itself. The essentially political nature of contemporary transnational human rights networks has been well-documented, which is something that should make us look – ethnographically and analytically – behind their discursively exalted outer appearances. I am not arguing that the emergence of human rights discourse, in Bolivia or elsewhere, masks a global conspiracy or project of normative or legal subterfuge (in which human rights cover "real" and increasingly unequal relations of production). But as scholars from Laura Nader (1999) to Berta E. Hernández-Truyol (2002) have shown, the current human rights regime either selectively brings attention to abuses that can be isolated and associated with international political and economic outliers (Nader), or justifies supplanting "traditional" moral or legal systems in the name of a benign "moral imperialism" (Hernández-Truyol). Moreover, and this is the real point I am trying to make here, the rise of human rights discourse over the last fifteen years cannot be separated from other key aspects of the continuing consolidation of liberalism (or, if you like, neoliberalism) as the dominant global frame of reference. The analysis of empires of law in Bolivia is an attempt to shine light on the relationship between human rights and these broader patterns.

The second thing that must be said – and this brings me back to resistance – is that if Hardt and Negri are right to make resistance an important part of their hypothesis, their relatively vague speculations don't help us understand developments in Bolivia over the last fifteen years, in which the rise of human rights discourse has been accompanied by a corresponding rise in new forms of social resistance. For the remainder of this chapter, I will flesh out the relationship between these two developments.

The most recent period in Bolivian history, one which has featured an intriguing mix of continuities and discontinuities, is rapidly building to something like a denouement. From the early to late 1980s, Bolivia's institutions and elites took some time readjusting to both national imperatives – the reemergence of civilian rule – and broader geopolitical realities, which included active US involvement/intervention in Latin America as part of the Cold War, in increase in International Monetary Fund demands to implement privatization and austerity programs as preconditions for massive loans, and the move by multinational corporations to take advantages of these first two by using the assistance of the US government (and the International Monetary Fund and World Bank) to make a play for a share of the international privatization largesse. Each of these interrelated developments took on new meaning in Bolivia after the election of Jamie Paz Zamora in 1989, and culminated with the election of his successor, Gonzalo Sánchez de Lozada in 1993. Between 1989 and 1997 (the end of Sánchez de Lozada's first term), a program that is understood in Bolivia as "neoliberal" was put into place, and it has endured through the turmoil of the post-1997 period right to the present, when its viability is now in doubt. This neoliberal program can be briefly described for my purposes here. Its first pillar was the pursuit of mixed or more pure forms of privatization, directed toward major utilities and resource sectors (water, natural gas, petroleum, mining) and transportation (mostly the railroad). Multinationals were either offered a significant ownership – short of a majority in some cases – in formerly state-owned companies, or they were (more recently) offered full control over certain concessions, which typically grant exclusive rights to maintain and operate an industry for extended periods.[17]

The second pillar of the neoliberal program was the embrace of human rights. This embrace took two main forms. First, there was the fact that the Paz Zamora and first Sánchez de Lozada governments opened Bolivia to human rights development work, from both international governmental and nongovernmental organizations.[18]

---

[17] For example, in 1999 a subsidiary of Bechtel Corporation – Aguas de Tunari – was awarded a forty-year contract to provide water to the entire Cochabamba Valley. And in El Alto, the epicenter of the current social movement in Bolivia, the water system was likewise taken over by Aguas del Illimani, a consortium jointly owned by the French utility megagiant Suez. As the journalist Jim Shultz explains, in one of his reports on the Bolivian "water wars," "by pegging rates to the dollar, [Aguas del Illimani] has raised water prices by 35% since it took over. The cost for new families to hook up their homes to water and sewage totals more than $445, an amount that exceeds more than six months of income at the national minimum wage" (Shultz 2004).

[18] An important symbol of this shift was the return of the Peace Corps to Bolivia in 1990.

For example, in the early 1990s UNICEF began a series of literacy and education projects in the north of Potosí Department that were organized within the new human rights paradigm. This was followed during the mid to late 1990s by what I have described elsewhere as an "influx" of human rights NGOs to Bolivia, who were eager to renew the material and moral development of Bolivia's poor within their radically transformed terms of reference (see Goodale 2001; for Cochabamba, see Goldstein 2004; for Santa Cruz, see Lowrey 2003). And second, there was a concerted effort to reinterpret especially the economic dimensions of the neoliberal project within a human rights framework. This was done quite formally, by either translating parts of different human rights provisions through new legislation, or by making the political decision to reframe longstanding social problems in Bolivia – access to land, control of natural resources, more decision-making by marginalized ethnic groups or social classes, etc. – in terms of human rights. Important examples of these would be new Articles 171 of the Constitution and 28 of the Code of Criminal Procedure, and the Law of Popular Participation (No. 1551, April 20, 1994).[19]

Beginning in about 1999, and continuing to the present, Bolivia entered a critical phase of the period of history that began in the early 1980s. Although this chapter is not the place for a full analysis of these developments, what is important for my purposes is the fact that new, hybrid forms of social resistance emerged in Bolivia, which combined an earlier discourse of structural revolution with a much more recent human rights discourse. For example, prominent leaders of the El Alto Federation of Neighborhood Assemblies, which played a major part in the recent blockades of La Paz which led to the

---

[19] Article 171 (No. 1615, February 1995) recognized the "cultural, economic, and social rights" of Bolivia's indigenous peoples and, even more radically, ceded jurisdiction to "natural authorities, indigenous communities, and peasants" in matters of administration and conflict resolution. Article 28 of the Code of Criminal Procedure (No. 1970, March 1999), which was largely missed by the public and scholars at the time, was in many ways even more (potentially) transformative. This article, subtitled "community justice," granted indigenous and peasant communities jurisdiction over criminal matters and recognized the right of communities to apply what it called "Indigenous Customary Law." The Law of Popular Participation was a longer and much more complicated piece of legislation, but it was anchored in the same broader shift toward human rights. For example, when Article 1 speaks of "perfecting a representative democracy" and "facilitating the citizens' participation and guaranteeing equality of representation at all levels," the Law is implementing key aspects of International Labor Organization Convention 169 (1989), the "Indigenous and Tribal Peoples Convention," which the Bolivian Congress ratified in 1991, making Bolivia the third country in the world to do so (after Mexico and Norway). For a more detailed analysis of the relationship between Convention 169, the Law of Popular Participation, and human rights development on the ground in Bolivia (especially in the *norte de Potosí*), see Goodale 2002.

resignation of President Carlos Mesa, frame their demands for complete nationalization of Bolivia's natural resources in terms of indigenous rights *and* Fausto Reinaga's classic 1969 book "La Revolución India," which exhorts Bolivia's indigenous population to "tear to shreds the infamous wall of 'organized silence' that . . . Bolivia . . . has built around me" (Reinaga 1969). As I will argue, this social resistance – both actual and potential – has been made possible in part by tensions (contradictions?) within the broader (neo-)liberal project of which human rights discourse is an important component.

Human rights and the Pandora's box of (neo-)liberalism

In the first place, the unfolding of the most recent iteration[20] of the liberal project, one which is coextensive with Bolivia itself as an independent nation-state, has revealed a tension between human rights and liberalism's economic imperatives. Beginning in the nineteenth century, Bolivian elites have sought to reconstitute Bolivia as a modern, industrialized nation which will achieve social and economic development on the basis of individual initiative, the creation of transmissible wealth, and private property (especially real property). On almost all counts, this project has failed, if we measure its history in terms of its stated goals: the development of Bolivia as a modern and liberal nation. However, given that Bolivia's landed and industrial (mostly mining and agribusiness) elites have managed to increase their wealth steadily over the last two centuries, all the while pursuing policies on behalf the "Bolivian people," we can say that economic programs instituted by a range of governments have achieved a kind of limited progress, one whose limitations have been justified by racial and class-based arguments. But, until quite recently, human rights were not explicitly embedded within liberal policies, even though they had always been part of Bolivian encounters with liberalism in different forms, from the "rights of man" language in the first Bolivian constitution of 1826, to the natural rights-based arguments behind the 1874 Law of Expropriation, which decreed the abolition and parsing of communally held lands, the distribution of titles to individuals (not communities) as private property, and a liberal and "rationalized"

---

[20] Again, I want to continue to emphasize the question of whether as a matter of social analysis it is more accurate to locate recent developments within a "new" version of liberalism, or as part of a much longer, and, in the broad outlines, continuous "pattern of intention" that emerged in the nineteenth century (see Goodale 2008). This is a separate, but obviously related, question from the ways in which "neoliberalism" is employed discursively in Bolivia (and elsewhere).

tax reform that replaced the decidedly non-liberal colonial tribute structure that continued to be so integral to many areas of rural Bolivia in particular (see Platt 1982).[21]

Since 1989, as I have already described, there has been a convergence between economic liberalism – or neoliberalism – and human rights in Bolivia. But this convergence has had the effect of unleashing forces that have the capacity to seriously transform the basic socio-economic relations of production in Bolivia perhaps for the first time. In other words, the rise of human rights discourse has shown liberalism to be a Pandora's box. Human rights discourse was formalized by the Bolivian state during the early to mid-1990s, and social movements across the range have drawn from this same discourse to attack economic relations that have their basis in the same liberal project from which human rights are derived. This has been true of social movements across the spectrum, from the class-based *Movimiento al Socialismo* (MAS) (Movement Towards Socialist party), led by the opposition firebrand and coca farmer Evo Morales (and Bolivia's new president), to the indigenist organizations based in El Alto, like the mostly Aymara Federation of Neighborhood Assemblies. Yet even as some MAS representatives attack "derechos humanos" as an expression of capitalism's hypocrisy (see Goldstein, chapter 1 in this volume), they do so through a hybrid discourse that invokes the rights of Bolivia's indigenous peoples to resist the abuses perpetrated in the name of individual rights expressed through economics. What is most important to underscore here is the way human rights consciousness comes to serve as a kind of abstract normative standard against which social and economic relations can be measured (and resisted if needed), even though, as a matter of political or legal theory, there is a certain paradoxical quality about one part of a rights framework being used to condemn the other. (Note that the critique of economic relations by social movements in Bolivia is not so much a critique of the results of these [human] rights-based relations, but a critique of the relations themselves.)

---

[21] As Silvia Rivera Cusicanqui explains about the liberal reforms of 1875–1900, of which the 1874 law was an important part: "the liberal reforms ... were preceded by a lengthy debate among the republication elite over the fate of the 'backward' territories possessed by the [indigenous communities] since pre-Hispanic times ... When a recovery in the mining sector generated new sources of revenue in the 1870s, the state was finally able to attempt reforms aimed at abolishing communal forms of land ownership, [and] legitimating its actions through a liberal rhetoric which equated the abolition of the tribute with the achievement of equal citizenship by the Indian population" (1991: 102).

Conclusion – human rights and normative pluralism

By way of concluding this chapter, let me describe what I see to be the relationship between human rights discourse, social resistance in Bolivia, and the emergence of normative pluralism. Universal human rights, as codified in instruments like the UDHR, represent a formally homogenous normative system. If we take the ontological assumptions of the UDHR at face value, as we must, particularly since the universality which underpins the UDHR is an *idea* that has tremendous discursive power for human rights actors across the range, then it is clear that there are only two possibilities: that systems of enforceable rules either align with human rights, or they do not. This is merely a descriptive problem. Of course those "local" normative systems that do not align with human rights can be altered or transformed – through many different means of varying degrees of legitimacy – but at any one point in time, the UDHR metric can be fairly easily applied. Another way to make this point is to say that the ontological universality that is expressed in the UDHR cannot, as a matter of theory – and theory is important here – tolerate diversity; it is not possible within the universal human rights framework for the right to life, say, to "exist" for a certain group of human beings in one place, but not to exist for another group somewhere else. Universal human rights are homogenous in this sense: because they are entailed by a common human nature, and are thus embedded in every human being, they are common to every human being. In a very literal (i.e., etymological) sense, human rights are formally homogenous ("of the same born").

But, of course, as the recent anthropology of human rights has shown, the homogenizing idea of universal human rights must itself "exist," in this case not just in the abstract, as a matter of jurisprudence or philosophy, but in social practice. And as my research in Bolivia shows, when the idea of human rights is rendered discursively, and enters the swirl of grounded legal universes, human rights discourse does not homogenize legal – or, more broadly, normative – practice. Rather, it both transforms the terms of reference through which the legal mediates social, political, and economic relations, which is to be expected, but, even more, creates new conditions in which individuals or groups can organize social resistance. And these conditions are not necessarily, as one might think, derived from the exalted and emancipatory vision associated with human rights, but, as the case of Bolivia shows, are enabled through the normative pluralism that counterintuitively follows in the wake of human rights discourse. Let me give an example of what I mean. In Alonso de Ibañez, the different sources from which rules are derived, the different normativities, were brought into sharper relief *after* 1998, when the human rights SLI had closed and Lucio Montesinos had been engaging in human rights advocacy for several years. When I say different sources, I am referring to a complicated network of "interlegalities" (Santos 1995), which include the following: the provincial *juzgado de instrucción*; the office of police; the five *defensores* or *qhelqueris* ("unofficial lawyers") who are based in provincial capital but work throughout the province; the *corregidor titular* of the canton in which the provincial capital is located; the rule systems administered by the so-called state authorities (*corregidores titulares* and *auxiliares*) outside of the capital; the *sindicatos campesinos*, or rural peasant unions, whose jurisdictional boundaries in the north of Potosí Department are usually coextensive with the boundaries of individual communities (called either *ranchus* or *estancias*); and, finally, the province's different *ayllus*, which can roughly be translated as "indigenous social structures," whose non-contiguous, and even non-geographical boundaries span the entire province and beyond and which are led by so-called natural authorities (*jilanqus* and *segundas*).[22]

Instead of suppressing (or homogenizing) the tremendous normative diversity in Alonso de Ibañez, the arrival of human rights discourse brought the idea that individuals – and, even more important, communities – had the right to organize themselves in ways that respected their inherent dignity. This was taken to mean that human rights promised a kind of freedom and respect for difference that didn't exist before, or, if so, had existed in a more circumscribed way. This was evident in the way the unions and ayllus, in particular, underwent a resurgence of power in relation to the other sources of normativity in the province through 1999 and into 2000. During conflict resolution processes, in which the relative importance of rules can be gauged, explanations based in union or ayllu traditions supplanted in many cases the formerly more influential "legal" explanations, which authorities throughout the province had always appropriated when resolving local disputes over property boundaries, fights between young men, damage to crops by animals, and so on (see Goodale 2001). Although this obviously involves a bit of speculation on my part, I would argue that the increase in normative diversity in the province was one effect

---

[22] For more on this complicated legal/normative universe, see Goodale 2001, 2002.

of the coming of human rights discourse in the 1990s, and, further, that this human rights – normative diversity connection establishes the conditions within which more organized forms of social resistance can structured. This last point actually leads back to my argument about the connotative power of human rights: if human rights express themselves as idea, as a kind of floating signifier that represents a new form of human dignity and moral worth, then it's clear how human rights can reinforce – and embolden – existing normativities, even if their provisions or rules or "laws" do not, strictly speaking, conform to specific human rights instruments. Even if the potential for social resistance that this connection makes possible has not "matured" throughout rural Bolivia, as it (perhaps) has in La Paz and other Bolivian cities over the last five years, the fact remains that human right discourse nurtures a new kind of diversity, and this, in turn, establishes the conditions for new forms of social resistance to very old forms of inequality and oppression.

REFERENCES

Baxi, Upendra. 2002. *The Future of Human Rights*. Oxford: Oxford University Press.

Berlin, Isaiah. 1997. *The Proper Study of Mankind*. Edited by Henry Hardy, and Roger Hausheer. New York: Farrar, Strauss and Giroux, p. 119.

Cueto, Marcus, ed. 1994. *Missionaries of Science: The Rockefeller Foundation and Latin America*. Bloomington: Indiana University Press.

Cueto, Marcus. 1995. *Saberes andinos: ciencia y tecnologia en Bolivia, Ecuador y Peru*. Lima: Instituto de Estudios Peruanos.

Donnelly, Jack. 2003. *Universal Human Rights in Theory and Practice*. Ithaca: Cornell University Press.

Escobar, Arturo. 1995. *Encountering Development: The Making and Unmaking of the Third World*. Princeton: Princeton University Press.

Goldstein, Daniel. 2004. *The Spectacular City: Violence and Performance in Urban Bolivia*. Durham: Duke University Press.

Goodale, Mark. 2001. "A Complex Legal Universe in Motion: Rights, Obligations, and Rural-Legal Intellectuality in the Bolivian Andes." Ph.D. diss., University of Wisconsin-Madison.

Goodale, Mark. 2002. "Legal Ethnography in an Era of Globalization: The Arrival of Western Human Rights Discourse to Rural Bolivia." In June Starr and Mark Goodale, eds. *Practicing Ethnography in Law: New Dialogues, Enduring Methods*. New York: Palgrave/St. Martin's Press.

Goodale, Mark. 2005. "Empires of Law: Discipline and Resistance within the Transnational System." *Social and Legal Studies* 14(4): 553–583.

Goodale, Mark. 2006. "Ethical Theory as Social Practice." *American Anthropologist* 108(1): 25–37.

Goodale, Mark. 2008. *Dilemmas of Modernity: Bolivian Encounters with Law and Liberalism* (forthcoming).

Hardt, Michael, and Antonio Negri. 2000. *Empire*. Cambridge: Harvard University Press.

Hernández-Truyol, Berta E., ed. 2002. *Moral Imperialism: A Critical Anthology*. New York: New York University Press.

Keck, Margaret, and Kathryn Sikkink, eds. 1998. *Activists Beyond Borders: Advocacy Networks in International Politics*. Ithaca: Cornell University Press.

Klein, Herbert S. 1982. *Bolivia: The Evolution of a Multi-Ethnic Society*. (Revised and reissued in 2003 as *A Concise History of Bolivia*.) Oxford: Oxford University Press.

Klug, Heinz. 2000. *Constituting Democracy: Law, Globalism and South Africa's Political Reconstruction*. Cambridge: Cambridge University Press.

Korey, William. 1998. *NGOs and the Universal Declaration of Human Rights: A Curious Grapevine*. New York: Palgrave Macmillan.

Lowrey, Kathleen. 2003. "Enchanted Ecology: Magic, Science, and Nature in the Bolivian Chaco." Ph.D. diss., University of Chicago.

Merry, Sally. 2005. *Human Rights and Gender Violence: Translating International Law into Local Justice*. Chicago: University of Chicago Press.

Merry, Sally. 2006. "Transnational Human Rights and Local Activism: Mapping the Middle." *American Anthropologist* 108(1): 38–51.

Nader, Laura. 1997. "Controlling Processes: Tracing the Dynamic Components of Power." *Current Anthropology* 38: 711–737.

Nader, Laura. 1999. "In a Women's Looking Glass: Normative Blindness and Unresolved Human Rights Issues." *Horizontes Antropológicos* (5)10: 61–82.

Nash, June. 1993. *We Eat the Mines and the Mines Eat Us: Dependency and Exploitation in Bolivian Tin Mines*. New York: Columbia University Press.

Platt, Tristan. 1982. *Estado Boliviano y Ayllu Andino: Tierra y Tributo en el Norte de Potosí*. Lima: Instituto de Estudios Peruanos.

Reinaga, Fausto. 1969. *La Revolución India*. La Paz: Ediciones PIB (Partido Indio de Bolivia).

Riles, Annelise. 2000. *The Network Inside Out*. Ann Arbor: University of Michigan Press.

Riles, Annelise. 2006. "Skepticism, Intimacy and the Ethnographic Subject: Human Rights as Legal Knowledge." *American Anthropologist* 108(1): 52–65.

Rivera Cusicanqui, Silvia. 1991. Liberal Democracy and Ayllu Democracy in Bolivia: The Case of Northern Potosí. *Journal of Development Studies* 26(4): 97–121.

Santos, Boaventura de S. 1995. *Toward a New Common Sense: Law, Science and Politics in the Paradigmatic Transition*. New York: Routledge.

Schultz, Jim. 2004. "Another Water Revolt Begins in Bolivia." Democracy Center on-line, December 18, 2004. Available on-line at www.cedib. org/accionandina/?module=displaystory&story_id=12984&format=print. Accessed February 7, 2007.

Speed, Shannon, and María Teresa Sierra (eds.). 2005. "Critical Perspectives on Human Rights and Multiculturalism in Neoliberal Latin America." Theme issue of *PoLAR: Political and Legal Anthropology Review* 28(1).

Turner, Terrence. 1997. "Human Rights, Human Difference: Anthropology's Contribution to an Emancipatory Cultural Politics." *Journal of Anthropological Research* (53)3: 273–291.

Van Cott, Donna Lee. 2000. *The Friendly Liquidation of the Past: The Politics of Diversity in Latin America*. Pittsburgh: University of Pittsburgh Press.

Wilson, Richard. 2001. *The Politics of Truth and Reconciliation in South Africa: Legitimizing the Post-Apartheid State*. Cambridge: Cambridge University Press.

4

EXERCISING RIGHTS AND RECONFIGURING RESISTANCE IN THE ZAPATISTA JUNTAS DE BUEN GOBIERNO

Shannon Speed *

> *What was lost in the promulgation of human rights theory in the 1990s was the connection between rights and subjects who can exercise those rights.* Chandler 2002: 114

> *Now, we have to exercise our rights ourselves. We don't need anyone's permission, especially that of politicians ... Forming our own autonomous municipalities, that's what we are doing in practice and we don't ask anyone's permission.*[1] Comandanta Esther August 2003

FROM GUNS TO SHELLS

Introduction

On an August day in 2003, I huddled beneath a plastic tarp through a typical afternoon downpour in the highlands community of Oventic, Chiapas. While the weather was not unusual, the day itself was far from typical: I stood, accompanied by several thousand others – indigenous people from throughout the state and activists from throughout the country and the world – listening to the speeches of Zapatista leaders. They spoke of the birth of the five "caracoles" (literally, shells, but indicating meeting points)[2] and the formation of the five *Juntas de Buen*

---

* Research for this article was supported by the SSRC-MacArthur Foundation, the Ford Foundation-Mexico, and two Mellon Faculty Research Grants from the Lozano Long Institute of Latin American Studies at the UT Austin. Minor portions of this text appeared previously in different forms in the *Political and Legal Anthropology Review (PoLAR)* 25(1), 28(1) and *LASA Forum* 35(1). The ideas elaborated here were developed in dialogue with, and owe an intellectual debt to, Miguel Angel de los Santos, Melissa Forbis, Charles R. Hale, Mariana Mora, Alvaro Reyes, María Teresa Sierra, and the participants in the MIT conference "Transnationalism and Human Rights" in June of 2005.
[1] Sound recording available on-line at fzlnnet.org. This and all translations herein are by the author.
[2] Subcomandante Marcos introduced the concept of "caracol" in July of 2003: "They say that the most ancient ones said that others, more ancient than they, appreciated the figure of the caracol. They say that they say that they said that the caracol represented entering the heart, that this

Gobierno ("Good Governance Councils," herein referred to as *Juntas*) to be seated in them. It was a major turning point for Zapatismo, signaling a transition from military to civilian governance and the formal end to their petition for state recognition of their collective right to autonomy. In the words of Rosalinda, "The government didn't pay attention to us. *Que se queden con sus pendejadas.*[3] We know how to make our municipalities work." From now on, the Zapatista communities would govern themselves – without state recognition – through the *Juntas*. The capacity to define whether or not indigenous people have rights to engage in autonomous practices had been taken out of the hands of the state.

In this chapter, I will examine the social meanings and effects of rights, law and state power in Zapatista philosophies and practices of resistance. Focusing in particular on the formation of the *Juntas*, I argue that, in the absence of possibilities for constructive dialogue with the state aimed at translating human and indigenous rights into concrete and effective policies, new forms of local governance are being created in order to exercise these rights. In the process, the actors involved are redefining concepts such as "autonomy" and "rights" as existing prior to and regardless of their recognition by the state. The Zapatista's assertion is that these rights exist in their *exercise*, not their establishment in the state's legal regimes. By eliminating the state as the external referent for rights, such conceptual reframings are challenging not only to the state itself, but liberal and neoliberal conceptualizations of rights and their relationship to the law. Based on ethnographic research in Chiapas, this chapter explores how people in the Zapatista autonomous municipalities are appropriating globalized discourses[4] such as human and indigenous rights, reconfiguring them based on their own

---

was what the first to have knowledge said. And they say that they say that they said that the caracol also represented the heart going forth to walk through the world, that was what they said, the first to live. And not only that, they say that they say that they said that with the caracol they called to the collective so that the word would be one and agreement would be born. And they also say that they say that they said that the caracol helped the ear to hear even the most distant word. That is what they say that they said." (Chiapas, la treceava estela: un caracol. *La Jornada*, Thursday, July 24, 2003.) The word refers both to a conch seashell and a snail shell. While the reference to shells for communication is for conch shells, used to call people to public meetings, in the Tzeltal communities of Chiapas, people use the word "pu'y" which means snail.

[3] Colloquial phrase meaning, roughly, "They can keep their bullshit."

[4] I utilize the term "discourse" in a Foucaultian sense. For Foucault, discourses promote specific kinds of power relations, by defining and regulating, setting the terms of what we can think about a particular set of relations. Discourse is not a text or an enunciation, but *its taking place*. Thus, for Foucault, "discourse is a complex, differentiated *practice* ..." (1972: 211, emphasis mine). Discourse, as I utilize it herein, is more than the way people talk about rights. It is the entire set of ways in which the notion of human rights can be understood and acted upon.

histories and subjectivities, and re-presenting them in ways that alter rights-based resistance and potentially challenge the logics of the neo-liberalizing state.

This chapter contributes to debates about human rights in the era of globalized neoliberalism. I agree with this volume's editors about both the problematic nature of categories such as global and local, and about the usefulness of retaining them for explorations social dynamics between the global and local. Rather than conceptualizing such dynamics in a spatial manner, either vertical or horizontal (though I believe they may be either or both in particular contexts), I prefer to conceptualize them as dialogic engagements, emphasizing that both globalized discourses and particular social actors in particular settings contribute to how that discourse will be understood and utilized. I recognize that such a dialogue is never free of power relations, and some social actors (such as states, multinationals, even transnational activists) may have more power to impose their interpretations than others social actors (such as indigenous communities). However, there is by no means a single, uni-directional influence flowing from global to local. People are engaging human rights in complicated ways in the ambiguous "betweens" of the global and local (Goodale, Introduction to this volume) and the nation-state. My argument is that these engagements are dialogic;[5] human rights discourses whether considered "global," "local," or "state" discourses, are products of continuous inter-pellation in which the others are implicated. The social actors involved are affected by the engagement and the power dynamics in which it is inscribed: appropriating and using a discourse of human rights affects how they understand themselves and how they effect their resistance. But at the same time, they bring to bear their own particular under-standings and goals in ways that reshape the meanings and functions of the discourse in interesting and at times contestatory ways. Even in cases where in some gross sense a dominant discourse of human rights is imposed, squashing local understandings, those social actors no longer think of human rights outside the context of that interaction. It is thus vital (and it is the goal of this chapter and this volume) to understand the workings of both the globalized discourse of human

---

[5] Bakhtin (1981) argued that every speech act implied a dialogic process, a response to others. Our discourse only exists in the context of previous or alternative discourses, and is in dialogue with them. Tedlock and Mannheim (1995) usefully apply this to culture, arguing that cultural systems and practices are constantly produced, reproduced, and revised in dialogues among their members, and in dialogue with other cultures and cultural expressions.

rights (itself multiplicitous) and its practice in local settings (how it is interpreted and acted upon in a particular context). Note that this is not a distinction between discourse (in the abstract realm of theory) and practice (what local people have). "Practice" in this analysis is a re-conceptualization of human rights based on the understandings and political processes of the social actors involved. This is what Goodale, in the volume's Introduction, refers to as an "organic theory" of human rights.

"Los Caminos de la Resistencia": from armed uprising to autonomous civilian governance, 1994–2004

> Ya ven, aquí estamos otra vez en la misma lucha, mejorando los caminos de la resistencia.
>
> Here we are once again in the same struggle, improving the paths of resistance
>
> Comandante Zebedeo, at the inauguration of the
> Juntas de Buen Gobierno. August 2003.

Most of us who have long held an interest in Mexico and its indigenous peoples remember the exact moment when we learned of the Zapatista uprising, which began on January 1, 1994. I was pounding the pavement in downtown San Francisco, heading into the office even on the holiday weekend, when I saw it on the front page of the newspaper: "Armed Indian Rebellion in Mexico." I was astonished to read that armed and unarmed troops of Tzeltal, Tzotzil, Tojolabal, Chol, and Mam Indians from the central highlands of Chiapas and the Lacandon jungle had taken over five county seats in the state. The group's name, "the Zapatista National Liberation Army," invoked the spirit of the Mexican Revolution and it put forward a broad platform of demands for work, land, housing, food, health, education, independence, liberty, democracy, justice, and peace. While the news was sketchy and it was hard to obtain reliable information about the tumultuous events, one thing seemed clear: the relationship between indigenous people and the state in Mexico would never be the same again.

After twelve days of armed confrontation between the poorly equipped Ejército Zapatista de Liberación Nacional (EZLN) (Zapatista Army of National Liberation) and the Mexican Army, and in the face of growing popular support for the insurgents, the government and the EZLN began peace negotiations. The negotiation process took place in the highlands community of San Andres Larrainzar. The preliminary talks took most of 1995. The process was lengthy, in part due to the Zapatistas' insistence that the proceedings be translated into the various languages of their members and that the base communities be consulted before any decisions were formalized. (As I will discuss further below, this type of direct democratic procedure is a keystone of the Zapatista conceptualization of power and authority.) In late 1995, it was agreed that there would be five "tables" of negotiations on different sets of topics; the first was on Indigenous Rights and Culture.

This set of talks ended optimistically in February 1996 with the signing of the San Andrés Accords on Indigenous Rights and Culture by the EZLN and the Mexican government. The accords specifically recognize the rights of indigenous peoples to "develop their specific forms of social, cultural, political and economic organization," "to obtain recognition of their internal normative systems for regulation and sanction insofar as they are not contrary to constitutional guarantees and human rights, especially those of women," "to freely designate their representatives within the community as well as in their municipal government bodies as well as the leaders of their pueblos indígenas in accordance with the institutions and traditions of each pueblo," and "to promote and develop their languages, cultures, as well as their political, social, economic, religious, and cultural customs and traditions" (San Andrés Accords on Indigenous Rights and Culture 1999: 35). Notably, the accords included commitments to constitutional recognition of indigenous peoples (pueblos indígenas) and "the right to self determination exercised in a constitutional framework of autonomy ..." (Hernández Navarro and Vera Herrera 1998: 58–59). From this point on, constitutional recognition of indigenous rights and autonomy became a key issue for the Zapatistas and their supporters.

Much needed as they were in order to address centuries of oppression, in the particular political juncture in which Mexico found itself at the time of the signing, there was nothing especially radical about the accords. They were based largely on international law, especially the International Labor Organization Convention 169 (considered by many to be the most complete international agreement on indigenous rights), which Mexico had signed and ratified in 1990, making them law at the level of the constitution. Further, in its neoliberal constitutional reforms in 1992, Mexico had made the shift from a corporatist, assimilationist model to a neoliberal, multicultural one, recognizing the pluriethinic makeup of the population (this is discussed in greater detail below). The accords, and the further constitutional reform that they mandated, would have been consistent with that transition, one which a number of Latin American countries made over the following five years.

However, the administration of President Zedillo backtracked on the accords. The legislative body that had participated in the negotiations process at San Andrés, called the Comisión de Concordia y Pacificación (COCOPA) (Commission of Concord and Pacification), prepared legislation to comply with the accords and forwarded it to the executive.[6] However, President Zedillo refused to submit the legislation, known as the "COCOPA initiative," and finally admitted that he had been unaware of the content of the agreements signed by his own Secretario de Gobernación (Secretary of the Interior).[7] This legislative and political debacle effectively ended the peace process and undoubtedly contributed to a strengthening of the demand for recognition of indigenous rights and autonomy in the Zapatista movement. The next set of talks, on "Democracy and Justice," was opened, but broke down without agreement. Shortly thereafter, the EZLN withdrew from the talks citing government non-compliance with the signed accords.

From this point on, demands for indigenous rights and self-determination began to take center stage in the Zapatista's public discourse, and broader national demands for resource redistribution and democratization became less prominent. In a four-year period of stalemate between the EZLN and the government, the Zapatistas continued to unilaterally construct their project for autonomy. Although the Zapatistas established thirty-eight "municipalities in rebellion" in 1994, it was from 1997 onward, after the failure of the San Andrés Accords, that these municipalities emerged as a principal space for the organization of resistance and a strategy for indigenous political participation (González Hernández and Quintanar 1999). Zapatista communities formed autonomous regions and began their own processes of implementing local governments and directing their energies to the task of developing their own systems of education, healthcare, agriculture, and more.

When Vicente Fox took office in 2000 – ending more than seven decades of PRI[8] party rule – he presented the four-year old COCOPA initiative to the Congress as a demonstration of the government's

---

[6] In Mexico, the vast majority of legislation is submitted to the Congress by the executive branch.
[7] La Jornada, January 1997.
[8] Partido Revolucionario Institucional (Institutional Revolutionary Party).

intention to honor the San Andrés Accords. The final outcome was a bitter disappointment to indigenous peoples throughout Mexico. Despite the march of thousands of Zapatistas and their supporters to Mexico City, a moving address to the Mexican Congress by Tzeltal Comandanta Esther and an outpouring of national support for the legislation, in April 2001 the Mexican Congress passed a greatly watered down version of the original accords. Whether the president intended the law to go through intact or had some responsibility for the outcome is a matter of political debate. But the Zapatistas, and indigenous people more generally, certainly interpreted the law as a betrayal. The fact that the president supported the law as it went through the process of state ratification, a process itself marked by irregularities,[9] made him at minimum a party to the treachery. The law places a series of restrictions on indigenous autonomy, including giving the authority for defining the specifics about how autonomy can be realized and by whom to individual state legislatures. It was rejected unanimously by indigenous peoples throughout Mexico; the Zapatistas issued a communiqué calling it a "legislative joke" (Marcos 2001). The content of the law will be discussed in greater detail below.

In August 2003, one year after the disastrous Indigenous Law, the Zapatistas announced the creation of five *caracoles* as the seats of five *Juntas de Buen Gobierno*. Each of the five *Juntas* includes one to three delegates from each of the already-existing Autonomous Councils in each zone. Currently there are thirty Zapatista Autonomous Municipalities in Rebellion that feed into the five *Juntas*. Among other things, the functions of the *Juntas* include: monitoring projects and community works in Zapatista autonomous municipalities; monitoring the implementation of laws that have been agreed to by the communities within their jurisdiction; conflict and dispute resolution within their jurisdiction; and governing Zapatista territory under the logic of *mandar obedeciendo* (lead by obeying), a keystone of "good"

---

[9] Regarding the state approval process (a legal requisite for the constitutionality of the reforms), Ramirez Cuevas (2002) cites Abigail Zuniga, advisor for the municipality of Tlaxiaco: "After Congress approved the reform, the PRI and the PAN [Partido Acción Nacional (National Action Party)] speeded up the process in the state legislatures ... On July 18, the Permanent Commission made the official count of the results, despite the fact that not all the legislatures had finished voting, and that two states had not even discussed the issue. The Commission totaled 19 state congresses in favor, and nine against (those with a majority indigenous population). Of the 19 states that voted in favor, irregularities and legal violations had been documented in eight. Chihuahua sent its results after the official count, and, despite that, it was included."

governance, which holds that authorities have a responsibility to carry out consensually arrived at decisions, rather than a mandate to make decisions on behalf of the population they represent.

At the celebration for the new *Juntas de Buen Gobierno*, Comandanta Esther, who had addressed the Mexican Congress two years earlier to urge them to implement the San Andrés Accords, expressed the Zapatistas' disillusionment with and rejection of the constitutional recognition process:

> The political parties conspired to deny us our rights, because they passed [the Law on Indigenous Rights and Culture] . . . Now, we have to exercise our rights ourselves. We don't need anyone's permission, especially that of politicians . . . Forming our own autonomous municipalities, that's what we are doing in practice and we don't ask anyone's permission.[10]

With the formation of the caracoles and the *Juntas de Buen Gobierno*, the Zapatistas were signaling a new phase in their renegotiation of the relationship between indigenous peoples and the Mexican state. No longer willing to "play by the rules" of petitioning for state recognition through the legal system, the Zapatistas were making a bold assertion that their rights to local autonomy as indigenous peoples already existed, even in the absence of the state's recognition of them. They existed because they were already being exercised in practice. This interpretation has important implications for the meanings attached to rights, law, and state power.

RIGHTS, STATE POWER, AND THE LAW

From modern liberalism to neoliberalism in Mexican law

Early Mexican constitutions were based on the classic liberal notion of "natural" rights developed by Enlightenment thinkers such as Locke and Hobbes in which certain rights were vested in human beings by virtue of the fact that they are human. These rights were understood to establish limits on existing political powers by asserting that there were natural rights and fundamental laws of governance that not even kings could overstep. Notable about these rights is that they are vested in the individual, and exist prior to their formal recognition or acceptance by the sovereign. The sovereign, in fact, was beholden to them.

---

[10] English text (translation may vary slightly from mine) available at: indymedia.org.uk/en/2001/ 03/2641.html. Last accessed March 5, 2006.

The precursory "Consitutional Decree for the Liberty of Mexican America" (also known as the Constitution of Apatzingán), issued in 1814 (although it never became law), stated in Article 24: "The happiness of the people and of every citizen consists of the enjoyment of equality, security, property, and liberty. The full preservation of these rights is the object of the institution of government and the only end (objective) of political association" (Terrazas 1996: 51). Note that in this framing, rights exist prior to the state, and it is the role of the state to ensure that its citizens can enjoy them. These ideas were also integral to the 1824 Federal Constitution of the United States of Mexico, which took its federalist framework and much of its language from the American Constitution. The Federal Constitution of 1857 was the first to actually mention "the rights of man," demonstrating in its language its roots in the French and German thought of the late eighteenth century, and particularly the influence of the French Declaration on the Rights of Man (Terrazas 1996; C. A. Hale 2000; Carozza 2003).[11] It was undoubtedly heavily influenced by the American Constitution, as well (C. A. Hale 2000). Like its predecessors, it took "the rights of man" to have their origin in natural law. The natural rights of man were primary, political power, social organization, and law existed to further these rights.

But rights discourses were moving in the direction of a distinct role for government. With the advent of secular legal realism, it was no longer tenable to justify moral rights by appeal to a natural order. There was a shift from moral or natural rights, which need not be enforceable by law in order to exist, to legal rights, which exist only when a preestablished legal rule provides an individual an entitlement enforceable by law. Thus, modern rights exist and can be appealed to only when they are established in positive law. When rights become a function of the law, the Kantian notion of duty on another party becomes a legal duty of states to fulfill that entitlement or refrain from denying it. This is a significant shift, which effectively puts the ability to establish rights in the hands of the sovereign (in the contemporary period, states) at that same time they are charged with protecting them.

Mexico became a modern liberal state in the decades following the Mexican Revolution. The Constitution of 1917 imposed a new system, "in accord with human dignity." It reflected a fundamental shift from

---

[11] Carozza (2003) argues that there was a heavy Rousseauian influence on Latin American constitutions that resulted in the notion of rights with corollary responsibilities characteristic of those documents.

the Federal Constitution of 1857 which still conceived these rights to have their origin in natural law (Terrazas 1996) There was, in fact, a debate at the time of the writing of this earlier constitution between those who defended natural law doctrine and those who held a positivist philosophy, who argued that rights were not in the nature of man, but were derived from positive law, and could not exist prior to society, or independent of positive law (C. A. Hale 1990). At that time, natural law conceptions prevailed. In Article 1, the 1857 Constitution was clear: "The Mexican people recognize that the rights of man are the basis and the objective of social institutions. Consequently, it declares that all laws and authorities of the country must respect and support the guarantees granted by this constitution." Social institutions and the law were thus products of rights, rather than the other way around. The natural rights of man were primary; political power, social organization, and law existed to further these rights.

This changed with the Constitution of 1917, in which positivist theory prevailed. Law was in accord with, but not subject to, the rights of man. Its opening statement, "Every person in the United Mexican States shall enjoy the guarantees granted by this Constitution" makes clear that, while individualist notions of rights are to be retained, they are guarantees grated by the state, through its constitution. The transition of the definition of rights to "guarantees" reinforcing the fundamental role of the state: one cannot have guarantees without a guarantor. The establishment of rights in the Mexican Constitution as a system of state "guarantees" to its citizens defined the paternalist state as the exclusive entity ensuring the existence and enforcement of those rights.

The Mexican Constitution of 1917 also established social rights based on premises of social justice and human dignity. This was consistent with emergent modern liberalism: the individual continued to be privileged but a variety of social and economic rights were added to the basic moral and political ones. Modern liberalism would of course reach its apex during the years of the New Deal and the welfare state, in which the state was understood to play an important role in mediating social inequality. But the 1917 Mexican Constitution was one of the earliest documents to enshrine such rights in law.[12] It

---

[12] These precepts are particularly notable in the post-World War II conceptualization, enshrined in the Universal Declaration of Human Rights, with its emphasis on rights aimed at protecting human dignity. In the Universal Declaration, a dignified life is conceptualized as requiring a degree of liberty, embodied by the civil and political rights of Articles 1–21, but also enjoying a measure of well-being, reflected in the list of welfare rights in Articles 21–28 such as social

included such a broad social rights platform that, in fact, it has often been characterized as "socialist." However, far from being a socialist document, it retained the liberal individualist orientation of rights and maintained intact the full range of liberal civil and political rights of the earlier constitutions. And the establishment of social rights did not imply group or collective rights: rather, these were rights that pertained to individuals within particular constituencies. This is distinct from the notion of group rights as they would pertain to an entire group, such as indigenous peoples.

Because the Constitution of 1917 was a product of the Mexican Revolution, social rights were required to address the demands of the groups that had formed the base of the Revolution: the traditionally marginalized populations of campesinos and workers. These rights were particularly manifested in Articles 27 and 123: agrarian law and labor law. The Constitution of 1917 provided the legal framework for the state-citizen relationship in the post-Revolutionary period. Notably, the emergence of social rights as guarantees granted by the state shifted conceptualizations of rights and rights-bearing subjects away from the agentive individual and onto the needy individual, paving the way for paternalistic political practice (Gourevitch 2004). This created a relationship between the state and civil society that was consolidated in the post-Revolutionary period: a paternalist, corporatist, state-dominated relationship.

This Constitution of 1917 thus provided a vital underpinning for the forms of governance that would be enacted in the post-Revolutionary period by the PRI party (initially by its precursor, the Partido de la Revolución Mexicana [PRM] [Party of the Mexican Revolution]). The ruling party consolidated power by engaging in a form of corporatist governance designed to draw potentially oppositional segments of the population into the state project through state-sponsored agencies and assistance programs. Corporatist rule worked relatively well for the PRI for several decades. The party enjoyed strong support from indigenous communities in many areas of the country in spite of their notable marginalization.

---

security, leisure, "food, clothing, housing and medical care and necessary social services" (Article 26), unemployment benefits, education, and cultural participation. In the modern liberal interpretation of rights, states – now charged with both creating rights through law and enforcing respect for them through law – also had a larger role to play in mediating economic and social relations, and in many cases placed controls on the economy. Carozza (2003) argues that Mexico and other Latin American countries played a significant role in ensuring that social rights were encompassed in the Universal Declaration.

This began to change with the neoliberal restructuring which began in the 1970s (Hernández 2001) and gained momentum in the late 1980s during the regime of Carlos Salinas de Gortari. The constitutional reforms implemented in 1992 effectively brought Mexico into the emergent global order and ended decades of corporatist rule. These reforms included the opening up of industries nationalized after the revolution to foreign investment, ending state protections on agricultural products, and terminating the agrarian reform. This meant, for many, the end of any hope of balancing out social inequalities through direct petitioning of the state (land reform, etc.), and signaled the demise of the established relationship with the national state. It was at this key juncture, in 1992, that the state formally altered this relationship through the reform of Articles 27 and 123 (land and labor). Notably, in the same set of reforms, Article 2 recognized for the first time that the Mexican nation had a "pluriethnic composition sustained originally by its indigenous peoples." The constitutional reforms of 1992 dramatically altered the Constitution of 1917, paving the way for a full-fledged neoliberal state, while creating a new legal framework for the relationship of the state to civil society, and especially to its indigenous population. The shift from modern liberalism to neoliberalism was formally underway.

Neoliberal logics of rule

Neoliberalism, the extension of liberal ideas that emphasize and privilege the "free market" to the entire realm of social interaction, entails a variety of government policies and practices designed to ensure that the workings of economic markets and social relations are unfettered by state mediation. It differs from classic and modern liberalisms by the philosophy that essentially all human interactions – not just economic ones – should be regulated by market forces. This has had significant implications for the modern interpretation of rights. The neoliberal state, as it has emerged in the last two to three decades, must downsize its social welfare undertakings and remove all restrictions on the economy designed to protect those citizens with less resources, a process epitomized by the "structural adjustment" measures pushed by international financial institutions in many countries in Latin America. Those rights, however, are now enshrined in law at the international level, which means that even as states alter their own legal frameworks to minimize them, groups within society continue to claim them, increasingly relying on international law as a basis for their claims. Many states continue to recognize their existence, but no longer are they interpreted as the responsible party for ensuring them. This function is "privatized," passed from the state to industry and business (corporate social responsibility), communities and individuals, and especially civil society organizations such as nongovernmental organizations (NGOs) (Deleuze 1994; Guehenno 1995; Hardt 1998). Thus, as the market is prioritized and the state is divested of responsibility for social welfare, relations between social groups are defined by market forces and mediated by civil society itself (Gill 2000).

However, this does not mean that the state disappears, or that its role as both granter and guarantor of rights is diminished. In this model, the state's primary responsibility is to ensure that the market operates freely. One of the principal ways that the state does this is by maintaining "stability," in particular through the maintenance of law and order. Nikolas Rose describes this process in what he terms "late liberalism":

> The relation of the state and the people was to take a different form: the former would maintain the infrastructure of law and order; the latter would promote individual and national well-being by their responsibility and enterprise.
>
> (1999: 139)

Neoliberalization entails not only the reduction of government's social functions and moves to "free" the economy, but a new set of governance practices for the state. On the one hand, the state maintains "law and order," while on the other it produces subjects who are autonomous and self-regulating:

> To govern better, the state must govern less; to optimize the economy, one must govern through the entrepreneurship of autonomous actors – individuals and families, firms and corporations. Once responsibilized and entrepreneurialized, they would govern themselves within a state secured framework of law and order.
>
> (Rose 1999: 139)

The neoliberal state thus governs by creating responsibilized and entreprenuerialized subjects, on the one hand, and maintaining the structure of law on the other. Neoliberalism, then, is not about "rolling back the state" but about inventing new strategies of governance that create "the legal, institutional and cultural conditions that will enable an artificial competitive game of entrepreneurial conduct to be played to best effect" (Burchell 1996: 27). Because these two aspects of neoliberal governance, controlling law and the formation of subjects, are so key, it is worth considering the ways that they come together in what Trouillot calls "the reworking of processes and relations of power so as to create new spaces for the deployment of power" (2001: 127).

The trouble with rights

There is no escaping the fact that the spread of neoliberalism in Latin America has taken place in tandem with the spread of other discourses, among them democratization, human rights and indigenous rights/ multiculturalism. Precisely as the triumphalist march of neoliberal capitalist democracy moved forward over the ruins of socialist projects and authoritarian governments, rights struggles became the primary form of contestation to state power and social injustice.

Because of the negative impact that neoliberal policies and practices have had on large numbers of people (as reflected in the growing poverty and income disparity),[13] some analysts have argued that the parallel spread of neoliberalism and the discourse of human rights is due either to a response to increasing needs as the welfare state is left behind (Donnelly 2003), or to horizontally-spreading resistance to the harsher consequences of neoliberalization (Ignatieff 2001).[14] These theorists understand the relationship between the globalization of human rights and that of neoliberalism to be fundamentally anta- gonistic: a process in which neoliberal policies, being antithetical to human rights, create conditions of increasing oppression, and civil society increasingly turns to human rights discourse and doctrine to defend itself. It is understood that, as a response to the negative impact of neoliberal globalization, human rights has emerged as an important discourse of resistance movements all over the world.

---

[13] The UN Economic Commission for Latin America and the Caribbean (ECLAC) reports that from 1980 to 1999, the percentage of households in poverty in Latin America grew from 34.7 percent to 35.3 percent. The percentage of individuals in poverty increased from 40.5 percent to 43.8 percent – meaning an increase of poor people from 136 million to 211 million. A later Comisión Económica Para América Latina (CEPAL) (Economic Commission for Latin America) report indicated that in 2003, there were 20 million more Latin Americans living in poverty than in 1997. Inequality also increased (see 2003 ECLAC report, discussed in the *Miami Herald*, July 16, 2002).

[14] The United Nations has specifically tied neoliberalization polices such as structural adjustment to human rights questions. A report by an independent expert to the United Nations High Commission of Human Rights (UNHCHR) discussed the effects of structural adjustment policies and foreign debt on the full enjoyment of human rights, particularly economic, social, and cultural rights (E/CN.4/2003/10) and the UNHCHR passed a resolution recognizing the negative impact of such policies (Resolution 2003/21).

Similarly, analysts have tended to see the growth of indigenous rights movement in Latin America as a response to centuries of oppression and the worsening of conditions for them as states neoliberalize (see, e.g., Bengoa 2000).[15] In part, this is because the liberal emphasis on the individual is retained in neoliberalism it is interpreted as "radically individualizing," and thus it logically follows that the demands of collectivities are innately challenging. For these reasons, it is easy to view indigenous rights movements as inherently contestatory to the state and anti-neoliberal in their orientation.

However, it is worth noting that the neoliberal reforms implemented in many countries were accompanied by constitutional reforms initiated by states such as Bolivia, Colombia, Ecuador, Guatemala, Brazil and, to a more limited extent, Mexico, which recognized indigenous rights (Assies, Van Der Haar, and Hoekema 2000; Van Cott 2000; Sierra 2001). This entails a shift from previous assimilationist approaches to governing diversity to a new recognition of distinct groups within society, and the permitting of some measure of self-regulation for these groups. This would seem to indicate that neoliberalism, far from being antagonistic to rights, in fact entails a wider recognition of human and indigenous rights.

Liberal political theorists have struggled to reconcile principles of individual freedom with the rights claims of collectivities through a "politics of recognition" (Kymlicka 1997; Taylor 1994). From a liberal perspective, collective rights are inherently in conflict with liberal individual equality, but this is an antagonism that states must nevertheless resolve in the interests of doing justice to the individuals that make up those groups, as well as doing justice to the collectivities that are, necessarily, made up of individuals but which assume a certain independent legal status. In an optimistic view, this is what newly-multicultural states are engaged in.

But other theorists suggest that state recognition and multicultural reforms in Latin America cannot be understood simply as the result of the gains made by indigenous rights movements, or the altruistic state's desire to do justice to all individuals. These analysts suggest that rights struggles, including collective indigenous rights, may in fact work to reinforce the underlying goals of neoliberal governance strategies and limit the force of collective indigenous demands (Gustafson 2002; C.R. Hale 2002; Postero 2001). From this perspective, recognition of collective rights is

---

[15] For a comprehensive recent discussion of indigenous rights movements in Latin America, and a survey of the different debates over their origins and meanings, see Jackson and Warren 2006. See also Warren and Jackson 2001; Warren 1998.

an integral part of neoliberal subject formation and the construction of neoliberal rule. Lesley Gill (2000), for example, argues that in democratization processes, the use of repression and force to maintain political power undermines legitimacy and credibility, and for this reason states increasingly deploy political discourses and strategies of inclusiveness. A similar argument may be made regarding the neoliberal mandate for reduced state intervention in social life. This mandate requires the participation of all subjects in managing and regulating society, thus rendering inclusive policies and processes of subject-formation the priorities of rule. If these analysts are right, there are serious risks for social movements framed as struggles for indigenous rights. First, pursuing social struggle by petitioning the state through the legal system for the establishment of "rights" may serve to buttress the neoliberal state's role as the purveyor and protector of rights, and as upholder of "law and order." Such forms of contestation and resistance may "reinforce the centrality of law as a mode of protest" (Merry 1992), and risk reinscribing the very forms and logics of power they are struggling against.

Second, law may provide a privileged space for the state to engage in neoliberal subject making, because of its inherent delimiting and regulating capacities. Menon argues that "modern forms of power do not simply oppress, they produce and regulate identity [and] law is an important technique by which this is achieved" (2004: 205). Gledhill has argued that it is risky to "settl[e] for the politics of rights alone under liberal political institutions which embody various kinds of regulatory power" (1997: 71), while Brown argues that "rights" "may become . . . a regulatory discourse, a means of obstructing or co-opting more radical political demands" (1995: 98). Geared to these narrow legal goals, legalism may actually reinforce structures and discourses of inequality, in part by "fixing" identities and delimiting culture in the law, subjugating them to "a stable set of regulatory norms" (Brown and Halley 2003: 24). These theorists emphasize the regulatory force of rights discourses in the current stage of capitalism. Importantly, this regulation is not only by the state, which holds the power to grant and take away rights, but also *self-regulation* on the part of those who seek to gain and or retain them.

C. R. Hale looks specifically at this process of subject constitution through the struggle for indigenous rights and multicultural policies in Guatemala. He argues that:

> Neoliberalism's cultural project entails pro-active recognition of a minimal package of cultural rights, and an equally vigorous rejection of the

rest. The result is a dichotomy between recognized and recalcitrant indigenous subjects, which confronts the indigenous rights movement as a "menace" even greater than the assimilationist policies of the previous era.

(2002: 485)

In Hale's analysis, "neoliberal multiculturalism" functions to limit the problem of collectivities, in part by dividing indigenous people, articulating them as those who are "acceptable" and those who are "unacceptable" to the state. More than just divide and conquer, such policies lead indigenous people to invest their energies in demonstrating their authentic belonging to the recognized group and away from focusing on existing inequalities in Guatemalan society. Thus, rights struggles, by encouraging a process in which the identities of the dissenters are "fixed" in legal regimes, may create a problematic need for subjects to continually fit themselves into these established legal categories, producing a self-regulatory policing of identity (see also Povinelli 2002; Dugan 2003).

Mexico's Law on Indigenous Rights and Culture provides an example of how neoliberal states use the law as a site for the production of subjects in light of these analyses. For example, in the Indigenous Law, the responsibility for determining both which indigenous people will be recognized and what form of autonomy of indigenous peoples will be granted is left in the hands of state-level legislatures. This interesting double move shifts responsibility from the centralized state, while retaining it within the purview of the state. Because these state-level legislatures can be expected to adopt restricted definitions of each, indigenous people would be placed in a similar position to what Hale describes, attempting to "prove" to the law makers that they and their practices are "authentically" indigenous in order to access whatever rights these bodies might grant. The Federal government is free of responsibility for this mediation. Perhaps the most transparent move to define indigenous subjects through the law resides in the clause that deems indigenous people to be "subjects of public interest" (*interés público*), a category also occupied by orphans, rather than "subjects of public right/law" (*derecho público*). This move meant that, even as rights for indigenous people were ostensibly being established, indigenous collectivities were being "undefined" as subjects of legal rights (see Regino 2001).

In this section, I have argued that definitions and interpretations of rights have shifted over time in accordance with shifting forms of governance. In the neoliberal era, the interpretation given to "rights" is distinct from that of the modern liberal era. Despite the reduction of the state's function for mediating social conflict, "rights" enjoy greater primacy today than in past eras. Law has become the privileged site of both contestation and regulation, and thus "rights" are the superlative mode for acceptable resistance. Neoliberalism reconfigures rights, taking collectives into the fold in the process of disciplining them. Disciplined citizen-subjects appropriately mediate themselves and the state is reinforced through the privileging of the legal system as the appropriate forum for dispute and the state as the appropriate arbiter.

Considering these characteristics of neoliberal rule, we can recognize the potential for rights-based claims to be seduced into a system where legal process is an empty signifier for the resolution of immediate conflict, while leaving the architecture of power that created those conflicts unquestioned. Similarly, the law's illusion that organized power can only be exercised through the state is combined with the desperation created by the social decay that accompanies the downsizing of the corporatist state, resulting in marginalized groups making claims to a sclerotic neoliberal state whose capacity to resolve social conflict is increasingly limited to its police function. Thus, although immediate conflict and violence may be temporarily resolved, this "resolution" may come at a heavy cost (see Agamben 1998; Guehenno 1995).

Those who are engaged in or support human and indigenous rights struggles may be profoundly uncomfortable with my argument at this point. Am I suggesting that rights struggles are inevitably compromised, and that as a form of resistance rights-based struggles can only serve state power? Certainly not. What I do wish to suggest is that it is vitally important, as we engage in these struggles, to remain critical of the larger structures and processes of power in which they are inscribed (see Goodale, chapter 3 in this volume). We cannot afford to assume that rights struggles, including human rights and indigenous rights, are inherently contestatory to neoliberal state power. In important ways, discourses of human rights and indigenous rights are intimately bound up with other discourses and practices of the latest stage of capitalism. However, this does not mean that discourses of rights are always or inevitably proscribed. In many places, indigenous people (and others) are appropriating discourses of rights and reformulating them in ways that are radically challenging to the particular forms and logics of power at work in neoliberal state: Bolivia is just one recent example (see Postero 2004; Goodale, chapter 3 and Goldstein, chapter 1 in this volume). In the following section, I wish to return to the Zapatista's autonomy process and the formation of the *Juntas de Buen Gobierno*, which I will argue is also an example of how local appropriations, reinterpretations, and redeployments of rights discourses can represent alternative forms of resistance.

EXERCISING RIGHTS, RECONFIGURING RESISTANCE: THE POWER OF "BUEN GOBIERNO"

> We the Zapatistas want to *exercise power*, not take it.
>
> Subcomandante Marcos

The Zapatista movement has pursued social change largely through the dominant discourse of rights. Even early on, when their demands remained broad – for reform of the state, democratization – they were couched in the language of rights. But the language of rights became more pronounced in their public discourse as the movement became increasingly focused on the struggle for indigenous autonomy.

This is perhaps not surprising: most disenfranchised groups in Mexico, and the NGOs that accompany them, have adopted the dominant discourse of rights and the practice of law to further their struggles. But what meanings do the Zapatistas invest in rights and law? What are the effects on the Zapatista movement of adopting this discourse? Is the movement inadvertently reinforcing the state's position as the purveyor of law by petitioning the state to recognize their "rights"? Do they waste valuable energy and resources on actions that further legitimate institutions and empty forms of social mediation that function to guarantee their ultimate subordination? In mobilizing the discourse of law, do they enter the ideal space of neoliberal subject making?

Dissing the state
As I stood listening to Comandanta Esther's words at the inauguration of the *Caracoles* – "Now, we have to exercise our rights ourselves. We don't need anyone's permission, especially that of politicians" – the words of another indigenous woman, spoken a year earlier, came back to me. In the San Cristóbal office of the *Red de Defensores Comunitarios por los Derechos Humanos*, Celerina,[16] a young Tzeltal woman from the Morelia region, commented on the newly-passed law: "[The passing of

---

[16] Celerina is a pseudonym.

the law] doesn't matter. Our autonomy doesn't need permission from the government; it already exists." Celerina's comment presaged Comandanta Esther's, and suggests that well before the establishment of the *Juntas*, even as they worked for the passage of the law, people in Zapatista communities were conceptualizing indigenous rights and autonomy as existing prior to and irrespective of their establishment in law. The sentiment, and certainly the autonomous structures and philosophies of Zapatista governance, were already in existence when the law was passed. As Celerina's comment suggested, the pursuit of constitutional recognition of indigenous rights was but one tactic in a much larger project of self-determination. The failure to gain adequate state recognition was unfortunate, but it was neither surprising, nor debilitating to this project. In fact, I suggest that it strengthened the Zapatista's project and debilitated the state.

Since its inception, the Zapatista movement has continually maintained an alternative project to that of negotiating with the state. This project entailed distinct conceptualizations and structures of power, governance, and law (Speed and Reyes 2002, 2005). As I noted above, the first autonomous municipalities were formed shortly after the uprising began in 1994. They have continued to grow and develop since that time, gaining momentum after the state's abandonment of the San Andrés Accords. Even as they continued to petition the state for legal recognition of indigenous rights, particularly the right to autonomy, they were engaging in autonomous governance practices within the Zapatista regions. With the failure of the Law on Indigenous Rights and Culture, which was uniformly rejected by indigenous peoples throughout the country, the Zapatistas dropped all pretense of petitioning the state as one avenue for pursuing social change. The autonomy project that had been in formation since 1994 was poised to demonstrate in practice their alternative logics of power and governance. With the establishment of the *Caracoles* and the *Juntas*, this alternative project was formalized, setting in motion a new dynamic of resistance. There are several points worth taking into consideration about the significance of the Zapatista project for our understandings of rights, the law, and the state in neoliberal Mexico, as well as the broader issues of power and resistance in the "between" spaces of global-local-state interaction.

The move to formally establish the *Juntas de Buen Gobierno* displaced and disempowered the state in important ways. First, because the neoliberal state's primary role is maintaining stability through the rule of law (a task the Mexican government had been failing at since the uprising began nearly ten years earlier), it was vital that stability be reinstated through the law, the state's principle site of legitimation. During his campaign, Vicente Fox asserted that if elected, he would resolve the Chiapas conflict in five minutes. Though resolving the conflict would clearly take longer than that, upon taking office he sought to deal with the problem by finally submitting the COCOPA legislation. However, the state failed in this task. As we have seen, the law's content was drastically altered by legislators, and the end result was rejected by indigenous people and created an outpouring of resentment and social discord. An astonishing 330 constitutional challenges to the law were filed by individuals, communities, and organizations (Ramírez Cuevas 2002). Needless to say, stability was not restored, "law and order" were destabilized, and the state suffered yet another blow to its legitimacy before civil society. Further, the new indigenous subject of neoliberalism that the law sought to create was never to be.

And second, more importantly, the failed law was the final event that compelled the Zapatistas to openly disregard the state as the source of their rights, and the law as the site for establishing them. This presented a radical challenge to the state: not, as some national analysts claimed, by seeking to secede and form a new sovereign state (for the EZLN position on this see Marcos 2001), but by unilaterally exercising their right to autonomy and self-determination – expressed as the capacity to control and affect their daily lives. This move effectively displaced the state as the sovereign power which can grant or retract rights through the law, a direct hit to the primary site of both legitimation and subject-making processes of the neoliberal state.

Alternative logics: reconceptualizing rights

There is more to the current mode of Zapatista autonomy than simply a response to the intransigence of the government in instituting reform on indigenous rights. There is a distinct conceptualization of those rights which functionally eliminates the legal regimes of the state as the external referent for the existence of rights. Bearing some resemblance to a natural law conceptualization of rights as prior to and irrespective of the laws of states, the Zapatista interpretation also eliminates the notion of nature/God as the source of those rights. The source of rights in this conceptualization lies in the actors themselves, who are collectively exercising them. This does not mean that the state is irrelevant – Zapatista autonomy, even when completely disengaged from interaction with the state, is still forged in silent dialogue with the state. However, by refusing to grant the state the power to designate who are rights-bearers and what rights they may enjoy, the Zapatistas articulate a radically distinct discourse of rights.

In the direct exercise of their right to self-determination, the Zapatista movement disengages from liberal conceptualizations of natural and positive law conceptualizations and redefines "rights" as existing *in their exercise*, not as designations from God/nature or the state/law. Further, they are exercised in Zapatista regions as a form of resistance, explicitly expressed in the term "Autonomous Municipalities in Rebellion." This notion of "rights" as the product of factors purely immanent to society, or as the product of particular relations of force is not exclusive to the Zapatistas. Theorists from Spinoza (see Deleuze 1993; Montag 2000; Negri 1990) to Foucault (1980) have considered the potential of "rights" as the product of factors purely immanent to society or as the product of particular social relations Spinoza argued: "Nature's right and its order ... forbids only those things that no one desires and *no one can do*" (cited in Deleuze 1993). That is, for Spinoza, a body's right was coextensive with what it could do. The only natural rights were those that were within a being's affect, its power to influence the world and be influenced by it. From this perspective, rights exist only when they can be exercised, not in their granting by a higher sovereign (the state, or God) (Speed and Reyes 2002). At a philosophical level, this conceptualization is distinct from, and thus presents a challenge to, the legal discourses that underpin the state power in the current global order.

Alternative logics: reordering rule

On the road to Oventic, there is a sign that reads: "Welcome to Zapatista Territory: Here the people command and the government obeys." Almost a year after the formation of the *Juntas*, I was again in Oventic, now home of the *Junta de Buen Gobierno "Corazón Céntrico de los Zapatistas delante del Mundo"* (Central Heart of the Zapatistas before the World). During a seemingly interminable wait for a decision on a project, I chatted with some members of the Junta. We sat in their meeting room, built of pine wood slats and lamina, perched about halfway up the steep incline from the basketball court/amphitheater to the road – the central artery of the *Caracol*. We talked about the *Juntas*, and "how things were going" in their first months. I couldn't resist interjecting a subtle complaint about the cumbersome process that seemed to be holding up approval – or even rejection – of my research project. One of the Junta members, looking me in the eye, said, "Well, yes. It's difficult. Sometimes things take time, because we make decisions, but we don't make them alone. We have to respond to others, we have to respond to *el pueblo. Asi es nuestro modo.*"[17]

This Junta member was pointing to a key Zapatista conceptualization of power and governance. Zapatista leadership style has been specifically constructed, both in discourse and practice, in a way that discourages the public role of individual leaders and heavily emphasizes collective processes. Through the structure of the CCRI,[18] the Zapatistas elaborated a notion of authority that downplayed the role of the leaders themselves, and highlighted collective decision making and the subjection of individual leaders' power to the collective will. Aspects of the Zapatistas' philosophy of governance, especially that of "lead by obeying," reflect their commitment to giving priority to the decisions of the many, rather than the chosen few. All major decisions in the communities are made after extensive deliberations in which all members have had the opportunity to speak (though women are often excluded from this process). Zapatista authorities, rather than having a right to make decisions for the communities, have a responsibility to carry out the collective decisions of the communities. If they use their position to do anything other than execute the decision of the people, they are removed from their positions.

This alternative logic of power was given new impetus and new visibility with the formation of the *Juntas de Buen Gobierno.* The Juntas, which deal with a range of issues for their regions from local disputes to major political policy, represented the transfer of power from military to civilian authorities in the autonomous regions. The five Juntas are made up of groups of from seven to fifteen members who rotate on a weekly or biweekly basis. This means that, for each Junta, there are between twenty-eight and sixty people participating in the decisions for their regions. The Junta draws its members from the councils of each autonomous township. Further, for each "turn" of the Junta, there are "suplentes" (alternates), who are also present and actively engaged. With their rotating structure of large groups that turn over frequently, the Juntas mark an important diffusion of leadership and authority.

---

[17] Conversation with the author, June 2004. Notes in possession of the author.
[18] Comité Clandestino Revolucionario Indígena – CCRI by its Spanish acronym (Indigenous Revolutionary Clandestine Committee). The CCRI is the leadership structure of the EZLN.

There is no need to romanticize this process. The positing of alternative logics of governance and a distinct framework of rights is a tall order, and on the ground their application and their results are uneven. The inverted power relations of *mandar obedeciendo* lead to complicated decision-making processes, and the rotating leadership model of the Juntas does give rise to confusion and inconsistencies. The concentration of authority and decision-making power in the hands of a few individuals would undoubtedly facilitate decision-making processes. However, the goal of the EZLN's autonomy project is not to promote efficiency. Although collective decision making and rotating members can be cumbersome, they reduce corruption, abuses of power and *protagonismo* – or individuals using their position to promote themselves and their interests. By positing these concepts as part of their autonomy project, Zapatistas articulate an alternative for social organization and rule.

The Zapatistas did not introduce the notion of collective decision making in Chiapas. The predominant mode of decision making in indigenous communities in Chiapas is through community assemblies in which issues are debated until a consensus of all those present is reached. Authorities are expected to act on these collective decisions, not make their own decisions about what is right or best for the community. That is, the authority vested in them when they achieve a leadership position is to carry out the collective decisions of the entire community (though women are frequently excluded from this process). The concept manifested in Zapatista philosophy as "lead by obeying" emerged from the communities themselves. "Lead by obeying" is one of the principal concepts of the Zapatistas' proposal for an alternative form of governance, which they call "*buen gobierno*," distinct from that of the Mexican state, or "*mal gobierno*."

The assertion of these alternative democratic practices challenges the emergent discourse of electoral representative democracy in Mexico, one that promotes certain types of citizenship and acceptable forms of political participation, such as voting and expressing dissent through the law. While many celebrated this liberalizing discourse as Mexico emerged from decades of authoritarian rule, others, like the Zapatistas, have recognized that it also forms part of the process of hegemonic construction by the neoliberal state – part of a set of rationalities and cultural logics that interpolate subjects and inform practices. The Zapatistas' discourse asserts a very different kind of logic, one that doesn't lend itself well to market logics and to notions of rational actor citizens out to maximize individual benefits, express their freedom of choice at the ballot box, and their dissent in the courts of the state. Zapatista philosophy presents a challenge to the dominant discourse of the Mexican state, not with arms, but with alternatives: alternative logics, subjectivities, and forms of power and authority.

Conclusions: reconfiguring resistance

The Zapatistas have mobilized global discourses of rights and waged their struggle on the legal terrain of the state in strategic fashion. I have argued that, by withdrawing their claims to indigenous rights from the realm of legal contestation, they have appropriated the discourses of human and indigenous rights, and are redeploying them with new significations in support of an alternative project that, rather than reinforcing state power, can be read as challenging it.

In the Zapatista's alternative project, rights exist in their exercise. This is a distinct conceptualization from that of liberal and neoliberal theory. This interpretation exposes the myth of liberal conceptions of law and the state: that the state will attempt to mediate social inequalities through the law and the establishment and defense of rights (when it may be engaged in just the opposite), and that rights, once established in law, *exist.* Indigenous people in southern Mexico are well aware that many rights established in law are functionally non-existent, precisely because the state refuses to enforce them and thus they cannot be exercised. The Zapatista movement has consistently channeled global discourses through their own local knowledge and understanding, and have put them into practice in new ways. They continue to claim their rights, but do not do so on the legal terrain of the state. In doing so, they are "improving the paths of resistance," making their rights struggle contestatory rather than accommodating to neoliberal state power.

Not all rights-based forms of resistance are simply reproducing the structures of power that maintain neoliberal global rule. Neither are all contesting it. I suggest that the Zapatista movement is one example of potential alternatives that break with the normalizing characteristics of legal discourse. These retooled conceptualizations make indigenous autonomy in the form elaborated by Zapatistas and their supporters challenging to the neoliberal state – not because of the much-debated risk of "separatism," but rather by providing both symbolic and material alternatives to neoliberal rule. They offer an alternative structure of power that is based on distinct logics of rule, in collective and consensus decision making, the concept of *mandar obedeciendo* and the assertion of pluriculturality or diversity within the collective. But in constructing their autonomy *en los hechos* (loosely, in practice) and outside state recognition, the Zapatistas can assert their own logic of rule, "good government" as posited against the "bad government" of the state, and in the process minimize the limiting, normalizing, and reproductive forces of the state and its legal regimes.

It is unclear what the limits of "rights in their exercise" would be. It is easy to celebrate such an argument when emanating from a movement one is sympathetic to, such as the Zapatista movement (to which I am indeed sympathetic). It might be less so if deployed, for example, by right-wing armed militia groups in the United States. But even if unsympathetic, such deployments might also be challenging to neoliberal power. Further, the strength of the Zapatistas' claim – and the force of its challenge – lies in the alternative project it is deployed to defend – a project that seeks to reconfigure power relations – not to hold power themselves, but to exercise it in ways that are more socially just for all within their territory.

REFERENCES

Agamben, Giorgio. 1998. *Homo Sacer, Sovereign Power and Bare Life*. Stanford: Stanford University Press.
Assies, Willem, Gemma Van Der Haar, and Andre Hoekema, eds. 2000. *The Challenge of Diversity: Indigenous Peoples and Reform of the State in Latin America*. Thela Thesis, Amsterdam.
Bakhtin, Mikhail. 1981. *The Dialogic Imagination: Four Essays*. Edited by Michael Holquist. Trans. Caryl Emerson, and Michael Holquist. Austin: University of Texas Press.
Bengoa, José, ed. 2000. *La Emergencia Indígena en América Latina*. Santiago, Chile: Fondo de Cultura Económica.
Brown, Wendy. 1995. *States of Injury: Power and Freedom in Late Modernity*. Princeton, NJ: Princeton University Press.
Brown, Wendy, and Janet Halley. 2002. *Left Legalism/Left Critique*. Durham: Duke.
Brysk, Alison, ed. 2002. *Globalization and Human Rights*. Berkeley: University of California Press.
Burchell, Graham. 1996. "Liberal Government and Techniques of the Self." In A. Barry, T. Osborne, and N. Rose, eds. *Foucault and Political Reason: Liberalism, Neo-liberalism, and Rationalities of Governance*. London: UCL Press.

Carozza, Paolo. 2003. "From Conquest to Constitutions: Retrieving a Latin American Tradition of the Idea of Human Rights." *Human Rights Quarterly* 25(2): 281–313.

Chandler, David. 2002. *From Kosovo to Kabul: Human Rights and International Intervention.* London: Pluto Press.

Constitución Política de los Estados Unidos Mexicanos. 2000. Mexico, DF: Instituto Federal Electoral.

Deleuze, Gilles. 1993. *Expressionism in Philosophy: Spinoza.* London: Zone Books.

Deleuze, Gilles. 1994. "Postscript on Societies of Control." In Gilles Deleuze, *Negotiations 1972–1990.* New York: Columbia University Press.

Donnelly, Jack. 2003. 1989. *Universal Human Rights in Theory and Practice.* Cornell: Ithaca.

Dugan, Lisa. 2003. *The Twilight of Equality: Neoliberalism, Cultural Politics, and the Attack on Democracy.* Boston: Beacon Press.

Esther, Commandanta. 2002. Speech before the Congress of the Union. Available on-line at fzlnnet.org. Accessed May 25, 2005.

Foucault, Michel. 1972. *The Archaeology of Knowledge.* Trans. A. M. Sheridan Smith. London: Tavistock.

Foucault, Michel. 1980. "Two Lectures." *Power/Knowledge: Selected Interviews and Other Writings.* New York: Random House.

Frankovits, Andre. 2001. "Why a Human Rights Approach to Development?" Paper submitted to the Parliamentary Commission of Inquiry into Swedish Policy for Global Development, April.

Gill, Lesley. 2000. *Teetering on the Rim: Global Restructuring, Daily Life, and the Armed Retreat of the Bolivian State.* New York: Columbia University Press.

Gledhill, John. 1997. "Liberalism, Socio-economic Rights and the Politics of Identity: From Moral Economy to Indigenous Rights." In R. Wilson, ed., *Human Rights, Culture and Context: Anthropological Perspectives.* London: Pluto Press, pp. 70–110.

González Hernández, Miguel, and Elvira Quintanar. 1999. "La reconstrucción de la region autónomo norte y el ejercicion del gobierno municipal." In Burguete Cal y Mayor, ed., *México: Experiencias de Autonomía Indígena.* Copenhagen: IWGIA, pp. 210–233.

Guehenno, Jean Marie. 1995. *The End of the Nation State.* Minneapolis: University of Minnesota Press.

Gourevitch, Alex. 2004. "Are Human Rights Liberal?" Available on-line at www.columbia.edu/cu/polisci/pdf-files/gourevitch.pdf. Accessed February 6, 2007.

Gustafson, Bret. 2002. "Paradoxes of Liberal Indigenism: Indigenous Movements, State Processes, and Intercultural Reform in Bolivia." In David Maybury-Lewis, ed., *The Politics of Ethnicity: Indigenous Peoples in Latin American States.* Cambridge, MA: Harvard University Press.

Hale, Charles A. 1990. *The Transmission of Liberalism in Late Nineteenth-Century Mexico*. Princeton, NJ: Princeton University Press.

Hale, Charles A. 2000. "The Civil Law Tradition and Constitutionalism in Twentieth-Century Mexico: The Legacy of Emilio Rabasa." *Law and History Review* 18(2): 257–280.

Hale, Charles R. 2002. "Does Multiculturalism Menace? Governance, Cultural Rights and the Politics of Identity in Guatemala." *Journal of Latin American Studies* 34(3): 485–524.

Hardt, Michael. 1998. "The Withering of Civil Society." In Eleanor Kaufman and Kevin Jon Heller, eds. *Deleuze and Guattari: New Mapping in Politics and Philosophy*, Minneapolis: University of Minnesota Press, pp. 23–39.

Hardt, Michael, and Antonio Negri. 2000. *Empire*. Cambridge, MA: Harvard University Press.

Hernández, Rosalva Aída. 2001. *Histories and Stories from Chiapas: Border Identities in Southern Mexico*. Austin: University of Texas Press.

Hernández Navarro, Luis, and Ramón Vera Herrera. 1998. *Los Acuerdos de San Andrés*. Mexico: ERA.

Ignatieff, Michael. 2001. *Human Rights as Politics and Idolatry*. Princeton, NJ: Princeton University Press.

Jackson, Jean E., and Kay B. Warren. 2006. "Indigenous Movements in Latin America, 1992–2004: Controversies, Ironies, New Directions." *Annual Review of Anthropology* 34: 549–573.

Kant, Immanuel. 1998. *Groundwork of the Metaphysics of Morals*, Mary J. Gregor, ed. (Cambridge Texts in the History of Philosophy). Cambridge, Cambridge University Press.

Kymlicka, W. 1997 *Multicultural Citizenship: A Liberal Theory of Minority Rights*. Oxford: Oxford University Press.

Locke, John. 1960. *Two Treatises of Government*. Cambridge: Cambridge University Press.

López Monjardín, Adriana, and Dulce María Rebolledo Millán. 1998. "La Resistencia en los Municipios Zapatistas, in Poder Local, Derechos Indígenasy Municipios." In Cobo, Rosario, Adriana López Monjardin, and Sergio Sarmiento, eds. *Cuadernos Agrarios 16*, Mexico. pp. 63–74.

Marcos, Subcomandante. 2001. "Communiqué from the Clandestine Revolutionary Indigenous Committee – General Command of the Zapatista Army of National Liberation. Mexico. April 29, 2001. Available on-line at www.ezln.org.mx/ Accessed February 6, 2007.

Menon, Nivedita. 2004. *Recovering Subversion: Feminist Politics Beyond the Law*. Illinois: University of Chicago Press.

Merry, Sally Engle. 1992. "Anthropology, Law, and Transnational Processes." *Annual Review of Anthropology* 21: 357–379.

Montag, Warren. 2000. *Bodies, Masses, Power*. London: Verso Press.

Negri, Antonio. 1990. *The Savage Anomaly*. Minneapolis: University of Minnesota Press.

Postero, Nancy. 2001. "Constructing Indigenous Citizens in Multicultural Bolivia." Paper in Possession of author.

Postero, Nancy. 2004. "Indigenous Responses to Neoliberalism: A Look at the Bolivin Uprising of 2003." In *Political and Legal Anthropology Review (PoLAR)*, co-edited special issue, Shannon Speed and Teresa Sierra, eds. 28(1).

Povinelli, Elizabeth. 2002. *The Cunning of Recognition: Indigenous Alterities and the Making of Australian Multiculturalism*. Durham: Duke University Press.

Ramírez Cuevas, Jesús. 2002. "The Mexican State on Trial." *Masiosare, La Jornada* May 7, 2002.

Regino Montes, Adelfo. 2001. "Negación Constitucional." *La Jornada*, April 28.

Rose, Nikolas. 1999. *Powers of Freedom: Reframing Political Thought*. Cambridge: Cambridge University Press.

San Andrés Accords on Indigenous Rights and Culture. 1999. Trans. Lynn Stephen, and Jonathan Fox. *Cultural Survival Quarterly* 12(1): 33–38.

Sierra, María Teresa. 2001. "Human Rights, Gender and Ethnicity: Legal Claims and Anthropological Challenges in Mexico." POLAR 23(2): 76–92.

Speed, Shannon. 2004. "Dangerous Discourses: Human Rights and Multiculturalism in Mexico." *Political and Legal Anthropology Review (PoLAR)*, co-edited special issue, Shannon Speed and Teresa Sierra, eds. 28(1).

Speed, Shannon, and Alvaro Reyes. 2002. "In Our Own Defense: Globalization, Rights and Resistance in Chiapas." *Political and Legal Anthropology Review (PoLAR)* 25(1).

Speed, Shannon, and Alvaro Reyes. 2005. "Rights, Resistance, and Radical Alternatives: The Red de Defensores Comunitarios and Zapatismo in Chiapas." *Humboldt Journal of Social Justice* 29(1): 47–82.

Taylor, Charles. 1994. "The Politics of Recognition." In Amy Gutmann, ed. *Charles Taylor. Multiculturalism*. Princeton, NJ: Princeton University Press, pp. 25–73.

Tedlock, Dennis, and Bruce Mannheim, eds. 1995. *The Dialogic Emergence of Culture*. Champaign-Urbana: University of Illinois Press.

Terrazas, Carlos R. 1996. *Los Derechos Humanos en las Constituciones Políticas de México*. Mexico: Miguel Angel Porrua Editorial.

Trouillot, Ralph. 2001. "The Anthropology of the State in the Age of Globalization: Close Encounters of the Deceptive Kind" *Current Anthropology* 42(1).

Van Cott, Donna Lee. 2000. *The Friendly Liquidation of the Past: The Politics of Diversity in Latin America*. Pittsburg: University of Pittsburg Press.

Warren, Kay B. 1998. *Indigenous Movements and their Critics: Pan-Maya Activism in Guatemala*. Princeton: Princeton University Press.

Warren, Kay B., and Jean E. Jackson, eds. 2001. *Indigenous Movements, Self-Representation, and the State in Latin America*. Austin: University of Texas Press.

Wilson, Richard, ed. 1997. *Human Rights, Culture and Context: Anthropological Perspectives*. London: Pluto Press.

PART THREE

CONDITIONS OF VULNERABILITY

INTRODUCTION: CONDITIONS
OF VULNERABILITY

Sally Engle Merry

Vulnerability is central to human rights activism and intervention. In identifying which individuals are understood as victims of human rights violations, those who are selected are typically those who are in some way helpless, powerless, unable to make choices for themselves, and forced to endure forms of pain and suffering. Women and children, indigenous people, poor people, and marginalized ethnic and racial groups are the most common categories of people who are identified as suffering human rights violations. Because this understanding of the human rights victim is so fundamental, advocates and even victims tend to define themselves in these terms. They do this even when they are not as helpless and vulnerable as the image of victim requires.

This conception of vulnerability hinges on the idea of agency. The vulnerable person is one who has little choice or capacity to escape pain and injury. Those who choose to put themselves in a dangerous situation are less deserving of the status of victim, as in the case of people who climb high mountains or engage in drug selling in drug-prone urban neighborhoods, for example, than those who have no choice. Risk-takers tend to elicit less sympathy when they are injured and are unlikely to be defined as victims of human rights violations.

Thus, in constructing the ideal victim, it becomes necessary to subtract dimensions of choice. The woman who deliberately provokes her partner and lands the first blow finds she is less acceptable as a victim of domestic violence than one who sits passively and is assaulted without apparent reason. Similarly, the victim of trafficking is quintessentially the young woman who is tricked into traveling to a brothel, from which she cannot escape, or kidnapped and forcibly carried to the site of sex work. A poor woman who deliberately moves to a wealthier country in the hope of finding a husband and doing sex work in the meantime is far less appealing as a victim of human rights violations. Yet, as an example, many women who go to Tokyo from the Philippines fall into this category, driven both by poverty at home and the hope of something better if they can marry a Japanese husband.

Work on humanitarianism has highlighted this dimension of human rights and humanitarian intervention, highlighting the way victims must be redefined as helpless and without agency in order to elicit help. For example, Lisa Malkki's study of the depiction of refugees of political violence shows how they are represented in a very specific way, as a "sea of humanity," a thickly massed body of people devoid of any particular characteristics or will (1996: 377). They are represented visually far more often than in voice, typically through images that are anonymous and focused on dead, starving, or homeless bodies. The predominance of women and children in these depictions emphasizes their helplessness and neediness. They need protection and someone to speak for them, in this rendition, not the opportunity to tell their stories. However, even as images of masses of suffering humanity appeal to universal experiences of suffering, they deny the kinds of particularities of culture, experience, and rootedness that make them people rather than merely human (1996: 389).

Refugees experience their situations quite differently from these images. Malkki discusses how the 1972 Hutu refugees from Burundi living in Tanzania eagerly claimed their legal status as refugees who fled based on a well-founded fear of persecution. But the staff of the international organizations administering the camp thought of them in far less political terms, reconstituting them as universal humanitarian subjects (1996: 376). She argues that this case is an example of a broader process of bureaucratized humanitarian intervention that disregards the specificities of individuals and their circumstances along with the particular historical experiences that brought them there. Instead, it reconstitutes refugees as "pure victims in general: universal man, universal woman, universal child, and taken together, universal family" (Malkki 1996: 378). They are transformed from historical actors to mute victims. This reduces their capacity to speak of their specific experiences in ways that will be heard. Thus, humanitarian interventions tend to redefine the space where they work as outside politics and construct the refugee as a universalized displaced person. In effect, this silences refugees (1996: 378).

More generally, refugees are always portrayed as vulnerable. They are typically described as consisting of mostly women and children.

Estimates of the world refugee population vary from 30 to 45 million people, of whom perhaps 70–75 percent are women and children (Wali 1995: 336; US Committee for Refugees 2004). While this framework emphasizes the vulnerability of the population, it distorts the gender divide. In fact, the populations are closer to half male and half female, although demographic information on refugees is very difficult to obtain and quite fragmentary. However, the women and children frame repositions the group into those who area vulnerable. As Kay Warren shows in her study of the ideology of the anti-trafficking documents, the phrase women and children is often imported in order to emphasize the vulnerability of trafficked victims.

Miriam Ticktin's analysis of the shift from a human-rights based immigration policy in France to one framed more by humanitarian concerns for illness offers a parallel story of how complex political questions of immigrant rights are transformed into a focus on charity for vulnerable persons (2006). Ticktin describes how the French emphasis on human rights as a way of thinking about immigration has been replaced by one of compassion, particularly through a 1998 law that added the right to "private and family life" to family reunification and asylum as conditions for legal immigration. This principle allowed health officials to exercise their discretion to determine when a person's physical illness evoked the compassionate response of allowing them to stay in France. Ticktin sees this shift to a humanitarian logic framed by the protection of what Agamben calls "bare life," the depoliticized body, as emblematic of a more general growth in humanitarianism in the 1990s. Under this humanitarian regime, undocumented immigrants must present themselves as ill and deserving of compassion instead of conforming to a legal regime of residence and therefore entitled to residence papers. The immigrant loses some level of predictability and entitlement and gains the possibility of compassion. However, the delivery of compassion is highly discretionary and variable in France, as in the United States. Indeed, American welfare regimes were historically grounded on notions of need and compassion, a situation of discretion and uncertainty that drove welfare recipients in the 1970s to insist on welfare as a right, not as a form of charity. Ticktin concludes:

> As the political body loses legitimacy in an increasingly globalized world in which national sovereignty is at stake and borders of all kinds are zealously guarded, the supposedly apolitical suffering body is becoming

the most legitimate political vehicle in the fight for a broader concept of social justice: our task is not only to understand the consequences of this shift but also to form a response to it.

(2006: 45)

The expansion of humanitarianism and its increasing centrality as a way of dealing with injustice and suffering influences human rights activism as well. As we have seen, human rights work also focuses on victims defined as vulnerable and in need of help. There are clearly many similarities between human rights and humanitarianism, with considerable slippage of ideologies and practices between them. Like humanitarianism, human rights activism has historically taken a neutral stance, focusing on the protection of individuals from state terror regardless of their political leanings. Similarly, the origins of humanitarianism were a concern for suffering on both sides of a battlefield, and the claim to immunity in combat by groups such as the Red Cross rested on the fact that their medical interventions focused on human suffering and did not take sides. This stance has proved difficult in some contemporary humanitarian interventions, yet serves as the basis for much of the work in this field. In a similar way, human rights advocates protest state repression regardless of the political stance of the state or the tortured victim. As a human rights advocate in Israel explained to me, they work to defend the rights of prisoners regardless of why they are there. It is this neutrality, this effort to rise above particular political struggles and assert the universal rights of all humans regardless of their political commitments, that provides an important part of the legitimation of both humanitarian and human rights intervention. Victims must, therefore, be vulnerable and suffering bodies rather than political persons.

Media representations often portray human rights victims as vulnerable and miserable. In her analysis of media representations of human rights violations, Meg McLagan notes that human rights claims are often represented through the frame of suffering (2006). They offer testimonies that present victims' bodies in ways that elicit sympathy from the audience. For example, Leshu Torchin shows how the 1915 Armenian genocide became an internationally recognized scandal in part through a 1919 film, *Ravished Armenia*, that focused on images of massacres, deportations, and rapes of Armenians by Turks (2006). The film included a depiction of a row of naked crucified women, showing their agony and suffering on the cross. Thus, it marshaled Christian images of martyrdom along with the sexual titillation of naked women (2006: 216–217). She argues that the film sought to elicit empathy for the suffering of the Armenian victims by connected the killings to the visual tradition of suffering in Christian iconography (2006: 215). Such depictions of victims of human rights violations, however, reify victimhood and fetishize it in a "mass-mediated economy of suffering"(McLagan 2006: 194).

What is the effect of this emphasis on the vulnerability of victims? It inevitably influences which individuals are defined as human rights victims and which are not. Indeed, deciding which person has experienced a human rights violation and which one a simple crime is often very complicated. Angelina Godoy argues, based on her study of crime and human rights in Guatemala, that the distinction between ordinary crime and human rights violations is quite blurred (2005). Many murders and other violent incidents can be defined both ways. The distinction is, however, of great consequence. The human rights victim receives widespread attention and concern along with an extensive investigation by human rights groups and sometimes the state, while the victim of an ordinary crime receives far less attention and the offense merits much less investigation or response from the state or other organizations. Thus, in many situations, earning the status and attention of being the subject of human rights abuses requires presenting one's self as suffering, helpless, and vulnerable.

Jean Jackson's account of the media representations of three cases concerning indigenous people in Columbia underscores the importance of focusing on the construction of claimants to human rights, both as they present themselves and as the media defines them. The self-presentation is important: she emphasizes the active way indigenous peoples shape an identity to generate a response from the state. Constructing themselves as eligible human rights claimants is particularly necessary since indigenous people are less familiar as claimants than other groups such as women or laborers. For example, they present themselves as isolated, marginal, and traditional in order to define themselves as entitled to human rights. Indigenous people must be culturally different in order to establish their legitimacy to make claims. At times they must focus on how different their customs and laws are from state law.

As Jackson shows through her analysis of particular cases, indigenous communities seek to establish the legitimacy and scope of indigenous systems of law and justice in order to assert a special indigenous jurisdiction. They emphasize their different legal approaches, which they claim are traditional, and stress how effectively they maintain community harmony and cohesion. For example, indigenous law includes punishments such as stocks or flogging which are not accepted in western law. Insistence on these punishments has the effect of emphasizing difference and the special status of indigenous peoples with their different "traditional" forms of justice and punishment. However, in emphasizing difference, they risk running afoul of western law. In one case, the use of flogging was defined by the state courts as torture.

Emphasizing tradition and cultural difference is particularly important since various groups' status as indigenous may be challenged. As the state calls for more purification and cleansing of the membership of indigenous communities, they respond by constructing images of themselves that fit more closely into the national imaginary, often through mimicry and camouflage. Indigenous communities are engaged in a complex dance of representation in the terms developed by the state in its multicultural vision; thus they must be different in the same way as the state imagines difference. That some people in Columbia think these strategies subvert state power, as Jackson points out, seems hardly uprising. Ironically, indigenous people who fail to fit a society's model of indigeneity, which typically expects them to be poor and marginal, disrupt established narratives. Eve Darian-Smith describes how Native Americans who become wealthy through casinos in the United States fail to fit into established categories of Indianness (2003). People in California, she points out, are not used to rich Indians.

The situation Jackson describes is full of ironies. This most vulnerable population in Columbia, confronting ongoing violence, must present itself as culturally different in the terms the state decides. It must strategize how to appear traditional in order to make claims to rights, yet retain its traditional innocence of strategizing in order to emphasize its harmoniousness and difference. It must appear vulnerable rather than powerful, innocent rather than strategic, in order to cope with the threats of violence and powerlessness that such indigenous communities face at all times. And yet, it is also depicted as using too much violence, in the form of stocks and floggings, in its efforts to assert difference. That the stocks came originally from the Spanish seems irrelevant to these debates about difference and violence.

In her study of the drafting of the United Nations' 2000 Protocol to Prevent, Suppress and Punish Trafficking in Persons, Especially

Women and Children, Kay Warren explores the many competing visions of how the problem of trafficking should be defined and what the solution might be. Warren tracks the discussions among governmental and nongovernmental actors in the drafting process in Vienna, showing the differences in the way the problem is represented and how these differences are hammered together to form a single, if sometimes obscure and contradictory, text. She argues that these differences are based on a variety of contradictory ideological positions such as those between nongovernmental organizations (NGOs) that seek to abolish prostitution versus those that want to improve the labor conditions of all workers. The fact that this discussion was lodged in the international crime part of the United Nations tended to focus discussion on problems of border control and criminals rather than on the human rights of the trafficked. The figure of the vulnerable victim, described as a woman or child, does important work in legitimating a protocol that is ultimately about strengthening border control and prosecuting organized crime.

Although there was general agreement that human trafficking means the use of coercion to transport people and force them to work in highly exploitative conditions, there was considerable disagreement about whether this was an issue of border control, the apprehension of organized criminals, or the human rights of victims. Clearly, the definition of the problem shapes the solution, whether this means tracking and identifying organized crime networks or providing alternative occupations for the poor who are driven to move. Despite the relevance of diminishing demand for trafficked persons as well as their supply, the discussion tended to ignore the problem of demand.

Warren emphasizes competing conceptions of "victims" in the document that emerged from this process. Although the image of the vulnerable victim is central to the document, the issue of who can consent and under what conditions is complicated. The drafters frequently describe victims as "women and children," thus implying that their purpose is to protect those who cannot protect themselves. At the same time, there are significant restrictions placed on the age and conditions under which a person can consent to being trafficked. Warren shows clearly that the various organizations and their institutional interests lead to quite different interpretations of what consent means and how vulnerability should be defined. The document itself is open to these multiple and conflicting interpretations and the debates continue long after the protocol is finalized.

Although the document endeavored to separate trafficking from smuggling, the actual circumstances of the lives of people who are trafficked do not fit easily into these categories. There is no doubt that some of the victims are vulnerable, of course, but portraying the entire project of controlling behavior that ranges from people who migrate for better jobs, people who are smuggled by coyotes by choice and who pay, people who move for sex work in the hope of marriage and a better life, people who move for jobs and end up doing sex work because there are no alternatives, misses the complexity of the story. To describe interventions for all of these groups as a matter of strengthening borders and catching criminals is clearly misleading. Most importantly, it misses the extent to which the alleged victims are themselves actively participating in the project, often investing substantial amounts of their own money in the attempt to move to what they hope will be a better situation. A stronger border control regime might be more difficult to implement in the absence of the legitimacy provided by the image of the trafficked victim, the young girl kidnapped from a loving home and dragged off drugged to a brothel.

As Warren points out, one of the key problematic features of efforts to control trafficking lies in the concept of consent itself. Trafficking is movement without consent but, as she notes, some people are considered unable to consent, either because they are too young or because they are being asked to do an activity that the drafters find beyond the possibility of consent. Thus, the centerpiece of the protocol is preserving the agency of vulnerable people. Yet there are substantial areas where consent, and therefore agency, is not even possible, such as in trafficking involving people under eighteen. Ironically, agency is denied in the name of protection. The protocol is framed around the image of the vulnerable victim who has little if any agency and who needs protection. Although there are activists who take a broader perspective on the issue, viewing it in terms of economic pressures that push people to move, it is those who are more interested in border policing and crime control who have taken over the project, using the vulnerable victim as a key legitimating figure.

These two chapters reveal the centrality of the image of vulnerability to the human rights project as well as to its humanitarian sister. They also show how this image fails to capture the agency and initiative of the those who endure violations. Victims are represented in ways that are appealing to funders and to governments, which seems to require a degree of neediness and passivity that fails to capture the dimensions of agency available to victims. The result is an ongoing lie: a misleading image of victims and a false set of expectations for those who feel called to protect the needy rather than to respect the active resisters.

REFERENCES

Darian-Smith, Eve. 2003. *New Capitalists: Law, Politics, and Identity Surrounding Casino Gaming on Native American Land*. Belmont, CA: Wadsworth.

Godoy, Angelina Snodgrass. 2005. "La Muchacha Respondona: Reflections on the Razor's Edge between Crime and Human Rights." *Human Rights Quarterly* 27: 597–624.

Malkki, Lisa H. 1996. "Speechless Emissaries: Refugees, Humanitarianism, and Dehistoricization." *Cultural Anthropology* 11(3): 377–404.

McLagan, Meg. 2006. "Introduction: Making Human Rights Claims Public." *American Anthropologist* 108(1): 191–195.

Ticktin, Miriam. 2006. "Where Ethics and Politics Meet: The Violence of Humanitarianism in France." *American Ethnologist* 33(1): 33–49.

Torchin, Leshu. 2006. "*Ravished Armenia*: Visual Media, Humanitarian Advocacy, and the Formation of Witnessing Publics." *American Anthropologist* 108(1): 214–220.

US Committee for Refugees World Refugee Survey. 2004. United States Refugee Commission. www.refugees.org/article.aspx?id=1156.

Wali, Sima. 1995. "Human Rights for Refugee and Displaced Women." In Julie Peters, and Andrea Wolper, eds. *Women's Rights, Human Rights: International Feminist Perspectives*. New York: Routledge, pp. 335–344.

5

RIGHTS TO INDIGENOUS CULTURE
IN COLOMBIA*

Jean E. Jackson

INTRODUCTION

This chapter uses three cases from indigenous Colombia to examine the at times awkward relationship between the set of "basic" human rights seen to reside in individuals (e.g., the right to be free from killing, torture, or forced exile) and a set of collective rights known as "rights to culture" (also known as "rights to difference"). Both sets of rights appear in various covenants and treaties to which the country has been a signatory, and they share some – but only some – of the same intellectual and moral underpinnings. I also examine the problematic way both the Colombian government and indigenous communities (henceforth *pueblos*[1]) appeal to a discourse of culture when disputes arise over who is entitled to claim the "right to culture." The conflicts these three cases illustrate have arisen in no small part due to the fact that campaigns supporting basic human rights, and the mobilizations around indigenous rights, have emerged out of significantly different histories.

* I would like to thank Mark Goodale and Sally Merry for organizing this project and seeing it through. I am also grateful to Joanne Rappaport, Margarita Chaves, Mark Goodale, Hugh Gusterson, and Sally Merry who read drafts and made useful suggestions. Advice and information provided during conversations with Floro Tunubalá in October 2004, and Luís Evelis Andrade in February 23–24, 2006 are also gratefully acknowledged. The usual disclaimers apply.
[1] *Pueblo*, a Spanish word meaning both "community," and "people," is shorter. All translations are my own.

I have been conducting research since 1968 on various topics in the Vaupés, a department[2] in the southeastern part of the country. In the early 1980s I became interested in the indigenous rights mobilizing taking place in the region, and subsequently expanded that interest to include the organizing at the national and international levels (see Warren and Jackson 2002; Jackson and Warren 2005). Security concerns have prevented me from returning to the Vaupés (my last visit took place in 1993) and, although I continue to travel to the country, I have not embarked on a new long-term, ethnography-intensive research project. In consequence, for the most part this chapter utilizes secondary sources.

Background

In Colombia, as elsewhere in Latin America, indigenous mobilizing at the national level took off during a period of political liberalization in the 1980s and 1990s known as the democratic transition. These reforms included a return to civilian rule and, with some exceptions, a reduction of repressive state responses to dissent. Sixteen Latin American countries instituted constitutional reforms.[3] Throughout Latin America, but especially in Colombia, the reforms were intended to address problems of corruption and lack of legitimacy, and to promote rights discourses that would go a long way toward solving the "crisis of representation" that characterized many governments in the region.

A key component of the reforms was the acknowledgment of the diversity found within Latin American countries, often described in the new constitutions in terms of a pluriethnic and multicultural citizenry. The reforms seriously challenged dominant imaginaries of the proper citizen as Spanish- (or Portuguese-) speaking, Catholic, and "modern." Many countries redefined their pueblos' legal status. In more general terms, the reforms ushered in an era in which the very meanings of citizenship, and of the state itself, were rethought.

Indigenous people have always been Latin America's most disadvantaged and powerless sector, and throughout the past five centuries mobilizations to protest exploitation, illegal appropriation of lands, and other forms of institutionalized discrimination have been mounted. A characteristic of the campaigns of the past twenty-odd years has been

---

[2] A Colombian *departamento* is the equivalent of a US state.
[3] Argentina, Bolivia, Brazil, Chile, Colombia, Costa Rica, Dominican Republic, Ecuador, Guatemala, Mexico, Nicaragua, Panama, Paraguay, Peru, Uruguay, and Venezuela (Van Cott 2000).

a shift in argument from a "rights as minorities" discourse to one claiming "rights as peoples." Pueblos that argue from a position that claims *inherent* rights, which derive from their status as autochthonous peoples, are employing a discourse that avoids the assimilationist implications of earlier appeals to minority rights. While the latter signals membership in a larger polity, the inherent rights argument strengthens claims to autonomy and self-determination. Demands at the top of activists' lists have included support for bilingual education, traditional medical systems, collective land titling, and self-government at local and regional levels. Legal leverage backing up these demands is provided by the various international covenants and treaties ratified by many Latin American states, among them the 1989 International Labor Organization's Indigenous and Tribal Peoples Convention 169.[4]

Somewhat difficult to pinpoint because of their diffuse nature are the effects on Latin American indigenous organizing of the embrace throughout the region of multiculturalism, a set of ideas that celebrates and works to protect ethnic and cultural diversity.[5] In many Latin American venues, certainly Colombian ones, indigenous otherness has come to be seen to involve a nonmaterialist and spiritual relation to the land, consensual decision making, a holistic environmentalist perspective, and a goal of reestablishing harmony in the social and physical worlds. Embedded in these values are critiques of occidental forms of authority, and the tendency to see nature as something to control and commodify. The notion that sovereignty should be invested in the nation-state has also been challenged, along with the state's monopoly on legitimate violence and claim to be the sole authority to define democracy, citizenship, penal codes, and jurisdiction (see Van Cott 2005). Unfortunately, although the region's recent

---

[4] Other agreements include the UN's draft Declaration on the Rights of Indigenous Peoples, and the draft Inter-American Declaration on the Rights of Indigenous Peoples (see Ramos 1998; also Swepston 1998).

[5] The earlier official discourse championed "universal and undifferentiated citizenship, shared national identity and equality before the law" (Sieder 2002a: 4–5; also see Yashar 2005). Needless to say, racial, ethnic and class inequities throughout the region have always revealed a considerable gap between the discourse and reality. The degree to which multicultural projects dovetail with neoliberal interests is hotly debated; see, for instance, Hale 2002, 2004; Povinelli 2002. Although multiculturalism does not constitute an ideology in the sense of masking a dominant class interest (Povinelli 2002: 25), an obviously crucial question remains as to why, in contrast to earlier hegemonic visions of the post-colonial state as culturally homogeneous and politically centralized, so many Latin American elites have found it in their interest to promote multiculturalism.

democratization does constitute a significant achievement, for the most part the impact has been confined to the formal domains of constitutional recognition of indigenous rights, a modest amount of protective legislation, and limited gains in the way of judicial decisions. Equally unfortunately, following the reforms, in response to directives from international lending agencies promoting neoliberal policies, legislation was passed in several countries, including Colombia, that decreased the effectiveness of the constitutionally mandated protections. All in all, despite the reforms, Latin America's indigenous people continue to make up the poorest sector, and many communities face a seriously eroding economic base.

In Colombia all of this change has taken place within the context of a sixty-year-old conflict that successive governments, corrupt and structurally weak, have not been able to end (see Chernick 2005). Several kinds of armed actors are involved, including Marxist insurgents, paramilitaries, and state security forces. Narcotraffickers have often complicated the picture through their large campaign contributions and other types of political and financial support which, although illegal, politicians and their supporters have often found hard to resist. Both the guerrillas and the paramilitaries have been heavily involved in the illegal drug trade since the early 1980s. The war has taken more than 350,000 lives, the vast majority of them civilians (Green 2005: 139), and created 3.2 million internally displaced people (out of a total population of 43 million). Speeded-up globalization and capitalist expansion have also played a part.

The country's pueblos took an adamant stance against the US-backed Plan Colombia (a six-year aid package begun in 2000[6]), protesting what they saw as a disproportionate part[7] of the aid package going to help the military and police effort to eradicate illegal drug cultivation. The strategy included aerial spraying of illegal crops, which resulted in complaints about negative health consequences and damage to food crops. Critics of the Plan argued in favor of a majority of the funds being used to promote economic and social development, in particular projects aimed at manual eradication of illegal crops and crop substitution.

---

[6] Developed by former President Andrés Pastrana (1998–2002) and the Clinton administration, Plan Colombia was implemented on July 13, 2000 and ended six years later. The Plan's stated purpose was to eradicate illegal drugs; additional goals were finding a way to end the country's forty-year-old armed conflict, and to promote economic and social development.
[7] In any given year between 68 and 75 percent of the funds; see Ramírez 2005: 54.

Many Latin American countries have been the recipients of various neoliberal economic restructuring packages mandated by international funding organizations like the World Bank and the Inter-American Development Bank. Most Colombian pueblos oppose the free-trade agreements the country has entered into, arguing that the poor are hit hardest by structural adjustment and other austerity measures intended to reduce fiscal and political instability and increase foreign investment. For example, leaders worry that new forest management laws being pushed by the Uribe administration would hand over territory controlled by pueblos to major corporate interests (Murillo 2006: 5–6). In October 2004 a campaign organized by the *Consejo Regional Indígenadel Cauca* (CRIC) (Regional Indigenous Council of Cauca) and the *Associación de Cabildos Indigenas del Cauca* (ACIN) (Indigenous Authorities Association from the North of Cauca), which called for a public vote on the free-trade agreement being negotiated between Colombia, Peru, Ecuador and the United States, resulted in 98 percent of some 50,000 participants voting "no" to the free-trade agreement.[8] Similar non-binding public referenda have been held more recently. Neither the government of Andrés Pastrana (1998–2002) nor of Álvaro Uribe Vélez (2002–2006) has been willing to enter into serious dialogue with the sectors that have organized these protests.

Indigenous activists throughout Latin America often speak of the importance of the concept of collective rights for achieving autonomy and advancing other demands (see, for example, Van Cott 2005: 235). Stavenhagen points out that granting rights to culture often presupposes collective rights "since some of these rights can only be enjoyed by individuals in community with others, and such a community must have the possibility to preserve, protect and develop its common culture" (2002: 37). Pueblos struggle to convince government bureaucrats and the courts of the validity of indigenous collective understandings of their *"usos y costumbres"* (uses and customs) – known as customary law. In general the concept of collective rights has been resisted by nation-states (see Rosen 1997). Western jurisprudence has consistently displayed an ambivalence toward the idea, which stems in part from the unfamiliar concepts underpinning the nature of those rights. Western notions of rights are based on an ideology that foregrounds the individual as the economic agent, bearer of rights and obligations, and owner of property, as well as the notion that policies

[8] Molano. 2004. Also see *Miami Herald*: "300,000 protesters jam Bogotá square" October 14, 2004.

and laws should (at least theoretically) apply to all citizens uniformly. An example of such resistance is the United Kingdom's decision in 2004 that collective human rights do not exist.[9] Another is a Canadian court's 1980 ruling that courts "cannot consider the merits of a case respecting the collective rights of an indigenous party until that party establishes to the satisfaction of the trial judge the extent to which 'they and their ancestors were members of an organized society' prior to the arrival of European settlers" – virtually impossible in Canada, given the criteria Europeans employed at the time to characterize "organized society."[10]

Goodale in his Introduction to this title points out that while western conceptualizations of human rights have for the most part located them in the individual, in fact the motivation for defining and protecting them came from vulnerable populations experiencing horrendous victimization throughout the twentieth century. The Colombian cases show how attempts to reduce one kind of group vulnerability – the ethnocide and genocide faced by Colombian pueblos (see Stavenhagen 2005; Jackson 2005) – clash with attempts to ease another kind of vulnerability through the recognition and legal protection of certain basic rights individuals are considered to possess by virtue of their membership in the human race.[11]

In sum, indigenous activists' insistence on collective rights, including control over resources, and pueblos' right to develop their institutions and development projects based on local *usos y costumbres*, challenge the foundational assumptions of official juridical systems throughout Latin America.

Perspectives and aims of essay

The three Colombian cases presented here were chosen in part for their ability to illustrate some of the on-the-ground effects of the importation of transnational human rights regimes into the country. The cases permit an exploration of "the extent to which not only national but

---

[9] "Collective Rights & the UK – 2004" www.survival-international.org/news.phi?id=171, accessed February 8, 2007.
[10] *The Hamlet of Baker Lake* (1980), as cited in Asch 2005: 432–433. Blackburn discusses the distinct "flavor of empire and of frontier" characterizing British Columbia (compared to the rest of Canada), which was, until very recently, reflected in disputes over land ownership (2005: 587–588).
[11] Speed's chapter in this book (chapter 4) provides a Mexican case that illustrates the tensions between universalism and relativism and between individual and collective rights. Also see Speed 2006: 72.

also international legal regimes ... dictate the contours and content of claims and even of identities" (Cowan, Dembour, and Wilson 2001: 11). In the Introduction to this volume, Goodale argues that the notion of "transcultural universal human rights is itself a product of particular histories and cultural imperatives, so that it is simply not possible to consider the idea of human rights 'in the abstract' ". Goodale also argues that the concept of transnationalism should not be confined to a literal meaning (i.e., involving interaction between two or more national states), which may lead to an over-emphasis on the activities "most symbolic of the trans-boundary and horizontal interconnections that define ... contemporary human rights networks" (Goodale, Introduction to this volume), and a neglect of other, less immediately visible, activities. In this chapter, "transnational" at times refers to indigenous "nations" (pueblos) interacting with other pueblos, the Colombian nation, or both. The cases I present provide instances of transnational human rights discourse penetrating into, and in turn being modified and transmitted out of, the most isolated and marginalized of locales, a clear instance of human rights theories being shaped and conceptualized "outside the centers of elite discourse" (Goodale, Introduction to this volume). They also illustrate Merry's point that the notion of "local" is "deeply problematic" (2006: 39). Each case illustrates how pueblo members and institutions creatively engage the specific logics of liberal multiculturalism, adopting what Wilson characterizes as "pluralizing strategies adopted by indigenous elites that employ the deceptively novel language of human rights" (2006: 79). The cases support Goodale's point that "the sites where human rights unfold in practice do matter, and these sites are not simply nodes in a virtual network, but actual *places* in social space, places which can become law-like and coercive" (Introduction, p. 13 above). Hence, the best theoretical framework for analyzing the Colombian materials proves to be a discursive approach to human rights, one that assumes that "social practice is, in part, constitutive of the idea of human rights, rather than simply the testing ground ..." (Introduction, p. 8 above).

We shall see that claiming and successfully securing these rights requires a performance on the part of Colombian pueblos that powerfully indexes such isolation and marginality, geographical and otherwise, in order to maximally promote the likelihood that they will continue to qualify as legitimate grantees of their rights to culture. Unlike many kinds of people who claim various rights – women's rights, children's rights, worker's rights, and so on – who are members of fairly unproblematic categories, the kinds of people claiming indigenous rights may be challenged as not indigenous, or not indigenous enough. The cases presented below, particularly the third, illustrate a pueblo strategy aimed at gaining official recognition, maintaining protection of *"usos y costumbres,"* and improving access to resources, including land. The strategy was developed upon pueblos' discovery that they needed to establish and regularly reestablish their legitimacy – legal and otherwise – through a rhetoric of cultural difference and continuity with a traditional past. We shall see that at times the rhetoric asserts an incommensurability between the western and pueblo rights systems. That is, not only is there at times no compelling reason for pueblos to translate their cosmologies or social practices into the westernized language of mainstream rights, at times pueblos will have strategic reasons to present their cosmologies and traditional *usos y costumbres* as simply untranslatable.[12] Adopting this position helps to establish and maintain claims to sovereignty, especially during disputes involving the interface between customary law and western law.

Finally, this chapter illustrates Goodale's point about scale, that notwithstanding the frequency with which human rights is articulated in global terms, in practice the scale within which human rights is actually encountered is far smaller. Of course a danger lurks, that of spiraling "into the regress of particularism that often characterizes accounts of human rights practice" (Introduction, p. 11 above). I believe these Colombian cases help us to address broader issues, for example, those concerned with the problematic arising from any effort to protect human rights through constitutional guarantees when sovereignty is located in an idea of "people" conceived of as diverse.

THE CASES

Colombia's 1991 Constitution and subsequent legislation confirm the country's status as a multicultural and pluri-ethnic nation.[13] Members of pueblos are rights-bearing autonomous citizens with special indigenous rights; that is, the Constitution guarantees pueblos' right to participate in civil society as ethnic citizens. The most recent phase of Colombian indigenous organizing, begun in the late 1970s, vividly

---

[12] See Graham 2002, and Rappaport 2005 on the notion of incommensurability.
[13] The actual language reads: "The state recognizes and protects the ethnic and cultural diversity of the Colombian Nation." *Constitución Política de Colombia* 1991, Art. 7.

illustrates the international turn toward a rights discourse. Rights language has deeply influenced the choices about what kind of demands to make and how best to articulate claims. Indigenous leaders have climbed on the rights rhetoric bandwagon in a number of ways.

The first way, claiming the "right to have rights," argues from the position of an excluded minority population (Ramírez 2002; see Dagnino 1998: 50). While at times protests have focused on an abusive, even terrorist, state, at other times the complaint has pointed to an absent state; in such locales residents find they are effectively non-citizens with next to no *de facto* rights, an especially acute problem in Colombia where the state is totally absent or minimally present (e.g., police garrisons in the larger towns) in a fourth of the national territory (see Ramírez 2001, 2002).

The second way concerns the right to participate in the political process by running for public office. Given that only two percent of the country's population is indigenous, the gains in this area have been nothing short of spectacular. Three indigenous representatives of national organizations served on the Constituent Assembly that wrote the constitution, and they significantly influenced parts of the resulting document (Laurent 2004; Gros 2000; Murillo 1996). Currently, indigenous representatives serve as legislators at both national and departmental levels, participate in municipal politics, and one, Floro Tunubalá, a Guambiano, served a term as governor of the department of Cauca in the southern part of the country. Indigenous candidates' platforms often crusade for openness and transparency and denounce "politics as usual" – usually seen to result in *de facto* disenfranchisement and a government of elites that serves elites.[14] Exclusionary rhetoric has often been avoided, particularly at the national level, and indigenous leaders have sought to form alliances with nonindigenous popular organizations, leftist cadres, and intellectuals. Such activist-politicians present an alternative that appeals to unattached, disaffected voters, both indigenous and nonindigenous.

The third way indigenous leaders have employed a rights discourse involves their insistence on the "right to difference," which opens the door to an expansive, heterogeneous definition of "rights." For example, some activists, indigenous and not, have championed "Andean democracy," which envisions the community assembly of heads of

---

[14] This discussion of indigenous politicians mainly comes from Van Cott 2005.

households as the authoritative decision-making body, working by consensus rather than majority rule (Assies 2000: 9).

In Colombia discourses about indigenous rights are often highly dynamic; close examination reveals processes of institutionalization in which actors mutually influence each other. Interactions between indigenous leaders and state functionaries will wring concessions from the latter, which in turn inspire activists to re-frame their demands in novel, often more expansive ways.

The 1991 constitution and subsequent legislation specify that "customary law" will have power within indigenous territories (known as *resguardos*, which are collectively owned and inalienable). The Colombian constitution recognizes locally elected councils called *cabildos* as the governing authority, in keeping with the communities' *usos y costumbres*.[15] This constitution promotes indigenous juridical autonomy to the greatest extent in Latin America (Stavenhagen 2002: 33).[16] In most countries, when the two systems interact, the national legal system has almost inevitably taken precedence, revealing the basic hierarchy, rather than parity, characterizing the relationship (see Yrigoyen 2002). We shall see that at times Colombia is an exception.

Constitutional recognition of customary law in Colombia (and elsewhere in Latin America) has been interpreted by many analysts as a covert critique of the state, an acknowledgment that the state itself needs to be restructured. Utterly ineffective and corrupt courts have been unable to act independently to carry out the rule of law in rural affairs, whether it be in land disputes, theft, or interpersonal violence.[17] The hope for a restructured Colombian state, especially palpable during the constitutional assembly deliberations in 1990, is understandable in a country suffering the effects of a long-running civil war and saddled with a weak government unable to administer a substantial part of its territory. One extraordinary critique of government legitimacy argues that indigenous people's highly participatory norms for decision-making can potentially help achieve democratization throughout the

---

[15] The actual wording of Article 330 reads: "In conformity with the Constitution and the laws, indigenous territories will be governed by councils created and regulated in keeping with the uses and customs of the communities . . ."

[16] Note that one should not conceive of indigenous "customary law" in terms of a single coherent body of indigenous customary law (see Sieder 2002a: 39).

[17] Donna Van Cott, personal communication February 2006.

country (Van Cott 2000; Rappaport 2003[18]). The same has been claimed for Colombia's indigenous juridical structures: one reason behind the official state support of local juridical systems is to reduce case backlogs, eliminate extra-institutional conflict resolution and violence, and formally recognize the legitimacy and effectiveness of local institutions that are often perceived as more legitimate than state courts (Van Cott 2000: 74, 112, 113–116).

The legitimacy of pueblo rule of law in the eyes of mainstream Colombian society has been strengthened by pueblo members' responses to the violence perpetrated on them. In 2001, for example, when members of the larger (of two) guerrilla armies, the *Fuerzas Armadas Revolucionarias de Colombia* (FARC) (Colombian Armed Revolutionary Forces), began firing homemade mortars on a police station in the Nasa (also known as Páez) community of Toribío, over 4,000 unarmed community members flooded its streets, ending the attack (Rappaport 2003: 41). On other occasions dozens of community members will travel to a guerrilla stronghold to obtain release of a kidnapped leader.[19] Following the demobilization in 1990 of an indigenous guerrilla organization known as Quintín Lame, the Nasa resolved to oppose the presence of all armed actors in their territory.[20] Beginning in the late 1990s they developed a campaign of pacific civil resistance, organizing an Indigenous Guard (*guardia indígena*), whose members are unarmed, save for ceremonial staffs.[21] The Guard currently numbers about 7,000 men and women.[22] This ability to arrive at a consensus and forge a collective will to act in the face of great danger has occasioned laudatory commentaries in the media,[23] church sermons, school lessons, and everyday conversations, as does pueblo members' obvious respect for leaders and traditional authorities.

---

[18] For a Mexican case, see Nash 2001.
[19] See "Colombia: FARC releases indigenous leaders," about four hundred Nasa obtaining the release of Arquímedes Vitonás, mayor of Toribío, in September 2004 (*Weekly Indigenous News*, culturalsurvival.org, reporting on a Reuters press release, September 17). Also see "Indígenas rescatan su alcalde." *El Tiempo*, April 14, 2003.
[20] Mercado. 1993.   [21] Valencia. 2001.
[22] Forero. 2005; Dudley. 2005; Klein. 2005. Also see Rappaport 2003; and Murillo 2006.
[23] An example is the interest displayed when governors of fourteen indigenous cabildos in northern Cauca received the National Peace Prize for their "Proyecto NASA" a coalition working to maintain community neutrality and autonomy in the face of threats by armed combatants: "'Más que neutrales, autónomos'." *El Espectador* December 12, 2000.

The case of Francisco Gembuel

Following the approval of the 1991 Constitution, the country's indigenous cabildos suddenly began to be presented with cases involving accusations of serious crimes. Although in the distant past local authorities had dealt with such cases, their legal machinery had long fallen into disuse, as prior to 1991 they had been handed over to the state. The pressure on cabildos to rise to the challenge of adjudicating cases like these has been substantial. To begin with, the bare fact of being able to exercise authority in this important domain has great appeal. Also, as the entire process that led to the codification of new ethnic rights came about through direct, successful engagement with the state and political elite (Van Cott 2005; Yashar 2005), by showing they could succeed here as well, leaders hoped to retain, and if possible increase, the overall political strength, moral capital, and public support they had acquired up to that point.

The Gembuel case is quite complex and aspects not relevant to my argument have been omitted.[24] Some of the complexities are crucial, however, as they illustrate how the resolution of such disputed sentences invariably occurs in extremely politicized contexts including, in the Colombian case, situations in which indigenous special jurisdiction is being created at the same time it is being applied. My concern here is to pay particular attention to the pueblos' perception that defending their jurisdiction and their juridical norms is crucial to the maintenance of their general legal status, both in the eyes of their fellow Colombian citizens and abroad. I particularly consider the general point made above: pueblos' evolving awareness that while at times they need to translate their legal and moral reasoning – often a very difficult task – into language that mainstream institutions can understand, at other times they need to argue that their reasoning is in fact too "other" to be able to be adequately translated. Asserting such incommensurability, what Rappaport terms "the expression of sovereignty through cultural difference" (2005: 236), strengthens their claim to being truly indigenous in the eyes of those who would challenge it.

The national media regularly report cases of "traditional" punishments being meted out. For example, one article in the daily *El Tiempo* titled "Stocks, to irresponsible fathers: Páez women do not tolerate being abandoned," describes the decision by a female governor of a

---

[24] Rappaport 2005, chapter 7 provides a much fuller discussion of this case. Also see Van Cott 2000: 114–116 Assies 2003: 174–177; Sánchez 2004: 421–436.

cabildo to impose a sentence of stocks on men who neglect their wives and children. The article notes that while stocks are a traditional punishment for homicide and theft, sentencing irresponsible fathers to this punishment is new.[25] The individuals punished with these stocks (introduced by the Spaniards[26]) hang upside down by the ankles (the *El Tiempo* article notes that "many of the punished remain with serious injuries on the ankles"). Another article relates how the former governor of a cabildo was given fourteen whip lashes (administered with a cattle whip on the legs) for the crime of adultery and neglect.[27] A third article reports on an adulterous pair receiving seventeen lashes. One of the whippers, the mother of the woman, said, "I'm sorry, daughter, but this is our law and we have to follow it."[28]

On August 19, 1996, the cabildo of Jambaló, a Nasa resguardo in the department of Cauca in the southwestern part of the country, found Francisco Gembuel Pechené, a Guambiano resident of Jambaló, and several companions guilty of murdering Marden Betancur Conda, a Nasa. Gembuel subsequently challenged the verdict, claiming procedural irregularities and insufficient evidence to convict. Gembuel said he supported the cabildo's use of these punishments in general, and that whipping and stocks had been used during his tenure as president of CRIC.[29] The case produced a great deal of discussion throughout the country. Gembuel and several other men (the number given by newspaper accounts varies from five to twelve; Van Cott [2000: 114] gives seven) had publicly accused Betancur of being a *pájaro*, a hired assassin in the employ of the paramilitaries in the area. The National Liberation Army (*Ejército de Liberación Nacional* – ELN), the smaller of Colombia's two guerrilla armies, had carried out the actual killing, gunning him down during a municipal celebration. The Jambaló cabildo accused the men as the intellectual authors of the crime. Both Gembuel and Betancur were well-known leaders; Gembuel had been a member of Jambaló's cabildo, and president of the CRIC, and Betancur was Jambaló's mayor when he was killed. The initial provocation was said to have been resentment on the part of Gembuel and his allies, who

---

[25] *El Tiempo* "Cepo, a padres irresponsables: mujeres paeces no tolerán el abandono" May 10, 2000.

[26] Rappaport 2005: 250; *El Tiempo*, " 'Siempre he obrado de manera limpia' " July 12, 1998.

[27] "The whip for an indigenous governor," *El Tiempo* May 14, 2000. Interestingly, the rector of the school defends the accused, Feliciano Valencia, saying he "shouldn't be blamed because women love him so much."

[28] "Castigan pareja indígena paez por infidelidad." *El Espectador*, June 5, 2000.

[29] Mompotes. 1997b.

belonged to a rival CRIC faction, that Betancur had won Jambaló's highly contested 1994 mayoral election. Gembuel was sentenced to fifteen minutes in the stocks, sixty whip lashes, and banishment from Nasa territory.[30] The others received the same or lesser sentences.

Residents of Jambaló were divided with respect to which authority should have conducted the trial – some believed the accused should have been turned over to the state judicial system. On December 24 Gembuel was given eight lashes, but his daughter and others physically blocked the administration of further punishment. The families and friends of the convicted individuals, a group of some ninety people, both indigenous and not, occupied a church in Popayán (the capital of Cauca), protesting both the sentence and the process.[31] The (non-indigenous) Public Defender of Cauca (*Defensor del Pueblo de Cauca*), a kind of ombudsman, also intervened, asking Gembuel to bring a constitutional suit ("*acción de tutela*") to avoid the punishment. He did, and the judge ruled that whipping was, in fact, torture, a decision upheld in an appellate court. International protests had been mounted; Amnesty International demanded that the sentence of whipping be suspended, and called on the civil authorities (the governor of Cauca) to prohibit further punishment of this nature.[32]

Subsequently, on January 11, an assembly of approximately a thousand Nasa decided to reopen the investigation. The assembly postponed the punishment to February 20, and stated that, come what may, they would complete the sentence on that date. A new commission was appointed to review the accusations and the entire process.[33] The cabildo governors reaffirmed that four men would receive sixty lashes, five would receive thirty, and all would be exiled. A protracted debate by representatives of sixty cabildos had preceded this decision,[34] during which many issues had surfaced, among them the dangerous influence of "white law" on indigenous law. By this time ELN had sent a communication to the cabildos saying that the killing of Betancur had

---

[30] For comparison, another article reported that cabildos in the north of Cauca carried out a sentence of fifty lashes on an Indian who had murdered his grandmother. He was also sentenced to five years of forced labor for the community. García. 1997d.

[31] "Protestan por pena de látigo a indígenas: Noventa nativos ocuparon la Basílica Menor de Popayán." *El Tiempo* January 9, 1997.

[32] On January 3, 1997 Susan Lee was cited as saying that: "the application of corporal punishment on a convict, no matter what nature of crime, constitutes a cruel, inhuman and degrading punishment, contrary to that established in Article 5 of the Universal Declaration of Human Rights." ("Amnistía rechaza latigazos a paeces." *El Tiempo* January 8, 1997).

[33] García. 1997c.   [34] García. 1997a.

been a mistake, as he had not been a hired assassin in the pay of the paramilitaries.[35]

The case wended its way to the Constitutional Court, which ruled on October 15, 1997 that concepts like human rights, due process, and torture are not universal, but context-dependent, and that the use of the whip "accorded with Nasa cosmovision and was, therefore, not an instrument of torture" (Rappaport 2005: 249). But while the appeals process was still underway, Gembuel left Nasa territory and was never punished.

The debate received widespread coverage in the newspapers and television. How the conflict was framed varied. One sympathetic article discusses how good a deterrent stocks are, for there reportedly had been only eighteen cases of robbery and infidelity in a community of around 4,600 inhabitants. After describing the stocks the article concludes: "although Colombian law does not understand this, these sanctions permit the rehabilitation of the person, because everyone witnesses the punishment being carried out, and a lesson is learned by all."[36] Another fairly sympathetic article, subtitled, "White law does not wash away the blame" quotes the Jambaló governor as saying that while they respect white law, they *have* to carry out the sentence passed down by their own judicial authorities.[37] However, accompanying this story are rather disturbing photographs of a whip and the town's stocks.

Nasa leaders defended the sentences by elaborating the intentions embedded in Nasa customary law, which, as we have seen, were picked up by the press. Unlike spending years in a penitentiary, the punishments allowed reintegration of the convicted into society. Luis Alberto Passú, governor of Jambaló, commented that even though the accused might prefer jail, "indigenous law affirms that jails are a cruelty that alienates the individual from his family and fills him with vices."[38] A nationally-known Nasa leader and former senator, Anatolio Quirá, complained that sixty-three natives were in Colombian jails, when they should have been working on behalf of their communities. He added that the only consequence of the punishment intended for Gembuel and his associates would be "the rehabilitation and reincorporation of the guilty."[39] Rappaport notes that the reconciliation between an individual and the community is achieved not only

[35] "Aplazan latigazos contra cinco indígenas paeces: Eln dice que fue un error asesinato de alcalde." *El Tiempo* January 11, 1997.
[36] Mompotes. 1997a.   [37] *El Tiempo* "Paeces levantarán 300 veces el látigo" January 10, 1997.
[38] Mompotes. 1997b.   [39] García. 1997d.

through the punishment itself but also through the four hours of ritual accompanying it, during which some cabildo officials briefly put themselves in the stocks, advice is provided, a shamanic ceremony is conducted, and, following the punishment, women ritually wash the offender's wounds (Rappaport 2005: 241).

Nasa questioned by journalists as to whether they saw their traditional punishment as torture replied in the negative; on the contrary, it was a way to secure harmony in the community.[40] Many Nasa reported being anxious about further bloodshed resulting from an inevitable deepening of the divisions between factions if the sentences were not carried out. As Passú put it, "it is possible that this [sentence] might be seen by western culture as a rebellion against the *tutela* and against ordinary law, but we are certain that it is this other law that is threatening the social equilibrium among the *indígenas*."[41] Interestingly, even one of the accused, Alirio Pitto, who was not sentenced to whipping but would lose his political rights and be exiled, confirmed that a main goal was to find a way "to end the opposition that questions the work of the governor."[42]

Another line of defense in favor of carrying out the sentences arose out of a fear that Gembuel's winning the *tutela* would set a precedent: "with this *tutela* and that *tutela* we'll eventually have to bury our stocks and our whips."[43] The stakes were high, due to a well-founded fear that the ruling in the Gembuel case would define once and for all who had the authority to judge crimes when both nonindigenous justice and indigenous justice were involved, thereby establishing the degree of autonomy permitted to the country's pueblos in this area of law. Arguments enlisted the themes of jurisdiction and incommensurability between the two legal systems. As Anatolio Quirá argued, "ordinary" (western) justice "didn't touch" the indigenous governors "because we are acting within indigenous law." Jesús Piñacué, then-president of CRIC (and future senator) said that Amnesty International's intervention "has created a confusion of laws because the Westerners don't understand indigenous law."

---

[40] García. 1997b. Note that Gembuel is quoted as saying that completing his sentence of sixty lashes on February 20 would definitely constitute torture "because one dies before all of the sixty lashes have been administered." He requests that sanctions not in violation of human rights be applied.

[41] García. 1997b.   [42] García. 1997b.

[43] *El Tiempo*, "Aplazan latigazos contra cinco indígenas paeces." January 11, 1997.

A final, crucial theme also appears: the pride felt by the Nasa of having reduced the influence of ELN in their territories. Cristóbal Secue, a Nasa leader and activist, emphasized how crucial it was that the cabildo successfully decide such cases, for failing to punish wrong-doers would virtually guarantee that "guerrilla justice" would be meted out. The wrongdoers would be killed and the influence of the armed groups in indigenous communities would once again be dramatically manifested (Rappaport 2005: 258). Rappaport concludes that a major causal factor behind the efforts to define and implement legal jurisdiction is "to establish a legitimate local authority in the face of the threat of guerrilla, paramilitary, and army hegemony, in the absence of efforts on the part of the Colombian state to contain armed actors" (2005: 244).

The Gembuel case illustrates several general themes, one of which is clearly the contradiction between *usos y costumbres* being understood as legitimate forms of legality "that must ultimately supplant Colombian legal usages in the resguardos" (Rappaport 2005: 229), and "indigenous people's individual rights as Colombian citizens to due process and to fair and reasonable punishment" (Rappaport 2005: 229). Both traditional authorities and the state juridical apparatus always play roles in cases involving indigenous and nonindigenous parties, as well as when convicted pueblo members appeal their sentence by turning to western courts, as we saw here. Disputes over jurisdiction frequently arise in such instances. Local decisions may be accused of being discriminatory, authoritarian, or intrusive into private space. Usually the underlying issue is a perceived incompatibility between local fact-finding procedures or the decision itself, and fundamental tenets of western law. In Colombia customary law involves issues of social citizenship, ethnic minority demands, and human rights, but also playing a role is a community's awareness that it needs a consensus about conceptions of, and proper performance of, "otherness" if their collective pueblo identity is to remain in good standing in everyone's eyes, their own and outsiders'. The effort to clarify the relationship between indigenous special jurisdiction and western law is still very much under construction, an effort taking place in grassroots legal committees, cabildo meetings, assemblies attended by authorities (from, as we have seen, as many as sixty cabildos), appellate courts, and the Constitutional Court itself (see Rappaport 2005: 235). It is clear that, no matter where the Colombian experiment in legal pluralism ends up, special indigenous jurisdiction will always exist in tension with the mainstream justice system, and such tensions will probably periodically "explode" in the future (Cowan, Dembour, and Wilson 2001: 10), as they did here.

In her discussion of the Gembuel case, Rappaport notes that the Constitutional Court decided not to conceive of Colombian indigenous jurisdiction in terms of ancient practices that have persisted across time and that need to be discovered and re-implemented. Rather, special jurisdiction must be seen as a kind of "counter-modernity," which incorporates a unique indigenous morality, something being instantiated and shaped in situations peopled with such a variety of agents, some of whom most definitely do not have Nasa interests uppermost in mind. The Gembuel case reveals a range of actors representing a range of interests – Jambaló residents, other Nasa resguardos, other Colombian pueblos, national indigenous organizations and their allies, state authorities, armed combatants, a curious public, and international organizations like Amnesty International. The degree to which pueblos will be allowed to *create* their own laws, as opposed to discovering them in past traditions and practices (Santos 2001: 208, as cited in Rappaport 2005: 240), is unknown. Individual Constitutional Court judges' decisions have varied in this respect, some taking into consideration what they term varying levels of cultural "purity" (degrees of acculturation), others not (Van Cott 2000: 113–116). The Jambaló decision received the attention it did in part because the ruling magistrate, Carlos Gaviria Díaz, did not take such "purity" questions into account. Rather, he allowed Nasa authorities to describe the intention behind their laws, which led to the finding that whipping did not constitute torture because its purpose was not to cause excessive suffering, but to ritually purify the violator and welcome him or her back into the community, thus restoring harmony.[44]

The case of Jesús Piñacué

During the 1997 presidential campaign, Jesús Enrique Piñacué Achicué, a Nasa senator in the Colombian parliament, voted publicly for the Liberal candidate, Horacio Serpa, despite having agreed with Nasa authorities and the *Alianza Social Indígena* (Indigenous Social Alliance – ASI – a coalition of left-leaning groups), one of two political parties supporting him, that he would cast a blank vote. Piñacué

---

[44] Quite pertinent to our concerns here, Gaviria maintained that "only a high degree of autonomy would ensure cultural survival" (Van Cott 2000: 115).

defended himself by saying that he had always worked in a "clean" manner in his public life.[45] A coalition composed of ASI and the *Franja Amarilla* (Yellow Stripe) party had put him up for office, and in the moment of choosing an option, Piñacué later stated that "in a conscious and free manner" he decided to vote for Serpa, *Franja Amarilla*'s candidate. Accusing Piñacué of "high treason," the president of ASI said that choosing to honor the other party's request constituted a violation of autochthonous laws.[46] According to ASI officials, Piñacué's action constituted a serious misstep, for he had bypassed indigenous honor codes as well as revealing an unacceptable attitude.[47] ASI was also angry about Piñacué's alliance with a traditional party (the Liberals), but what had really hurt them, officials said, was the fact that he had not kept his word. Piñacué announced that he would not assume the senate seat he had been elected to, scheduled for July 20, because he considered himself "morally impeded to represent the indigenous community before the country" until the matter could be resolved.[48] He commented that he did not repent of renouncing his senate seat because he preferred losing it to losing his fatherland: "*Asistiré a Paniquitá y me someteré al fallo para no perder mi patria.*"[49]).

An assembly was scheduled for July 15 to consider ASI's demand. During the ensuing discussions, ASI held firm, but it became clear that various cabildos supported Piñacué, who noted that it was ASI that was questioning his vote for Serpa, rather than the overall indigenous community, and that "although ASI requests the punishment, not everyone in the indigenous community is in favor of it."[50] CRIC subsequently scheduled another assembly for both the 15th and 16th, in a town in Paniquitá (Totoró) in the eastern part of Cauca, some four hours by road from the location of the assembly ASI had scheduled. The ASI assembly was cancelled after Piñacué asserted that he would not attend it. Piñacué had said that, rather than ASI, his "legitimate judges are the indigenous communities, with their governors."[51] Although he did not explicitly refer to ASI's juridical legitimacy, this statement clearly challenged ASI's authority to conduct such a meeting, its cancellation an obvious loss of face for the organization. Piñacué

---

[45] *El Tiempo*, " 'Siempre he obrado de manera limpia' " July 12, 1998.
[46] *El Tiempo* "Piñacué no se posesionará como senador," July 9, 1998.
[47] Mompotes. 1998b.   [48] *El Tiempo* "Piñacué no se posesionará como senador," July 9, 1998.
[49] Mompotes. 1998b.   [50] *El Tiempo* "Piñacué no se posesionará como senador," July 9, 1998.
[51] *El Tiempo*, "Juicio 'político' indígena: Jesús Piñacué será juzgado en su comunidad por votar por Serpa," July 12, 1998. The rest of this paragraph is taken from the same article.

said he respected the decision to punish him according to Nasa law, and he would not dodge the judgment, even if he were sentenced to be whipped.

Prior to the meeting possible punishments were discussed: physical (whip and stocks), and "moral." The latter would consist of not allowing Piñacué to assume public office. Such "moral" punishment is a form of ostracism: while the convicted are not forcibly exiled, they are politically isolated.[52] Twelve cabildo governors from the north favored whipping, and discussed a sentence of fifty lashes. During this period Piñacué spoke with many Nasa, analyzing the possibility of his being absolved in light of Nasa law.

Piñacué requested punishment in the form of being thrown into the sacred lake of Juan Tama in the eastern part of Cauca, a traditional ritual that had lapsed at the beginning of the twentieth century but revived in 1983. Piñacué cited a statement by culture hero Juan Tama: "the Nasa should never permit external visions to intrude into Nasa spirituality."[53] Juan Tama had made these remarks before disappearing into the lake 200 years earlier, out of desperation about divisions within the Nasa pueblo.[54]

On the appointed day of July 15 the deliberations, in the form of private discussion (no cameras or tape recorders), began.[55] In the middle of the discussions the judges found that no whip could be located; none of the 500 who attended the Paniquitá session had brought one.[56] Although the governor of Paniquitá commented that "during the decision-making it is better to have a whip ready at hand," he himself hadn't whipped "even his children." In fact, no one had been punished in this manner in Paniquitá. Several authorities left to look for a whip. Another reason given as to why no one had thought to bring a whip was because many people felt that Piñacué did not deserve to be punished "for acting in a democratic manner."

Thirty-five governors agreed to a sentence of a "sacred wash" in Juan Tama lake, a ritual of "refrescamiento" ("cooling").[57] This ritual would be secret and conducted in silence, preceded by deep meditation.[58] Piñacué would first walk for more than six hours to get to the lake, a difficult journey that needed permission from various Nasa shamans and required very experienced guides. At dawn, after he and ten

[52] *El Tiempo* "Una justicia de dolor y leyenda" July 12, 1998.
[53] Mompotes. 1998b.   [54] Campo. 1998.   [55] Mompotes. 1998a.
[56] Mompotes. 1998b. The rest of this paragraph draws on this article.
[57] Campo. 1998.   [58] García 16. 1998. The rest of this paragraph draws on this article.

shamans had spent the night in the freezing cold (at 4,400 meters) they would throw him, nude, into the water. This dunking would bring new energy to him "in order to begin to walk the road back" to re-incorporation within the Nasa community. In the process of getting out of the extremely cold lake Piñacué would use up every bit of energy, liberating him from the "bad spirits." Following the punishment Piñacué would be able to assume his seat in the senate, and continue to represent indigenous cabildos. He would also have to acknowledge his error in front of the governors and the public, both indigenous and nonindigenous, as well as agree to improve his conduct. Finally, Piñacué would have to visit all of the resguardos to beg pardon and ratify his commitments with his community. ASI agreed with this punishment. Piñacué subsequently did ask for forgiveness "before public opinion," and acknowledged that he had committed an infraction of the rules. But he also excused himself somewhat by saying the mistake happened due to the impossibility of consulting with the authorities in time.[59]

The Gembuel and Piñacué cases have a lot in common, although the outcomes differed fundamentally, and electoral politics played a major role in the latter. Once again, newspapers and television turned their gaze to customary law. Once again questions were raised about the legitimacy of these laws: because they had been passed down orally from generation to generation, "details about amount and manner of administering or about the kinds of crimes that warranted the punishments were lacking."[60] Once again justifications were proffered based on rehabilitating the accused by punishing and shaming them before the community.

Once again, voices were heard expressing anxiety that serious internal divisions might be exacerbated. And although debates on the degree of ASI's juridical legitimacy were not referred to in the national media, clearly they represented another potential source of ill will. Once again the importance of arriving at a correct solution was described as crucial to the maintenance of traditional order and justice. Once again the press reported pueblo members' conviction that indigenous customary law was superior in several important respects – an example being ASI member Manuel Santos Poto's comment that being thrown in prison "far from one's community and lands" was worse than whipping.[61]

[59] Mompotes. 1998a.   [60] *El Tiempo* "Una justicia de dolor y leyenda" July 12, 1998.
[61] *El Tiempo* "Una justicia de dolor y leyenda" July 12, 1998.

The Piñacué case demonstrates many of the complications that can arise when indigenous communities attempt to apply traditional justice systems in highly visible, politicized contexts. An insistence that Nasa laws be followed and Nasa traditional authorities be respected stood side by side with worries about increased factionalization and concerns to minimize negative publicity produced by punishments seen by mainstream society to violate basic human rights.[62]

The case also produced instances of a discourse encountered in the larger society about the valuable lessons to be learned from the life ways of the country's indigenous citizens. In a piece titled "Social laboratory," the columnist Manuel Hernández begins by speaking about how the new constitution finally provides "recognition and identity to Colombia's ethnic communities, which suffered discrimination and abandonment."[63] Under continuing great hardships, he continues, Colombia's pueblos are working hard, and have constructive lessons to teach the rest of the country. The "moral sanction" Piñacué underwent demonstrates the vitality of indigenous customs. Hernández criticizes the way some journalists sensationalized the story, saying they intended to "damage the relations within the [indigenous] community, as well as advance the media's political ends." Hernández comments that in the Piñacué case, unlike mainstream society, punishers and the accused had joked among themselves during the long walk, and although the punishment was indeed meted out, "the power of individual jurisdiction remained intact." Also, he continues, the antagonism and ill will, so frequent in judicial proceedings "of the so-called 'civilized' sectors" were absent. "This demonstrates that pueblos know to withstand the siege mounted by the mass media, which so often attempts to put words in the mouths of people in the news, a morbid fascination actually invented by the journalists themselves."

The role played by whips, stocks and coerced exile in both cases resonates with Elizabeth Povinelli's employment of the concept of "repugnance" in her examination of Australia's multiculturalist laws and federal policies. When behaviors become "repugnant" they threaten to "shatter the skeletal structure" of state law. The resulting experience of "fundamental alterity" transforms the subaltern into

---

[62] See Sierra (1995), for a Mexican judicial proceeding involving somewhat similar discussions.
[63] Hernández. 1998. The rest of this paragraph is based on this article.

something so profoundly "not-us" that an impasse is reached (2002: 17).[64] Like Australian Aborigines, the Nasa and their customs not only need to be seen by the dominant society as a "real acknowledgment of traditional law and real observance of traditional customs" (2002: 39, 45), they must be acceptable – no "repugnant" features allowed (2002: 34). For Povinelli, indigenous people face society's impossible demand "that they desire and identify with their cultural traditions in a way that just so happens, in an uncanny convergence of interests, to fit the national and legal imaginary of multiculturalism" (2002: 7–8). The Piñacué case in particular shows Nasa leaders expending a great deal of effort to present a radically different cultural system that manages to fit Colombian society's multiculturalist imaginary. While journalist Hernández attempts to convince readers that Nasa forms of cultural difference are indeed "acceptable," the debates over whether or not Nasa punishments constitute torture demonstrate what can happen when a sense of "repugnance" enters the picture. We are reminded of Goldilocks' quest: neither too much nor too little, but, if you try hard enough, you can get it just right. However, Povinelli says that real indigenous people will never manage to do this; they will invariably fail to qualify for inclusion in the nation's imaginary of indigeneity. The hegemonic domination characteristic of postcolonial multicultural societies, she argues, "works primarily by inspiring in the indigenous subject a desire to identify with a lost indeterminable object – indeed, to be the melancholic subject of traditions" (2002: 39). Inculcating this motivation results in actions that "always already constitute indigenous persons as failures of indigeneity as such" (2002: 39).

The case of contested indigenous status in Putumayo

Margarita Chaves's research in the Putumayo department of southern Colombia has focused on several communities that petitioned the government to grant them official indigenous status. The state's rejection of these claims reveals an unstable notion of indigeneity, illustrating an important underlying question that also arose in the Gembuel case: in disputed cases, who is authorized to decide who is entitled to which rights?[65]

---

[64] Also see Strathern on the problem of "repugnant" customs in the Western Highlands of Papua New Guinea (2004: 230).

[65] See Occipinti 2003 and Speed 2002 for examples of such debates in indigenous Argentina and Mexico, respectively.

Chaves documents a process of re-indigenization of communities of *colonos* (settlers) in the region (2003, 2005; also see Ramírez 2002). These were ethnically diverse families who arrived in successive waves from various parts of the country over the past seventy-odd years, many of them fleeing the mid-century bloody conflict raging in Andean areas known as "*La Violencia*" that left 200,000 dead (Chernick 2005: 178). National and regional Indigenous Affairs Offices (*División de Asuntos Indígenas* – DAI) are in charge of creating and implementing government policy for the country's pueblos. Successive Putumayo censuses had shown that both numbers of indigenous individuals and of cabildos had been rapidly increasing (Chaves 2003: 122, also see Chaves 2005), producing great consternation among regional and national DAI authorities. Members of recognized cabildos in the region also were expressing dismay, for they considered these reindigenized cabildos competitors for scarce state resources (which include benefits in the areas of health, scholarships, exemption from the military, availability of certain economic resources, and a greater likelihood of obtaining land [see Jackson 1996, 2002b]). Chaves argues that these processes of recovery and "recreation" of identity should not be seen only in instrumental terms, as the shift that had taken place during the previous twenty-five years (particularly during the constitutional process) from a valorization of *blanqueamiento* (whitening) to a valorization of indigenization, had had powerful effects, both symbolic and emotional (2003: 192).

Chaves notes that the dynamic identitarian discourses in these remote places reflect similar ones taking place at national and international levels; the latter enter regions like the Putumayo via many routes. An example is the different "qualitative scales" of indigeneity that were being created to pinpoint the "quality" or "grade" of indigenousness of recognized indigenous communities.[66] Long-time resident Putumayo Indians were increasingly becoming aware of ways in which the *colono* was also being excluded from the world of "white" domination (2003: 209), an ever-growing exclusion due to oil exploration in the area. From the perspective of the state, Chaves comments, all groups continued to occupy positions of subalternity, in which all rights were subject to challenge – *anyone's* "right to have rights" could increasingly be impugned.

[66] Chaves 2001: 172. Recall the criterion of "level of purity" employed by some Constitutional Court magistrates in the Gembuel case.

Unlike many indigenous communities in the area, which had often wanted to marginalize themselves further to escape the reach of the state, Chaves comments that *colonos* had always resisted their marginalization (also see Ramírez 2002); what was new in Putumayo is that the most recent resistance has taken the form of reindigenization, including the creation of new cabildos. Chaves documents the way in which a process that resulted in an increasingly "objective reality" of the "*indio*" ironically emerged out of the state's requirement that petitioner *colonos* demonstrate their indigeneity, with the obvious goal of setting standards they could not meet. The state required a "purification" of the censuses of already existing cabildos, in essence a form of ethnic cleansing; everyone had to demonstrate they were indigenous by language and *usos y costumbres* (Chaves 2003: 126). (Note that many of the petitioner *colono* families saw themselves as always having been indigenous, as their forbears originally came from highland pueblos like the Nasa, seeking land and fleeing the conflict).

When the state, represented by the DAI regional director (a member of the Inga pueblo, one of the several local pueblos opposed to the formation of new cabildos), decreed that multi-ethnic cabildos were not permitted, the *colonos* continued to push, asking why such cabildos did not qualify. When DAI obliged with ever more precise specifications, these cabildos proceeded to meet them and reapply. Chaves likens this back-and-forth process to a hall of mirrors (2003: 134). The *colono* groups increasingly valorized and talked up those physical characteristics and indigenous-derived practices – *usos y costumbres* – that would mark them as ethnically different in the eyes of both the state and the other pueblos in the area. At one point, over the space of only three months, DAI sent out four *circulares/ordenanzas* (policy statements) intended to halt the formation of new cabildos and end the emergence of new ethnicities. But these circulars had the opposite effect, for each proclamation detailing the increasingly precise requirements allowed the *colonos* to more precisely adjust their cultural identity. The petitioners began to find genealogical "footprints" in their shared last names, and began to rename their cabildos, sometimes several times. For example, one first went from *Cabildo Multiétnico Urbano de Puerto Caicedo* (consisting of Nasa, Awa, Inga and some Afro-Colombians from Cauca) to the *Cabildo Páez de la Zona Urbana de Puerto Caicedo* (indicating a cabildo made up only of Páez [Nasa]), and then to *Nasa Ku'esh Tata Wala*, a Nasa name intended to convey that the "purification" of the cabildo was complete (2003: 129).[67] Another cabildo created a name that joined the first syllables of the ethnicities they shared: the acronym QUIYAINPA signals that its members are Quillacingas, Yanaconas, Ingas and Pastos. However, as the name sounds like an Inga name, the cabildo received legal recognition (Chaves 2003: 129).

Unfortunately (because Chaves' account makes for fascinating reading), space does not permit going into more detail. What is important for our purposes is that these back-and-forth interactions, in which the state called for increasing levels of "purification" and "cleaning" (as well as an increased consultation of authorized sources – anthropological studies, for example[68]), resulted in ever-greater amounts of ingenious camouflage and mimicry being generated, which mounted an effective challenge of colonial (here neocolonial) discourses about rights. Chaves argues that these colonos brought about a "profound and disturbing" subversion of state authority because of the imperfect quality of their performative strategies. The goal of convincing themselves and others of their indigenous identity was almost, but not entirely, achieved. Chaves comments that such subversion is especially upsetting to state functionaries, regional elites, and the sector of academe characterized by a love of "the idea of alterity at all costs" that Amazonian Indians embody (2005: 147).

The colono communities that had requested official recognition as indigenous cabildos responded to the state's denial of their rights claims by hoisting the state on its own petard. Their imaginative strategies disclosed the inner workings and discursive practices of DAI, as well as those of the local municipalities actually in charge of granting cabildo status. The case illustrates how variable, situational, and political the criteria for being granted the "right to indigenous rights" can be.

As many scholars have pointed out (Scott 1990, Aretzaga 2003), the state is not a unitary center of power, but in fact is composed of institutions like legislatures and judiciaries whose individual actors engage in discourses and practices of power, the multiple effects of which give the appearance of a state (also see Trouillot 2001). In the

---

[67] According to Joanne Rappaport (who discussed this with Abelardo Ramos, a Nasa linguist), the name has no meaning in Nasa (personal communication February 13, 2006).
[68] One group rediscovered an origin myth telling of their having originated in Putumayo, only later migrating to Cauca; their subsequent migration to Putumayo was in effect a homecoming (Chaves 2003: 132).

Putumayo case the actors are (1) the petitioners, (2) the national and regional directors of DAI, who unsuccessfully called upon an accepted *modus operandi* to achieve their goals, and enlisted still other actors as allies, these being (3) the municipal government functionaries, and (4) the members of traditional Putumayo pueblos. The fluidity revealed by Chaves' investigation of actual rights practices, a back-and-forth interaction in which, à la Alice in Wonderland, the rules and their application seemed to continually change, were the result of the complex relations between local and national state agencies, as well as the transnational indigenous movement and its various allied nongovernmental organizations (NGOs). The latter have created a global indigenous rights discourse that is continually being incorporated and reworked at these various levels, merging with notions about indigeneity already present in the region. Chaves (2001: 242) outlines easily identifiable areas where the reethnicized *colonos'* representations are hybrid: "the influence of cultural images of very diverse origins and of wide circulation in regional, national and international levels" is quite apparent. These images include that of the "indigenous defender of the tropical forest,"[69] and the "wise *curandero*" (shaman). In the end, the reethnicized cabildos, now with all sorts of evidence of their otherness, having in fact reorganized themselves politically and culturally and recovered traditional festivals, origin myths and the like – in short, having come to fit the "fixed" state definition of the "other" – can successfully claim that they are being discriminated against. For Chaves, these cases reveal the impossibility of defining that which is indigenous as something not political, as well as the impossibility of defining the essentializations employed by the state as not ideological (2003: 134).

The Putumayo case resonates with Povinelli's discussion of cultural differences considered by mainstream society to be "too hauntingly similar to themselves to warrant social entitlements – for example, land claims by indigenous people who dress, act, and sound like the suburban neighbors they are" (2002: 13). Neither mainstream Colombian society (represented by the national DAI), nor traditional Putumayo pueblos accepted the new cabildos' petitions at first. But Putumayo indigeneity emerges from interactions between state agents

---

[69] Speed makes a similar point in her discussion of a Mexican community: essentialized ideas about indigenous people having a special relationship to the land may result in some communities finding it difficult "to meet those definitions and thus 'qualify' for rights" (2006: 72–73).

and citizens, both indigenous and nonindigenous, both nearby and far away, and over time the new pueblos become indigenous for most intents and purposes. These communities provide a superb example of subjects creatively engaging "the slippages, dispersions, and ambivalences of discursive and moral formations that make up their lives" (Povinelli 2002: 29). The Colombian materials confirm Cowan's point that "the recent revision of political and legal structures to recognize 'culture' and 'multiculturalism' has its own transformative effects, shaping and at times creating that which it purports merely to recognize" (2006: 17–18).

CONCLUSIONS

We see that in Colombia, as well as in many other countries, debates about the recognition of customary law have opened up spaces for citizens, indigenous and not, to rethink the state in its entirety, and to contest the parameters of government and other political institutions. If a nation's citizens are so diverse, a diversity legally recognized by the most fundamental law of the land, what does citizenship, in fact, consist of? Clearly, any comprehensive analysis of identity politics in Latin America must include discussion of how the identity of the state itself is being reformulated (see Warren and Jackson 2002: 20).

The two Nasa cases contain a worry one finds throughout the literature on indigenous customary law: that a pueblo's "culture," or their "otherness" will be restricted or otherwise diminished as a result of increased participation in modern life. "Culture" is not the same as autonomy, but the two are deeply imbricated. Most Colombian pueblo members do not want their indigenousness diminished; not only would they lose something of value, but they would run the risk of losing their right to occupy the "savage slot" created for them by the nonindigenous Colombian society (and international actors[70]). Pueblos and their allies know that successful representation of indigenous authority and authenticity must occur if leaders are to be granted the right to represent their pueblo.[71] The enactment of indigenous law and the

---

[70] See Trouillot 1991; Merry 2001: 41; also see Castañeda 2004 on the Yucatec Maya's unwillingness to occupy this "slot."

[71] I do not mean to imply that pueblos are not riddled with conflicts, nor suggest that local hierarchies do not result in unequal access to resources and power. Decision-making mechanisms that exclude and marginalize result in some members – most often women, poorer families, the younger generation – having less of a voice. A romantic view of pueblos as

231

subversion of federal and municipal law are clearly two very important sites at which successful performance of self-authenticating practices helps to achieve this goal. But the cultural content of such performances needs to be "acceptable"; these cases illustrate what can happen when "repugnance" intrudes, for when liberal members of mainstream society confront "intractable" social differences that their moral sensibility rejects, their experiences of "moments of fundamental and uncanny alterity" result in impasses (Povinelli 2002: 13).

All three cases, especially the Putumayo one, illustrate "the complex and contradictory consequences of being granted rights on the basis of having a culture and a cultural identity" (Cowan 2006: 18). Coming up with acceptable forms of cultural difference, not too "other" (which runs the risk of "repugnance"), yet different enough to offer the best possible likelihood of a pueblo's claims being recognized, is quite a balancing act. Communities are requested to produce "a detailed account of the content of their traditions and the force with which they identify with them – discursive, practical, and dispositional states" (Povinelli 2002: 39) congruent with mainstream society's imaginary of "real" indigeneity. Povinelli characterizes "dominant multiculturalism" as inspiring subaltern and minority subjects "to identify with the impossible object of an authentic self-identity ... a domesticated nonconflictual 'traditional' form of sociality and (inter)subjectivity" (2002: 6). A close examination of the above cases has allowed us to better understand how Colombia's particular version, visible in the actions taken by various kinds of judges, policies implemented by state officials, and articles written by journalists, works.

These cases, especially the third, reveal a dynamic process of appropriation, contestation, and re-fashioning of western meanings, in particular that of "culture." The diverse meanings and roles the culture concept takes on can resist elements of its western ideological underpinnings, and become a subaltern political tool. As such these cases pose challenges to conventional boundaries of cultural and political representation and social practice (Alvarez, Dagnino, and Escobar 1998: 8), as well as to the international community's use of "culture,"

cohesive and consensus-based communities can be sustained only from a distance; up close they reveal actions and underlying values that are anything but fair or democratic. How these more vulnerable sectors feel about the status quo, or even about the desirability of transforming their culture according to their own normativity and rules must, of course, be investigated ethnographically in each case. Assies, vander Haar, and Hoekema point out that "indigenous women may contest aspects of their culture without abandoning the defence of a culture of their own" (2000: 313).

"peoples," "rights," and other concepts (e.g., "democracy," "citizen"), which continue to compel indigenous groups to repackage their concerns and identities for wider audiences in order to facilitate communicating claims and enlisting support. The growth of rights discourses and the linking up (sometimes done so awkwardly that we should perhaps say "lashing up" (see Li 2005: 386)) of indigenous culture-specific collective rights regimes (e.g., rights to culture) with other kinds of rights regimes, will inevitably result in tensions and periodic "explosions."[72]

Helping us to understand these processes are the approaches to studying rights regimes outlined at the beginning of this chapter. Scholars have been problematizing the notion of "culture" to better understand these processes. One kind of problematization involves examining the ways in which indigenous movements, like all social movements, challenge the boundaries of cultural and political representation and social practice (Alvarez, Dagnino, and Escobar 1998: 8). These three Colombian cases illustrate that culture is "a dimension of all institutions, 'a set of *material* practices which constitute meanings, values and subjectivities'" (Jordan and Weedon, 1995: 8, as cited in Alvarez, Dagnino and Escobar 1998: 3).

The Colombian examples illustrate how the concept of human rights, although often seen as universal, is coming to be seen by some scholars and activists as a product of Western cultural and intellectual history (see Speed, chapter 4 in this volume). Scholars like Merry (1997: 28) propose such notions; authorities like magistrate Gaviria Díaz put them into practice. We see the wisdom of Wilson's recommendation to pay attention to "human rights according to the actions and the intentions of the social actors, within the wider historical constraints of institutionalized power" (Wilson 1997: 4).

We have seen that certain Colombian Constitutional Court judges take their charge to respect the intent of the 1991 Constitution quite seriously (see Sánchez 1997, 1998, 2000). Of course, the Constitution was framed within the context of western democratic ideals and practices, so the Court's perceived mandate to respect the country's pluri-ethnic and multicultural nature extends only so far (see Benavides 2004: 414–417). Some of the Court's decisions are nonetheless surprisingly open to fundamentally different visions of justice, surprising

---

[72] See Merry 2001 for a discussion of the international rights community's essentialization of both "culture" and "rights."

particularly in a country characterized by excessive amounts of impunity and immunity. But this receptivity is perhaps not as paradoxical as it seems at first. May be, in a setting where 98 percent of crimes go unpunished, attention will very likely be riveted on cases that *presume* a well-intentioned and functional judicial system, one capable of seriously considering what indigenous special jurisdiction might mean. Colombian citizens are seeing in action new forms of governmentality that involve dispersed, graduated sovereignties. Some authors, like Manuel Hernández, suggest that *these* judicial processes, albeit unusual and highly circumscribed, are providing an embryonic vision of a just, tolerant, multicultural and intercultural[73] state and civil society – as well, we must add, as a discomfiting vision of unintended consequences[74] that may appear when robust intercultural definitions of justice and tolerance are actually put into practice.

My methodology has not allowed me to provide direct evidence of the transnational influences on these interactions, but the indirect evidence is compelling. We have seen how social actors in Colombia have envisioned the legal and ethical frameworks implied by the idea of human rights (see Goodale, Introduction, p. 22), "which requires the projection of the moral imagination in ways that not only contribute to how we can (and should) understand the meaning of human rights, but also, at a more basic level, suggest that the emergence of transnational networks takes places 'in our minds, as much as in our actions'" (Goodale, quoting from Boaventura de Sousa Santos 1995: 473).

Vulnerable indigenous populations in rural Colombia, in their effort to find and maintain stability in a situation of tremendous violence and government neglect, enlist particular traditions and authorize particular actors to carry out actions that without doubt challenge the transcultural scaffolding of the human rights regime. If the opposite of vulnerability is stability, we need to keep in mind that in Colombia indigenous communities are anything but stable, and that the war is a backdrop to every single event that led to the various packages of legislation, treaty-signings, and governmental policy promulgations that gave pueblos the territory and degree of autonomy they presently enjoy.[75]

---

[73] See Rappaport 2005 and Whitten 2004 for discussions of interculturality.
[74] As Povinelli asks, "On what basis does a practice or belief switch from being an instance of cultural difference to being repugnant culture?" (2002: 4).
[75] See Jackson 2002a.

A great irony derives from the fact that war-weary Colombians have perceived certain pueblos to be presenting ways to resist violence (despite at times terrible costs): ways to achieve consensus and act, thereby conquering, if only temporarily, the fear-induced paralysis that a civil war can produce. These pueblos have shown the courage to declare to those who violently challenge their autonomy, "*hasta aquí, no más*" ("you will not advance farther"). In the eyes of a pueblo like the Nasa, something "more terrible than death" (Kirk 2003) would be to give in to the guerrillas, paramilitaries and repressive state security forces, and abandon their project of securing at least some of their rights. In their vulnerability, but also in their conviction and determination to not yield, we indeed have a "messy"[76] set of symbols, a "messy" series of actions, and a "messy" set of moral and ethical imperatives, in large part due to the "messy" and inadequate government response to the violence perpetrated on the country's pueblos over the last sixty years.

REFERENCES

Alvarez, Sonia E., Evelina Dagnino, and Arturo Escobar. 1998. "Introduction." In Alvarez, Dagnino, and Escobar, eds., *Cultures of Politics Politics of Cultures: Re-visioning Latin American Social Movements*. Boulder: Westview Press.

Aretxaga, Begoña. 2003. "Maddening States." *Annual Review of Anthropology* 32: 393–410.

Asch, Michael. 2005. "Lévi-Strauss and the Political: *The Elementary Structures of Kinship* and the Resolution of Relations between Indigenous People and Settler States." *Journal of the Royal Anthropological Institute* (N.S.) 11: 425–444.

Assies, Willem. 2000. "Indigenous Peoples and Reform of the State in Latin America." In Willem Assies, Gemma van der Haar, and André Hoekema, eds. *The Challenge of Diversity: Indigenous Peoples and Reform of the State in Latin America*. Amsterdam: Thela Thesis, pp. 3–22.

Assies, Willem. 2003. "Indian Justice in the Andes: Re-rooting or Re-routing?" In Ton Salman and Annelies Zoomers, eds. *Imaging the Andes: Shifting Margins of a Marginal World*. Amsterdam: CEDLA, pp. 167–186.

Assies, Willem, Gemma van der Haar, and André Hoekema. 2000. "Diversity as a challenge: a note on the dilemmas of diversity." In Willem Assies,

[76] Goodale points out that while the abstract idea of human rights may lend itself to projects concerned with definition, classification and modeling, when emerging within situated normativities it is an inevitably messy and contradictory idea (see p. 25 of his Introduction).

Gemma van der Haar, and André Hoekema, eds. *The Challenge of Diversity: Indigenous Peoples and Reform of the State in Latin America.* Amsterdam: Thela Thesis, pp. 295–315.

Benavides, Farid Samir. 2004. "Hermeneutical Violence: Human Rights, Law, and the Constitution of a Global Identity." *International Journal for the Semiotics of Law* 17: 391–418.

Blackburn, Carole. 2005. "Searching for Guarantees in the Midst of Uncertainty: Negotiating Aboriginal Rights and Title in British Columbia." *American Anthropologist* 107(4): 586–596.

Campo, Carlos. 1998. "Misterioso Baño de Piñacué: la Laguna de Juan Tama es una Leyenda." *El Tiempo*, July 19.

Castañeda, Quetzil E. 2004. "'We are not indigenous!' The Maya Identity of Yucatan, an Introduction." *Journal of Latin American Anthropology* 9(1): 36–63.

Chaves, Margarita. 2001. "Conflictos Territoriales o la Política de la Ubicación: Actores Étnicos, Re-etnizados y no Étnicos en Disputa por un Territorio en el Putumayo." In Beatriz Nates, ed. *Memorias II Seminario Internacional sobre Territorio y Cultura: Territorios de conflicto y cambio sociocultural.* Manizales: Universidad de Caldas, pp. 167–186.

Chaves, Margarita. 2003. "Cabildos Multiétnicos e Identidades Depuradas." In Clara Inés García, ed. *Fronteras: Territorios y Metáforas.* Medellín: Hombre Nuevo Editores.

Chaves, Margarita. 2005. "'Qué va a Pasar con los Indios Cuando todos Seamos Indios?' Ethnic Rights and Reindianization in Southwestern Colombian Amazonia." Ph.D. thesis, University of Illinois at Urbana-Champaign.

Chernick, Marc. 2005. "Economic Resources and Internal Armed Conflicts: Lessons from the Colombian Case." In Cynthia J. Arnson and I. William Zartman, eds. *Rethinking the Economics of War: the Intersection of Need, Creed, and Greed.* Washington, DC and Baltimore: Woodrow Wilson Center Press and The Johns Hopkins University Press, pp. 178–205.

Cowan, Jane K. 2006. "Culture and Rights after *Culture and Rights*." *American Anthropologist* 108(1): 9–24.

Cowan, Jane K., Marie Bénédicte Dembour, and Richard A. Wilson. 2001. "Introduction." In Jane K. Cowan, Marie-Bénédicte Dembour, and Richard A. Wilson, eds., *Culture and Rights: Anthropological Perspectives.* Cambridge: Cambridge University Press, pp. 1–26.

Dagnino, Evelina. 1998. "Culture, Citizenship, and Democracy: Changing Discourses and Practices of the Latin American Left." In Sonia E. Alvrez, Evelina Dagnino, and Arturo Escobar, eds. *Cultures of Politics Politics of Cultures: Re-visioning Latin American Social Movements.* Boulder: Westview, pp. 33–63.

Dudley, Steven. 2005. "Indians Battle Rebels." *Miami Herald*, April 21.

Forero, Juan. 2005. "Colombia War Spills into Indians' Peaceful World." *New York Times*, May 2.

García, Yimy Melo. 1997a. "El Castigo será en Febrero: los Indígenas Aplazaron un mes el Cumplimiento de la Sentencia a Implicados en Crimen." *El Espectador*, January 11.

García, Yimy Melo. 1997b. "Es Mejor el Fuete que una Cárcel: Castigo Paez no es una Tortura, es la Forma de Asegurar Armonía en la Comunidad." El Espectador, January 12.

García, Yimy Melo. 1997c. "Por Tutela se Aplazaron los Fuetazos en Jambaló." *El Espectador*, January 11.

García, Yimy Melo. 1997d. "Sí les 'dieron' los Fuetazos en Toribío." *El Espectador*, January 13.

García, Yimy Melo. 1998. "Le Cambian Fuete por Agua a Piñacué." *El Espectador*, July 16.

Graham, Laura R. 2002. "How should an Indian speak? Amazonian Indians and the Symbolic Politics of Language in the Global Public Sphere." In Kay B. Warren and Jean E. Jackson, eds. *Indigenous Movements, Self-Representation and the State in Latin America*. Austin: University of Texas Press, pp. 181–228.

Green, W. John. 2005. "Guerrillas, Soldiers, Paramilitaries, Assassins, Narcos, and Gringos: The Unhappy Prospects for Peace and Democracy in Colombia." *Latin American Research Review* 40(2): 137–149.

Gros, Christian. 2000. *Políticas de la Etnicidad: Identidad, Estado y Modernidad*. Bogota: Instituto Colombiano de Antropología e Historia.

Hale, Charles. 2002. "Does Multiculturalism Menace? Governance, Cultural Rights and the Politics of Identity in Guatemala." *Journal of Latin American Studies* 34: 485–524.

Hale, Charles, 2004. "Rethinking Indigenous Politics in the Era of the 'Indio Permitido'. " *NACLA* 38(1): 16–20.

Hernández, Manuel. 1998. "Laboratorio Social." *El Espectador*, September 8.

Jackson, Jean E. 1996. "The Impact of Recent National Legislation on Tukanoan Communities in the Vaupés Region of Southeastern Colombia." *Journal of Latin American Anthropology* 1(2): 120–151.

Jackson, Jean E. 2002a. "Caught in the Crossfire: Colombia's Indigenous Peoples during the 1990s." In David Maybury-Lewis, ed. *Identities in Conflict: Indigenous Peoples and Latin American States*. Cambridge, MA: Harvard University Press, pp. 107–134.

Jackson, Jean E. 2002b. "Contested Discourses of Authority in Colombian National Indigenous Politics: The 1996 Summer Takeovers." In Kay B. Warren, and Jean E, Jackson, eds. *Indigenous Movements, Self-Representation and the State in Latin America*. Austin: University of Texas Press, pp. 81–122.

Jackson, Jean E. 2005. "Colombia's Indigenous Peoples Confront the Armed Conflict." In Cristina Rojas, and Judy Meltzer, eds. *Elusive Peace: International, National, and Local Dimensions of Conflict in Colombia.* New York: Palgrave/Macmillan, pp. 185–208.

Jackson, Jean E., and Kay B. Warren. 2005. "Indigenous Movements in Latin America, 1992–2004: Controversies, Ironies, New Directions." *Annual Review of Anthropology.* Palo Alto: Annual Reviews, pp. 549–573.

Jordan, Glenn, and Chris Weedon. 1995. *Cultural Politics: Class, Gender, Race, and the Postmodern World.* Oxford: Blackwell.

Kirk, Robin. 2003. *More Terrible than Death: Violence, Drugs, and America's War in Colombia.* New York: Public Affairs.

Klein, Naomi. 2005. "The Threat of Hope in Latin America." *The Nation,* November 21, p. 14.

Laurent, Virginie. 2005. *Comunidades Indígenas, Espacios Políticos y Movilización Electoral en Colombia, 1990–1998: Motivaciones, Campos de Acción e Impactos.* Bogota: Instituto Colombiano de Antropología e Historia, Instituto Francés de Estudios Andinos.

Li, Tania Murray. 2005. "Beyond the State and Failed Schemes." *American Anthropologist* 107(3): 383–394.

Mercado, Bibiana. 1993. " 'Estamos en el Centro de una Guerra': Indígenas." *El Tiempo,* November 21.

Merry, Sally E. 1997. Legal Pluralism and Transnational Culture: The Ka Ho'okolokolonui Kanaka Maoli Tribunal, Hawai'i 1993." In R. A. Wilson, ed. *Human Rights, Culture and Context: Anthropological Perspectives.* London: Pluto Press.

Merry, Sally E. 2001. "Changing rights, changing culture." In Jane K. Cowan, Marie-Bénédicte Dembour, and Richard A. Wilson, eds. *Culture and Rights: Anthropological Perspectives.* Cambridge: Cambridge University Press, pp. 31–55.

Merry, Sally E. 2006. "Transnational Human Rights and Local Activism: Mapping the Middle." *American Anthropologist* 108(1): 38–51.

Molano, Alfredo. 2004. "La Fábula del Cóndor y el Colibrí." *El Espectador,* September 20.

Mompotes, Andrés. 1997a. "El Cepo Evita los Crímenes en Pitayó." *El Tiempo* January 10.

Mompotes, Andrés. 1997b. "Ley Blanca no Lava las Culpas: Paeces Insisten en Castigar hoy con Latigazos a Implicados en Crimen." *El Tiempo,* January 10.

Mompotes, Andrés. 1998a. "Gota fría para Piñacué: Fué condenado a sumergirse en la laguna Juan Tama." *El Tiempo,* July 16.

Mompotes, Andrés. 1998b. "En Paniquitá Buscan un Fuete: Hoy es el Juicio a Jesús Piñacué." *El Tiempo,* July 15.

Murillo, Mario. 1996. "Confronting the Dilemmas of Political Participation." *NACLA Report on the Americas* 29(5): 21–22.

Murillo, Mario. 2006. "Colombia's indigenous caught in the conflict." *NACLA Report on the Americas* 39(4): 4–7.

Nash, June. 2001. *Mayan Visions: The Quest for Autonomy in an Age of Globalization.* New York: Routledge.

Occhipinti, Laurie. 2003. "Claiming a Place: Land and Identity in Two Communities in Northwestern Argentina." *Journal of Latin American Anthropology* 8(3): 155–174.

Povinelli, Elizabeth A. 2002. *The Cunning of Recognition: Indigenous Alterities and the Making of Australian Multiculturalism.* Durham: Duke University Press.

Ramírez, María Clemencia. 2001. *Entre el Estado y la Guerrilla: Identidad y Ciudadanía en el Movimiento de los Campesinos Cocaleros del Putumayo.* Bogota: Instituto Colombiano de Antropología e Historia.

Ramírez, María Clemencia. 2002. "The Politics of Identity and Cultural Difference in the Putumayo: Claiming Special Indigenous Rights in Colombia's Amazon." In Maybury-Lewis D., ed. 2002. *The Politics of Ethnicity: Indigenous Peoples in Latin American States.* Cambridge, MA: Harvard University Press, pp. 135–168.

Ramírez, María Clemencia. 2005. "Aerial Spraying and Alternative Development in Plan Colombia: Two Sides of the Same Coin or Two Contested Policies?" *ReVista* Spring/Summer, pp. 54–57.

Ramos, Alcida R. 1998. *Indigenism: Ethnic Politics in Brazil.* Madison: University of Wisconsin Press.

Rappaport, Joanne. 2003. "Innovative Resistance in Cauca." *Cultural Survival Quarterly,* Winter, pp. 39–43.

Rappaport, Joanne. 2005. *Intercultural Utopias: Public Intellectuals, Cultural Experimentation, and Ethnic Pluralism in Colombia.* Durham: Duke University Press.

Rosen, Lawrence. 1997. "Indigenous Peoples in International Law." *Yale Law Journal* 107(1): 227–259.

Sánchez, Esther. 1997. "Conflicto entre la Jurisdicción Especial Indígena y la Jurisdicción Ordinaria (enfoque Antropológico)." In Ministerio de Justicia y del Derecho/Dirección General de Asuntos Indígenas, *"Del olvido surgimos para traer nuevas esperanzas": La jurisdicción especial indígena.* Bogota: 287–292.

Sánchez, Esther. 1998. *Justicia y Pueblos Indígenas de Colombia.* Bogota: Universidad Nacional de Colombia.

Sánchez, Esther. 2000. "The Tutela-system as a means of Transforming the Relations between the State and the Indigenous Peoples of Colombia." In Willem Assies, Gemma van der Haar, and André Hoekema, eds. *The Challenge of Diversity: Indigenous Peoples and Reform of the State in Latin America.* Amsterdam: Thela Thesis, pp. 223–245.

Sánchez, Esther. 2004. *Justicia y PueblosIindígenas de Colombia Segundo Edición: Jurisprudencia Actualizada*. Bogota: Universidad Nacional de Colombia & UNIJUS.

Santos, Boaventura de Sousa. 1995. *Toward a New Common Sense: Law, Science and Politics in the Paradigmatic Transition*. New York: Routledge.

Santos, Boaventura de Sousa. 2001. "El Significado Político y Jurídico de la Jurisdicción Indígena." In Boaventura de Sousa Santos, and Mauricio García Villegas, eds. *El Caleidoscopio de las Justicias en Colombia*, vol. 2. Bogota: Siglo de Hombre editores, pp. 201–216.

Scott, James C. 1990. *Domination and the Arts of Resistance: Hidden Transcripts*. New Haven: Yale University Press.

Sieder, Rachel. 2002a. "Introduction." In Rachel Sieder, ed. *Multiculturalism in Latin America: Indigenous Rights, Diversity and Democracy*. New York: Palgrave Macmillan, pp. 1–23.

Sieder, Rachel. 2002b. "Recognising Indigenous Law and the Politics of State Formation in Mesoamerica." In Rachel Sieder, ed. *Multiculturalism in Latin America: Indigenous Rights, Diversity and Democracy*. New York: Palgrave Macmillan, pp. 184–207.

Sierra, María T. 1995. "Articulaciones entre ley y Costumbre: Estrategias Jurídicas de los Nahuas." In Victoria Chenaut, and María T. Sierra, eds. *Pueblos Indígenas Ante el Derecho*. Mexico City, Mexico: Centro de Investigaciones y Estudios Superiores en Antropología Social; Centro Francés de Estudios Mexicanos Centroamericanos, pp. 101–123.

Speed, Shannon. 2002. "Global Discourses on the Local Terrain: Human Rights and Indigenous Identity in Chiapas." *Cultural Dynamics* 14(2): 205–128.

Speed, Shannon. 2006. "At the Crossroads of Human Rights and Anthropology: Toward a Critically Engaged Activist Research." *American Anthropologist* 108(1): 66–76.

Stavenhagen, Rodolfo. 2002. "Indigenous Peoples and the State in Latin America: an Ongoing Debate." In R. Sieder, ed. *Multiculturalism in Latin America: Indigenous Rights, Diversity and Democracy*. New York: Palgrave Macmillan, pp. 24–44.

Stavenhagen, Rodolfo. 2005. "Human Rights and Indigenous Issues." Report of the Special Rapporteur on the Situation of Human Rights and Fundamental Freedoms of Indigenous People. United Nations Economic and Social Council, Commission on Human Rights.

Strathern, Marilyn. 2004. "Losing (out on) Intellectual Resources." In Alain Pottage and Martha Mundy, eds. *Law, Anthropology, and the Constitution of the Social: Making Persons and Things*. Cambridge: Cambridge University Press, pp. 201–233.

Swepston, Lee. 1998. "The Indigenous and Tribal Peoples Convention (No. 169): Eight years after Adoption." In Cynthia Price Cohen, ed.

The Human Rights of Indigenous Peoples. Ardsley, NY: Transnational Publishers, pp. 16–36.

Trouillot, Michel-Rolph. 1991. "Anthropology and the Savage Slot: The Poetics and Politics of Otherness." In Richard Fox (ed.). *Recapturing Anthropology.* Santa Fe: School of American Research Press, pp. 17–44.

Trouillot, Michel-Rolph. 2001. "The Anthropology of the State in the Age of Globalization: Close Encounters of the Deceptive Kind." *Current Anthropology* 42(1): 125–138.

Valencia, José Luis. 2001. "Indígenas Prohibirán paso a Actores Armados," *El Tiempo,* May 16.

Van Cott, Donna Lee. 2000. *The Friendly Liquidation of the Past: The Politics of Diversity in Latin America.* Pittsburgh: University of Pittsburgh Press.

Van Cott, Donna Lee. 2005. *From Movements to Parties in Latin America: The Evolution of Ethnic Politics.* Cambridge: Cambridge University Press.

Warren, Kay B., and Jean E. Jackson. 2002. "Introduction." In Kay B. Warren, and Jean E. Jackson, eds. *Indigenous Movements, Self-Representation and the State in Latin America.* Austin: University of Texas Press, pp. 1–46.

Whitten, Norman E. 2004. "Ecuador in the New Millennium: 25 Years of Democracy." *Journal of Latin American Anthropology* 9(2): 439–460.

Wilson, Richard, A., ed. 1997. *Human Rights, Culture and Context: Anthropological Approaches.* London Pluto.

Wilson, Richard A. 2006. Afterword to "Anthropology and Human Rights in a New Key": The social life of human rights." *American Anthropologist* 108(1): 77–83.

Yashar, Deborah J. 2005. *Contesting Citizenship in Latin America: The Rise of Indigenous Movements and the Postliberal Challenge.* Cambridge: Cambridge University Press.

Yrigoyen, Raquel. 2002. "Peru Pluralist Constitution, Monist Judiciary – a Post-reform Assessment." In R. Sieder, ed. 2002. *Multiculturalism in Latin America: Indigenous Rights, Diversity and Democracy.* New York: Palgrave Macmillan, pp. 157–183.

Legal case

Case cited: *The Hamlet of Baker Lake* v. *Minister of Indian Affairs and Northern Development* (1980) 1 FC 518 (FCC).

6

THE 2000 UN HUMAN TRAFFICKING PROTOCOL: RIGHTS, ENFORCEMENT, VULNERABILITIES

*Kay Warren**

"What are the consequences of the invisibility of many types of violence?" asks Balakrishnan Rajagopal in his critique of human rights discourse and state power (2003: 186). He observes that unrecognized violence is, by default, allowed to continue unchallenged; in that sense it is "authorized." This chapter looks at attempts by the international community to name and combat human trafficking as a form of transnational violence invisible to many until recently but, in the mind of some, surging out of control. Responding to Rajagopal in this context leads me to pose an alternative set of questions: "What are the political dynamics of making violence visible, the consequences of naming and circumscribing human trafficking through a new round of international norms? How does this trajectory of international law become problematic for activists who claim that the wrong kinds of violence may be targeted by these norms?

To address these issues, this chapter examines the UN anti-trafficking protocol as a living document whose final language is consulted by parties around the globe who may know little about its genesis. In the genealogy of human trafficking as an urgent problem that requires international attention, the 2000 UN Protocol to Prevent, Suppress, and Punish Trafficking in Persons, Especially Women and Children has played the formative role as the generator of international norms.

* My thanks to Sally Merry and Mark Goodale for the opportunity to join this research group on human rights and for their suggestions and feedback on this analysis. Special appreciation goes to Annelise Grimm for excellent research assistance and to Andrea Mazzarino for interesting questions. I have also benefited from Johan Lindquist's critical engagement with this analysis.

In the genealogy of human trafficking as an urgent problem that needed to be addressed, the 2000 UN Protocol to Prevent, Suppress, and Punish Trafficking in Persons, Especially Women and Children played the formative role as the generator of international norms. This chapter examines how "human trafficking" was officially defined and strategies for combating it authorized through UN meetings of government delegations to create an overarching international convention on organized crime and a supplementary protocol on human trafficking. The process was not unchallenged. From very different ideological positions, two nongovernmental organizations (NGO) networks were active in lobbying for distinctive constructions of human trafficking, and other international organizations and UN offices entered the fray.

Knowledge production in this case did not finish when the convention and protocol were signed and ratified. Rather, NGOs of different stripes reintensified their pressure, in effect, creating alternative versions of the protocol through their own interpretive analyses and annotations of the official document. Their goal is to spur their networks of activists who, in many instances, become parties to the protocol's implementation on a country-by-country basis throughout the world. Yet, human trafficking has also been a challenge because of its dynamic character, on-the-ground complexity, and transnational routes from "source" to "destination" countries.

It is clear to me that making something called human trafficking "legible"[1] (Scott 1998) as a crime has been a challenge because it is a category for a complex, transregionally coordinated, and continually morphing chain of activities that involves both legal and illegal workers. In the early 2000s it was constructed as a new crisis of transnational violence with distinctive histories in different parts of the world. The United Nation's quest to establish universal patterns in the organization of trafficking can be seen as an attempt to tame this heterogeneous reality so it could be comprehended as an entity appropriate for a certain set of interventions.

This chapter analyzes the protocol both as a legal text in-and-of-itself and as a living document, with a history and ongoing political relevance. Charged by the UN General Assembly with the drafting process, the Ad Hoc Committee, understood its project as formulating a consensus document for the Convention against Transnational

---

[1] See Scott 1998 on the issue of legibility.

Organized Crime and protocol supplements to the convention[2] designed to criminalize trafficking in women and children; illegal trafficking in and transporting of migrants; and illicit manufacture of and trafficking in firearms, their parts and components and ammunition.[3] After three preliminary sessions, the committee met in Vienna for eleven sessions, initially convening on January 19–29, 1999 and wrapping up in October 2–27, 2000.[4] The committee was open to all states in the United Nations, and government officials from some forty-nine countries participated in the human trafficking sessions under the leadership of delegations from Argentina and the US Major NGOs colations with well articulated positions expressed their expert views along the way. The signing conference for the convention was held in Palermo, Italy, on December 12–15, 2000. By December 2003, the protocol had gathered the 40 state ratifications necessary to be put into force as a binding international legal instrument. As of September 7, 2006, the protocol has 117 signatories and 106 parties that have ratified, accepted, approved, or accessed the agreement.

First, this chapter raises the issue of the balance in the trafficking protocol between what I will term a "law enforcement paradigm," which focuses on policing and border control strategies to criminalize traffickers, and a "human rights paradigm" that stresses the importance of the recognition of the rights held by all individuals who have been trafficked. Second, the chapter examines the ways in which gendered images of vulnerability became central to the protocol's constructions of trafficking and the terms in which these images were contested by different organizations as the protocol was drafted. Third, the analysis outlines the ways in which the protocol has been used to inform anti-trafficking campaigns, or to put it another way the alternative ways that anti-trafficking campaigns have appropriated the protocol. Since 2002, my research has centered on campaigns to combat human trafficking for sexual exploitation between Colombia as a "sending country" and Japan as a "receiving country." While this research is still in progress, my preliminary results show that anti-trafficking campaigns adhere to the protocol in different ways and that they negotiate complex organizational fields and political pressures as the implementation of different aspects of the protocol takes place.

---

[2] See UN General Assembly 2000. The texts are available in five languages.
[3] This wording comes from the first session's annotated provisional agenda and proposed organizational of work, distributed December 14, 1998 for the first session one month later (UN General Assembly A/AC.254/1).
[4] See UN General Assembly A/AC.254.

EXAMINING THE TRAFFICKING PROTOCOL AS A LEGAL TEXT REFLECTING ITS GENESIS

As an anthropologist, my goal in this chapter is to trace the complex genesis of international norms in an emerging arena of transnational concern. Initially, this analysis considers the protocol in its own terms, seeking a "presentist" understanding of the norms. I argue that, while on first reading the protocol seems to be a very progressive document promising the "victim of trafficking" substantial services and support, a closer reading that the text reveals signs of tension in the drafting process. The protocol loses focus when it is forced into compromises between alternative ideological understandings of trafficking. There are striking silences on important issues, problems that are raised only to be neglected, and ambiguities about the beneficiaries. The text also appears to reflect cultural routines – localized practices that guide consensus building – employed by transnational elites and knowledge brokers working within the UN system to facilitate meetings and decision making under the pressure of major deadlines.

The 2000 UN trafficking protocol is regularly cited by governments, NGOs, activists, and scholars as the prime source for defining human trafficking. The situating of the trafficking protocol within the UN Convention against Transnational Organized Crime ties it to a specific field of criminalizing interventions. By definition, we are dealing with the nether world of organized crime that illegally smuggles and traffics people for profit, just as it markets drugs, weapons, and other contraband. Organized crime syndicates combine illicit and legal enterprises[5] that cultivate ties with corrupt state officials as it exploits globalized commerce, inequality, migrants' search for better work in remittance economies, and the ease of moving people through different transportation corridors to a particular destination only to shift destinations whenever necessary or expedient.

Article 3 of the protocol characterizes trafficking in the following terms, using gender neutral language, beginning with the violent and coercive means traffickers use:

> (a) Trafficking in persons shall mean the recruitment, transportation, transfer, harbouring or receipt of persons, by means of the threat or use of force or other forms of coercion, of abduction, of fraud, of

---

[5] See Carolyn Nordstrom (2004) on the heterogeneity of transnational criminal enterprises.

deception, of the abuse of power or of a position of vulnerability or of the giving or receiving of payments or benefits to achieve the consent of a person having control over another persons, for the purpose of exploitation.

In this formulation, the *means* of trafficking are heterogeneous as are the *forms* that exploitation takes:

> Exploitation shall include, at a minimum, the exploitation of the prostitution of others or other forms of sexual exploitation, forced labour or services, slavery or practices similar to slavery, servitude or the removal of organs;

The broad scope of this formulation of exploitation is confusing given the lack of definitions and possible overlaps in significance of prostitution and sexual exploitation, forced labor, slavery-like working conditions, servitude, and trafficking of people in conjunction with the commodification of organs.

"Consent" is the final issue treated in Article 3's definition of trafficking:

> (b) The consent of a victim of trafficking in persons to the intended exploitation set forth in subparagraph (a) of this article shall be irrelevant where any of the means set forth in subparagraph (a) have been used;
>
> (c) The recruitment, transportation, transfer, harbouring or receipt of a child for the purpose of exploitation shall be considered trafficking in persons even if this does not involve any of the means set forth in subparagraph (a) of this article;
>
> (d) Child shall mean any person under eighteen years of age.

In my view, it is not consent but the negation of consent that is the primary issue in this statement.[6] As one commentator observed, "You cannot consent to a lie." The manipulative means, including threats, force, coercion, abduction, fraud, deception, and abuse of power or vulnerability, or debts to compel the consent of the person negates any imputed consent the individual might have expressed. Children under international law cannot give their own consent if they are less than eighteen years of age.[7]

---

[6] In many legal systems, though it varies by state in the United States, there is an age of consent for sexual relations below which minors cannot legally express their consent.
[7] This universal norm ignores and negates very different standards for adulthood in other societies.

I would suggest that a close reading of the text reveals the subtle terms in which the protocol slips between the wider construction of exploitation flowing from the use of the gender neutral language of "persons" and a narrower understanding that focuses on women and foregrounds their vulnerability along with children's vulnerability. This effect is achieved by repeated reference in the title, preamble, and Article 9 to "victims of trafficking in persons, especially women and children" and the "exploitation of persons, especially women and children." The abuse of vulnerability is defined as a situation in which an individual has "no acceptable alternative but to submit to the abuse involved."[8] Coupling vulnerability with the female gender and dependent children is a very potent imagery for the construction of worthy victims.

The protocol emphasizes that these norms are designed to deal with a transnational phenomenon, one that is pursued by international webs of organized crime, rather than labor recruiting for domestic markets or the involvement of friends, family, and neighbors, which in practice are very common forms of local labor recruitment. It is hard for those of us who have done research on this issue not to critique any transnational/domestic distinction as problematic because local and transnational recruiting efforts are interconnected in practice. The people involved in trafficking others are not inevitably threatening strangers. One is left with the impression that the constructed contrast between transnational/domestic spheres in the protocol represents a nod to the UN policy of non-interference in the affairs of other sovereign states – which was indeed important to these delegates. It was an ironic move in this case but repeatedly reaffirmed in the instrument and correspondence between the delegates and the Ad Hoc Committee.

The body of the protocol in Articles 5–8 articulates a striking set of issues, reforms, and remedies for the "receiving" state to assume: legal reforms to criminalize trafficking as a unified phenomenon and afford "victim" protection especially for privacy and physical well-being. Receiving states are encouraged to promote a wide-ranging assistance to those who have been trafficked: legal counseling, a voice in legal proceedings against their traffickers, housing, medical and financial assistance, employment and training, compensation for damage suffered, and rights to temporary or permanent residence.

---

[8] This definition is drawn from the UN interpretive notes which are meant to be read with the protocol although they are not conventionally printed with the document. Cited in this instance in Jordan 2002b, p. 7, n. 12.

The repatriation of trafficking victims to "sending" countries is another facet of the protocol. Home countries are obligated to take part in the speedy return of the victims, with concern for their safety, verification of their nationality, and reissuing documents for the victim's return as these have often been taken from them overseas.

Norms for the prevention of trafficking and revictimization, "especially for women and children," receive substantial attention in the protocol. Here states are encouraged to establish new policies and programs, in cooperation with NGOs, civil society, and other forms of bilateral and multilateral cooperation. At issue are the factors which make individuals "vulnerable":

> States Parties shall take or strengthen measures, including through bilateral or multilateral cooperation, to alleviate the factors that make persons, especially women and children, vulnerable to trafficking, such as poverty, underdevelopment and lack of equal opportunity.
>
> (Article 9, No. 4)

This is an open-ended commitment since nothing is added about how to go about dealing with these fundamental issues.

The state's role in reducing "demand" is also mentioned in this section on prevention:

> States Parties shall adopt or strengthen legislative or other measures, such as educational, social or cultural measures, including through bilateral and multilateral cooperation, to discourage the demand that fosters all forms of exploitation of persons, especially women and children, that leads to trafficking.
>
> (Article 9, No. 5)

The final issue dealt with in Articles 9 through 11 is prevention and training to strengthen the coordination of state officials in law enforcement and immigration. The protocol makes sweeping and often vague statement about states' obligations to "undertake measures such as research, information and mass media campaigns and social and economic initiatives to prevent and combat trafficking in persons." State officials are encouraged to share information with their counterparts in other states "as appropriate" and "in accordance with their domestic laws." The major interventions advocated by the protocol becomes one of monitoring trafficking routes, borders, and checking travel documents at key points of entry such as airports. The goal is to identify and distinguish perpetrators and victims along the international routes used by organized crime groups. States are urged to consider measures to deny or revoke the visas of those implicated in trafficking. Increased surveillance and border security measures are advocated to make it more difficult to falsify or alter travel and identity documents.

Before I further contextualize the UN Protocol against Trafficking in Persons by examining contending histories of its drafting process and its life as a normative document that circulates in a variety of social fields, it is possible to note some very interesting attributes of this formulation as it stands. The protocol hints at the issues debated in its formulation and the kind of discipline required of states so that they can protect themselves. In my view, what is so striking in the text is the representational strategy that idealizes the coupling of state self-protection with the protection of "vulnerable victims" – signaled in the refrain of "especially women and children" – that serves as the protocol's gloss for vulnerability. The imagined remedies outlined in the document evoke the image of the paternal state, watching over the welfare of a gendered victim. The strong and well-prepared state protects itself and its citizens by watching over its borders and protecting the nation from the entry of threatening "others" – especially illegal travelers of other nationalities. Combating traffickers means bureaucratically monitoring identities and documents in order to sort out those involved in trafficking networks from the general public and differentiate traffickers and victims as they attempt to penetrate the state's security system.

Yet, the playing field established by the protocol's definition of exploitation is in theory more comprehensive. *Any person* – read any worker – transnationally recruited through slavery, slave-like practices, or arrangements that involve extending debts coercively collected as part of an exploitative regime of forced labor or demand for services has, by this definition, been victimized by the crime of human trafficking. The measure of criminal wrong-doing is the recruitment, transportation, or receipt of persons achieved through coercive force, deception, abuses of vulnerability, or the use of debt to achieve control over another with the goals of exploiting them for profit. Consent in this formulation is a non-issue when any of these forms of coercive, deceptive, or manipulative means of achieving control are used or, alternatively, if the person is a minor under international law, "a child."

As I see it, the result of this formulation is a vacillating definition of the problem and scope of the beneficiaries of the protocol. All laborers working under coercive circumstances are covered by these new strategies for criminalizing traffickers rather than their "victims" and entitled to available protections and remedies. Yet the protocol returns repeatedly to focus on women and children, and by implication to trafficking for commercial sexual exploitation. This channeling of universality to narrower constructions repeatedly takes on a gendered imagery. While the choice between a universal and a much more particular framing is kept in play, trafficking for sexual exploitation seems fated to edge toward center stage. In fact, many states interpret it as dealing exclusively with the transnational prostitution of women, with "sex slaves" who work in extremely abusive, degrading, and violent circumstances. Here the fact that the protocol was originally designated by the General Assembly in 1998 as a legal instrument to dealing specifically with women and children continues to suffuse the document even as the mandate was widened during the drafting process to include other issues and the gender neutral language of personhood.

I was struck with the silences[9] and long lists of issues in the protocol's definition of trafficking. One can see at different junctures – such as in the characterization of forms of exploitation – evidence in the protocol of the piling on of issues. Sally Merry (2006) describes this process in her work on transnational consensus building at UN meetings. At international women's rights sessions, she identifies the delegates' common practice of contributing to lists of issues without offering justifications or suggesting substitutions and the tendency to keep alive alternative wordings in working drafts. This representation combines consensus decision-making and conflict resolution:

> Although there were often proposals to eliminate sections or to streamline language, there was a tendency to take an additive approach to resolving differences, producing very repetitive texts. Strong sentences were often qualified and lost their punch. Clear timelines for action and obligations on governments were shifted to vague normative recommendations. Code phrases such as "as appropriate" or "as soon as possible," were used to diminish nations' responsibilities to accomplish goals.
>
> (Merry 2006: 42)[10]

---

[9] There are interesting omissions such as the forced recruitment of irregular militias composed of male child soldiers and female sex slaves who served them in some recent African wars.

[10] Merry found other strategies in the crafting of UN documents, such as recognized power differentials of different blocs of countries playing out in the process of textual production, and some delegates' very adroit importing of selections of other UN documents that by definition had already been vetted and thus considered to have already passed through the UN consensus-making process (2006: 42–44).

One can see many of these code phrases in the trafficking protocol, particularly in the implementation section which waters down legal obligations for states with very undemanding calls to action: "to the extent possible according to domestic law," "in appropriate cases," "return . . . shall preferably be voluntary," "States Parties shall endeavor to undertake measures . . .," "Each State Party shall consider . . ."

Finally, Merry (2006) takes note of the ways that consensus phrasing from earlier UN documents can be skillfully appropriated by delegates in the present, tactically taking advantage of their status as having successfully passed the test of consensus approval. One sees this process throughout the wording of the protocol, as key phrasings are borrowed from earlier documents such as the 1949 Convention for the Suppression of the Traffic in Persons and the Exploitation of the Prostitution of Others. This combination of a genealogy of terms associated with politicized cleavages in the present accounts for some of the awkward wording in the text which, as I will illustrate later in this chapter, marks ideological positions for those in the know and leaves other readers puzzled and confused.

The protocol text can be seen as the product of highly participatory state delegations acting within an ad hoc committee structure, a power structure that gives leadership roles to certain countries, bolstered by cross-cutting lines of representation via regional blocks and blocks of developed and underdeveloped states in addition to interest group networks. This mode made room for NGOs, UN bodies, and other interests to lobby government delegations with suggestions for the drafting process stemming from their own agendas. The underlying conventions for consensus decision making allow a great deal of debate but tend to channel outcomes in a risk adverse manner. Sometimes the result is an inconsistent, heterogeneous statements or vague overgeneralizations with little actual content rather than a precise specification of issues that would call for more appropriate and far-reaching interventions. In some ways one can see the protocol as undermining itself even as it makes violence visible in telling ways. With its stress on national borders and the privileging of domestic law and state discretion in implementing reforms, with only a nod toward encouraging interstate cooperation, the protocol acts to elevate state power at the moment of its continuing compromise given intensified globalization and transnationalism.

For instance, I was struck with how the issue of "demand," when mentioned, is left unspecified and ambiguous or is subtly sexualized by the chain of associations created with the lead-off concern with trafficking as prostitution and sexual exploitation and the refrain "especially women and children." While the protocol focuses on the "supply" side of the issue and the criminalization of trafficking there, the domestic "demand" as a driver of this commerce remains oddly underexplored as a point of intervention.[11] Article 5 on criminalization pictures this as an interpersonal rather than an institutional issue. Little is said about how demand would be characterized in the different cases of exploitation or how demand is entrepreneurially, institutionally, and politically cultivated. Missing is the broad scope of organized trafficking entrepreneurs and corporatized "entertainment" industries. To some extent this is the consequence of having an umbrella convention against Transnational Organized Crime, which explicates transnational organizational and financial issues in a generic way and has other agendas such as money laundering in mind. But this seems distant from the issues at hand in the protocol.

Rather, in the trafficking protocol, there is emphasis on boundaries as the major locus of state intervention and reform. The state's efforts to protect itself through protecting vulnerable others, in my view, displaces the issues of domestic demand, internal markets, and state complicity or indifference. While dangerous recruiter-transporters are the primary target for criminalization, the demand for trafficked migrant labor is marked as a special issue tied on the domestic scene with the "educational," "social" or "cultural" issues appropriate to the national situation:

> States Parties shall adopt or strengthen legislative or other measures, such as educational, social or cultural measures, including through bilateral and multilateral cooperation, to discourage the demand that fosters all forms of exploitation of persons, especially women and children, that leads to trafficking.
>
> (Article 9, item 5)

It is interesting that the call for interventions becomes most sensitive to local culture when demand issues are raised.

DRAFTING THE TEXT IN VIENNA

Drafting the trafficking convention and protocols took the better part of two years. One can begin to get a sense of the drafting process in this

---

[11] On demand, see Anderson and O'Connell 2002, Eckberg 2004, and Raymond 2004.

particular situation from the government delegates' drafts, commentaries produced for discussion, and reports from NGOs with consultative status, along with our background on the cultural routines that guide UN knowledge production.[12] There are a variety of accounts of the drafting process, most all of them partisan ones.[13] Here we have the chance to see the influence of the context on the production of the protocol's text and the social fields that were activated and rejuvenated in the process.

At the first session of the Ad Hoc Committee, delegates who had participated in the preparatory meetings submitted drafts of the instruments under consideration for circulation and discussion. Almost immediately there was anxiety over potential overlaps between the "illegal trafficking and the transport of migrants" for the smuggling protocol and the "illicit trafficking in women and children" for the trafficking protocol. This seems to be a predictable moment in the development of long-term consensus building, an attempt to delimit the object of study and establish the appropriate segmentation of this market of crises in need of regulation and reform. Some felt the trafficking and smuggling instruments should be discussed together, others felt they raised different issues and should be discussed separately.[14] In reality, the blurring of the experiences of smuggled migrants and trafficked workers continues to be an important issue, made all the more significant because under the new legal regime wider rights are accorded to individuals who are deemed by emigration and police authorities to have been "trafficked" rather than "smuggled."

Some delegates thought there might be overlap between the present project and the work of the Committee on the Rights of the Child.[15] In a telling observation, it was explained that the findings of the Committee on the Rights of the Child were a non-issue for these deliberations because the Ad Hoc Committee was considering the issues "from the perspective of international criminal law and cooperation in criminal

[12] This overview is based on a careful review of the UN documents concerning the trafficking protocol sessions in Vienna, governmental reports, and NGO input critiquing the drafting process at the meetings. I plan future interviews with delegates and NGO representatives.
[13] See, for example, Ditmore and Wijers 2003; Doezema 2002, 2005; Human Rights Caucus 2002, 2000a, 2000b; Jordan 2002a, 2002b; Kanics, Reiter, and Uhl 2005; Kemapdoo 2005; Raymond 2001, 2002; Sanghera 2005; Sullivan 2003; and UN General Assembly 2000.
[14] See Bhabha 2005 on the blurring of trafficking and smuggling experiences in practice.
[15] The meeting notes read like this passage in that proper names are not generally used, unless one is talking of leadership positions where recognition is important, and people are usually subsumed, if identified, in the name of their state.

matters" rather than from a human rights perspective. In the end, a compromise reached directing discussions of related protocols to take place in sequential meetings so that any overlap could be easily taken care of (A/AC.254/3, p. 3).

In fact the venue for the meetings – in Vienna, the center of international law enforcement policy and research, rather than New York or Geneva, the center of human rights institutions and advocacy – was for some the determinative issue for the whole process. From the onset, the delegates and observers were quite aware of the political geography in which they were working, even as some resisted the local dominance of law enforcement perspective. In the case of human trafficking, it is clear that this initial allocation of the process to the UN Crime Commission and its inclusion within the Organized Crime convention set the tone for a similar law enforcement emphasis.[16] Nevertheless, human rights issues were very much on the minds of the human rights NGOs who lobbied during the drafting process.

Over the course of the meetings, there was an ebb and flow of delegates, representatives of UN Secretariat units, UN bodies and affiliated institutions, specialized organizations in the UN system, intergovernmental organizations, and NGOs, some with general consultative and special consultative statuses. Given the diverse topics of this convention and the protocols, there was a very heterogeneous mix of institutions and interest groups.

Delegates at the planning session for the first session Ad Hoc Committee meeting came from forty-nine countries, ninety-one came for the first session (and larger numbers came for many of the later sessions). UN Secretariat units and agencies included the UN High Commissioner for Refugees Office, UN Children's Fund, and International Maritime Organization. Regional institutes were also in attendance, including the Latin American Institute for the Prevention of Crime and the Treatment of Offenders, International Centre for Criminal Law Reform and Criminal Justice Policy, and International Institute of Higher Studies in Criminal Sciences. Intergovernmental organizations were also represented including the European Union, International Organization for Migration (IOM), International Criminal Police Organization, International Federation of Red Cross and Red Crescent Societies, Organization for Economic Cooperation

[16] See Jordan 2002: 2–4.

and Development, and Organization for Security and Cooperation in Europe (A/AC.254/3, 1999, pp. 4–5).

Finally there were NGOs with consultative status, general or special, with the Economic and Social Council, statuses that were carefully annotated in the attendees reports. These NGOs included the International Council of Women (general consultative status), Pax Romana (International Catholic Movement for Intellectual and Cultural Affairs) (International Movement of Catholic Students) with special consultative status; the National Rifle Association (NRA) of America's Institute for Legislative Action, and the Sporting Shooter's Association of Australia (roster) (A/AC.254/3 1999, pp. 4–5). Clearly the variety of issues raised in the protocols brought very different groups to the meetings.

Representatives of UN organizations and major NGOs, including the Office of the High Commissioner for Refugees, UNESCO, Amnesty International, Anti-Slavery International, International Human Rights Law Group, and Pax Romana among others, were involved in the trafficking and migrant smuggling protocol sessions, as I will discuss below.

Early in the proceedings there was a flurry of drafts for the trafficking protocol. The United States offered one at the first session and Argentina replied with a draft of additional considerations. By the second session on May 8–12, 1999, the decision had been made that the delegations from the two countries would produce a combined text with different wordings bracketed in the text to facilitate the discussion of the options (A/AC.254/9, p. 6). Argentina had begun with the "especially women and children" phrasing for the discussion of traffick- ing, while the United States had favored the gender neutral and inclusive framing of "persons." As is clear from my analysis discussion of the final protocol, the resolution in this instance was to make the final document a blend of both representational strategies.

As the sessions progressed areas of intense interest emerged for the state delegates. Defining the key terms of the convention and protocols occupied a great deal of time. Defining trafficking took a whole year of deliberation with serious discussions over whether the trafficking protocol should be worded as initially intended "for women and children" or for the more inclusive "persons," and many differences of opinion over the distinction between trafficking and smuggling were aired. An interesting convention exercise that captured the imagin- ation of a variety of delegations was the task of compiling a master list of transnational crimes – a good case of piling on in the group exchanges though one that was not carried through to the convention itself (A/AC.254/4/Rev. 2, pp. 48, 49; A/AC.254/13, p. 6).

Some delegates and NGOs were experts in marshalling phrases from early texts as sources for the protocol wording. The history of white slavery and early anti-trafficking campaigns, with their driving interest in abduction for forced prostitution, were introduced by some who tied the gendering of the protocol to earlier moments of international law, such as the 1949 Convention for the Suppression of the Traffic in Persons and the Exploitation of the Prostitution of Others, the 1926 Slavery Convention, the 1953 Protocol Amending the Slavery Convention, and the Platform for Action of the Beijing Fourth World Conference on Women (A/AC.254/4/Rev. 2, p. 48).

Two sets of social fields were mobilized in the drafting process, beyond the substantive interest groups who were by definition more involved in one drafting enterprise than the others. As in other UN deliberations, there was a conventionalized stratification of delegations into "donor countries [invited] to cooperate with developing countries" to insure that everyone was represented on the Ad Hoc Committee. Several unnamed delegations raised the issue at the first two sessions, as did representatives of the Group of 77 plus China. The UN Secretariat made a call for countries to help fund this wider participation. Apparently, only Japan and the United States replied to the request, leaving some of the forty-eight least developed countries without support and the opportunity to attend the Ad Hoc Committee. Faced with this shortfall, the Secretariat called on the regional blocs to help with additional funding. These classical regional groupings, used by the United Nations encourage fuller representation, were an integral part of the convention and protocol meetings (A/AC.254/13, p. 4). These were among the other axes of transnationalism in the drafting process, other ways to stratify and segment leadership and the production of knowledge and transnational norms. One wonders if, during the discussions of trafficking, the asymmetry between "sending" countries, which tend to be the economically disadvantaged, and "receiving" countries, which tend to be economically privileged, came ever closer to home on the trafficking issue than the delegates might have anticipated.

In the drafting process, one can trace a series of social fields, status hierarchies, and geopolitical divisions, not to mention the institutional contexts and cultural norms that propelled the drafting process. The major cleavage in this drafting, however, was an ideological one between three sets of NGOs, two of which regarded themselves as deeply embedded in debates over the interpretation of human rights and gender concerns and one of which was ambivalent about participating in a trafficking protocol which might well adversely affect them.

THE LIVING HISTORY OF THE ANTI-TRAFFICKING PROTOCOL

One can go a step further in the analytical process, using historical and anthropological approaches to examine the debates that surfaced during the drafting and the representational strategies used by advocates in their anti-trafficking campaigns to establish wider authority. Diverse social fields and institutional interests were activated in the process. To provide a window on the clashing arguments, I consulted a range of advocacy documents, commentaries by contending parties in the drafting process beyond the delegate drafts, including commentaries from NGOs, UN offices, and other international organizations.

It is clear that NGO advocates weighed in with important suggestions during the process and that they contributed something more than the evident piling on of issues, formulaic abstractions, overgeneralizations, and ambiguities in the final document. Through widely circulated position papers and annotations of the protocol, several sets of groups allied with major social movements sought to compel legal and policy reforms to promote support for individuals who had been trafficked. International NGO networks are often involved in providing expert consultants and researchers for country studies, assessments, and evaluations called for by international organizations. They may act locally as direct service providers for the implementation of interventions called for by the protocol. As a result of their continuing engagement with the issues, NGO appropriations of the protocol have important ramifications for state reform and community involvement long after the ratification process is over. Developing media, publicity, and workshops for anti-trafficking educational campaigns involves engaging different publics and government agencies. The question, of course, is how those multiple publics are conceptualized and reached by different perspectives.

This examination of the NGO protocol debates begins with Janice Raymond, the executive director of the Coalition against Trafficking in

Women (CATW), who lobbied during the Vienna meetings from a neo-abolitionist perspective, sought delegate allies, and promoted protocol wording to reflect this ideological position. She has published "Guide to the New UN Trafficking Protocol" (2001), "The New UN Trafficking Protocol" (2002), and essays on such issues as "Prostitution on Demand: Legalizing the Buyers as Sexual Consumers" (2004), essays that have been widely translated. These advocacy pieces represent the views of the Human Rights Network, an umbrella group composed of CATW; the Movement for the Abolition of Pornography and Prostitution (MAPP), France; the European Women's Lobby (EWL); the Association des Femmes de l'Europe Meridionale (AFEM); Article One, France; and Equality Now, United States. These groups worked on statements reflecting their anti-prostitution commitment and mobilized a network of 140 NGOs, which included a wide range of international participants, who supported their views.[17]

Janice Raymond was an active lobbyist throughout the drafting of the trafficking protocol. Although she diplomatically embraced the protocol's inclusive list of different forms of exploitation (2001: 1), her network's primary interest centered on "the exploitation of the prostitution of others or other forms of sexual exploitation" and specifically on gendered violence against "women and children." To add authority to this position, she drew from the 1949 Convention for the Suppression of the Traffic in Persons and the Exploitation of the Prostitution of Others.

Harkening back to the early work of Kathleen Barry (1979, 1995), the founder of CATW, Raymond seeks to marshal feminist NGOs to fight against the growing crisis of the legalization and regulation of prostitution. She argues that there is really no significant difference between domestic and international trafficking, and that legalization or regulation of prostitution does not reduce the numbers of women who are internationally trafficked for prostitution:

> Governments which have rejected this false solution of legalization and chosen to address prostitution as a violation of women's rights are in a key position to create forums and model regional legislation in which prostitution is put back on the policy agenda ... [M]any countries in Europe and the new independent states are rushing to redefine prostitution as legal work in the misguided attempt to regulate and control

---

[17] For a listing of the 140 organizations affiliated with the abolitionist cause through the International Human Rights Network, see Raymond 2001: 11.

what they allege are the abuses of prostitution without recognizing that
the system of prostitution itself is the abuse.

(Raymond 2001: 8)

She argues that where prostitution has been legalized in Europe a two-
tier system has developed and the sex industry has flourished with
growing regional tourism, creating structural inequalities between
women citizens who work with some protection in official establish-
ments and large numbers of internationally trafficked women who work
in marginal brothels for lower pay without the official services, in
situations where they are doubly exploited. For her, the legalization
of prostitution means that there will be greater investment in and
government support of the sex industry which makes the physical and
psychological abuse and control of women central to business.[18] The
cooptation of western governments as "destination countries" means
that they are corrupted in their dealings with developing countries
even as they fund direct service projects in countries in political and
economic crisis. The NGOs working where prostitution is legalized
must hide their critical views of prostitution or risk losing government
funding (Raymond 2002: 498–499). Countries with legalized or regulated prostitution such as Holland and Germany become, in effect,
dangerous, corrupt, and immoral.

As Raymond argues, "The Protocol promises to contest the world's
organized crime networks and combat the trade in human beings and
transnational prostitution." The issue for these organizations is a construction that protects "all victims of [sexual exploitation and] trafficking, not just those who could prove they had been forced" (Raymond
2001: 3). In this formulation, there is no separation to be made between
prostitution and trafficking. Consent is a non-issue because all victims
of prostitution and trafficking fall into a protected class because of the
extreme violence of their abuse, according to Raymond's reading of
Article 3. This framing means that, by definition, a sex worker cannot
be seen as working *of her own volition*. Coercion is a non-issue in the
sense because it is unreasonable to require women who have been
violently abused to provide legally accepted proof of the intentions of
their abusers; thus, there is no individual burden of proof of trafficking
in this reading of the official document. Abolitionists want to disman-
tle the sex industry and are especially concerned with the protection

[18] See Farley 2000.

rather than criminalization of women and children as victims, the prosecution of traffickers, and the targeting of men to diminish the demand for prostitution (Raymond 2002, 2004). In this formulation, it is prostitution not the transportation of victims that is the crucial issue for interventions. This movement strongly opposes the legalization of prostitution and seeks the criminalization of the "male buyers of women" and the sex industry, rather than the women who have been victimized in prostitution. The abolitionists promote a human rights perspective focusing on the protection of victims of trafficking.

Ann Jordan, a lawyer, head of the International Human Rights Law Group (IHRLG), offered direct challenges to Raymond's Human Rights Network in Vienna. Jordan has a long history of activism as a lobbyist and legal advisor for the adoption of the UN Convention on the Elimination of All Forms of Discrimination Against Women. She produced the "Annotated Guide to the Complete UN Trafficking Protocol" (2002b) and "Human Rights or Wrongs?: The Struggle for a Rights-Based Response to Trafficking in Human Beings" (2002a), and consulted on "Human Rights and Trafficking in Persons: A Handbook" (Pearson 2001). Her interpretive guide reflects the views of the Human Rights Caucus, a network of eleven international NGOs including the IHRLG, Foundation Against Trafficking in Women, Global Alliance Against Traffic in Women (GAATW), Asian Women's Human Rights Council, La Strada, Ban-Ying, Fundación Esperanza, Foundation for Women, KOK-NGO Network Against Trafficking in Women, Solomon Foundation, Women's Consortium of Nigeria, Women, and Law & Development in Africa (Nigeria). One can see in this list the involvement of a wide range of international rights groups.

Created to inform human rights activists from a labor perspective, Jordan's multi-layered guide to the protocol weaves together strands of the protocol's text and relevant selections from the wider UN Convention against Transnational Organized Crime, its parent document. In addition, the Travaux Preparatoires (official notes routinely formulated to accompany protocols to guide their interpretation) and the IHRLG's "Unofficial Annotations" are included in the text as distinctive strands that explain the significance of the official text for advocates of a human rights framing of anti-trafficking law and policies.

Jordan's view stresses the issue of worker rights in the global economy, and refuses to see prostitution and sexual exploitation as special gendered issues that stand over and above other kinds of work place exploitation. In fact, Jordan lobbied to delete both phrases from the protocol, arguing that the rest of Article 3 adequately covered all coerced and bonded labor. In contrast to the abolitionist position, consent and choice are the fundamental issues for the Human Rights Caucus. If workers freely consent to sex work or other kinds of labor and the terms of their work agreements are legal then they have not been trafficked. In this view, the transnational trafficking of workers by organized crime and the state's complicity in depriving trafficked laborers of legal rights after their arrest and detainment, most often for visa overstaying, are major concerns. In contrast to states' emphasis on border monitoring and visa enforcement, Jordon wants to secure support for individuals who had been trafficked against their will, to work in slavery-like conditions, and be held in bondage until huge debts for transportation and other exaggerated expenses as debts are repaid. Among the rights she is concerned with are the right of women and men to testify in court in proceedings against their traffickers, just compensation for their mistreatment and violations of their rights, and their choice (rather than the state's mandate) of whether to remain where they are with legal residency papers or to return home, as individual evaluations of circumstances warranted. The Human Rights Caucus favors policies that open borders to workers so they can weigh their own migration options rather than depend on illegal traffickers.

Representatives of the Network of Sex Work Projects (NSWP), including writer and sex worker activist Jo Doezema, joined Jordan's Human Rights Caucus in a loose and low profile coalition of their own making. Their views as sex workers complicate any neatly polarized view of the anti-trafficking debates. Doezema produced her own critical evaluation of the proceedings. Her writings include "Who Gets to Change?: Coercion, Consent, and the UN Trafficking Protocol" (2002), "Now You See Her, Now You Don't: Sex Workers at the UN Trafficking Protocol Negotiations (2005a), and "Sex Worker Rights, Abolitionism and the Possibility for a Rights-based Approach to Trafficking" (2005b). These publications describe the conditional support that NSWP's advocates expressed for the protocol's reforms and questions they have raised about the utility and efficacy of the language of rights for the aspirations of this sex worker social movement. With very different arguments, the NSWP contests both the abolitionist and the workers' rights advocates.

The NSPA asserts that sex work is another legitimate form of labor. They reject the special status and moral stigma attributed to prostitution by abolitionists who see prostitution as evil, by states that criminalize sex work rather than the abusers of sex workers, and by other feminists who see the male violent sexual exploitation of women's bodies as a reflection of women's sexual and economic subordination and growing income gaps with globalization. Doezema (2005) points out that sex workers include men, women, and transgendered people. In this formulation, children are the protected class, lacking legal consent until they reach the age of eighteen. She argues that sex workers are concerned with alternative constructions of their political project that would provide more fluid ways to express choice. Many activists are ambivalent about the liberal rights-based language which, in effect, contrasts "voluntary prostitution as work" versus "forced prostitution as violence" (2005: 70). In practice, the consent denied by neo-abolitionists (yet central to the NSWP's construction of freedom) turns out to be consistent with liberal feminist thinking. What troubles sex work activists is the unintended consequence of this language, especially with the renewed international politicization of trafficking. From their point of view, the contrast between "free workers" and "forced workers" can easily slip into a distinction between free workers who need rights and forced workers who need rescue. Suddenly liberalism is transformed into another variant of neo-abolitionism.

This danger and the association of many anti-trafficking organizations with an implicit, if not explicit, anti-prostitution politics pushed sex work activists, who were welcomed as active allies in the Human Rights Caucus, to the margins of the protocol deliberation of IHRLG and GAATW. To the extent that anti-trafficking discourses continue to limit sex workers' mobility and their rights as voluntary migrants, there will continue to be tension between the movements (Doezema 2005: 70–72, 76). In the end, the NSWP went on record at the protocol deliberations as opposing the trafficking protocol at the same time as it privately collaborated with the Human Rights Caucus. Doezema's provocative analysis demonstrates the way in which sex workers' outsider position and their tensions with both currents of feminism reveal a great deal about the dynamics and presuppositions in international anti-trafficking campaigns.

Both Raymond's and Jordan's networks identified themselves with human rights perspectives attempting to influence government delegation work by providing their own statements for key sections of the protocol, most importantly with regard to the definitional section in Article 3, and critical appraisals of final document to give impetus to alternative forms of activism. They have also been active in critiquing each other's constructions of trafficking. In the end, one could argue that neither side received the protocol they wanted because the final document incorporated so many moments of compromise. Each side's guide, however, makes the best case for its triumph in the final version of the protocol. As I argued earlier in the chapter, these maneuvers are more than spin; rather, they are aggressive attempts to claim ownership and harness the protocol as impetus for state and transnational reforms from radically different points of view. What becomes apparent as we see the groups in action is the *interplay* of the key terms in the protocol – consent, coercion, and vulnerability – and their liberal and moralized heritage.

CONCLUSIONS

At the beginning of this chapter, I replied to Rajagopal's question about the consequences of the invisibility of so many types of violence with the suggestion that we also confront the political and epistemic dynamics through which violence is recognized. This chapter argues that making violence visible for the world community is a profoundly historical and collective organizational act. To shed light on a new generation of global efforts to define and combat human trafficking, this chapter traces the production of knowledge behind the creation of 2000 UN Protocol to Prevent, Suppress, and Punish Trafficking in Persons, Especially Women and Children. In the process, I consider Sally Merry's observation[19] that making victims of human rights abuses visible involves casting them as worthy victims, as vulnerable individuals who have been stripped of their agency. This certainly appears to be the case in mass media portrayals of trafficking and in the outcome of the protocol drafting of new international norms. Yet, this examination of major NGOs and their debates during the Vienna meetings reveals a more complicated picture, including organized resistance to gendered images of vulnerability in some quarters, and very different strategies for intervention.

This chapter traces the emergence of a rediscovered formation of violence. Unlike 1949, when the Convention for the Suppression of

---

[19] See Merry's Introduction to Part III in this volume for her commentary on vulnerability.

the Traffic in Persons and the Exploitation of the Prostitution of Others attracted little attention and very few signatures, in 2000 human trafficking, phrased as an international organized crime issue along with migrant smuggling and small arms control, commands wider international audiences. NGOs, UN offices, transnational organizations like the International Organization of Migration (OIM), and the World Health Organization (WHO), and the Catholic Church, all with longer track records than the General Assembly's Ad Hoc Committee, are midwives of this document.

My analytical strategy for this study of the creation of international norms for human trafficking has been to peel back multiple layers in the production and codification of knowledge, moving from examining the protocol as an official text to engaging the complex transnational contexts – historical, organizational, political, and ideological – that influenced the crafting and interpretation of these norms. One can identify abstract forces that play a role in the current situation – economic globalization and expanding markets that create demands for trafficked migrant labor; political and economic instabilities at home that force people to look elsewhere for their livelihoods and greater opportunity; and the transnational circulation of goods, people, businesses, social movements, and ideologies that tie different world regions together. But this list of forces and currents of change begs the question of how the perceived crisis of human trafficking has taken the shape that it has and choices made among interventions imagined "combat" it.

The legal recognition of "human trafficking" is a good example of how much work it takes to create a unified object, a distinctive formation of violence which, despite its heterogeneous history in different parts of the world and diverse contemporary manifestations, requires global norms and standardized transnational interventions to criminalize certain acts and decriminalize others. The trafficking protocol took the form it did through two years of deliberations influenced by the United Nations template for international legal instruments, the transnational elite culture of consensus decision making and conflict resolution at the Vienna meetings where it was developed, and the compromises that emerged during the delegates' deliberations which were informed by polarized debates among NGO networks that politicize trafficking in different ways.

As this analysis has shown, the meetings were influenced by two contending "authorized" views of trafficking, the fruits of human rights movements with contrasting feminist roots, each with a distinctive ideology and its own international networks of NGOs. Added to this mix was a subaltern "unauthorized" view with its own libratory agenda and networks that wound up rejecting the trafficking framework itself. Each movement was committed to distinctive definitions of who is vulnerable, what coercion involves, and what lack of consent signifies. Each had its own definition of exploitation. Remedies flowed from distinctive definitions of the problem. Movement identities were not autonomous as much as they were mutually revealing elements of each other's ideologies that played off each other for a sense of threat and urgency.

The neoabolitionists, like Janice Raymond, named and circumscribed the violence of trafficking as female prostitution, forcing other forms of labor to the margins of the protocol's agenda, to create a gendered vulnerability that renders consent irrelevant because, by definition, women prostitutes are the objects/products of male violence. By contrast, the workers' rights advocates like Ann Jordan, in effect, made the claim that the protocol was in danger of representing and delimiting the wrong kind of violence. For them, trafficked labor rests on a key contrast between forced labor against an individual's will and labor to which individuals consent. The quest for recognized rights, voice, and agency for male and female workers poses an alternative to the archetypes of trafficked women who must be rescued from their abuse. Organized sex workers like Jo Doezema who were involved in the protocol debates with a lower profile by choice rejected the protocol on the grounds that made no room for their work to occupy a space of choice beyond stigma, violence, and the limits of liberal constructions of rights. One can see in these constructions the way that the groups were mutually revealing, some marking the protocol's boundaries from a position situated, at that point, largely but not completely outside its scope.

The protocol itself situates trafficking in relation to transnational organized crime, the surveillance of state borders, and law enforcement practices focused on monitoring passports and visas. While giving a nod to interstate cooperation, it reaffirms state powers by dwelling on the image of states in control of their own borders. Greater weight is given to the "enforcement paradigm" and to the strengthening of border surveillance at the very moment when the quickened pace of globalization and transnationalism has deeply eroded state sovereignty in many ways. The result of concentrating on policing and emigration reforms to monitor entry points is an emphasis on detecting dangerous foreigners – criminalizing the trafficker, trafficked, and the migrant alike despite the language of the protocol. In this discourse, the dangers are projected outside the borders rather than configured as complicit with domestic organized crime and policing structures within the country. At issue will be the capacity of activist NGOs to reassert more of the "human rights paradigm" as the protocol is implemented, particularly the capacity to define their work futures and residence.

This particular essay leaves the protocol project in midstream as texts are transformed into state policy and interventions. To follow this contemporary history through, one would have to look at the post-ratification process as states create their own Action Plans to demonstrate their compliance with new international norms and best practices. Let me hasten to add from my research in Japan and Colombia and discussions with Eastern European activists that individuals and NGOs spend a great deal of their time working in the political space between the polarized positions I explore in this chapter. Nevertheless, there are powerful political forces that demand signs of compliance with one construction or the other for access to jobs and funding.[20]

To pursue transnational anti-trafficking campaigns, one would have to examine the monitoring of state compliance with international norms after the protocol's ratification. Although the UN protocol has only weak provisions for monitoring compliance, the US State Department moved into this vacuum to produce the annual TIP (Trafficking in Persons) reports of country-by-country compliance with the goal of publicly punishing non-compliance and rewarding efforts to respond to the protocol's framing of effective ways to combat trafficking. I am working on these issues as this research project turns to the interplay of global norms and local responses at the state level to demonstrate the way the accords are appropriated as they are propelled through new sites of national politics and anxiety in different parts of the world.[21]

REFERENCES

Anderson, Bridget, and Julia O'Connell Davidson. 2002. *Trafficking – A Demand Led Problem?: A Multi-Country Pilot Study.* Stockholm: Save the Children.
Barry, Kathleen. 1979. *Female Sexual Slavery.* New York and London: New York University Press.

[20] This includes the US development establishment which is fully committed to an anti-prostitution stance.
[21] For insightful comparative research on this issue, see Munro 2006.

Barry, Kathleen. 1995. *The Prostitution of Sexuality*. New York and London: New York University Press.

Bhabha, Jacqueline. 2005. "Trafficking, Smuggling, and Human Rights." *Migration Information Source*. March 1: pp. 1–6. Available on-line at www.migrationinformation.org

Buss, Doris, Ruth Fletcher, Daniel Monk, Surya Monro, and Oliver Phillips. 2005. "Introduction to 'Sexual Movements and Gendered Boundaries: Legal Negotiations of the Global and the Local.'" *Social and Legal Studies* 14(1): 5–15.

Ditmore, Melissa, and Warjan Wijers. 2003. "The Negotiations on the UN Protocol on Trafficking in Persons." *Nemesis* 4: 79–88.

Doezema, Jo. 2002. "Who Gets of Choose?: Coercion, Consent, and the UN Trafficking Protocol." *Gender and Development* 10(1): 20–27.

Doezema, Jo. 2005. "Now You See Her, Now You Don't: Sex Workers at the UN Trafficking Protocol Negotiations." *Social and Legal Studies* 14(1): 61–89.

Ekberg, Gunilla. 2004. "The Swedish Law that Prohibits the Purchase of Sexual Services." *Violence against Women*, 10(10): 1187–1218.

Farley, Melissa. 2000. *Prostitution, Trafficking and Traumatic Stress*. New York: Haworth Press.

Human Rights Caucus. 2000a. "UN Trafficking Protocol: No Commitment to Protect the Rights of Trafficked Persons." Press Release. Available at, www.december18.net. Accessed 8 February 2007.

Human Rights Caucus. 2000b. "*Stop-traffic* UN Trafficking Protocol: Lost Opportunity to Protect the Rights of Trafficked Persons." October 23. Available at www.friends-partners.org/lists/stop-traffic/1999/1207.html

Jordan, Ann. 2002a. "Human Rights or Wrongs?: The Struggle for a Right-Based Response to Trafficking in Human Beings." *Gender and Development* 10(1): 28–37.

Jordan, Ann. 2002b. "The Annotated Guide to the Complete UN Trafficking Protocol," International Human Rights Law Group (IHRLG). Available at www.walnet.org/csis/papers/UN-TRAFFICK.PDF

Kanics, Jyothi, Gabriele Reiter, and Bärbel Heide Uhl. 2005. "Trafficking in Human Beings – A Threat under Control? Taking Stock Four years after Major International Efforts Started." *Helsinki Monitor* 1: 53–67.

Kempadoo, Kamala, ed. 2005. *Trafficking and Prostitution Reconsidered: New Perspectives on Migration, Sex, Work, and Human Rights*. Boulder: Paradigm Press.

Merry, Sally Engle. 2006. *Human Rights and Gender Violence: Translating International Law into Local Justice*. Chicago: University of Chicago Press.

Munro, Vanessa. 2006. "Stopping Traffic: A Comparative Study of Responses to the Trafficking in Women for Prostitution." *British Journal of Criminology* 46: 318–333.

Nordstrom, Carolyn. 2004. *Violence, Power, and International Profiteering at the Twenty-First Century.* Berkeley: University of California Press.

Pearson, Elaine. 2001. *Human Rights and Trafficking in Persons: A Handbook.* Bangkok, Thailand: Global Alliance against Trafficking in Women.

Rajagopal, Balakrishnan. 2003. *International Law from Below: Development, Social Movements and Third World Resistance.* Cambridge: Cambridge University Press.

Raymond, Janice. 2001. "Guide to the New UN Trafficking Protocol" North Amherst, MA: Coalition Against Trafficking in Women.

Raymond, Janice. 2002. "The New UN Trafficking Protocol." *Women's Studies International Forum,* 25 (5): 491–502.

Raymond, Janice. 2004. "Prostitution on Demand: Legalizing the Buyers as Sexual Consumers." *Violence against Women,* 10(10): 1156–1186.

Sanghera, Jyoti. 2005. "Unpacking the Trafficking Discourse." In Kampala Kempadoo, ed., *Trafficking and Prostitution Reconsidered: New Perspectives on Migration, Sex, Work, and Human Rights.* Boulder: Paradigm Press, pp. 3–24.

Scott, James. 1998. *Seeing Like a State: How Certain Schemes to Improve the Human Condition Have Failed.* New Haven: Yale University Press.

Sullivan, Barbara. 2003. "Trafficking in Women: Feminism and New International Law" *International Feminist Journal of Politics,* 5(1): 67–91.

Taylor, Ian, and Ruth Jamieson. 1999. "Sex Trafficking and the Mainstream of Market Culture." *Crime, Law and Social Change* 32: 257–278.

United Nations General Assembly. 2000 "UN Convention against Transnational Organized Crime," "UN Protocol to Prevent, Suppress and Punish Trafficking in Persons, especially Women and Children," and "UN Protocol against the Smuggling of Migrants by Land, Sea and Air." www.uncjin.org/Documents/Conventions/dcatoc/final_documents_2/index.htm

United Nations Ad Hoc Committee on the Elaboration of a Convention against Transnational Organized Crime. 1999. "Draft Protocol to Combat International Trafficking in Women and Children Supplementary to the United Nations Convention on Transnational Organized Crime." Item 4 of the provisional agenda. Proposal Submitted by the United States of America at the First Session January 19–29. V.98–57505 (E). A/AC.254/4/Add.3. New York: United Nations, pp. 1–5.

United Nations Ad Hoc Committee on the Elaboration of a Convention against Transnational Organized Crime. 1999. "Consideration of the Additional International Legal Instruments against Trafficking in Women and Children." Item 5 of the provision agenda. Submitted by Argentina at the First Session January 19–29. V.98–80243 (E). A/AC.254/8. New York: United Nations, pp. 1–5.

United Nations Ad Hoc Committee on the Elaboration of a Convention against Transnational Organized Crime. 1999 "Revised draft Protocol to Prevent, Suppress and Punish Trafficking in Women and Children, Supplementing the United Nations Convention against Transnational Organized Crime." Item 4 of the prvision agenda. Proposal submitted by Argentina and the United States at the Second Session. March 8–12. v.99–81266 (E) A/AC.254/4/Add.3/Rev. 1. New York: United Nations, pp. 1–10.

PART FOUR

ENCOUNTERING AMBIVALENCE

INTRODUCTION: ENCOUNTERING AMBIVALENCE

Balakrishnan Rajagopal

During the past decade, the relationship between anthropology and human rights has been reinvented, if one judges by the academic output that explains and documents it (American Anthropological Association (AAA) 1999; Cowan, Dembour and Wilson 2001; Engle 2001; Goodale 2006a, 2006b, 2006c; Mamdani 2000; Merry 2003, 2006a, 2006b; Riles 2000, 2006; Wilson 1997; Wilson and Mitchell 2003). With this reinvention, the contours of traditional debates in international human rights law such as the tension between universality of human rights and cultural relativism, have also been transformed, although this not fully reflected in the dominant human rights scholarship produced within the legal academy. Anthropology used to be identified with a strong Herskovitsian defense of cultural relativism, as exemplified in the famous 1947 AAA statement against universal human rights (AAA 1947). That statement famously declared that "[s]tandards and values are relative to the culture from which they derive so that any attempt to formulate postulates that grow out of the beliefs or moral codes of one culture must to that extent detract from the applicability of any Declaration of Human Rights to mankind as a whole" (AAA 1947: 542). This emphatic Boasian pronouncement was based on an anti-colonial and anti-racist stance which, with the exception of many anthropologists, virtually no other social scientists shared at that time. After almost fifty years, the anthropology profession has turned almost completely around, according to the AAA itself, which adopted a Declaration on Anthropology and Human Rights in 1999 (AAA 1999) in which it purported to reconcile itself with the anti-activist and relativist implications of the 1947 statement. While there are doubts as to how much the views of the anthropology profession has genuinely turned around from the Boasian relativism of its 1947 statement (Engle 2001; Goodale 2006a), there is little doubt that the academic study of anthropology as well as the role of anthropologists in the practice of human rights have significantly altered, with important implications for the legal scholarship on human rights. But this new-found enthusiasm for universal human rights among anthropologists has been accompanied by a rising level of ambivalence about the practice of human rights and the place of anthropology and anthropologists in that practice. The two chapters in this section by John Dale (chapter 7) and Sari Wastell (chapter 8) point to some of that ambivalence. The ambivalence can be seen in the changing attitudes towards the role of "outsiders" (especially westerners) in "local" cultural struggles; notions of legitimacy and violence; competing universal discourses such as development; politics of representation; and the relationship between activism and theory. These sets of ambivalence lead, in turn, to different conceptions of "practice" and power, that have significant implications for anthropologists on the one hand, and dominant human rights scholarship on the other.

On the positive side, I must begin by noting the contributions of anthropology to the study of human rights, which surely exceed its limited contribution to the topic of relativism. Mainstream or dominant human rights – by which I mean the official version of the source, purpose and the content of human rights as well as the production of knowledge by scholars and other actors that bolster the official version through the manufacture of a history, theory, method and criticism that confirms the official version – starts from several premises which are relevant to my discussion of its link with anthropology here:

(1) That the human rights discourse is a distinctly post-World War II modern discourse, which resulted from a Euro-American elite reaction to the atrocities committed by the Nazis and owes little to the struggles against colonialism.

(2) That human rights is to modernity what culture is to tradition; as a language of social transformation and even emancipation, rights interventions are teleologically focused on the transformation of tradition to modernity, and of culture to rights; that culture is about difference while rights are about leveling and sameness

(3) That international law is the official language of human rights, quite distinct from customary or even constitutional rights

regimes; that this language is the only, sole, legitimate discourse of resistance recognized by law, which will mean that any other form of resistance which is not recognized as human rights, stands the risk of being ignored or being met with a fierce backlash from organized modes of violence such as the state.

(4) Following from (2) to be recognized as "rights" scholarship or practice, the approved actors and languages of international human rights need to be used. Chief among those actors is the state, which defines the meaning of "practice".

Much of the ambivalence about human rights emerges from the tension between the dominant human rights approach to the issues mentioned above, and the views of anthropologists and other social scientists influenced by its methodological attention to what happens on the ground and an ethical commitment to understand the views of the non-elite and the subaltern.

While it is true that modern human rights institutions such as the United Nations are post-World War II creations, human rights *ideas* and *practices* predate World War II. A major element of this prehistory is the struggle against colonialism and racism, which motivated the 1947 AAA statement. I have written recently that a new social history of human rights that departs from its Euro- and State-centric historiography, is yet to be written, but the elements of that task already exist, thanks to the effort of anthropologists among others (Rajagopal 2003: ch. 7). The anticolonial revolt against Empires led to the recognition of the core human rights principles of our time including that of right to equality and the right to self-determination. The labor movements and the women's movements, not to mention the earliest "human rights" movements such as the antislavery movement, have been active at least since the nineteenth century in several countries. As ideas, and as concrete practices in the social, cultural, economic, and political domains, human rights can hardly be dated from World War II. Yet another element of the dominant narrative about human rights is that the rights revolution was begun by elites, such as Eleanor Roosevelt through her role in the drafting of the Universal Declaration on Human Rights (UDHR) at the United Nations. An anthropological reading of history can move away from this elitist focus and focus on the role played by ordinary people in the construction of human rights, through their everyday practices.

While much of this may be unremarkable to anthropologists, they also need to understand more clearly why the dominant position on human rights has a hard time comprehending even the possibility of a non-elitist historiography of human rights. First, perspective of dominant historiography, which is primarily in the field of international law, is that human rights was born as a Euro-American concept, which was then be exported to the less civilized, backward peoples of the non-western world, as they became civilized and were admitted to the community of nation-states. This was indeed the theoretical and doctrinal position of international law until World War II, but its influence still shadows the way human rights is imagined in the West. The global democracy-promotion agenda, the grammar of the United States-led imperial order now, is rooted in this fantasy. After World War II, the system of international law had to be revived from its acknowledged failures to prevent either wars or atrocities during the preceding several decades, and was seen to lack legitimacy due to its complicity with colonialism. As the former colonies gained independence, a new self-understanding of the discipline of international law was sought to be generated by its scholars and practitioners. According to this understanding, the new international law was different from the old international law of colonialism, and the idea of human rights was the main marker of this break, of its entry into a new modernity. This self-understanding was combined with the national interests of imperial powers to maintain their moral standing – essential for hegemonic leadership – in the difficult transitions from colonialism. This is one major reason why the image of human rights as a post-World War II gift from the West, is so central to a Euro-American dominated view of human rights. This view had no place for political agency exercised by non-elites, that too from the non-western world, thus continuing its attitude of contempt for the masses that was evident during the previous decades of colonial rule.

Second, dominant human rights approaches in scholarship and practice operate on simplistic, Manichean views of the distinction between tradition and modernity, and between rights and culture. Most human rights advocacy strategies, for example on issues such as Female Genital Mutilation (FGM) in Africa or the place of Shariat as a source of law in the new Iraqi Constitution, operate with this view of culture, wherein culture is somehow seen as organic and purely endogenous. Human rights scholarship, which rehearses the legal instantiations of these advocacy strategies, through court cases in which the advocates are victorious for example, unproblematically reproduces these understandings of a "bad" culture which needs to be disciplined by a modern, rational, "good" rights discourse, thus reaffirming images of redemption. Part of the reason why this is so has to do with the methodology of the discipline, which is legal and focused on macro-level strategies aimed at elites, so that they will be shamed into saving the "victims." But this Manichean image is also the logical result of the structure of human rights work in which sharply defined and simple images of destitution or exploitation or violence are more likely to lead to results because of the attention span and the crowded agendas of the elites who are called upon to act.

Thus, when anthropologists become human rights advocates or simply identify with their ethnographic subjects while doing "human rights research" as Riles points out (Riles 2006), they are also entering this Manichean world of isolated backward cultures in need of a dose of modernity from human rights. The problem for anthropologists is, of course, that this view of culture is no longer shared by their field. They may begin with the idea that culture is about difference, which is an article of faith among anthropologists. As the 1947 AAA statement declared, "[t]he individual realizes his personality through his culture, hence respect for individual differences entails a respect for cultural differences" (AAA 1947: 541). This emphasis on respect for cultural difference continues even in the 1999 statement of the AAA (AAA 1999; Engle 2001: 553). But now anthropologists do not equate respect for cultural difference with a respect for cultural autonomy. This is partly because their understanding of culture itself has changed, at least since the 1970s, to mean a more hybrid, open-ended term. It is also because their field has become thoroughly transnationalized, wherein no "local" and authentic cultures exist in isolation from transnational flows of actors, ideas or resources (Merry 1992). This disciplinary dissonance between anthropology and international law can produce ambivalence in the field of human rights towards goals, strategies, resources, and alliances.

At one level, anthropology provides a corrective to the dominant human rights view that human rights norms are first generated in a distinct transnational space, presumably through an amazing court ruling (such as *Filartiga* v. *Pena Irala*, a prominent US case that gave rise to litigation of the type discussed in John Dale's chapter) or by a heroic international lawyer (such as Judge Keba M'baye of Senegal who is reputed to have articulated the "right to development"), and then travel to the local level and are applied in practice. Rather, anthropology sees social practice itself as constitutive of the very idea of human rights, as Goodale points out in his Introduction to this volume (see pp. 8–9). I have argued in recent work that the struggle of social movements at the local level in fact inscribe and give content to transnational norms of human rights (Rajagopal 2003: ch. 8). The question for human rights law then becomes: how does one write the multiverse of resistance into international law? An attempt to engage in that writing remains one of the few ways in which a hegemonic international law can be thwarted in this age of empire and violence (Rajagopal 2006).

At another level, their continuing disciplinary emphasis on respect for local cultural difference and local political agency can lead anthropologists to deemphasize international norms, which may already be constituting the "local" human rights domain through various fields such as public international law (norms on recognition, treaty accession, incorporation into domestic law, minority rights, etc.) or private international law (rules on arbitration, investment, etc.). Perhaps it is due to this that anthropologists have had relatively little to say about how norms travel from one level to another, from the local to the global and back. Much of that explanation has come, regrettably, only from international relations scholars (for example Risse, Ropp and Sikkink 1999). This is a rich field in which anthropologists can contribute much.

Third, the dominant view of human rights is that it needs to be expressed in international law to be considered official. Thus, alternative articulations of rights in domestic law, or customary law, are treated as secondary or even suspect. From this premise, it also follows that to be recognized as legitimate, any form of resistance or even difference needs to be expressed in terms that are approved by the legally-sanctioned rights discourse; otherwise, organized violence in the form of state repression can be the result. Of course, there is a hegemonic move here wherein it is only the residents of weak, Third World countries, who are compelled to conform their resistance to global emancipatory scripts such as human rights, and not the citizens of the West (Rajagopal 2006).

Anthropology has done much to uncover alternative articulations of rights. By paying close attention to everyday practices and by uncovering states' failure to discharge their responsibilities to protect human rights through institutional ethnographies that view the state from below and by documenting the actions of social movements on the ground, anthropologists have contributed to the understanding of "rights in action" in informal, customary or even illegal arenas.

However, little of this has affected the dominant rights discourse, which remains fixated on official pronouncements of statist structures, both within and beyond state boundaries. The main reason for this disjuncture between legally-driven human rights and anthropology-driven approaches is their differing attitudes towards politics, and the function of politics. Lawyers see the main function of politics as the legitimation of social, economic and cultural arrangements, and therefore see the state as the main arena for producing this legitimation through both "hegemonic" tactics (such as human rights) as well as other tactics that draw on the state's monopoly of force and violence. Anthropologists, on the other hand, had very little engagement with the political, until a few decades ago, imagining "culture" as the dominant and the primary domain in which people lived their lives. This relative inattention to the political has changed, as can be seen in the attention to the concepts of "political culture" as well as "cultural politics", especially in social movement literature (Dagnino, Alvarez, and Escobar 1998: 1–25). But this focus remains somewhat new, and is yet to percolate the dominant understanding of the "proper" domain of anthropology, which remains culture.

Many anthropologists also misunderstand the way international law, and therefore human rights, works as a political device. The differences between scalar representations of reality – between the global, national, and local, for example – are often exaggerated by anthropologists in their desire to ensure the distinctness of local culture, and thereby enhance the chances of its survival. But international law itself provides mechanisms through which the transnational norms are contained in their application or scope, often precisely tracking the national and local cultural domains, and exempting them from the application of international law. States achieve this through the device of reservations, understandings, and declarations, a method allowed under international law. The purpose of these devices is to restrict the application of international norms by exempting some domains within states which are regulated by their own national, religious or customary law. Thus, the United States has reservations to the International Covenant on Civil and Political Rights (ICCPR), which prevents the treaty's application to the death penalty of minors, a practice that remains legal under US law despite ratification of the ICCPR. Kuwait has reservations that prevent the principle of equality from being applied with regard to the right of females to political participation, and also prevent human rights norms being applied when there is a conflict with the *Shariat*. Thus, states have many tools under international law – the ostensible language of universal human rights – to protect local culture. This complicates the situation for anthropologists and raises the possibility of ambivalence towards the whole issue of application of human rights norms in practice. In other words, the issue may not always be a tension between a universal hegemonic law and local culture, as the terms of adherence to the universal norms may be circumscribed by the state itself precisely to protect the local culture in question. At that point, the more relevant question is not the protection of culture, but the moral and political evaluation of the particular act in question which is sought to be defined in terms of 'rights' or 'culture'. Wastell's chapter points out this kind of ambivalence quite well, by pointing to the tension that exists between attempted scalar representations versus cultural representations of citizenship in Swaziland.

A major question for anthropologists who work on human rights is the relationship between the human rights discourse and other more vernacular discourses of justice or emancipation or dignity. Another way of thinking about this might be to think of the local-global normative interaction, through familiar interpretive tools such as the notion of legal pluralism (Merry 1992). Recent work in anthropology shows that "global" human rights may indeed be vernacularized under particular circumstances (Merry 2006a). It may also be the case that certain discourses of justice or rights are in fact incommensurable with the dominant modernist, rationalist discourse of human rights. In the enactment of cultural politics of social movements in Latin America, scholars of social movements note that some movements pose the question of how to be both modern and different in ways that may not be strictly defined within the terms of dominant discourses of western modernity such as human rights (Dagnino, Alvarez, and Escobar 1999: 9). Wastell's chapter draws attention to the latter phenomenon in Swaziland during its constitution-making process. If vernacularization and incommensurability are possible in the operation of human rights, what then can explain why one or the other happens in particular instances? From the perspective of international law, vernacularization is more easily explained than incommensurability.

Yet another major issue for anthropologists is the relationship between a global discourse such as human rights and other circulating global discourses, such as "development", "security" or "environment". Many of these discourses also serve as arenas of cultural construction, identity formation and resource mobilization, very similar to and sometimes overlapping with the human rights discourse. Indeed, the same social phenomenon might well be "represented" differently by different universal discourses. For example, during the lead up to the Iraq war, the low status of Arab women in their societies was used to bolster the case for intervention, so that Arab states could be truly modernized, starting with the case of Iraq. *New York Times* columnist Thomas Friedman referred to a UNDP regional report on the status of Arab women to lay the ground work for intervention (Friedman 2002). Meanwhile, the lack of women's rights in Arab societies was also being pushed as a human rights issue by many human rights organizations, both inside Arab countries, and in the West. The correspondence and the disjunctures between these globalist discourses, and the politics that these representations spawned, need to be sufficiently problematized. For anthropologists, the encounter with development has led, in recent years, to deeper questions of this kind (Gardner and Lewis 1996). Unlike in 1947, now the key tensions are between the various globalist discourses themselves, and not merely between a "universal" rights discourse and "local" culture.

Finally, there is the question of how one defines "practice." As I have noted already, dominant legal approaches to human rights place their emphasis on the practice of statist institutions from the local to the global levels, to the exclusion of everyday practices or other forms of non-official conduct. This is a consequence of both the methodology and purpose. Methodologically, lawyers have a hard time figuring out how to even find out what unofficial conduct counts, and their professional training prepares them to focus better on official texts such as court rulings. In that sense, they remain quite juro-centric. This methodology enables them to impose a framework on "facts," selecting what is relevant for decision making (which is one of the final goals of the legal approach) from that which is irrelevant (Santos 1987). Of course, the facts that are chosen depend on the purpose or goal of the legal system in question. A "global" legal system such as international law may choose only those facts which enable a practice to be comprehensible within its own terms, while a "customary" legal system may choose very different facts from the same practice, for the same reasons. The ethnographic focus of anthropologists yields thicker, more empirical accounts of reality, but the sheer "messiness" of real life produces a form of human rights narration which does not yield itself to decision making, regulation of other pragmatic outcomes. This brings us to the question of purpose, which is central to how one defines practice.

For lawyers, a principal purpose of human rights is to govern, as it sets the terms of the relationship between the governed and the governors. Depending on who is supposed to govern – an international criminal court, judge, bureaucrat, or a village chief – lawyers have no trouble picking the facts that suit their goal. For anthropologists, the meaning of "practice" is not so clear and it raises much ambivalence. While methodologically they may focus on everyday practices, the statist nature of human rights compels them to pay more attention to statecraft. John Dale's attention to the way the US court became a battleground for holding Unocal and the Burmese government responsible for human rights abuses in Burma, through the Alien Tort Claims Act, is emblematic of this. Yet, his chapter does not adequately capture the various registers of power that are evident in the difficult relationships between Washington-based international rights advocates, a US court enforcing American law in a hegemonic manner to conduct that occurs outside its borders, the logics of global corporate conduct and the strategies of poor, Burmese "victims." Indeed, his account shows an earnestness to identify with the victims in the way that Annelise Riles has discussed recently (Riles 2006), and pays relatively less attention to documenting the practice in all its ethnographic intensity. In such a mode, anthropologists become indistinguishable from human rights advocates, as they provide a narrative that empirically "confirms" the logic behind international human rights, saving its status as the sole discourse of resistance. Perhaps that is what some anthropologists would like their work to do, but for others it may raise a sense of ambivalence, not least about their own roles. The "messiness" of the ethnographic account is here given up for an account that is much more congruent with dominant versions of human rights "practice."

All this does not take away anything from the fact that in order to overcome the functionalist orientation that is inherent in a purely legal approach to "practice," the insights that obtain from anthropological inequiries of practice are crucial. There is a dire need to comprehend the content of human rights inductively, by deploying the tools of anthropology to investigate how struggles for justice, dignity, or power constitute what we may later call human rights. As Baxi puts it, human rights are then "protean forms of social action, assembled, by convention, under a portal named 'human rights'" (Baxi 2002: v). It is unfortunate that dominant approaches to human rights fail to register this reality yet.

REFERENCES

American Anthropological Association, Executive Board. 1947. 'Statement on Human Rights', *American Anthropologist* 49: 539.

American Anthropological Association (AAA). 1999. "Declaration On Anthropology And Human Rights" available on www.aaanet.org/committees/cfhr/ar95.htm

Baxi, Upendra. 2002. *The Future of Human Rights*. Oxford: Oxford University Press.

Cowan, Jane K., Marie-Bénédicte Dembour, and Richard A. Wilson, eds. 2001. *Culture and Rights: Anthropological Perspectives*. Cambridge: Cambridge University Press.

AAA. See American Anthropological Association. Dagnino, Evelyn, Sonia E. Alvarez, and Arturo Escobar, eds. 1998. *Cultures of Politics/Politics of Cultures: Revisioning Latin American Social Movements*. Boulder, CO: Westview Press.

Engle, Karen. 2001. "From Skepticism to Embrace: Human Rights and the American Anthropological Association from 1947–1999." *Human Rights Quarterly* 23(3): 536–559.

Friedman, Thomas. 2002. "The Arabs at the Crossroads." *New York Times*, 3 July.

Gardner, Katy, and David Lewis. 1996. *Anthropology, Development and the Post-Modern Challenge*. London: Pluto Press.

Goodale, Mark. 2006a. "Toward a Critical Anthropology of Human Rights." *Current Anthropology* (47)(3): 485–511.

Goodale, Mark. 2006b. "Introduction to 'Anthropology and Human Rights in New Key.'" *American Anthropologist* (108)(1): 1–8.

Goodale, Mark. 2006c. "Ethical Theory as Social Practice." *American Anthropologist* 108(1): 25–37.

Mamdani, Mahmood. 2000. *Beyond Rights Talk and Culture Talk: Comparative Essays on the Politics of Rights and Culture*. New York: St Martin's Press.

Merry, Sally Engle. 1992. Anthropology, Law and Transnational Processes. *Annual Review of Anthropology* 21: 357–379.

Merry, Sally Engle. 2003. "Human Rights Law and the Demonization of Culture (And Anthropology Along the Way)." *Polar: Political and Legal Anthropology Review* 26(1): 55–77.

Merry, Sally Engle. 2006a. *Human Rights and Gender Violence: Translating International Law into Local Justice*. Chicago: University of Chicago Press.

Merry, Sally Engle. 2006b. "Transnational Human Rights and Local Activism: Mapping the Middle." *American Anthropologist* 108(1): 38–51.

Rajagopal, Balakrishnan. 2003. *International Law from Below: Development, Social Movements and Third World Resistance*. Cambridge: Cambridge University Press.

Rajagopal, Balakrishnan. 2006. "Counter-hegemonic International Law: Rethinking Human Rights and Development as a Third World Strategy." *Third World Quarterly* 27(5): 767–783.

Riles, Annelise. 2000. *The Network Inside Out*. Ann Arbor: University of Michigan Press.

Riles, Annelise. 2006. "Skepticism, Intimacy and the Ethnographic Subject: Human Rights as Legal Knowledge." *American Anthropologist* 108(1).

Risse, Thomas, Stephen C. Ropp, Kathryn Sikkink, eds. 1999. *The Power of Human Rights: International Norms and Domestic Change*. Cambridge: Cambridge University Press.

Santos, B. de Sousa. 1987. "Law: A Map of Misreading: Toward a Postmodern Conception of Law." *Journal of Law and Society* 14: 279–302.

Wilson, Richard A., ed. 1997. *Human Rights, Culture and Context: Anthropological Perspectives*. London: Pluto Press.

Wilson, Richard A., and Jon P. Mitchell, eds. 2003. *Human Rights in Global Perspective: Anthropological Studies of Rights, Claims, and Entitlements*. London: Routledge.

7

TRANSNATIONAL LEGAL CONFLICT BETWEEN PEASANTS AND CORPORATIONS IN BURMA: HUMAN RIGHTS AND DISCURSIVE AMBIVALENCE UNDER THE US ALIEN TORT CLAIMS ACT

*John G. Dale**

INTRODUCTION

In the 1990s, Unocal Oil Corporation made a deal with the author-itarian government of Myanmar (Burma)[1] to build the Yadana Project,

* This chapter is based in part on field research that I conducted in Burma and Thailand in 1997 and 1998. But I am deeply indebted to many people who volunteered their time and effort, shared their food and homes, and in some cases risked their lives, to assist me in collecting data for this project. To many I have promised confidentiality. To the other generous and courageous individuals and organizations I offer my *kadawt* – especially Zaw Min (All Burma Students' Democratic Front); Ko Kyaw Kyaw (and other members of the National League for Democracy); Teddy Buri and Aung Myo Min (National Coalition Government of the Union of Burma); Ah Moe Zoe, Zaw Zaw Htun, and Min Min Oo (Democratic Party for a New Society); U Ba Kyi; Bo Thakhin Sa; Lu Maw; Saw Cit Oo; Dr Guy Morineau (Medecins du Monde); John C. Bradshaw (US Embassy in Myanmar); Max Ediger and Chris Kennel (Burma Issues); Faith Doherty (Southeast Asian Information Network); Debbie Stothard (Alternative ASEAN Network on Burma); Lyndal Barry, Sitthipong Kalayanee, and Htet Khai (Images Asia); Jackie Pollock (Empower and the Migration Assistance Program); Veronika Martin (Women's Education for Advancement and Empowerment); Peter Halford, Pippa, and James (Burmese Relief Centre); Justin Sherman (International Rescue Committee); Sally Thompson (Burmese Border Consortium); Kevin Heppner (Karen Human Rights Group); Annette Kunigagon; and many brave friends in Hsipaw, Shan State. Outside of Burma and Thailand, more individuals and organizations than I have space to list also provided me with critical assistance. However, I must thank Burma Centre Nederlands for allowing me liberal access to their archives in Amsterdam, the Netherlands. In the United States, I am grateful to Simon Billenness and Robert Benson for providing me with substantial insight into their work on transnational legal campaigns that have contributed to the Free Burma Movement. I also wish to thank Fred Block, Jack Goldstone, and Michael Peter Smith for their insightful comments on earlier versions of this work, and their intellectual support throughout the progress of this research. For their additional comments, I would also like to extend thanks to Andy Nathan and my other co-participants in the Seminar on Human Rights in an Age of Globalization, supported by the National Endowment for the Humanities, and hosted by Columbia University during the Summer of 2005.

1 In 1988, under Ne Win's dictatorship, the military reconsolidated power when it violently repressed a domestic pro-democracy movement that was deploying "people power" tactics in an effort to end the military's rule. In the wake of international condemnation for its action, the

a natural gas pipeline. As part of that deal, the military junta that runs Myanmar forced local villagers to work for Unocal under some of the most deplorable conditions imaginable. The junta forced the peasants from their homes and made them work literally at gunpoint. Soldiers from Myanmar's army raped, tortured and, in some cases, murdered the forced laborers. *Doe v. Unocal Corp.*, 963 F Supp 880 (C.D. Cal. 1997). They also used the workers as human shields and munitions porters against other peasants, often from their own villages, who the government had branded as rebels. The peasants working for Unocal on the Yadana Project were slaves – joining the ranks of the 27 million other people held as slaves in the world today (Bales 1999: 8–9).

Peasants such as those forced to work on the Yadana Project have little power within Burma. In 1988, they participated in a statewide pro-democracy movement that the military junta brutally crushed. The crackdown in Burma was bloodier than the one the following year in Tiananmen Square in Beijing, China. However, it received little international attention because it was not televised. Best estimates suggest that the death toll ranged from 3,000 to 5,000 citizens.

Burma's pro-democracy movement emerged initially within a national scope of action. The movement's participants targeted the practices of the Myanmar military which, under an isolationist economic policy called the "Burmese way to Socialism," had come to increasingly dominate the state and economic activity within its territory since General Ne Win's *coup d'état* in 1962.[2] However, statewide protest by hundreds of thousands of citizens, living in both urban centers and rural villages, did not secure a democratic future for Burma. The Myanmar military not only violently and indiscriminately repressed public protest, but also heavily restricted non-military access to communications and transportation infrastructure, and vigilantly censored all civilian information flows (Lintner 1990; Mya Maung 1992; Schock 1999; Martin Smith 1991).

Burmese military's ruling party, the State Law and Order Restoration Council (SLORC), initiated a series of measures intended to sublimate any collective memory of the illegitimate means by which it had secured its political domination over the state. One of the first measures that SLORC took was to rename the country that it ruled – from Burma to "Myanmar." I will use Myanmar to refer to the post-1990 military government; yet, to resist playing too easily into the questionable intentions of this regime's project of collective forgetting, I retain the name "Burma" to refer to the country, and "Burmese" to refer to the state's citizens.

[2] Forty years later, in December 2002, and well into his nineties, Ne Win died of natural causes. After formally relinquishing his political office in 1988, he became progressively reclusive and devoted to Buddhist meditation. He continued to reside in Burma until his death.

Popular democratic aspirations were temporarily revived in 1990, when the military agreed to hold "free and fair" elections. The main opposition party, the National League for Democracy (NLD), won over 60 percent of the popular vote and 82 percent of the parliamentary seats under the leadership of Aung San Suu Kyi, daughter of the country's first post-colonial national hero General Aung San, who was assassinated by his domestic political rivals in 1948. But once again, democratic reform was forestalled as the military refused to honor the election results and tightened its authoritarian grip. It outlawed opposition parties and systematically imprisoned or "disappeared"[3] members of the NLD (Fink 2001: chs. 3, 4 and 8). This time, however, injustice found no expression in mass protest. Instead, the movement slipped temporarily into abeyance (V. Taylor 1989; Meyer 1999). The students and Buddhist monks, who had primarily led the movement, subsequently joined with peasants in ethnic minority villages in rural areas near the Thai-Burma border.

What makes this case so sociologically interesting is that some victims of Myanmar's violent policies then did something non-traditional. The slaves forced to work on the Yadana Project, with the help of activist lawyers in the United States, and working within a more comprehensive transnational "Free Burma" movement, created a transnational legal space within which to address their grievances. It is on the construction of this transnational legal space, and its implications for the practice of human rights, that I focus in this chapter.

---

[3] The term "disappeared," refers to the human rights violation and crime of enforced or involuntary disappearance, and is widely interpreted by civilians in Burma to be a euphemism used by the military to suggest that the arrested person has been executed by the military. Use of the term, however, allows the military to simultaneously signal a threat to any civilians who may clandestinely participate in or affiliate with oppositional political parties, and avoid accepting legal responsibility or providing official justifications for executing civilians challenging the military's rule (Human Rights Documentation Unit 1996: 91–125; Amnesty International 2004, 2006). According to Laifungbam Debabrata Roy (2002): "Modern history has credited Adolf Hitler for [the] invention [of the practice] in his Nacht und Nebel Erlass (Night and Fog Decree) of December 7, 1941. The purpose of this decree was to seize persons in occupied territories suspected of 'endangering German security' who were not immediately executed, to transport them secretly to Germany, where they disappeared without trace. In order to achieve the desired intimidating effect, it was prohibited to provide any information as to their whereabouts or fate. The phenomenon reappeared as a systematic policy of state repression in the late 1960s and early 1970s in Latin America, starting first in Guatemala and Brazil. The term 'enforced disappearance' was first used by Latin American NGOs and is a translation of the Spanish expression 'desaparición forzada.' The UN Commission was the first international human rights body to respond both in general terms and also in specific cases which had occurred in Chile since the military coup d'état on September 11, 1973."

I examine how movement activists have used this space to shape an important legal mechanism, the Alien Tort Claims Act, for reigning in the power of transnational corporations that violate human rights. I also examine how this space has generated discursive ambivalence among a wide range of social actors, particularly corporate and state agents, who have voiced support for human rights within this space. I argue that the discursive ambivalence of corporate and state agents results from their combining human rights discourse with other discourses that are meant both to protect corporations from being held accountable for their abusive human rights practices, as well as to minimize the state's vulnerability to international legal standards.

To better understand the complex discursive practice of human rights that I discuss below, it is helpful to distinguish between two broad discourses that anthropologists often conflate: the globalization discourse and the transnationalist discourse. The globalization discourse, writes Michael Peter Smith, "... draws attention to social processes that are largely de-centered from specific national territories ... and often explicitly assumes the growing insignificance of national borders, boundaries, and identities" (2001: 3). Smith points out that this discourse is grounded in the assumption that globalization and the nation-state are "mutually exclusive and antagonistically related conceptual categories" (2001: 3).

In contrast to the globalization discourse, Smith distinguishes the "transnationalist discourse." The transnationalist discourse, he explains, not only challenges the binary distinction between globalization and the nation-state but, furthermore, "insists on the continuing significance of borders, state policies, and national identities even as these are often transgressed by transnational communication circuits and social practices" (2001: 3). According to Smith's distinction, the transnationalist discourse emphasizes transnational practices rather than global processes. Moreover, this discourse does not treat the nation-state and transnational practices as mutually exclusive social phenomena nor even as binary conceptual categories. Instead, the transnationalist discourse depicts nation-states and transnational practices as contributing to the constitution of each other. It sees nation-states as not only being transformed by transnational practices, but as often participating in and even promoting these very practices that are transforming nation-states.

State actors, as well as their targets and challengers, may deploy both kinds of discourse, even combining aspects of each, when representing their own power and choices to act in various contexts. It matters how actors (including collective actors, both state and non-state) represent their power, choices, and even interests, because, as Alison Brysk writes, they are "increasingly constituted from the meanings assigned to them by interacting subjects" (2000: 43). Furthermore, the new social subjectivities that are produced through practices connecting social networks in more than one national territory are not necessarily transgressive agents of change. As Smith asserts, "[T]ransnational political, economic, and sociocultural practices are embodied in historically specific, culturally constituted, social relations, i.e., they are networks of meaning, established between particular spatially and temporally situated social actors" (2001: 167). Attention to the meanings and intentions of transnational practices (including discursive practices) helps us to usefully distinguish between different types of transnational networks, some of which have allied with Burma's military state, and others which have challenged those alliances. Cumulatively, these transnationalist discursive challenges have transformed the context of the pro-democracy movement's struggle in a way that has created new opportunities for meaningful collective action both within and beyond Burma's territorial boundaries.

FROM NATION-CENTERED TO TRANSNATIONAL MOVEMENT

In order to appreciate how this transnational legal space was created, we must begin by understanding how this court case was embedded within a broader transnational movement. After 1990, the activists came to understand that their "people power" movement tactics had failed. More and more pro-democracy activists were forced into exile. Signs of organized, large-scale, non-violent, public protest reappeared briefly in the 1996 student demonstrations, and the 1998 tenth-year anniversary of the "8-8-88" uprising,[4] and again in the symbolic "9-9-99" demonstration in 1999 (Dale 2003: ch. 3).[5] Yet, the military quickly

---

[4] Burmese activists commonly refer to the commencement of the statewide general strike that launched the pro-democracy movement as Shitlay Loan A-Yay A-Hkin, or the "Four Eights Affair (8-8-88)" because it began at precisely 8:08 a.m. on August 8, 1988.

[5] Although Burma's dictator General Ne Win was over ninety years old in 1999, the wealthiest person in Burma, and rarely appeared in public anymore, many believed that he was still the most powerful person in the country, and still influenced the military's top cadre of generals and state officials. Ne Win was said to be obsessed with astrology and numerology to the extent that

and easily repressed all of this collective action without significant casualties. Although the claim to legitimate state representation in Burma remains contested (Yawnghwe 1995; R. H. Taylor 1998), the military has remained in power to this day.

However, from 1990 through 1994, several factors combined to alter the conditions challenging the pro-democracy movement: (1) the Myanmar state's refusal to acknowledge the victory of the country's powerful opposition party in the 1990 elections; (2) the state's sudden adoption of an economic liberalization policy; (3) the rapid consolidation of neo-liberal "free trade" as a hegemonic discourse on globalization as the Cold War was ending; and (4) a massive influx of foreign investment by transnational corporations seeking to build a natural gas pipeline through Burma. During this period, the pro-democracy movement's leaders came to realize that the Myanmar state was not the only obstacle to domestic political change. The investments of transnational corporations and foreign states in Burma also buttressed the Myanmar state's power to repress the movement. In response, the pro-democracy movement began to organize transnational campaigns with other movements. Those movements were less centered on the Myanmar state, and instead centered on foreign democratic states and transnational corporations chartered within them that sought to profit from Burma's opening market.

many major tactical decisions at the national level are based on consultations with horoscopes and obscure number charts. It was popularly understood that Ne Win revered the number "9" as the most auspicious of all numerals. "*Ko nawin kane*," a phrase which means "the astrological calculation of the number '9'," is invoked playfully in teashop conversation as a pun [nawin/Ne Win], playing on Ne Win's name. For example, when the military retook control of the state on September 18, 1988, it is widely believed that the date was deliberately chosen on the basis of *ko nawin kane*. September is the ninth month of the year. The number 18 is divisible by 9 and, moreover, the first digit (1) and the second digit (8), when added together, equal 9. Underground pro-democracy activists in Burma creatively manipulated the Burmese commoner's attentiveness to Ne Win's obsession with numerology, particularly the number 9, in its deployment of symbolic politics to mobilize the "9-9-99 uprising," which it launched on September 9, 1999. In contrast to the mass direct action of the Four Eights Affair eleven years prior, the activists deployed new forms of collective action, including "cat and mouse" guerilla tactics, symbolic protests, and dozens of transnationally coordinated demonstrations with activists in countries around the world, that were designed to get the Myanmar state to "jump at shadows" and demonstrate to an international audience the military's willingness to use repressive measures that could be easily exploited by activists in transnational media campaigns. The intention was not to mobilize citizens to take to the streets. Rather, it was to create the impression in the minds of state authorities that such a conventional uprising might take place. The state predictably responded by ordering soldiers to occupy the streets to intimidate citizens into remaining in their homes, and by indiscriminately arresting hundreds of citizens who were not even engaged in protest. The timing of the protest coincided with Myanmar's recent induction to the Association of Southeast Nations (ASEAN), whose member states justified Myanmar's inclusion based on the argument that they could constructively engage and steer the junta toward more democratic rule.

Foreign states have been reticent to publicly ally themselves closely with the Myanmar state since 1988. Nevertheless, many of them, including the United States, have helped to sustain it. The Myanmar military's response to the revolutionary crisis that it faced in 1988 quickly became the target of two different globalization discourses deployed by foreign actors. One of these globalization discourses promoted "free trade," and the other proclaimed support for "human rights." The resulting discursive contention yielded two polarized international foreign policy positions: (1) "constructive engagement," which prescribes international economic trade and development as the surest route to political stability and democratization; and (2) multilateral "economic sanctions" implemented through the coordinated action of individual nation-states against rogue-state challengers to the international community's new global order.

The transnational networks of actors supporting each of these foreign policies all proclaimed their support for human rights, while simultaneously jockeying for favorable economic partnerships and trade relations with the Myanmar military ruling the state. Moreover, these foreign policy discourses were mediated by a cultural structure of neo-liberalism that channeled state power toward positions of discursive stalemate, and toward practices that sustained the structures of military repression in Burma. That is, although these two foreign policies have become polarized as competing discourses at the international level, taken together they effectively channel discursive contention within a framework of conceptual distinctions that re-inscribes the hegemonic power of the globalization discourse. In practice, however, neither of these international foreign policies curbed, nor were they intended to curb, transnational oil and gas corporations from seeking highly profitable new investment and development opportunities in Burma. For these corporations, Burma represented a crucial link to future natural gas markets in Southeast Asia and, most importantly, China (Dale 2003: chs. 4 and 6).

Although the Burmese pro-democracy movement has not mounted a significant internal challenge to the Myanmar state since 1988, a good deal of pro-democracy movement activity has been taking place outside of Burma. By 1994, the Burmese pro-democracy activists-in-exile had forged alternative transnational networks that strategically chose to target the new transnational trade relations being forged by the military state. Instead of focusing their protest efforts on the military state of Burma, they expanded the scope of their collective action to target the foreign states, transnational corporations, and international trade organizations that were conducting business (and, in some cases, allegedly colluding in abusive human rights practices) with the Myanmar state. In my broader study of the Free Burma Movement (Dale 2003), I identify several transnationalist "Free Burma" discourses generated by these alternative transnational networks that have intentionally challenged both the neo-liberal dimensions of the discourse on constructive engagement and the nationalist dimensions of US federal discourse on economic sanctions that had become institutionalized in foreign policy toward Burma.

Under the banner of the "Free Burma" movement, and linking grassroots movements in both the East and West, the Burmese pro-democracy activists-in-exile have helped organize transnational legal campaigns waged in alliance with local state and municipal governments in the United States and Australia, as well as non-state actors, including regional governing bodies like the European Union, nongovernmental organizations (NGOs) throughout East and Southeast Asia, international nongovernmental organizations (INGOs), and voluntary associations on every continent and in over twenty-six countries (Dale 2003: 5). The movement has also attracted pre-existing transnational advocacy networks that defend issues like human rights, women's rights, the degradation of the natural environment, labor rights, indigenous people's rights, and socially responsible corporate investment, and has even created new principled-issue networks, like those now forming around the international "right to know" (about the labor conditions and environmental impact of proposed development projects that are financed through transnational corporations in partnership with the state) (Dale 2003: 113).

It is also at this time that the Free Burma movement began to develop and voice a transnationalist discourse on human rights and their protection against the abusive practices of corporations partnering with the Myanmar state. It is a discourse reflecting several transnational strategies deployed by the Free Burma movement that move beyond holding accountable the Myanmar state for its human rights abuses, economic mismanagement, and political illegitimacy.[6] It articulates an alternative understanding of the relationship between

---

[6] Dale (2003) describes several of the transnational legal campaigns that the Free Burma movement activists organized, including a selective purchasing campaign comprised of over thirty cities in the United States and the State of Massachusetts, all of which adopted "Free Burma laws that forced corporations to *choose* between doing business with the Myanmar junta or with

political processes in Burma and global market dynamics, and depicts a variety of ways in which actors outside of Burma have helped to sustain the Myanmar state's repression of democratic change.

CREATING A TRANSNATIONAL LEGAL SPACE

In 1996, a dozen ethnic-minority peasants from Burma sued the Unocal Corporation in a US court in a case titled *Doe v. Unocal. Doe v. Unocal Corp.*, 963 F Supp 880 (C.D. Cal. 1997); 27 F Supp 2d 1174 (C.D. Cal. 1998); 67 F Supp 2d 1140 (C.D. 1999); 110 F Supp 2d 1294 (C.D. Cal. 2000); and 403 F 3d 708 (9th Cir. 2002). They alleged that Unocal had been complicit in human rights abuses against them and demanded that Unocal stop the human rights abuses and pay money damages. For eight years, this case wound its way through the courts. Then, suddenly, in December 2004, Unocal announced that it had reached a settlement with the plaintiffs (Lifsher 2005; EarthRights International 2005a). This was clearly a victory for the peasants.

What makes this transnational legal action significant is that, had the court been left to decide the case, and had it ruled in favor of the peasants (an outcome that Unocal clearly thought likely), it would have been the first time that foreigners had won a case against a transnational corporation in a US court for an injury that took place in another country. The peasants filed the suit under the United States Alien Tort Claims Act, 28 USC §1350. Since *Doe v. Unocal*, over a dozen similar suits have been filed against other corporations on the model of the transnational legal strategy used in the Unocal case.

The judicial struggle of the *Doe v. Unocal* case, in itself, represents a stunning achievement for the Free Burma Movement. This long shot of a transnational legal strategy soon became a landmark suit. The publicity from the suit brought stories of Burma's struggle for democracy into living rooms across the United States. But the negative publicity that this case generated is not ultimately what threatens Unocal's corporate conduct. Rather, this case threatens Unocal's "bottom line" of profitability by forcing it to build into its calculus the costs of litigation and liability for violating the human rights of foreign nationals in foreign countries in which it does business. It also sends a clear message to other corporations: if the activists win, corporations must

these US municipal and regional-state governments. The National Foreign Trade Council ultimately sued the State of Massachusetts in a case that went to the US Supreme Court, which forced Massachusetts to later rescind this legislation.

consider these costs in deciding whether to partner with rogue states. This could provide an important tool for weakening the authoritarian grip of Burma's ruling junta and others like it which depend upon foreign corporate investment. Most importantly, this campaign created what I call a "transnational legal space."

What I mean by transnational legal space are the discourses constructed at the interstices of existing state legal systems that identify institutional arrangements or legal mechanisms that present opportunities for making crimes or torts committed in one state *actionable* in the legal system of another state. Transnational legal space therefore also provides an opportunity for mediating how the emerging rules of global markets are politically, legally, and morally constructed. While this space may include international fora, (i.e., contexts that represent states and their agents interacting among themselves), it is especially meant to include transnational interactions, (i.e., contexts that represent interactions including at least one non-state actor). For example, by bringing a lawsuit against Unocal Corporation, otherwise powerless Burmese peasants were able to create a transnational legal space in which they could argue for the institutionalization of democratic market practices such as those that ban slavery.

What is important to grasp here is that the notion of "transnational legal space" represents a contested terrain of legal discourse. As Mark Goodale argues in the Introduction to this volume, "discursive approaches to human rights assume that social practice is, in part, constitutive of the idea of human rights itself, rather than simply the testing ground on which the idea of universal human encounters actual ethical or legal systems" (pp. 8–9 above). Transnational legal space is a discursive field. A discursive field is in part bounded by norms. But, the symbolic dimension of any given norm is never completely fixed. We can speak of norms that have varying degrees of durability or stability, but there is no reason to assume that this underlying symbolic dimension of a norm is fixed once and for all. As soon as we begin to question why a norm exists, or why it should be enforced to address a given social condition, we are entering the world of discourse.

Discourse structures the symbols that give meaning to norms. Symbols have no inherent meaning. They are polysemous. It is only when a symbol is brought into relation with another symbol that meaning emerges. That is, meaning derives from how we give structure to symbols. Discursive action provides such a structure. Discourse has the potential to transform the meaning of a given norm by bringing together polysemous symbols in new combinations – in new relation-ships to each other – and altering the original meaning of these symbols. Thus, discursive action can provide new ways of understanding norms, and serve as a vehicle for bringing new interpretive claims regarding norms into the mix.

Also, Goodale reminds us of a key fact about human rights discourse: "the sites where human rights unfold in practice do matter, and these sites are not simply nodes in a virtual network, but actual *places* in social space, places which can become law-like and coercive" (p. 13 above). If we think of "place" as spaces that have become embedded with mean-ing, and understand that meaning is produced, reproduced, and trans-formed within social relations and through social practices, then we can begin to understand the importance of transnational legal space and transnationalist discursive practices for the construction and progres-sive development of human rights norms.

Transnational legal space suggests a site for examining proce-sses through which economic globalization becomes institutionally embedded in legal, moral, and political relations that are discursively constituted through conflicting and contradictory legislative, judi-cial, and administrative struggles. The focus here is on the discur-sive struggles of a not-yet-institutionalized space of globalization in which any existing transnational norms, like the prohibition against the use of slave labor, are culturally refracted through competing interests and experiences. The judicial, administrative, and legislative dimensions of discursive struggle among state and non-state actors shape the institutional boundaries of the emerging transnational legal terrain.

This very premise is an interrogation of the globalization discourse: first, because it assumes that states are still critical actors in the con-struction of a regulatory infrastructure for globalization; and, second, it assumes that markets, especially global markets, are always embed-ded to a greater or lesser extent in social relations of governance. The neo-liberal idea that markets could be "free" of (or completely dis-embedded from) such relations is a utopian impossibility (see Block 1990, 2001). In this case, it is the transnational legal action (inclu-ding discursive action) of the Free Burma movement's participants and allies who initiate and sustain these struggles through conflict with their targets and challengers, whose norms of neoliberal eco-nomic "free trade" and "constructive engagement" (among others) they contest.

USING THE ALIEN TORT CLAIMS ACT TO SUE CORPORATIONS

The *Doe* v. *Unocal* suit, filed under the Alien Tort Claims Act (ATCA), deploys a transnational strategy through which the Free Burma movement attempts to use the statute *for the first time* to hold liable in a US court *transnational corporations*, not just state actors or private individuals, for their complicity in human rights abuses committed outside the United States in furthering their transnational joint ventures with states like Burma. The original legislators of this statute had never, nor could have, imagined using it for this purpose. Yet, movement activists, deploying a transnationalist discourse, creatively appropriated this statute to address relations among states, citizens, corporations, and human rights that had significantly changed over the two centuries since ATCA's adoption. This suit illustrates how movement activists created a transnational legal space to shape the meaning and application of the ATCA for reigning in the power of transnational corporations that violate human rights.

An appreciation for how the *Doe* v. *Unocal* suit brought under the ATCA provides an example of a transnational legal space begins with understanding the historical development of the Act itself, and how the peasants and their lawyers reappropriated it in a new way. In 1789, the First Congress of the United States adopted the ATCA. It remained largely unused for the next two centuries. The text of the Act is short. It reads simply, "The district courts shall have original jurisdiction of any civil action by an alien [non-United States citizen] for a tort only, committed in violation of the *law of nations* or a treaty of the United States." 28 USC §1350. The ATCA is not a human rights law per se, but it allows for civil suits for violations of the law of nations. The "law of nations" is the law of international relations, embracing not only nations but also individuals, such as those who invoke their human rights or commit war crimes.[7]

The members of the United States' First Congress were obviously cognizant of the "law of nations" as they crafted their nascent nation's Constitution. Yet, they could not have anticipated, in 1789, the extent to which the law of nations would develop over the course of the following two centuries. Nor, for that matter, could they have imagined

---

[7] This is the definition of the law of nations that the Ninth Circuit Court of Appeals used in *Doe* v. *Unocal Corp.*, 395 F 3d 932, 944 n. 12 (9th Cir. 2002).

the radical development of two other legal concepts that have significantly transformed the context within which contemporary actors have begun to interpret the ATCA: "human rights" and "the corporate rights of personhood."

The Law of Nations

Although litigation under the ATCA remained dormant for two centuries following its passage, lawyers in the United States appropriated it during the past two decades to challenge the abuses of foreign state-agents, and even non-state actors, that were committed in foreign states between non-US citizens. While some have cheered these ATCA cases as a progressive step forward in the development of international norms, others have decried the very same cases as a creeping American imperialism which threatens to export the legal standards of the United States to other nations, raising the question of whether these ATCA cases represent an erosion of state sovereignty in sheep's clothing.

In 1980, lawyers at the Center for Constitutional Rights rediscovered ATCA and put it to modern use in the landmark case of *Filartiga v. Pena-Irala*, 630 F 2d 876 (2d Cir. 1980).[8] The decision in that case interpreted the ATCA to provide jurisdiction for US courts in cases where the perpetrator (even though not a US citizen) is properly served within the United States' borders, but it left open whether the ATCA applies only to state actors or also to non-state actors. In addition, this decision drew attention, amidst increasing international concern with human rights issues, to a new legal tool that human rights advocates might find workable in a variety of related cases. As Andrew Ridenour explains: "The resulting body of jurisprudence has slowly expanded over the past twenty years to deal with an otherwise open area of law: civil remedies for certain violations of international law" (2001: 584).

Subsequent courts in the United States have generally followed the interpretation set out in *Filartiga*, holding that the ATCA not only provides jurisdiction, but also authorizes plaintiffs to base their substantive claims on international law norms. *In re Estate of Ferdinand E. Marcos Human Rights Litig.*, 25 F 3rd 1467, 1475 (9th Cir. 1994), *cert. denied*, 513 US 1126 (1995). Courts also have relied on this

---

[8] As Ridenour (2001) explains, although plaintiffs had invoked the alien tort statute in numerous suits prior to 1980, only two suits had been successful under the statute (see *Abdul-Rahman Omar Adra* v. *Clift* 1961; *Bolchos* v. *Darrel* 1795).

interpretation to suggest that plaintiffs do not have to base their causes of action on the municipal law of the forum or of the site of the tort. *Xuncax v. Gramajo*, 886 F Supp 162, 181–183 (D. Mass. 1995).

However, courts have debated whether the statute provides a cause of action against a party that has violated *international* law. One of the most difficult issues facing the courts has been that of determining what constitutes a violation of the law of nations. In *Tel-Oren v. Libyan Arab Republic*, the District Court for the District of Columbia reasoned that:

> The law of nations never has been perceived to create or define the civil actions to be made available by each member of the community of nations; by consensus, the states leave that determination to their respective municipal laws ... In consequence, to require international accord on a right to sue, when in fact the law of nations relegates decisions on such questions to the states themselves, would be to effectively nullify the 'law of nations' portion of [ATCA].
>
> (*Tel Oren v. Libyan Arab Republic*, 726 F 2d at 778 [D.C. Cir. 1984])

That is, the law of nations itself does not provide rights of action, thus Congress must have intended for ATCA to grant a cause of action to a foreign national to remedy a violation of the law of nations by another party. Yet, as the district court pointed out, this raises a further issue: how are the courts to derive from an amorphous entity (i.e., the "law of nations") standards of liability that are applicable in concrete situations? The *Tel-Oren* court proposed an alternative approach to that of the *Filartiga* court. While ATCA can provide federal court jurisdiction to aliens alleging torts framed as a violation of the law of nations, the substantive right on which this action is based must be found in the domestic tort law of the United States.

In 1991, the US Congress passed the Torture Victim Protection Act (TVPA) with the intention of augmenting the *Filartiga* approach and extending it to citizens of the United States.[9] The TVPA states that:

> An individual who, under actual or apparent authority, or color of law, of any foreign nation, subjects an individual to torture shall, in a civil

---

[9] The House of Representatives stated: "The TVPA would establish an unambiguous and modern basis for a cause of action that has been successfully maintained under an existing law, section 1350 of the Judiciary Act of 1789 [the Alien Tort Claims Act], which permits Federal district courts to hear claims by aliens for torts committed 'in violation of the law of nations' ... Judge Bork questioned the existence of a private right of action under the Alien Tort Claims Act, reasoning that separation of powers principles required an explicit – and preferably contemporary – grant by Congress of a private right of action before U.S. courts could consider cases likely to impact on U.S. foreign relations ... The TVPA would provide such a grant ..." (US House Judiciary, Committee 1991: 3–4.)

action, be liable for damages to that individual; or subjects an individual to extra judicial killing shall, in a civil action, be liable for damages to the individual's legal representative, or to any person who may be a claimant in an action for wrongful death.

(Torture Victim Protection Act of 1991, 28 USC § 1350 *et seq.*, *affirmed by* 470 US 1003 (1985))

Since Congress passed this statute, courts have held, that regardless of the original intent that Congress may have had in adopting ATCA, the TVPA demonstrates a contemporary legislative intent that ATCA does create a private cause of action for violations of international law. See, e.g., *Xuncax* v. *Gramajo*, 886 F Supp 162, 179 (D. Mass. 1995). In other words, the TVPA gave new meaning to the law of nations, permitting non-state actors to be sued under ATCA for violations of international law, provided that the tort represents the violation of a norm that is universal, specific, and obligatory.

In 1995, the Court of Appeals for the Second Circuit Court drew upon Congress' explicit intention in passing the TVPA to hold that certain forms of conduct violate the law of nations whether undertaken by those acting under the auspices of a state or only as private individuals. *Kadic* v. *Karadzic*, 70 F 3d 232, 241 (2d Cir. 1995). This in turn opened ATCA to being used to sue private individuals – not just states and their agents – who violate the law of nations. Even "private" individuals, that is, individuals who are *not* acting as agents of the state per se, but those who are found to be acting in cooperation with government officials or significant government aid when they allegedly committed a violation of the law of nations, were also within US court jurisdiction under the ATCA (Walker 1997).[10]

Thus, it is the intersection of ATCA, which is almost as old as the Republic, with recent developments in the domestic appropriation of international law that created the legal opportunity, or critical

---

[10] In this case filed against Radnovan Karadzic following civil war in former Yugoslavia, the court provided a reasoned analysis of the scope of the private individual's liability for violations of international law. The Second Circuit court disagreed with the proposition "that the law of nations, as understood in the modern era, confines its reach to state action. Instead, [the court held] that certain forms of conduct violate the law of nations whether undertaken by those acting under the auspices of a state or only as private individuals." *Kadic* v. *Karadzic*, 70 F 3d at 239 (1995). While *international law* proscribes crimes such as torture and summary execution only when committed by state officials or under their legal authority, the *law of nations* has historically been applied to private actors for the crimes of piracy and slavery, and for certain war crimes. *Kadic* v. *Karadzic*, 70 F 3d at 243 n. 4 (1995). Thus, individual liability may apply when torture or summary execution are perpetrated as a war crime. *Kadic* v. *Karadzic*, 70 F 3d at 239 (1995).

discursive space, for suing the Unocal Corporation. The activist attorneys representing the Doe plaintiffs pushed the argument further. As individual private actors, corporations too, they asserted, are capable of violating and being held liable for a new class of international norms which had emerged officially in only the past two decades: *jus cogens* norms.

The human rights regime and corporate personhood

An important factor that has influenced the changing relationship between state sovereignty and the law of nations is the development of the international human rights regime. As Sarah Cleveland has cogently argued, this regime has been

> enunciated through a loose network of general treaties promulgated by the United Nations; rights-specific regimes which are promoted by intergovernmental entities and international organizations [e.g., the International Labor Organization]; regional regimes of conventions and oversight; and universal customary prohibitions that have evolved through treaties, the practices of states, and the efforts of nongovernmental and private actors.

(Cleveland 2001: 20)

Emerging from these efforts has been an unevenly developed global system of normative rules relating to human rights. Not all human rights are equal before the law. Comprising this global system of rules are two tiers of human rights: (1) *jus cogens* norms and (2) treaty rights and customary obligations *erga omnes* (Cleveland 2001). This has implications for those filing suits under the ATCA.

Treaty rights, of course, are detailed in the formal instrument of the human rights regime. These international treaty obligations cover a wide range of protections for human rights by creating binding obligations between party states. A state which accedes to these conventions becomes obligated to every other state to uphold the promises of the treaty and "submit[s] its performance to scrutiny and to appropriate, peaceful action by other parties ..." (Henkin 1981: 1, 15). It should be noted that Myanmar is a member of both the United Nations and the International Labor Organization (ILO).[11]

[11] The ILO, which is the international body responsible for defining and implementing international labor norms, has played a significant role in helping certain labor rights, including the prohibition against slavery and forced labor, to attain broad recognition among states as fundamental human rights. Its eight conventions explicitly setting forth "fundamental

Beyond those human rights formally expressed in these treaties, the law of nations recognizes certain rights to be universally accepted and binding on all sovereign states as either *jus cogens* or *erga omnes* principles of customary international law. *Jus cogens* norms (literally meaning "the highest law") hold the highest hierarchical position among all other norms and principles (Bassiouni 1996: 67). In 1969, the Vienna Convention on the Law of Treaties first defined *jus cogens* norms as principles "accepted and recognized by the international community of States as a whole as a norm from which no derogation is permitted and which can be modified only by a subsequent norm of general international law having the same character" (Vienna Convention of the Law on Treaties, 1155 UNTS 331, 344, Art. 53). They represent the higher of the two tiers of human rights to which I alluded above. As a consequence of this standing within the law of nations, nearly all courts around the world (including US courts) deem *jus cogens* norms to be "peremptory" and "non-derogable." In other words, *jus cogens* norms are norms of international law that are binding on nations even if they do not agree with them. Any international agreement that would violate them would be void (Vienna Convention of the Law on Treaties, 1155 UNTS 331, 347, Art. 64). Any *jus cogens* violation, therefore, is also, by definition, a violation of the law of nations. The legal literature discloses that the following are broadly recognized rights that no state officially claims the right to violate and may be considered *jus cogens* principles of the human rights system: aggression, genocide, crimes against humanity, war crimes, torture, piracy, and slavery and slavery-related practices.[12]

Human rights obligations that enjoy the status of *erga omnes* norms share with *jus cogens* norms their universal character and are binding on all states. However, unlike *jus cogens* norms, *erga omnes* norms are not peremptory norms which prevail over all other rules of customary law.

human rights" have been almost universally embraced, with the notable exception of the United States. The United States has, however, ratified the ILO's Convention No. 105 regarding the abolition of forced labor. In 1998, the ILO made further progress toward universalizing these norms by adopting its Declaration on Fundamental Principles and Rights at Work, which binds all ILO members to the core labor principles, regardless of whether the member has ratified the relevant conventions. Commitment to these core ILO principles is a condition of ILO membership. Moreover, the basic, non-specific, labor rights have been incorporated into foundational international human rights instruments, all of which have received nearly universal acceptance.

[12] Although identifying the international human rights principles that constitute *jus cogens* can be controversial, the Restatement (Third) of the Foreign Relations Law of the United States § 702 (1987) recognizes the following *jus cogens* norms: genocide; slavery or slave trade; summary execution or causing the disappearance of individuals; torture or other cruel, inhuman, or degrading treatment or punishment; prolonged arbitrary detention; systematic racial discrimination; and a consistent pattern or gross violations of internationally recognized human rights.

Thus, we can think of treaty rights and *erga omnes* norms together as comprising the lower of the two tiers of human rights.

In the summer of 2004, the US Supreme Court held in the case of *Sosa v. Alvarez-Machain* that only a human rights violation of the highest and most agreed upon magnitude qualifies for consideration under ATCA. In other words, only ATCA claims based on violations of *jus cogens* norms qualify (*Sosa v. Alvarez-Machain*, 542 US 692 (2004)). This institutionalization of *jus cogens* presupposes that some laws are inherent and inalienable, reflecting the notion that there are ultimately fundamental moral choices, and thus that there are non-economic boundaries which market participants should not be permitted to transgress; for example, that slavery is immoral. This case illustrates how transnational legal space mediates the process through which global markets become embedded in morality. This case also highlights discursive contention around a statute that confers jurisdiction in a US federal court, but which does not create a substantive right. Yet, the ambiguity of this statute is powerful when combined with *jus cogens*.

The US Supreme Court ruled that ATCA can be used for *jus cogens* violations. But the question raised in *Doe v. Unocal* was whether a party could sue a corporation for these *jus cogens* violations. Over the course of the nineteenth and twentieth centuries, US courts have increasingly granted corporations the rights of personhood, allowing them to be treated legally as private individual persons, separately from the individuals who own or operate them, and providing them with the same rights to due process under the law enjoyed by human persons (Benson 1999; Lamoreaux 2000). The plaintiffs in *Doe v. Unocal* essentially argued that with the rights of personhood also come responsibilities. Thus, they argued, corporate violations should be held liable under the ATCA for *jus cogens* violations in the same way that individuals are. The district court ruled that the plaintiffs in *Doe v. Unocal* have a legitimate *cause of action*, and agreed to hear the case. However, what remained at issue was whether Unocal should be held *liable* for the *jus cogens* violations suffered by the peasants. But Unocal settled the suit before this question was ever decided by the courts, and it remains to this day a central question for ATCA claims against corporations.

DISCURSIVE AMBIVALENCE

This transnational legal space has been significantly shaped by a transnationalist discourse on human rights. But the struggle to give this space meaning has also generated discursive ambivalence among some of the very actors who have voiced support for human rights within this space. In particular, corporations and states have diluted human rights discourse by combining it with others meant to protect corporations from being held accountable for their abusive human rights practices, and to minimize the state's vulnerability to international legal standards.

The discursive ambivalence created by corporations

Corporations have deliberately created discursive ambivalence on two fronts: first, by resisting attempts to subject corporations in general to an enforceable legal framework; and second, by actively consolidating a self-regulatory regime of "corporate social responsibility" that is based on a host of voluntary and non-enforceable instruments.

For example, in its effort to have *Doe* v. *Unocal* dismissed, Unocal deployed two main discourses, one relating to corporations' liability for human rights abuses, and the other relating to the United States' present foreign policy toward Burma. Unocal consistently proclaimed its support for human rights. At issue, they argued, was whether they should be held liable for the abusive human rights practices of the Myanmar junta. First, Unocal argued that it had a civil right to freely contract,[13] and that holding it "vicariously liable" for the actions of its state partners would interfere with that right. Unocal fought for the use of a weaker domestic standard of liability (based on direct and active participation), rather than the more stringent standard (based on aiding and abetting abusive human rights practices) that is used in international law.

Second, Unocal asserted that it could both profit from doing business with a repressive regime, and promote human rights. Moreover, Unocal has maintained that only continued trade and investment in Burma will restore democracy. However, this case presents a difficult challenge to the general proposition asserted by "free trade"

---

[13] The District Court stated that the "plaintiffs' allegations of Unocal's complicity in forced labor do not meet the standard of liability used in U.S. civil proceedings." That is, the plaintiffs could not show that Unocal "actively participated" in the forced labor. In effect, the District Court ruled that, because Unocal did not "actively and directly participate" in the alleged torts, they could not be held liable for those torts under the ATCA. Unocal subsequently asserted on its website that this ruling confirmed that they were not "vicariously liable" for the military's torts. On appeal, the attorneys and *amici curiae* for the *Doe* plaintiffs successfully argued that the lower court had failed to properly use the international standard of "aiding and abetting" the alleged tort in testing Unocal's liability. *Doe* v. *Unocal Corp.*, 395 F 3d 932 (9th Cir. 2002).

economists – that is, the proposition that trade liberalization policies promote economic growth and are therefore beneficial to countries that embrace them. Unocal argued that their presence in Burma and partnership with the Myanmar state was ultimately a positive force, because it was providing greater wealth for the country and jobs for Burmese citizens. They also argued that such economic growth would ultimately contribute to the democratization of Burma and empower its citizens to demand from its political institutions greater adherence to human rights norms.

However, this discursive ambivalence reveals a kind of disingenuous support for human rights in Burma. As Aung San Suu Kyi pointed out repeatedly, the vast percentage of wealth generated by foreign investment is not used to improve the economic conditions of Burma's citizens, but only to strengthen the military whose primary enemies are the economic minorities and pro-democracy activists within their country. It is also unclear how Unocal's use of slave labor in the construction of its $1.5 billion dollar gas pipeline project is providing "jobs" for Burma's citizenry in any meaningful sense. Nor is it clear how such corporate practices – despite the economic "growth" that they might create – would ultimately contribute to Burma's democratization, much less promote human rights.

Indeed, the National Foreign Trade Council (NFTC), an association of over 680 transnational corporations (chartered in the United States), intervened in the lawsuit, arguing that the federal court should not hold Unocal liable because it could deter companies from economic engagement with the oppressive regime (Dale 2003: 279–285, and ch. 4). Although Unocal has repeatedly claimed to support human rights, they have continued to aid and abet the Myanmar state's use of coerced labor, and have intentionally exploited the situation for profit.

Unocal argued before the District Court of California that granting jurisdiction over the *Doe* v. *Unocal* suit would interfere with the United States' present policy on Burma, which Unocal stated was to refrain "from taking precipitous steps, such as prohibiting all American investment that might serve only to isolate the [Myanmar state] and actually hinder efforts toward reform" (*Doe* v. *Unocal Corp.*, 963 F Supp 880, 894 FN 17 (C.D. CA 1997)). In short, Unocal claimed that any court decision that might threaten the existence of such a previously established partnership (like that established between Unocal and the Myanmar Government) is an inappropriate intrusion by the court into United States' foreign policy.

The discursive ambivalence created by states

The state too has shown discursive ambivalence with respect to human rights. The federal court refused all requests to dismiss the *Doe v. Unocal* case. Indeed, in response to Unocal's claim that is has a civil right to freely contract, the Ninth Circuit Court pointed out that it is has a civil obligation to uphold the Thirteenth Amendment as well, which includes "forced labor" in its prohibition against slavery. "The fact that the Thirteenth Amendment reaches private action," explained the court in its written decision, "in turn supports the view that forced labor by private actors gives rise to liability under [the] ATCA" (*Doe v. Unocal Corp.*, 395 F 3d 932, 946 n. 18 [9th Cir. 2002]).

The federal court also explained that because forced labor is a *jus cogens* violation, not only can a private party be held liable, but they should be subject to the stronger international, not the weaker domestic, civil standard of liability, namely, "aiding and abetting" rather than "direct and active participation."[14] Under the international standard of aiding and abetting a *jus cogens* violation, the test for whether Unocal is liable is based not on their exercise of "control" over the Myanmar military's actions, but rather on whether Unocal could, or should, have been able to foresee a reasonable likelihood of the Myanmar military's using the material support and information that Unocal provided them to commit a *jus cogens* violation.[15]

As evidence of Unocal's "aiding and abetting" the Myanmar military's policy of forced labor in connection with the pipeline, it pointed to the testimony from numerous witnesses, including several of

[14] The District Court incorrectly borrowed the "active participation" standard for liability from war crimes before Nuremberg Military Tribunals involving the role of German Industrialists in the Nazi forced labor program during World War II. The Military Tribunals applied the "active participation" standard in these cases only to overcome the defendants' "necessity defense." In the present case, Unocal did not invoke – and could not have invoked – the necessity defense. The court notes that the tribunal had defined the necessity defense as follows: "Necessity is a defense when it shown that the act charged was done to avoid an evil both serious and irreparable; that there was no other adequate means to escape; and that the remedy was not disproportionate to the evil." *Doe v. Unocal Corp.*, 395 F 3d 932, 948 n. 21 (9th Cir. 2002).

[15] "We require 'control' to establish proximate causation by private third parties only in cases . . . where we otherwise require state action. In other cases – including cases such as this one – where state action is *not* otherwise required, we require no more than 'foreseeability' to establish proximate causation. This requirement is easily met in the present case, where Unocal Vice President Lipman testified that even before Unocal invested in the Project, Unocal was aware that the 'option of having the [Myanmar] [M]ilitary provide protection for the pipeline construction . . . would [entail] that they might proceed in the manner that would be out of our control and not be in a manner that we would like to see them proceed,' i.e., 'going to excess.'" *Doe v. Unocal Corp.*, 395 F 3d 932, 954 n. 32 (9th Cir. 2002).

the plaintiffs themselves, that they were forced to clear the right of way for the pipeline and to build helipads for the project before construction of the pipeline began, which were then used by Unocal to visit the pipeline during the planning stages, as well as to ferry their executives and materials to the construction site. In terms of Unocal's practical assistance, Unocal hired the Myanmar military to provide security and build infrastructure along the pipeline route in exchange for money and food. Unocal also provided the Myanmar military with photos, maps, and surveys in daily meetings to show them where to provide the security and build the infrastructure which Unocal had hired them to do (*Doe v. Unocal Corp.*, 395 F 3d 932, 952–953 [9th Cir. 2002]).

The court further pointed to admissions made by Unocal representatives in two separate contexts that support the conclusion that Unocal's assistance had a "substantial effect on the perpetration of forced labor, which most probably would not have occurred in the same way without someone hiring the Myanmar military to provide security, and without someone showing them where to do it." The first admission was that of Unocal Representative Robinson to the US Embassy in Rangoon (in the once-classified "Robinson cable" that was forwarded to the US State Department), which read: "Our assertion that [the Myanmar military] has not expanded and amplified its usual methods around the pipeline on our behalf may not withstand much scrutiny" (*Doe v. Unocal Corp.*, 395 F 3d 932, 953 [9th Cir. 2002]).

The second admission was that of Unocal President Imle who, when confronted by Free Burma and human rights activists in January 1995 at Unocal's headquarters in Los Angeles, acknowledged to them that the Myanmar military might be using forced labor in connection with the project by saying that "[p]eople are threatening physical damage to the pipeline," that "if you threaten the pipeline there's gonna be more military," and that "[i]f forced labor goes hand and glove with the military yes there will be more forced labor" (*Doe v. Unocal Corp.*, 395 F 3d 932, 941 and 953 [9th Cir. 2002]). Notably, the court observed that on the basis of the same evidence, Unocal could even be shown to have met the standard of "active participation" erroneously applied by the District Court (*Doe v. Unocal Corp.*, 395 F 3d 932, 948 n. 22 [9th Cir. 2002]).

Responding to Unocal's claim that this ATCA suit represents an unconstitutional intrusion by the judiciary into the United States' foreign policy toward Burma, the District Court disagreed with Unocal's argument. First of all, instead of interpreting the State Department's foreign policy intentions for itself, the court asked the State Department directly to clarify its foreign policy position regarding Burma. In the "Statement of Interest of the United States," the State Department wrote that "at this time the adjudication of claims based on allegations of torture and slavery would not prejudice or impede the conduct of U.S. foreign relations with the current government of Burma."[16]

Second, the court reasoned that, even if Unocal is correct in drawing upon the Congressional debates over whether or not to impose sanctions on Burma as a valid indicator of the Congressional and Executive foreign policy position, that debate revolved around how to *improve* conditions in Burma by asserting *positive* pressure on the SLORC through investment in Burma.[17] Yet, this lawsuit does not question this foreign policy. Instead, the court explained:

> The [*Doe*] Plaintiffs essentially contend that Unocal, rather than encouraging reform through investment, is knowingly taking advantage of and profiting from [the] SLORC's practice of using forced labor and forced relocation, in concert with other human rights violations, including rape and other torture, to further the interests of the Yadana gas pipeline project. Whatever the Court's final decision in this action may be, it will not reflect on, undermine or limit the policy determinations made by the coordinate branches with respect to human rights violations in Burma.
>
> *Doe v. Unocal Corp.*, 963 F Supp 880, 895 (C.D. Cal. 1997).

In other words, the District Court asserted that the foreign policy of the United States, regardless of its position on the influence of corporate investment in Burma, does not intend to protect corporate activity that violates human rights violations. The District Court rejected

---

[16] *National Coalition Government of the Union of Burma v. Unocal, Inc.*, 176 FRD 329, 362 (C.D. Cal. 1997). Judge Paez initially authored the orders granting in part and denying in part Defendants' Motions to Dismiss. *See Doe v. Unocal Corp.*, 963 F Supp 880 (C.D. Cal. 1997). Judge Lew later authored the order granting Defendants' consolidated Motions for Summary Judgment. *See Doe v. Unocal Corp.*, 110 F Supp 2d 1294 (C.D. Cal. 2000).

[17] Statement of Sen. John McCain, 142 *Cong. Rec.* § 8755 (daily ed. July 25, 1996), quoted in *Doe v. Unocal Corp.*, 963 F Supp 880, 894 n. 17 (C.D. Cal. 1997). As Paez stated in his published court opinion, "Even accepting the Congressional and Executive decisions as Unocal frames them, the coordinate branches of government have simply indicated an intention to encourage reform by allowing companies from the United States to assert positive pressure on SLORC through their investments in Burma."

Unocal's argument to have the suit dismissed on the grounds that it represented an impediment to the federal government's foreign policy (*National Coalition Gov't of the Union of Burma v. Unocal, Inc.*, 176 FRD 329, 354 n. 29 [C.D. Cal. 1997]).[18]

However, we have also seen how the US Supreme Court has sought in *Sosa v. Alvarez-Machain* to contain the extent to which international human rights law might become enunciated within the United States' federal court system. Furthermore, the executive and legislative branches of the Federal Government have been exercising additional power to delimit ATCA. For example, bowing to the political pressure of corporations, Congress could easily create limitations on the use of ATCA. In October 2005, California Senator Dianne Feinstein, who serves on the Senate Energy and Natural Resource Committee, introduced S. 1874, a bill to reform the ATCA. Human rights groups like EarthRights International (ERI) were quick to denounce the bill as the "Torturer's Protection Act" (EarthRights International 2000b).

The bill prohibits any suit where a foreign government is responsible for the abuse within its own territory. ERI points out that this alone would eliminate most ATCA cases. The bill excludes from lawsuits war crimes, crimes against humanity, forced labor, terrorism, and cruel, inhuman and degrading treatment. It also requires that the defendant be a "direct participant" in the abuse. In essence, it argues that courts should use civil rather than international standards (of "aiding and abetting" the abuse) in assessing liability. Also, as ERI correctly warns, "Feinstein's bill gives the [Bush] Administration a blank check to interfere [in court cases] and have any case it chooses dismissed" (EarthRights International 2000b). Among the corporate beneficiaries would be Chevron, who has donated $30,800 to Feinstein's senatorial campaigns since 1989, according to the Center for Responsive Politics (Baker 2005). Also noteworthy is that Unocal maintained its headquarters in California since 1890, until it merged with Chevron Texaco (now Chevron) on August 10, 2005. Unocal is now a wholly-owned subsidiary of Chevron Corporation.

---

[18] The Ninth Circuit Court stated: "We agree with the District Court's evaluation that '[g]iven the circumstances of the instant case, and particularly the Statement of Interest of the United States, it is hard to imagine how judicial consideration of the matter will so substantially exacerbate relations with [the Myanmar Military] as to cause hostile confrontations." *Doe v. Unocal Corp.*, 395 F 3d 932, 959 (9th Cir. 2002).

This is not to suggest that the bill's passage is a foregone conclusion. Only one week after introducing S. 1874, Feinstein submitted a formal letter to Chairman of the Senate Committee on the Judiciary Arlen Specter requesting that he not proceed with the legislation at this time. Feinstein's letter explains:

> The legislation in question is designed to address concerns about the clarity of the existing Alien Tort Claim statute in light of the recent Supreme Court decision *Sosa v. Alvarez-Machain*, 542 U.S. 692 (2004). However, I believe that the legislation in its present form calls for refinement in light of concerns raised by human rights advocates, and thus a hearing or other action by the Committee on this bill would be premature.

Although several California corporations would benefit from S. 1874, it is not yet clear that these corporations will ultimately wield more influence over Senator Feinstein than human rights advocates.

There are, however, also pressures from the executive branch bearing on the future application of ATCA. The federal court's decision to hear *Doe v. Unocal* prompted other transnational activist networks to help file more such ATCA suits against corporations – particularly, though not exclusively, oil corporations.[19] Chevron is a defendant in one ATCA lawsuit relating to its complicity in the killing of peaceful protestors by the Nigerian military[20] (*Bowoto v. Chevron Texaco Corp.*, 312 F Supp 2d 1229 [N.D. Cal. 2004]). An ATCA suit was also filed in New York by the family of late Ogoni activist playwright Ken Saro-Wiwa against Royal Dutch [Shell] Petroleum alleging that the corporation had conspired with the military tribunal in Nigeria which hanged Wiwa, along with eight other activists who were organizing opposition to Royal Dutch Shell operations in their native Ogoniland on the delta

---

[19] There have been other ATCA cases against corporations outside the oil industry. Coca-Cola, for example, have been sued under ATCA for their complicity in the murder and intimidation of union members from their Columbian factory. And, although the courts rejected their first ATCA claim in 1989, the new flurry of ATCA cases against corporations has encouraged a renewed effort by citizens in Bhopal, India, to hold Union Carbide liable for the 1989 gas-leak disaster that caused thousands of deaths and permanent health problems.

[20] The suit, which the plaintiffs originally filed against a pre-merger Chevron, seeks to hold the company responsible for both the deaths of protesters who occupied a Nigerian oil drilling platform in 1998, and the attacks on residents of two Nigerian villages in 1999. The protesters were shot and killed by Nigerian security forces who were flown to the site in helicopters that were used by the joint venture that ran the platform. Both cases involve projects of companies that were Chevron Texaco's subsidiaries, rather than the parent company itself. Attorneys and activists have asserted, however, that liability for these wrongdoings should rest with the parent corporation and be pursued in the country where that parent corporation is chartered.

of the Niger River (*Wiwa* v. *Royal Dutch Petroleum Co.*, 226 F 3d 88 [2d Cir. 2000]).[21] Also, in 2001, eleven plaintiffs from the Aceh province of Indonesia's Sumatra Island, with the help of the International Labor Rights Fund, filed a suit using the ATCA against the Exxon Mobil Corporation in a suit titled *Doe* v. *Exxon Mobil* (*Doe* v. *Exxon Mobil Corp.*, 393 F Supp 2d 20 [D.D.C. 2005]).[22]

Yet, it is not clear whether these cases strengthened ATCA as a tool for addressing human rights abuses against corporations, or simply provided legal fodder that enabled the Supreme Court to justify narrowing the spectrum of human rights abuses committed by corporations for which the federal district courts may serve as a venue in ATCA suits. As the ATCA case against Unocal lumbered through the appeals court, the swifter decisions in these other ATCA cases provided useful discursive resources for Unocal's struggle to influence the courts to decide these legal conflicts in its favor. This became a significant factor after the new US administration (with its strong ties to the oil industry under George W. Bush, Dick Cheney, and Condoleezza Rice) began to discursively redefine its foreign policy around "counter-terrorism."

In early August 2002, the State Department warned the District Court of the District of Columbia that the *Doe* v. *Exxon Mobil* case "would hinder the war on terrorism and jeopardize U.S. foreign investment in a key ally [Indonesia]" (Alden 2002). The *Financial Times* reported that "a former State Department official," had stated that the Department's legal affairs office "saw an irresistible opportunity to strike a blow against the Alien Tort Claims Act" (Alden 2002). Yet, the official also reported that the State Department's letter came "after a heated debate inside the agency, with its human rights bureau arguing that U.S. intervention in the case would mar U.S. credibility on issues of corporate social responsibility," while other officials were "worried

---

[21] The case is still working its way through the Federal District Court after the US Supreme Court refused to hear arguments for the dismissal of the suit in March 2001, effectively granting the New York court jurisdiction.

[22] Exxon and Mobil merged in 1999. The International Labor Rights Fund is an advocacy organization dedicated to achieving just and humane treatment for workers worldwide, and the same organization who helped the National Coalition Government of Burma file their case against Unocal. The suit alleges that Exxon Mobil had been complicit in human rights violations committed by Indonesian military units who were hired to provide security for their natural gas field located in the Aceh province. Since 1975, the Indonesian military has had a history of violence and repression toward the Aceh ethnic minority and their Islamic separatist movement. While under contract with Exxon Mobil, allege the *Doe* plaintiffs, these military units committed widespread abuses, including murder, torture, rape, and kidnapping of the Aceh local population.

that the spate of court cases is angering US allies and interfering with the government's foreign policy authority" (Alden 2002). Publicly, however, the government issued a statement that claimed that "letting the case go to trial would harm the national interest, including the war on terrorism, and efforts to improve the Indonesian military's record of human rights abuses" (Efron 2002). During the same week, Unocal lawyers asked California State Superior Court Judge Chaney, who is presiding over a California "Unfair Business Practices" claims in a case based on the same facts as *Doe* v. *Unocal*, to seek a similar government opinion, asserting that many of the arguments in the *Doe* v. *Exxon Mobil* case were "equally applicable" to the *Doe* v. *Unocal* case.

These examples also highlight how economic globalization, and the transnational legal space for regulating it, are always subject to politics. This law, interpreted by a court and subject to amendment by a federal congress, reminds us of the vital role that states play in the process of globalization. All of these dimensions of state action (legislative, administrative, and judicial) remain crucial to the unfolding struggle over the rules and institutional arrangements of economic globalization.

Because human rights discourse is so often invoked as a political, legal, and moral resource for addressing (and diffusing contentious challenges to) the dehumanizing consequences of economic global-ization, it is important to focus on its many forms of practice – including the discursively ambivalent practices of corporate and state agents that combine human rights discourse with others that are meant to protect corporations from being held accountable for their abusive human rights practices, as well as those that are meant to minimize the state's vulnerability to international legal standards. Transcending the parti-cularities of any specific lawsuit under the ATCA, we may there-fore speak of a strategy that employs powerful discursive, ideological, and practical devices designed to stabilize this transnational legal space around voluntary and legally non-binding practices of social responsibility.

CONCLUSION

This case study has implications for existing theory on transnational movements and their relationship to human rights. Keck and Sikkink's *Activists Beyond Borders* (1998a) has arguably influenced the theoretical discussion of transnational movements more than any book published in the past five years. This influence is all the more impressive since the focus of their research is not on transnational movements per se, but rather on what they call "transnational advocacy networks" – that is, transnational networks of activists, distinguishable from other transnational networks largely by the centrality of principled ideas or values in motivating their formation (Keck and Sikkink 1998a: 1; Keck and Sikkink: 1998b: 217). Despite their efforts to distinguish such transnational social formations from transnational movements (see, e.g., 1998b: 236), their metaphor of the "boomerang pattern" to describe the influence characteristic of transnational advocacy networks – particularly under conditions in which channels between the state and its domestic actors are blocked – has itself channeled the interpretations of many observers of transnational social movements.

When channels between the state and its domestic actors are blocked, the boomerang pattern of influence characteristic of transnational networks may occur: domestic NGOs bypass their state and directly search out international allies to try to bring pressure on their states from outside. This, claim Keck and Sikkink, is most obviously the case in human rights campaigns (1998a: 12). Their model actually illustrates an additional step in this process whereby the domestic NGOs that have been blocked by their state activate the network *whose members pressure their own states* and (if relevant) a third-party organization, which in turn pressure the blocking, i.e., target, state.

This model focuses almost exclusively on interactions between states and civil society. They provide no conceptual space for examining interactions between markets and society. Corporations and market relations do not appear in Keck and Sikkink's conceptual model of how transnational social movements or transnational advocacy networks exert pressure for changing the human rights conditions that motivated their action. Yet, as we have seen in the case of the Free Burma movement, the trade relations between states and transnational corporations may constitute a very different kind of target and may require a different kind of pressure for affecting social change than that presumed by Keck and Sikkink's model.

Keck and Sikkink correctly emphasize the continuing significance of states, their reasons for doing so betrays, in light of the empirical evidence presented in this chapter, a questionable assumption regarding human rights practices and their implications for transnational movements. They claim that governments are the primary violators of rights (1998a: 12). Based upon this assumption, they build the conceptual logic of their boomerang pattern: "When a government violates or refuses to recognize rights, individuals and domestic groups often have no recourse within domestic political or judicial arenas. They may seek international connections finally to express their concerns and even to protect their lives" (1998a: 12).

One of the lessons that we should take from the transnational campaigns of the Free Burma movement is that transnational corporations, as much as governments, may also be significant violators of human rights. In some cases, transnational corporations may even work together with states in violating them. Moreover, the *Doe v. Unocal*, and other cases filed against both corporate- and state-violators of human rights under the ATCA reflect a transnational legal space where individuals and groups outside the United States may well find recourse within the judicial arenas of the US federal courts. That is, the domestic state in which human rights victims hold their citizenship does not necessarily have a monopoly on their access to a judicial arena. Each of these points taken on their own may seem like trivial tinkering with Keck and Sikkink's model. Taken together however, they begin to suggest an alternative pattern of transnational pressure that is distinctly different from the "international pressure" depicted in their model.

Keck and Sikkink's treatment of "international pressure" seems to suggest practices whereby foreign states are persuaded – via combinations of various types of politics (information, symbolic, leverage, and accountability) – to intervene in the affairs of the target state either directly or else through a mediating intergovernmental organization. However, the case study that I present in this chapter suggests a different pattern of pressure whereby foreign states neither intervene directly in the affairs of the target state, nor through a mediating intergovernmental organization. The various types of politics identified by Keck and Sikkink are still important to this alternative pattern of pressure, but they are deployed within a transnational legal space over legislative, administrative, and judicial maters of US law that mediate how global markets (in this case linking corporations chartered in the United States with the Myanmar state) become embedded in politics, law, and morality. It is through these legislative, administrative, and judicial *dimensions* of state action, and at multiple spatial *levels* of state action (municipal, regional, and federal) that the United States exercises pressure – *transnational*, as opposed to international, pressure – on the transnational corporations that buttress the power of the Myanmar state. That is, Keck and Sikkink focus on international pressure that states exert on other states (sometimes mediated through intergovernmental organizations), but they provide no conceptual space for considering the transnational pressure that states exert on transnational corporations. Such pressure may well contribute to social change within the blocking state that has forged business relations with the targeted transnational corporations. Only with substantial conceptual stretching might one suggest that this pattern of pressure represents a state exerting pressure on another state.

The case of the Free Burma movement illustrates how transnational movements that focus on influencing domestic policies in democratic states are not necessarily less effective in enhancing representation of groups suffering under authoritarian rule. Although a transnational movement campaign's focus on *jus cogens* violations may seem overly narrow or obscure, it may have a very significant impact on global governance. The transnationalist discourse deployed by the Free Burma activists has effectively problematized the discursive fusion of "free trade" and "human rights" asserted by the discourse on "constructive engagement" in the context of addressing the abusive practices of the Myanmar state. This case also illustrates how groups suffering under authoritarian rule may be repressed by not only the domestic policies of authoritarian states, but also by the domestic policies of democratic states that facilitate the undemocratic practices of the transnational corporations that collaborate with authoritarian states in repressing groups that live there. When we pay closer attention to these transnational connections between democratic and authoritarian states, their domestic policies, and their citizens, as well as to the transnational corporate practices and partnerships that span the boundaries of democratic and authoritarian states, it blurs the binary conceptual distinction through which we differentiate states as either "democratic" or "authoritarian." This provides the first analytical step toward creating new possibilities for imagining transnational legal action that effectively challenges the dominant relations and discourses sustaining such a reified conceptual distinction between democratic and authoritarian states.

ATCA is a potentially useful tool for furthering human rights. But it is also one that, when combined with other countervailing discourses, may become so diluted or de-clawed that it fails to retain the power or scope to reach some of the most egregious violators and violations of human rights. The struggle over ATCA illustrates the ambivalence and discursive dilemmas of foreign policy conservatives who have appropriated the language of international human rights for their own purposes. The consequence is that they are in an awkward position in trying to draw a line that immunizes US firms from complicity in such abuses. Yet, I have argued, even in the current political environment there are reasons to believe that this transnational legal strategy, using ATCA to hold liable corporations that aid and abet human rights violations, has legs.

This legal strategy represents one of the most significant efforts of the past century to reign in the power of transnational corporations. The case of *Doe* v. *Unocal* dramatically demonstrates the potential for using transnational legal action to challenge neo-liberal understandings of globalization. Rather than allowing the proponents of neo-liberal globalization to dismiss human rights concerns as "artificial obstacles to free trade," the federal courts have been providing a venue for discussing corporations' responsibilities and liabilities with regard to human rights. By shaping the moral boundaries within which corporations compete for profits, these venues have provided an important institutional mechanism and discursive resource for further discussion of how and why global markets are not self-regulating, but rather are (and must always be) institutionally constructed through and embedded in politics, law, and morality.

Despite the ambivalent discursive practices of both corporate and state actors who have donned the mantle of human rights, we should resist insisting that human rights discourse itself is necessarily hegemonic. Doing so serves ultimately to further empower those who seek to instrumentally subordinate human rights norms to the control of markets and particular nation-states. Rather we must focus on the ways that competing social actors – including corporations and states – draw upon human rights discourse and combine it with diverse configurations of multiple discourses to insert their own networks' social arrangement of power, practice, and meaning. Human rights discourse is not oppressive; but *how* we institutionalize the legal arrangement of human rights in practice can be.

This case, therefore, speaks not only to the discursive ambivalence of human rights practice, but also to what Goodale refers to as the "betweenness" of human rights discourse:

> the ways in which human rights discourse unfolds ambiguously, without a clear spatial referent, in part through transnational networks, but also, equally important, through the projection of the moral and legal

imagination by social actors whose precise locations – *pace* Keck and Sikkink – within these networks are (for them) practically irrelevant.

(Goodale, Introduction, p. 22 above.)

An approach highlighting transnational legal discourse is important precisely because the state's legal discourse and norms are so often hegemonic. Appreciation for the success of these transnational legal campaigns begins not with an accounting of victory or defeat in the court, or on the floor of the legislature, nor merely with an assessment of their direct role in transforming existing international law or global norms, but rather with the capacity of their participants to create an alternative discursive space in the legal records of the transnational struggles that take place in these institutions of the state.

These records, combined with the experiences of allied movement participants supporting the campaigns from outside the legal institutional arena, provide critical resources for sustaining the kind of public collective memory that future transnational campaigns and movements will have to draw upon in the inevitably incremental struggle for democratic global change. Transnational discursive strategies help us to re-conceptualize the relations within which we institutionalize economic globalization, as well as the way that we imagine the possibilities of participating in its institutionalization.

REFERENCES

Alden, Edward. 2002. "Unocal wants Government to Assess Labour Lawsuit." *Financial Times*, August 9, p. 3.

Amnesty International. 2004. "Appeals for Action: Myanmar: End Crackdown Now", April 5. Available on-line at web.amnesty.org/pages/mmr-040603-action-eng, accessed February 8, 2007.

Amnesty International. 2006. "Urgent Action: Myanmar: Possible 'disappearance'/Fear of torture/Arbitrary detention", January 20. Available on-line at web.amnesty.org/library/Index/ENGASA160012006?, accessed February 8, 2007.

Baker, David R. 2005. "Chevron Donates to Lawmakers against China Bid; Politicians Deny Link to Stance on Oil Firm's Unocal Offer." *San Francisco Chronicle*, July 23, p. C1.

Bales, Kevin. 1999. *Disposable People: New Slavery in the Global Economy.* Berkeley, Los Angeles, and London: University of California Press.

Bassiouni, Cherif. 1996. "International Crimes: *Jus Cogens* and *Obligatio Erga Omnes*." *Law and Contemporary Problems* 59: 63–74.

Benson, Robert. 1999. *Challenging Corporate Rule: A Petition to Revoke Unocal's Charter as a Guide to Citizen Action*. New York: Apex Press.

Block, Fred. 1990. *Postindustrial Possibilities: A Critique of Economic Discourse*. Berkeley, Los Angeles, and London: University of California Press.

Block, Fred. 2001. "Introduction." In Karl Polanyi. 2001 [1944]. *The Great Transformation: The Political and Economic Origins of Our Time*. 2d Beacon Paperback edn, with a foreword by Joseph E. Stiglitz and new introduction by Fred Block. Boston: Beacon Press.

Brysk, Alison. 2000. *From Tribal Village to Global Village: Indian Rights and International Relations in Latin America*. Stanford, CA: Stanford University Press.

Cleveland, Sarah H. 2001. "Norm Internalization and U.S. Economic Sanctions." *Yale Journal of International Law* 26: 1–92.

Dale, John Gilbert. 2003. "Transnational Legal Space: Corporations, States, and the Free Burma Movement." Ph.D. diss., University of California, Davis.

EarthRights International. 2005. "Common Questions and Answer for ERI: What are the terms of the settlement?", April 5. Available on-line at www.earthrights.org, accessed February 8, 2007.

EarthRights International. 2005b. "Senator Feinstein Introduces Bill to Protect Perpetrators of Human Rights Abuses", October 20. Available on-line at www.earthrights.org/, accessed February 8, 2007.

EarthRights International. 2005c. "Senator Feinstein Puts the Breaks on Anti-ATCA Bill S. 1874." October 25. Available on-line at www.earthrights.org/index.php?option=com_content&task=view&id=126&Itemid=41& lang=, accessed February 8, 2007.

Efron, Sonni. 2002. "Judge Lets Unocal Ask State Dept. to Intervene in Myanmar Lawsuit." *Los Angeles Times*, August 9, p. C2.

Fink, Christina. 2001. *Living Silence: Burma Under Military Rule*. New York: Zed Books.

Henkin, Louis, ed. 1981. *The International Bill of Rights: The Covenant on Civil and Political Rights*. New York, NY: Columbia University Press.

Human Rights Documentation Unit (National Coalition Government of the Union of Burma) (1997), Human Rights Yearbook: 1996 Burma. Nonthaburi, Thailand.

Keck, Margaret E., and Kathryn Sikkink. 1998a. *Activists Beyond Borders: Advocacy Networks in International Politics*. Ithaca, NY and London: Cornell University Press.

Keck, Margaret E., and Kathryn Sikkink. 1998b. "Transnational Advocacy Networks in the Movement Society." In David S. Meyer, and Sidney Tarrow, eds., *The Social Movement Society: Contentious Politics for a New Century*. Lanham, Boulder, New York, and Oxford: Rowman & Littlefield Publishers.

Lamoreaux, Naomi R. 2000. "How Corporations Acquired Legal Personhood: Language and Economics in the Late-Nineteenth-Century United States." Paper presented at the University of California, Davis Center for History, Society, and Culture, May 4.

Lifsher, Marc. 2005. "Unocal Settles Human Rights Lawsuit over Alleged Abuses at Myanmar Pipeline; A deal ends a landmark case brought by villagers who said soldiers committed atrocities." *Los Angeles Times*, March 22, p. C1.

Lintner, Bertil. 1990. *Outrage: Burma's Struggle for Democracy*. London and Bangkok: White Lotus.

Maung, Mya. 1992. *Totalitarianism in Burma: Prospects for Economic Development*. New York: Paragon House.

Meyer, David S. 1999. "Tending the Vineyard: Cultivating Political Process Research." *Sociological Forum* 14(1): 79–92.

Ridenour, Andrew. 2001. "Doe v. Unocal Corp., Apples and Oranges: Why Courts Should Use International Standards to Determine Liability for Violation of the Law of Nations under the Alien Tort Claims Act." *Tulane Journal of International and Comparative Law* 9: 581–603.

Roy, Laifungham Debabrata. 2002. "Enforced Disappearance," March. Available on-line at www.manipuronline.com/Features/March2002/disappearance08_2.htm, accessed February 20, 2007.

Schock, Kurt. 1999. "People Power and Political Opportunities: Social Movement Mobilization and Outcomes in the Philippines and Burma." *Social Problems* 46(3): 355–375.

Smith, Martin. 1991. *Burma: Insurgency and the Politics of Ethnicity*. London and New Jersey: Zed.

Smith, Michael Peter. 2001. *Transnational Urbanism: Locating Globalization*. Oxford: Blackwell.

Taylor, Robert H. 1998. "Political Values and Political Culture in Burma." In Robert I. Rotberg, ed. *Burma: Prospects for a Democratic Future*. Washington, DC: Brookings Institution Press, pp. 33–47.

Taylor, Verta. 1989. "Social Movement Continuity: The Women's Movement in Abeyance." *American Sociological Review* 54: 761–775.

US House Judiciary Committee. 1991. *H. R. Report*, No. 102–367, Pt. 1.

Walker, John M., Jr. 1997. "Domestic Adjudication of International Human Rights Violations Under the Alien Tort Statute." *Saint Louis University Law Journal* 41(2): 543–549.

Yawnghwe, Chao-Tzang. 1995. "Burma: The Depoliticization of the Political." In Muthiah Alagappa, ed. *Political Legitimacy in Southeast Asia: The Quest for Moral Authority*. Stanford: Stanford University Press, pp. 170–192.

Legal cases

Adra (*Abdul-Rahman Omar*) v. *Clift*, 195 F Supp 857 (D.Md. 1961).

Bolchos v. *Darrel*, 3 F Cas 810 (DSC 1795).

Bowoto v. *Chevron Texaco Corp.*, 312 F Supp 2d 1229 (N.D. Cal. 2004).

Filartiga v. *Pena-Irala*, 630 F 2d 876 (2d Cir. 1980).

In re Estate of Ferdinand E. Marcos Human Rights Litig., 25 F 3rd 1467, 1475 (9th Cir. 1994), *cert. denied*, 513 US 1126 (1995).

Doe v. *Exxon Mobil Corp.*, 393 F Supp 2d 20 (D.D.C. 2005).

Doe v. *Unocal Corp.*, 963 F Supp 880 (C.D. Cal. 1997).

Doe v. *Unocal Corp.*, 27 F Supp 2d 1174 (C.D. Cal. 1998).

Doe v. *Unocal Corp.*, 67 F Supp 2d 1140 (C.D. Cal. 1999).

Doe v. *Unocal Corp.*, 110 F Supp 2d 1294 (C.D. Cal. 2000).

Doe v. *Unocal Corp.*, F 3d 915 (9th Cir. 2001).

Doe v. *Unocal Corp.*, 395 F 3d 932 (9th Cir. 2002).

Doe v. *Unocal Corp.*, 395 F 3d 978 (9th Cir. 2003).

Doe v. *Unocal Corp.*, 403 F 3d 708 (9th Cir. 2005).

Kadic v. *Karadzic*, 70 F 3d (2d Cir. 1995).

National Coalition Government of the Union of Burma v. *Unocal, Inc.*, 176 FRD 329 (C.D. Cal. 1997).

Sosa v. *Alvarez-Machain*, 542 US 692 (2004).

Tel-Oren v. *Libyan Arab Republic*, 726 F 2d (D.C. Cir. 1984).

Tel-Oren v. *Libyan Arab Republic*, 470 US 1003 (1985).

Wiwa v. *Royal Dutch Petroleum Co.*, 226 F 3d 88 (2nd Cir. 2000).

Xuncax v. *Gramajo*, 886 F Supp 162 (D. Mass. 1995).

Model statute

American Law Institute, Restatement (Third) of the Foreign Relations Law of the United States § 702 (1987).

Reports

142 Cong. Rec. § 8755 (daily ed. July 25, 1996).

Statutes and treaties

Abolition of Forced Labor Convention (ILO No. 105), 320 UNTS 291, entered into force January 17, 1959.

Torture Victim Protection Act of 1991, 28 USC § 1350 *et seq.*

United States Alien Tort Claims Act, 28 USC §1350 *et seq.*

Vienna Convention of the Law on Treaties, 1155 UNTS 331, entered into force January 27, 1980.

8

BEING SWAZI, BEING HUMAN: CUSTOM, CONSTITUTIONALISM AND HUMAN RIGHTS IN AN AFRICAN POLITY*

Sari Wastell

In 1995, the government of His Majesty, the King of Swaziland, began the process of consultation that would eventually lead to the adoption and implementation of a new constitution for the small African king-dom a full decade later. Each year witnessed an annual increase in international pressure to fill the void left by the previous King when he repealed the Independence constitution by Royal Decree in 1973.[1] And many observers, from both inside and outside of Swaziland,

* This contents of this chapter were first discussed at a conference on Abnormal Justice convened by the Unit for Global Justice within the Sociology Department at Goldsmiths College, University of London. Many thanks to Kate Nash for her kind invitation to present the work there and for the many useful comments offered by members of the audience. Thanks also to Kirsten Campbell, Mlungisi Dlamini, Mark Goodale, Martin Holbraad, Vito Laterza, Sally Engle Merry, Musa Sibandze, and Marilyn Strathern for their careful readings and stimulating comments at various points in the chapter's maturation. I only regret that I was sometimes unable to rise to the challenge of these critical interventions; all failings of the work are very much of the author's own making. The research for this paper was undertaken in 2004–2005 under the auspices of a British Academy Small Research Grant, but builds on research I began in Swaziland in 1997.
[1] As much of the following will imply, if not directly address, any distinction between an autocratic polity of absolute monarchical rule as opposed to a law-governed state proves spurious in the Swazi instance. For example, the encompassment of the state by the monarchy was initially promulgated in law (albeit a royal decree) and continued to be articulated in the constitutional framework, which was the only document that addressed Swaziland's constitutional dispensation up until the July 2005 adoption of the new constitution. In the constitutional framework, it is clear that the King supercedes the law – which is to say, that a law existed for many years to state that the King is above the law. After the new constitution was accepted, the Royal Decree of 1973 remained in place for some time, as the new constitution did not include a provision allowing for the parliamentary repeal of royal decrees (although further extra-parliamentary law-making was to stop). Thus, for a period of some months, the country – legally – lived under two disparate, parallel, authoritative and largely incommensurable con-stitutional dispensations, a state of affairs which mirrors the elision of the autocracy/law-governed state divide one witnesses across Swazi society.

presumed that those committed to the political and legal reforms deemed necessary to end the thirty-two year state of emergency would welcome the document's long awaited arrival into law. Indeed, although probably a vocal minority, self-ascribed political progressives had long hoped the constitutional drafting process might usher in a return to multiparty democracy. Monarchical supporters, on the other hand, clearly envisioned the constitution's adoption in terms of a consolidation of absolute royal power and had engineered much of the consultation and drafting process in this direction. However, in the final months of the document's gestation, the geography of interests around the new constitution proved far more complex than one might have anticipated, and the ambivalence over the "rights" it was supposed to enshrine – and the nation it was said to constitute – proved profound.

This chapter aims to explore some of these "ambivalent encounters" with the Swazi constitution by interrogating the presumptions and prejudices of scale inherent in the perspectives of local and transnational actors involved in the document's realization. I will focus in particular on the interface of custom, constitutionalism and human rights under the new constitution's dispensation, with an eye towards arguing that one's understanding of that interface is still hugely over-determined by colonial registers of value. In particular, it is the entrenched presumption that Custom is both an analogue to ("western", received) law and, at the same time, a more atomistic, particular and context-dependent modality for legal claim-making and dispute settlement, that leads many to presume that a new era of constitutionalism in Swaziland will efface, assimilate or nominally accommodate custom within the embrace of a new Swazi Bill of Rights. Indeed, the question has been put to me repeatedly – always couched in terms of what I predict will *become* of custom once the new constitution has been adopted. My answer has met with varied reactions, but underwrites much of what follows: I am curious to see what becomes of constitutionalism (both its legal forms and the political subjectivities it cultivates) once custom is through with *it*.

SCALES OF JUSTICE AND JUSTICE WITHOUT SCALES

If the remit of the current volume has been to track the workings of rights discourses in the in-between space of the transnational, then the current contribution proposes a mildly mischievous intervention. On the one hand, the *question* of scale is central to the current chapter's concerns. On the other, the work seeks to query the appropriateness of presuming a *single* scale as the analytical frame through which rights practices can be studied, or indeed perhaps the appropriateness of a scalar framework at all in some instances.

Let us be clear. When one locates rights somewhere *between* the global and the local, one is not moving between scales per se, but between the levels of a single scale which takes the global as its ceiling and the local as its floor. "The transnational" then emerges as an interim between those two points, presumably one of many interims (or 'levels' in the language of scalar theory[2]) measured by its propor-tionate relationship to other levels of the scale. To move between scales is another matter entirely (and perhaps more akin to the anthro-pological practice of analogy). For disparate scales are rendered incom-mensurable by the very fact that their proportions can never be understood as homologues to one another.[3] Put another way, any time one scale can actually be mapped onto another, one comes to realize that one is not looking at distinct scales, but a more expanded or contracted version of the same scale (see Wastell 2001).

So the first proposition of this contribution is that the under-examined middle space of the transnational might present both conceptual and pragmatic challenges precisely because it is only available to a single scalar imagining of rights discourses. The second proposition suggests that the apparent tension – the lack of "fit" – between "rights" and various other formulations of "social justice" derives from the absence of true scalar analysis, where one would have to be moving between absolutely disparate scales or between the presence and absence of scale altogether. One of the things this contribution will endeavour to accom-plish is a very different imagining of that "fit" (between "rights" and "social justice") by exploring the possibilities and constraints posed by the evocation of rights discourses in the context of divine kingship.

Where this piece very clearly aligns itself with the volume as a whole is in its rejection of a retreat into the "bounded cultural universe" or

[2] Scalar theory has been most rigorously elaborated in the ecological sciences (see Peterson and Parker 1998), and I am most indebted to Paul Richardson for first directing me to this body of literature.
[3] And here one can already see certain parallels between scalar theory's concern for the non-homologous character of proportion and Luhmannian social system theory's similar preoccupa-tion for the non-homologous character of system codes – a point I will return to towards the end of the chapter.

"worldview" approach to rights which has long been considered the purview of the anthropologist on this topic. My intention is not to "capture" rights in their moment of realization inside of an essentialized Swazi culture. Rather, I submit that the political ontology of divine kingship makes rights available within the context of its own – non-scalar – imagining, and that it is only by moving between the scalar (global-transnational-local) imagining with which we are familiar and the non-scalar imagining fostered by divine kingship, that we can make sense of the ambivalent encounters Swazis themselves experience with respect to human rights.

The question of political ontology presents two immediate problems in the Swazi case: that of the legislator of law and that of the legal subject. Let us take each in turn briefly, although the two points are virtually inseparable.

Within the political ontology that underpins the rule of law, law comes into being – is legislated – as a product of free will. In a variety of different guises, "western" jurisprudence presumes that "modern" aggregates of individuals, unable to agree on the common good, submit to a legal framework which allows them to "agree on how to disagree."[4] Hence, "society" can be "realized." Indeed, the social contract model is particularly relevant with respect to human rights, where – critiques by Burke and Marx notwithstanding[5] – rights have long been understood to exist "when a duty bearer owes an obligation to the right-holder because of a prior *promise*" (Douzinas 2000: 232, emphasis mine).[6] What is of particular import to the current discussion, is the way in which a contractual framing of rights not only underscores the legislator (state) as a duty-bearer bound by mutual agreement to a rights-holder (individual), but the extent to which that relationship is insular and circumscribed. Contract does not create chains of relationships. Each contract binds only the two parties concerned; contracts are not transitive in the way that tort is.[7]

---

[4] With particular respect to the concerns of this work, see Douzinas and Warrington 1994, where they argue that justice has come to be replaced by the administration of justice.
[5] For the most complete and eloquent exploration, see Douzinas 2000: ch. 7.
[6] See Douzinas 2000 for an abbreviated explication of power theories and interest theories respectively.
[7] While it is largely outwith the scope of the present work, it would be interesting to see how much mileage could be gained by applying the contract–tort distinction to those ethnographic case studies where the "modern" legal subject (who is the precondition) of human rights, comes into competition with the person whose constitution is understood *only* through the complex of relationships and obligations in which they are enmeshed. For the most compelling of ethnographic examples, one should see Strathern 2004, an analysis of a Papua New Guinean

However, the other point to note, which brings us to the issue of the rights-holder or legal subject, is that the legislator and legislatee in this case mutually constitute each other. Put another way, each is the axiological foundation of the other. As Douzinas observes: "rules create rights and rights belong to people, they exist only with the support of a subject" (Douzinas 2000: 233). The conjuring of this denuded legal subject – abstract and stripped of his/her relationships to anything but the law[8] – is part of what Douzinas refers to as the law's anthropogenetic power (2000: 234; and see Pottage and Mundy 2004). However, in terms of the analytical concerns of the current chapter, this formulation of the relation between legislator and legislatee firmly positions rights on the gobal-local scale, only choosing to focus on that bit of the scale which takes the state as its ceiling and the individual as its floor. All we have managed to do is to shift levels in our analysis – not the scale itself (see Wastell 2001).

What we shall see in the following section is how poorly this rendering of law's legislator and its subject maps onto the political ontology inherent in divine kingship. For in Swazi kingship at least, what appears to be the legal domain – "custom" so-called[9] – simply emanates from the immanent presence of kingship itself. And far from appearing as an implicit contract between the King and His subject, that is, as a precondition which establishes that relation, the mobilization of Swazi law and custom constitutes one's participation in, and incorporation into, the substance of the kingship. In scalar terms then,

---

compensation payment (agreed in custom), which was forestalled on the grounds that it included the transfer through matrimony of a woman, Miriam, from one clan to another as part of the payment. The concern was that Miriam's human rights, as guaranteed in the country's constitution, were being infringed upon, and that the practice represented the "bad" face of custom. Appealing to the "traditional"/"modern" distinction, Strathern argues, allowed kinship to be "bundled away" under the mantle of tradition (2004: 208) – together with "a whole set of suppositions summed up in the term kinship – the nature of relationships as a matter of people's conduct and obligations towards one another" (2004: 225). While I will also be arguing against the modernist disposition towards believing one can pick and choose between "good" and "bad" custom by the end of this chapter, I imagine there could also be some purchase in thinking through human rights-as-contract versus custom-as-tort, since contract and tort are not intrinsically incommensurable within the rule of law, whereas human rights and custom invariably are.
[8] Again, see Strathern 2004.
[9] Up to this point, I have used "custom" in a vernacular fashion, only hinting that I remain unconvinced that custom is an obvious analogue of law. From here on in, I would like to differentiate between "custom" as that ideational construct of the received law as its own "other", and Swazi Law and Custom (as the Swazis themselves refer to it), which comprises a constellation of normative practices that emanate from kingship. While some of these practices have a legal character at times, the sum total of the practices cannot be reduced to "law" any more than Swazi kingship can be reduced to politics.

there is no scale because there is no differentiated entity that could be recognized as the legislator, nor a legal subject to whom rights might be attributed.

I am not arguing that Swazis are incapable of the scalar imaginings of justice which derive from the political ontology of the rule of law. Far from it. I am suggesting that Swazis move between two seemingly incommensurable positions, between the scalar void of their kingship and the scalar scaffolding of Euro-American modernism. So my "in-betweenness" is sited in *that* interchange and the various ambiguities to which it gives rise, rather than in the "in-betweenness" found somewhere between the global and the local. As we will see, there is nothing "local" about Swazi kingship from its own perspective, and being Swazi might be of a type – of the same value magnitude – with being human. Most Swazis, I argue, are uncomfortable with the implicit proposition inherent in the discourse of human rights that they must choose between their rights as humans and their responsibilities as Swazis, since the latter is not conceived of as a sub-level category enveloped by the former.

LOOKING FOR SWAZI CITIZENS AND SWAZI SUBJECTS: THE THEORETICAL INVERSIONS SUGGESTED BY SWAZI DIVINE KINGSHIP

Returning to Swaziland in October 2004 after some years away, and with my attentions focused by a remit to study the constitution's final months of gestation, I was greeted by a frenzy of activity. The constitution would soon be debated in the two houses of parliament, from whence a joint session would be convened before the bill proceeded to the Royal Palace at Lozitha for assent. A strict deadline of January 2005 was said to have been imposed by the commonwealth – a deadline which would prove hard to meet as it impinged on the King's obligation to go into seclusion in preparation for the sacred *iNcwala* (or first fruits) ceremony. The exact date of his withdrawal into seclusion is never specified in advance, but would coincide with the day that the Bemanti water parties would be dispatched from the country to collect waters from the Indian Ocean and the Lusaba, Mgwenya, Komati, and Mbuluzi Rivers. In any event, the date, astrologically ordained, always falls between the start of October and the end of November. Thus, the fact that the parliamentary debate over the constitution had not begun before my arrival in mid-October did not auger well. And from the

King's entrance into seclusion forward, all political activity in the country would halt for the full duration of the ritual cycle, a period which varies but usually lasts at least five weeks. Throughout this interim, courts and ministries are closed, parliament does not meet and all activity of a political nature remains in suspension. Even those who challenge the omnipotence of monarchical authority in the country seem to accept as given the necessary cessation of "politics" as the nation awaits the restoral and rejuvenation of their King and collectively offers thanks to Mvelinchanti (the Swazi Creator-God or "First to Appear").

In November 2004, this abrupt and non-negotiable recess was all the more noticeable for the backdrop of political overdrive it interrupted. A consortium of local nongovernmental organizations (NGOs), labour unions, and civil organizations such as the executive of the Swaziland Law Society had banded together to form a coalition[10] to obstruct the adoption of the new constitution. Concerned that the document was neither representative of many Swazis political aspirations nor capable of significantly changing the current status quo (in which the King is vested with full executive, legislative and judicial authority) members of the coalition remained convinced that the absolute power of the Swazi monarchy would only be further enshrined should the document become law. Urgent applications were made to the High Court to interdict debate of the constitution in parliament, and every aspect of the document's progress into law was scrutinized during emergency meetings convened over breakfast before long days of lobbying commenced. Lobbying was aimed at damage control; most recognized that the constitution's eventual success was a foregone conclusion.

The legal efforts made by the coalition notwithstanding, other impediments stood in the way of the time-strapped parliamentary debate. The bicameral parliament was not legally authorized to undertake the debate unless it could be raised to the level of a constitutional assembly, and there seemed to be no shortage of confusion within the Ministry of Justice as to how this might be effected. In the final instance, the status of parliament was left unchanged, and the status

---

[10] Henceforth, I will refer to this group of activists simply as "the Coalition," as they themselves did. It should be noted that while I was not formally acknowledged as a member, my position vis-à-vis the coalition was not entirely neutral either. As a result of my longstanding association with the Women and Law in Southern Africa Research Trust (WLSA-Swaziland chapter), I was involved in a considerable amount of lobbying and research on behalf of the coalition throughout my stay in October to December 2004.

of the document was changed instead. The draft constitution was "re-drafted" by the (then) Attorney General, Phesaya Dlamini, into a bill, on a certificate of urgency, which parliament would then be able to debate. The change in the document's status, however, also raised new concerns in some quarters. The draft constitution, it was understood, had been legitimized only a month earlier when the King called the people to *sibaya* (the royal kraal at Lobamba, which the Swazi historian J. S. M Matsebula likens to a "spiritual temple" of the Swazi people (1988: 331)[11]) to convene a "people's parliament." This was the final opportunity for the Swazi people to either accept the document as "truly Swazi" (the Independence constitution having been repealed on the grounds that it was "un-Swazi" and a foreign imposition[12]) or to reject it. Official accounts reported a near unanimous endorsement – a point to which we will return.

However, when the draft constitution was re-rendered as a bill, a number of changes were interpolated, such that the document acceded to by the nation at *sibaya* was subtly – but significantly – different from the document which arrived in parliament. Some alterations, despite their sweeping implications, merited comment in only the most constricted of circles and never featured in the parliamentary debate that eventually did take place. For example, a legally-trained colleague of mine at WLSA (Women and Law in Southern Africa Research Trust – Swaziland office) noted that where in section 12(a) the King was originally granted immunity from any "suit or legal process in any *civil* cause in respect of all things done or omitted to be done by him in his *private* capacity" (emphasis mine), the newly modified bill conferred immunity in *both* civil and criminal proceedings arising from actions undertaken (or not undertaken) in *both* his public and private capacities. The effect of the change was to underscore that all actions by the

---

[11] *Sibaya* does not only denote the physical space in which the Swazi nation gathers to present views on the King on pressing matters of concern, but, like many other siSwati terms, simultaneously refers to the politico-juridical body itself. Thus, *sibaya* is synonymous with the Swazi National Council, described in the Draft Constitution as "the highest policy and advisory council (*Libandla*) of the nation" (section 233(1)). It is comprised of all senior princes, chiefs and all adult "citizens" (the wording used in the Draft Constitution, section 233(2)) of Swaziland.

[12] Mlungisi Dlamini, in an unpublished essay, has compellingly argued that the abrogation of the 1968 Independence (or Westminster) constitution by Royal Decree in 1973 was the dénoument of a longstanding campaign on the part of King Sobhuza II to not only regain independence for the Swazi nation, but to do so exclusively under the sovereign power of the Swazi King. Such an arrangement had originally been acknowledged in the 1881 Pretoria Convention, which not only recognized Swazi independence, but integrally tied this independence to the sovereignty of their kingship (pers. comm.)

King are understood as "supra-legal" – arguably conferring more power and autonomy on him than he might enjoy within the boundaries of Swazi law and custom (the so-called "customary" law).[13] This was but one of many such changes that emerged, and while the changes themselves garnered little or no attention outside of the coalition,[14] the anti-constitution contingency argued that the sum effect of the document's change in status was to undermine the alleged "success" of the people's parliament. Critics of the constitution could now rightfully claim that the document presented for consideration to parliament was a substantially different entity from the one accepted by the Swazi nation.

However, the political progressives (self-ascribed) who now queried the legitimacy conferred by *sibaya*, had earlier expressed reservations about the capacity of the "people's parliament" to offer a wholly representative endorsement of the constitution on behalf of all Swazis. Observing that the congregation at *sibaya* was a self-selecting sample of Swazi society, as only "traditionalists" and monarchists would answer the King's summons in the first place, they explained that attendance at *sibaya* was akin to accepting an invitation into someone's home – except that this was the home of the Swazi nation-in-kingship. "When you go to someone's house and eat their food, do you criticize the host?" The critics of the people's parliament may have been contesting the representative character of those who had "accepted" the constitution on behalf of the nation, but what they simultaneously refused to contest was the nature and protocols of *sibaya* itself.

My motive in highlighting the ways in which coalition members offered distinct readings of *sibaya*'s endorsement of the draft constitution

---

[13] To the extent that a King is understood always to be a mouthpiece of his people and that the nation is understood to be one in the body and person of the King, the limits of kingly caprice are believed to be tightly circumscribed within Swazi law and custom. Additionally, the Swazi system of "traditional" government comprises a highly articulated system of checks and balances on royal power, including a dual monarchy with a division of labour between the King and Queen Mother as well as a system of decision making by the King-in-Council, which further limits the King's ability to govern autocratically. In practice, there is no doubt that many kings have been noted for their abuse of privilege, but it is also a point of fact that being a "bad" king does not make you any less of a king. Ultimately, the comparison (of the limits or extent of kingly power as between received law and Swazi law and custom) is largely spurious, I would contend, as it involves the assumed equivalency of two unlike social phenomena. However, my larger point here would be that it is the King himself who brings these two disparate entities into the same analytic frame, and that it is just this sort of political improvisation which has long ensured his position.

[14] The significant exception to the general disinterest in changes unilaterally undertaken within the Ministry of Justice as the draft constitution re-emerged as a parliamentary bill was the furore that erupted over the deletion of a clause stating that Christianity was to be the country's official religion.

before and after the document was presented as a bill to be debated in parliament speaks directly back to my surprise at the sudden stillness and inertia which overcame Swaziland as the King went into seclusion for *iNcwala*. Just as it seemed to me that the hiatus with respect to "official" political activity might well prove a particularly fecund window of opportunity for "unofficial" activity, I originally presumed that coalition supporters would want to attend *sibaya* to give the lie to any absolute consensus performed there. However, many of my colleagues in the coalition, while critical of absolute monarchical rule and the absence of multiparty democracy in Swaziland, are the first to acknowledge the very palpable thrall of divine kingship. As one friend and colleague admonished me, "I can arrive at Lozitha [the Royal Palace] with someone at my side that I know and leave standing next to a stranger. I don't know what that place does to you, but I've seen it happen to many people."

In larger analytic terms, the failure of *sibaya* as a site for political agitation, and of the King's term of seclusion as a time for subversive campaigning, can be read as the failure of "bifurcation" as a descriptive device for the (allegedly) dual forms of law and governance that obtain in Swaziland (as well as the disparate populations to which each of the forms could be said to attach[15]). Mahmood Mamdani's seminal account of the bifurcated states spawned by indirect rule in the British African colonies (1996) proves instructive in this respect for both its correspondences and its divergences in the Swazi instance. Of course Swaziland was something of an exception in many respects. Its kingship was maintained, albeit in the diminished form of a paramount chief, and continued to exert a centralizing effect throughout the colonial period due to the size of the population and the cultural homogeneity that was the legacy of at least two centuries of state formation under a succession of Swazi kings.[16] Even Mamdani notes that the absolute autonomy of indirect rule in Swaziland was extraordinary given the

---

[15] By this I simply mean the commonplace presumption on the part of many observers of Swazi politics that Swazi custom and the "traditional" system of governance organized through the dual monarchy down through chiefs, their governors, and runners must pertain to rural Swazis, while urbanized Swazis conduct their affairs predominantly through the received law and the bicameral parliament. For a critique of the dual characterization of Swazi polity more generally, see Wastell 2007.

[16] Both Matsebula (1988) and Bonner (1983) offer very comprehensive accounts of the strategies of the earliest Swazi kings which helped to not only consolidate their power politically, but integrate their kingdoms culturally – the emphasis on assimilation falling away in the past century.

country's strong settler population (1996: 89).[17] However, the political identities of Swazis that were legally constituted during the colonial period (which Mamdani wants to argue exist in a dynamic tension with the economic identities created by colonial policies[18]) were less clear-cut and produced less fragmentation in the social body than what Mamdani describes for many other African post-colonies. Thus, Swaziland's road to independence was significantly different and its post-colonial government grappled with a very different set of concerns.[19] The reason for this goes directly back to the nature of Swazi kingship and the significant ways in which it differs from other subsaharan African forms of charismatic and/or "traditional" authority.

Mamdani's central thesis is that rural-based Africans under indirect rule were incorporated *ethnically* under the regime of Custom as administered by native authorities, while their urban counterparts were included or excluded *racially* from the civil law and regime of rights which governed the settler populations and colonial administrators. On the one hand, it is true that in Swaziland longstanding recourse to custom in the rural areas has fostered political identities more akin to "subjects" than "citizens." But even here the term "subject" would need to be qualified. For rural Swazis do not identify ethnically so much as culturally, and their identities as subjects refer back to their relations to chiefs. In respect of their relation to the King, rural Swazis – like their urban counterparts – understand that they are one in the person and body of the King and that they participate in the essence of Kingship – not least through their mobilization of custom itself. It is for this reason that Swazis, both rural and urban alike, *lobola* (pay bridewealth) to kingly marriages, such that the Swazi nation is said to have claims on all

---

[17] Proclamation 70 of 1950 recognized the Swazi King as the sole authority in matters customary, a state of affairs which largely mirrors Swazi sensibilities. Swazis assert that their custom comes from the imminent authority of the King rather than a practice or norm legitimized by its duration through time, and few would see the 1950 legislation as the source of this formulation. However, Mamdani's understanding of this relationship (between the immanent character of Swazi kingship and their custom) is lost by the end of his book, where he falls back into a discussion of "custom then versus custom now" – implying that the former is more authentic than the latter (1996: 172).

[18] For Mamdani's strongest and most concise statement of his position on this point, see Mamdani 2000.

[19] Mamdani's account of Swaziland's conservative return to custom through a policy of forced compulsions is not entirely satisfactory in this respect (2000: 177–178). It is largely based on Richard Levin's work (1997), which convincingly charts the financial consolidation of Dlamini power. However, Levin's Marxist rendering of Swazi society-as-class-struggle fails to address why the Dlaminis (and King Sobhuza II in particular) were capable of imposing the drastic reforms that facilitated Dlamini hegemony. In short, the work refuses to engage seriously with the resonances and cosmological implications of divine kingship for the Swazi people.

the offspring of royal couplings, and by extension, on the future King. So the term "subject" is not entirely apt in this context.[20] On the other hand, with reference to urban Swazis, while racially identified (and largely excluded) throughout the colonial era, they too share a cultural and spiritual bond to the kingship which often overrides their identities as *mere* Swazi citizens. It is not that the "citizen/subject" divide does not obtain at all in Swaziland. It is simply the case that its salience is mediated by the practices of kingship, which is precisely why the protocols of *sibaya* and kingly ritual seclusion are not solely the provenance of "rural subjects."[21]

The import of such an observation to a discussion of custom, constitutionalism and human rights in Swaziland cannot be underestimated. A recurring theme of this volume has been to critically investigate the articulation of human rights with alternative normative frameworks, and many of the contributions have put paid to the presumption that this articulation is a unidirectional one. Rather, the alleged universality of human rights, when confronted with the contingency of their application in contexts informed by alternative normative frameworks, initiates a process of cycling, which reinforms and destabilizes the unity of human rights as a monolithic discourse. So, in the first instance, we could posit the practices of divine kingship as one such "alternative normative framework" in which almost all Swazis participate (albeit in varying degrees), irrespective of whether they appear to be rural "subjects" or urban "citizens."

But what of the notion of "cycling"? The question remains, what exactly is being cycled? Are the elements emanating from the discourse of human rights of a type with those that are returned from those very sites of practice (here the practices of kingship)? The question turns on a dog-eared dichotomy that underpins the discipline of anthropology itself, that of the distinction between humanism and alterity.[22] Human rights presumes a self-evidence of what it is to be human and protects

---

[20] For a more extended discussion of the problematic nature of the term "subject" in relation to Swazi kingship and of the concept of "sovereignty" in this respect, see Wastell 2006: *passim* and Wastell 2007: chs 3 and 8.

[21] It is also the case that rural and urban communities are vastly more integrated in Swaziland – not least through royal ritual migrations to the *iNcwala* and *umhlanga* ceremonies – such that only 17 percent of Swazis live exclusively on Swazi nation land (or land held in trust by the crown and allocated by chiefs) (Russell 1990 cited in Mamdani 1996: 172, see also Wastell 2007: ch. 6).

[22] Many thanks to Martin Holbraad for framing the matter in this way and for the many discussions and collaborations we have undertaken along these lines.

that essence or quality against the compromising and dehumanizing practices of states in particular. Anthropological analyses of human rights take for granted the self-evident diversity of contexts into which human rights discourse is introduced (see Wastell 2001). Whether framed in terms of a structure/agency opposition or the proliferation of cultural difference in the face of a cosmopolitan world society harbingered by globalization, the "inputs" from either side of the equation are not of a type. Take, for example, the oft-repeated argument that globalization has the correlative effect of producing cultural differentiation, or – in its more provocative guise – "cultural fundamentalism" (see Stolcke 1995). While no doubt true in many respects, it also has to be noted that the observation is contingent on the potentially infinite divisibility of the term "culture" as against the absolute indivisibility of the term "global." In the case of Swazi kingship, where what is Swazi is understood to be of the same value magnitude as what is non-Swazi (i.e., rather than Swazis being a small part of the teeming globe, Swazi kingship posits the nation-in-kingship as the coequal counterparts to "the Globe") the calculus breaks down. And here we see the invisible hand of scale.[23] For the scale presumed by Swazi kingship disallows an analysis of parts to wholes – or better put, obviates scalar imagining because the proportions are deemed binary and commensurable.

Now, one might reasonably counter that there is no shortage of scholars who have queried and problematized and deconstructed the presumed universalism and unity of human rights, just as most commentators on globalization do not take the term to – self-evidently – refer to a single, empirically observable set of practices which are historically unprecedented. Rather, both are understood as "discourses" or "concepts," the sorts of lenses through which we apprehend and constitute objects of knowledge, rather than objects of knowledge in and of themselves.[24] This volume is an excellent example of this (necessary) critical move. The problem, however, arises on the Swazi side of the equation. Having countenanced the possibility of human

---

[23] The global and the local is all too often glossed as the international versus the domestic, betraying our post-Westphalian predilections. However, as the "western," "white," and "global" can all be collapsed into a Swazi measure of Swazi versus non-Swazi in the idioms and distinctions harboured by divine kingship, already our scalar imaginings are challenged by the revisions presented by a sort of "anti"-scalar imagining.

[24] In the case of human rights, the distinction could be teased out by considering those works which focus on human rights as a discourse or concept (such as the present volume) versus those which approach human rights as law.

rights discourses – very much in the plural – what do we do when confronted with an "alternative normative framework" which presumes the very sort of unity and material character of which human rights has only recently been divested? The very model of alternative normative frameworks belies the Swazi perspective – for the Swazi (non)-scalar imagination creates binary unities which sit in an orthogonal relation. Therefore, not only does the Swazi social imagining (as fostered by participation in divine kingship) of "normative frameworks" only entertain a single alternative, it is predisposed to presuming its other is equally as unified and as indivisible as itself. Thus, to understand what is happening when Swazis negotiate the interlocutions of Custom, constitutionalism and human rights, one has to incorporate this register as well. It is not that Swazis are not also consummate modernists, with a cartographical imagination which can locate the "local" as a part inside of the "global" whole. It is that they continually operate in an inter-change between these two disparate epistemic positions, a fact which confers a distinct ontological vantage on them from many of the non-Swazi actors with whom they collaborate.

So my first theoretical move is to problematize the humanism/alter-ity dichotomy which often remains unenunciated in discussions of the global and the local or the relation of human rights-as-discourse to human rights-as-(multiple) discourses resulting from the actual prac-tice of Human Rights "on the ground." However, my next theoretical move – again trying to tease out the various predicates with which the term "cycling" might be freighted – would be to query the opposition of "discourse" to "practice." For in this model of "cycling," it is assumed that abstractions are materialized in concrete sets of practices under-taken in specific locations of engagement, an innocent enough starting point it would seem. Indeed, in the case of Swaziland, the repeated concern for what is to become of custom once the country finds its constitutional voice betrays this very mapping of the problematic. The *principles* of constitutionalism (together with the human rights to be enshrined in constitutional form) are understood to be the abstract concerns that will come to colonise the concrete and particular prac-tices of custom. However, by raising the question of kingship and the ways in which it obviates a subject/citizen binary, I hope to have set the stage for a very different sort of discussion of scale in relation to these issues. For divine kingship comes attendant with its own constellation of concepts, concepts which, as in the case of human rights-as-concept, take on disparate forms and distinct inflections when operationalized in discrete locations and sets of practices. So, even as kingship presents a sort of limiting condition to human rights – those "existing relations of meaning and production" (Goodale, Introduction to this volume) in which human rights are always embedded in practice – so too can one understand divine kingship as the very determinate conceptual repertoire which finds itself pressed into service in the concrete practices and locations of human rights.

AMBIVALENCE AND ITS RELATION TO THE SCALES OF JUSTICE

Like myself, many non-Swazi actors involved in either observing or facilitating the realization of the Swazi constitution found themselves a bit flummoxed by the response of those Swazis they hoped would be their natural allies in the battle to restore constitutionalism to the country. Anticipating that the very constituencies who had long pressed for multiparty democracy, the observance of the rule of law and the recognition of human rights in the country would welcome the constitution's passage into law, many were surprised by the vehemence with which the document was roundly rejected. Advice on the "local sentiments" was commissioned from a variety of quarters, and various commentators were asked to explain why "progressive" Swazi activists were quick to renounce the document out of hand.

One such advisor, sent by the American Bar Association, explained the situation in no uncertain terms. Emboldened by a recent return from Afghanistan where, she explained, she had being doing "similar work" with considerable success, she held forth at a number of different coalition-sponsored events on the inadequacy of Swaziland's new constitution. It was, she offered, "a chicken," insofar as it flapped around and made a lot of noise but could not be said to be a constitution in any straightforward sense of the word. Indeed, a legally very gifted scholar, her excoriation of the document was both precise and accurate in its own terms, and few had either the cause or inclination to disagree with her on any of the substantive points made. And yet, nonetheless, a simmering disagreement subtended across the tight network of the coalition.

The discomfort was largely put down to the tone of her critique. Some felt that she was implying that Swazis – generally – did not understand or could not accomplish a "suitable" constitutional dispensation. Obviously, such a suggestion, whether an accurate reading of her assessments or not, affronted a body of activists who not only recognized the shortcomings of the Draft Constitution, but had spent much of the last nine years endeavouring to bring a very different sort of document into being. Their efforts thwarted, they were now faced with the unenviable task of trying to subvert the realization of a project to which they had long been committed – for fear of actually ratifying the very state of affairs they had sought to overcome. Ambivalence in relation to the document was shared out in spades for this very reason.

However, I would suggest that there was also another register at which the "chicken" comments gave rise to ambivalence. And this other register was directly implicated in shared concerns over how human *rights* might be imagined and mobilized within a country where Custom suffuses all discourse with a concern for (Swazis') *responsibilities* to one another. For Swazi Law and Custom (SLC), like human rights, centers on the conservation of an essence. In the case of SLC, what is being conserved is the quality of being Swazi, whereas for human rights, it is the quality of being human which is at stake. And remember that under the rubric of divine kingship, being Swazi is of a type with its counterpart, being human, not merely a sub-level distinction suggesting that one is a particular "type" of human being.[25] Both, as I have said, have the same value magnitude. But whereas human rights is predominantly concerned with protecting incursions into the integrity of each individual's humanity, Swazi law and custom safeguards the quality of being Swazi through a fortification of the family.[26]

Bearing this in mind, the ferocious polemic over section 29(3) in the Senate debate of the Constitutional Bill begins to take on a variety of meanings. The section pertains to the rights and freedoms of women, and subsection (3) reads: "A woman shall not be compelled to undergo or uphold any custom to which she is in conscience opposed." Now,

---

[25] I would suggest that the same formulation has been seen in the legal musings of "the West," most forcefully in the indictment of the World War II war criminal, Adolf Eichmann, on charges including "crimes against humanity" and "crimes against the Jewish people." Many thanks to Hannah Starman for first alerting me to these parallels and for ongoing discussions, with Kirsten Campbell, about their significance in relation to human rights and humanitarian law worldwide.

[26] This is in no way to deny the vast catalogue of abuses – especially with respect to women – which have been promulgated under the banner of "custom." It is simply to note that jurisprudentially, SLC is operationalized through relations (and very especially kin relations), which act as a juridical framework of responsibilities. Where custom can be bowlderized and used in the service of oppression, I have long argued it could also be marshaled as a platform for the protection of women and girl-children as well.

there are any number of customs which the authors of this clause might have had in mind, including the practice of *emalobola* (bridewealth payments), forced marriages through the *tekwa* of young brides or the levirate practices of *inhlanti*, whereby a husband may take as his wife the sister of his deceased spouse. None of these was submitted for discussion to the floor. Rather, a senator railed against the clause as un-Swazi, provocatively "explaining" that were this clause accepted into law, a wife would have the *legal* right to deny her husband sex when and as she felt so inclined. While the media made much of the example, the larger question around various senators' ambivalence to the clause – and to the minatory evocation of its un-Swazi nature – was left unexplored. For the larger point here turns on the belief that a woman could only ever be a woman by virtue of those relations which constitute her as mother, sister, daughter or wife within SLC. And in respect of each of these roles, she both assumes various responsibilities, and – in theory – enjoys the protection of a concomitant set of responsibilities which sustain her position. Thus, the abstract "woman" of section 29 could hardly be seen to be in a position to elect between those customs which constituted her *as* a woman and those customs which she felt threatened her personal integrity particularly *because* she was a woman.

Such observations, between the ways in which human rights preserve an essence through the safeguarding of individuals' rights as opposed to Custom's efforts to preserve an essence through the maintenance of reciprocal and relational responsibilities,[27] prove familiar territory for anthropologists by now. However, what I would like to pursue in respect of the Swazi example are the implications for constitutionalism in the country and why the many parties involved in the constitutional melée might have felt ambivalent for very disparate reasons. Both human rights and SLC are intrinsically implicated in what we now like to call a concern for social justice. By this I simply mean that both take as their axiological foundation the preclusion of any compromise to the qualities they protect. In this way, they both differ radically from law, insofar as the law operates on a binary code of

---

[27] F. P. van R. Whelpton, a specialist on Swazi law and custom writes: "When the Swazis speak of 'our way of life' and of 'our traditions' they refer to the social relationships and social actions which take as their point of departure age-old customs validated by the ideology of traditionalism and legitimized by the king" (1997: 147). I would take issue with his rendering of custom as a matter of temporal duration and am more than a bit uncomfortable with the conceptualisation of "tradition" as an ideology, but his recognition of the social and relational nature of the Swazi way is apt. (See also Vilakati 1977.)

legal/illegal more than right/wrong or good/bad (see Luhmann 1995, 1998). The very point of the rule of law is to create a framework within which members of a differentiated "modern" society, unable to reach consensus on the nature of "the common good," can agree on how to disagree. As Luhmann (amongst many others) has long noted, pronouncements as to the "justice" accorded by a legal decision derive from outside the law itself. They comprise a mere overlay of communication on top of what the law has said, which can only ever be that an act was a legal one or an illegal one.

The reason the good/bad or just/unjust distinction does not emanate from the law is because it is a moral communication. And in Luhmannian terms, the moral system (as opposed to say, the social systems of politics, art or economics) is a particularly unique and problematic entity. The reason for this is that morality has come, in the modern, functionally-differentiated society, to detach itself from religion, such that the good/bad code is no longer housed inside of an autonomous, self-referential system. Thus, it presents its own code as the unallowable homology of system codes (Rasch 2000: 145–146).

The impossibility of homologous codes is an important predicate of systems theory. For social systems, in Luhmann's terms, are matrices that inform observation, each operationally closed and autopoetic, locations from which distinctions issue and "the world" – whatever is not deemed part of the system[28] – is configured in a way that directly correlates to the system's own *raison d'être*.[29] System codes, like

---

[28] In Luhmannian terms, whatever is not the system is its (undifferentiated) "environment."

[29] Pottage, in his compelling and articulate Introduction to the volume *Law, Anthropology, and the Constitution of the Social* (2004) suggests that "contemporary theories of society are faced with the difficulty of changing their theoretical 'instrumentation' from a schema of 'division' to a schema of 'distinction'" (2004: 8). What this implies is a theoretical shift from models of "foundational oppositions" to those based on distinctions which are wholly contingent on the location from which an observation is made. The emphasis on positionality and the contingency this introduces has obviously been explored under the mantle of Foucauldian discourse theory of course, but Luhmann's formulation is vastly more radical. Amongst many other dissimilarities, social systems, as opposed to discourses, allow for no "inputs" from outside of themselves, nor recognize the existence of other social systems. Indeed, their productivity comes from their extreme degree of closure – from their absolute inability to communicate in the sense of engaging in an intercourse with other social systems. This itself is a product of system's necessary streamlining of their environment into an undifferentiated domain, which allows the system to elaborate its own internal complexity and closely – one might note – approximates what I describe for Swazi kingship's operational distinction between what is understood as Swazi versus non-Swazi. Where the Swazi instance differs from Luhmann's description of modernity is in the absence of a proliferation of functionally differentiated systems, as Swazi kingship not only cannot "see" or register the existence of other systems, but that those other systems simply do not exist.

legal/illegal, make sense only to the system from which they derive because all communication is system internal. That is, from any system's perspective, the system is only ever faced with an undifferentiated environment (see Schutz 1997) – not with the cacophony of other systems and their various codes. All communication is deeply embedded and makes sense only to the system which produces it. Meaning attribution and interpretation can never feature then, because system differentiation is only ever successful in a state of profound noncommunication.

But what happens with the binary code of the moral system? A historical casualty of the rise in the system differentiation which is modernity, morality threatens the integrity of other functionally differentiated social systems. For example, if the political system is operationalized by a binary code of government/opposition, the very identity of the system dissolves where "good" attaches to one side of the equation and "bad" to the other. "Politics" would cease to exist.

So for Luhmann, the floating "good/bad" distinction must only attach to the ability of systems to make distinctions at all.[30] And what I would like to argue here is that the ambivalence that many non-Swazi (transnational) actors face when contending with the pressing concern of how to integrate human rights into a new constitutional dispensation originates from the very anxiety raised by the spectre of "justice." While discussions about a woman's "right" to opt out of those customs she might find repugnant to her personal and bodily integrity distract attention away from the paradox, it is the very fact that "justice" implies de-differentiation – and the concomitant collapse of "modernity" – which proves unsettling. For custom is in no way opposed to social justice. Quite the contrary, custom implicates a level of participatory parity to which democracy could barely hope to aspire. However, it does so by means of effacing the differentiation of society into discrete realms of activity – the political, the religious, the economic and so forth. So the ambivalence experienced by many non-Swazis (and sometimes shared by their Swazi counterparts, but unevenly and not as a singular and overriding concern) is the ambivalence of those who are both committed to social justice, but also unswerving in their belief that such justice must prove the byproduct of a constitution which socially distinguishes between the constituent domains of society in a way kingship cannot.

---

[30] This, for Luhmann, is the proper work of ethics – to guard against de-differentation (Rasch 2000: 149).

So what would the dedifferentiated society of the Swazi-Nation-in-kingship look like by comparison? For Swazis, it would comprise two elements, each an intrinsic component of their Custom. Swazi law and custom comprises two parts, *imihambo* and *emasiko*, both glossed in English as "tradition," but very distinct in their siSwati rendering. *Imihambo* is a matter of process and procedure, and like the framework of the rule of law is immutable in character. It is the journey taken, the route traveled to arrive at the substantive content of custom. *Emasiko*, by contrast, are those customs which emerge from that journey. Thus, my basic contention with respect to the interlocutions of custom, constitutionalism and human rights in Swaziland is that the *imihambo* (process) of Swazi custom will come to determine the *emasiko* (substantive content) of constitutionalism.

In terms of the "justice" many actors hope to see activated by a Swazi Bill of Rights in their constitution then, one must look to the very form of the law itself. If being Swazi is of a type with being human, to sacrifice the former in order to preserve the latter is a replication of the very violences wrought by colonialism and the scalar imagining it imposed. For how Swazis have come to arrive at their constitutional arrangements very much matters here.[31] Justice will be fundamentally "legal" in character where it inheres not only in the substantive content and possible outcomes derived from legal interactions, but also – and perhaps primarily – in the very forms the law might take. Thus, by allowing the practice of human rights to be overdetermined – concretized as a Swazi legal form – by the constellation of concepts inherent in Swazi divine kingship, one begins to recognize justice in other terms. It is not that custom is an alternative legal form jostling for space within constitutionalism. Rather, custom takes its rightful place as the extra-legal conceptual framework in which the existing relations of meaning and production that are human rights can be realized in uniquely Swazi ways.

That such a project will necessarily confound our expectations of what a constitution is and what it exists to do seems inevitable. But I contend this is not a self-evident threat to the practice of 'rights' in Swaziland (and likely elsewhere). Rather, such a formulation simply insists that the instruments of justice and of change are not forged solely

---

[31] Many thanks to Kimberley Hutchins for her input on this point in a symposium on "Abnormal Justice" convened by Kate Nash at Goldsmiths College in March 2006.

in the fires of western liberal democracy and the tenets of international human rights to which those fires gave birth. With humility, and cognizant of the fact that there are as many Swazis invested in realizing the values of human rights in their country and in their laws as there are international donors and activists trying to facilitate such an enterprise, we may yet see an experiment in social justice whose lessons will prove vital in the ongoing maturation of rights-practices generally. If we are willing to take seriously the Swazi non-scalar perspective which dictates that being Swazi and being human are binary complements, and endeavour to explore how this non-scalar approach might articulate with modernist, Euro-American scalar imaginings, we might better understand the uneven and shifting terrain of Swazi constitutionalism as it evolves and to appreciate the variety of opportunities such an experiment opens up, in lieu of focusing solely on those avenues of possibility it might close down.

REFERENCES

Bonner, Philip. 1983. *Kings, Commoners and Concessionaires*. Johannesburg: Raven Press.

Douzinas, Costas. 2000. *The End of Human Rights*. Oxford: Hart Publishing.

Douzinas, Costas, and Ronnie Warrington. 1994. *Justice Miscarried*. Edinburgh: Edinburgh Universty Press.

Levin, Richard. 1997. *When the Sleeping Grass Awakens*. Johannesburg: University of Witswatersrand Press.

Luhmann, Niklas. 1995. *Social Systems*. Stanford: Stanford University Press.

Luhmann, Niklas. 1998. *Observations on Modernity*. Stanford: Stanford University Press.

Mamdani, Mahmood. 1996. *Citizen and Subject: Contemporary Africa and the Legacy of Late Colonialism*. Princeton: Princeton University Press.

Mamdani, Mahmood. 2000. "Indirect Rule and the Struggle for Democracy: a Response to Bridget O'Laughlin." *African Affairs*, 99(394): 43–46.

Matsebula, J. S. M. 1988. *A History of Swaziland*. 3rd edn. Cape Town: Longman.

Peterson, David L., and V. Thomas Parker. 1998. *Ecological Scale*. New York: Columbia University Press.

Pottage, Alain. 2004. "Introduction: the Fabrication of Persons and Things." In Alain Pottage, and Martha Mundy, eds. *Law, Anthropology and the Constitution of the Social*. Cambridge: Cambridge University Press.

Pottage, Alain and Martha Mundy (eds.). 2004. *Law, Anthropology and the Constitution of the Social: Making Persons and Things*. Cambridge: Cambridge University Press.

Rasch, William. 2000. *Niklas Luhmann's Modernity: The Paradoxes of Differentiation*. Stanford: Stanford University Press.

Russell, Margo. 1990. "African Freeholders: A Study of Individual Tenure Farms in Swazi Ownership." Working Paper, December. Land Tenure Center, University of Wisconsin.

Schutz, Anton. 1997. "The Twilight of the Global Polis: On Losing Paradigms, Environing Systems and Observing World Society." In Gunther Tuebner, ed., *Global Law without a State*. Aldershot: Dartmouth Press.

Stolcke, Verena. 1995. "Talking Culture: New Boundaries, New Rhetorics of Exclusion in Europe." *Current Anthropology* 36: 1–24.

Strathern, Marilyn. 2004. *"Losing (out on) Intellectual Resources." Law, Anthropology, and the Constitution of the Social: Making Persons and Things*. Cambridge: Cambridge University Press.

Vilakati, A. L. 1977. "Swaziland and Lesotho: From Traditionalism to Modernity." G. Carter, ed., *Southern African Crisis*. Bloomington: Indiana University Press.

Wastell, Sari. 2001. "Presuming Scale, Making Diversity: On the Mischiefs of Measurement and the Global/Local Metonym in Theories of Law and Culture." *Critique of Anthropology*. 21(2): 185–210.

Wastell, Sari. 2006. In "The Legal Thing in Swaziland: *Res Judicata* and Divine Kingship." In Amiria Henare, Martin Holbraad, and Sari Wastell, eds., *Thinking through Things*. London: University College London Press/ Routledge.

Wastell, Sari. 2007. *The Mouth that Tells No Lies: Kingship, Law and Sovereignty in Swaziland*. Walnut Creek, CA: Left Coast Press (forthcoming).

Whelpton, F. P. van R. 1997. "Swazi Law and Custom in the Kingdom of Swaziland." *South African Journal of Ethnology*, 20(3): 145–151.

Legal document
The Draft Constitution of the Kingdom of Swaziland. Nkhanini: 2003.

341

TYRANNOSAURUS LEX: THE ANTHROPOLOGY OF HUMAN RIGHTS AND TRANSNATIONAL LAW

Richard Ashby Wilson

INTRODUCTION

This chapter seeks to complement the emphasis in this volume on the discursive and social aspects of human rights by focusing on their legal character, and how this shapes the responses of local actors who generate innovative discursive and political strategies within a rights paradigm. Law is not the only viable setting for an ethnography of human rights, nevertheless anthropologists need to have better analytical tools for understanding the institutional environment in which rights are generated and enforced. Law is the focal point of studies of human rights in international relations, political science and international law, and anthropologists cannot afford to neglect the legal aspects of human rights, if their insights are going to have a salience beyond the discipline.

The question then becomes, what conceptual ideas can the field of legal anthropology offer to the study of human rights in transnational and domestic law? While the origins of legal anthropology can be traced back to Maine, Morgan, and Marx,[1] the history of the anthropology of human rights in transnational legal processes is relatively recent. Less than twenty years old, the anthropology of transnational law came into its own in the 1990s during an epoch of the rapid globalization of law and the rise of a more robust international human rights legal framework. Anthropologists responded to this

---

[1] See Sally Falk Moore 2005 for an excellent reader on the anthropology of law, with commentaries that provide valuable insight into the historical development of this field.

resurgence of global humanitarianism by studying a number of its manifestations, from refugee camps to HIV/AIDS clinics to local courts. This chapter reviews the emergence of this new sub-field, discusses some of its main theoretical contours and dilemmas and offers some thoughts on how to move our analysis forward. It argues that the anthropology of the legal instantiations of human rights would benefit if it refrained from modeling the relationship between legal levels or systems and instead emphasized the social agency and global processes that pervade and cut across many domains of law. Finally, it encourages legal anthropologists to venture into the central sites of the international legal order, so as to complement recent studies of international law's impact upon human rights struggles outside North America and Western Europe.

The anthropology of human rights as a subcategory of transnational law really begins with Sally Engle Merry's 1992 review essay "Anthropology, Law and Transnational Processes" in the *Annual Review of Anthropology*. Ostensibly a review essay summarizing prior research on transnational legal processes, this was in fact a landmark essay which drew together a field that barely existed at the time and laid the theoretical groundwork for the rise of a more transnational legal anthropology in the 1990s. It encompassed a wide range of related phenomena under the rubric of law and transnational processes," including human rights, indigenous rights, colonial and customary law, culture and legal consciousness, legal pluralism, popular justice, and administrative law.

Merry focused significant attention on colonialism in the essay and how anthropologists had attempted to understand the relationship between customary law and colonial rule. A guiding assumption in the paper was that colonialism was, by and large, an early form of transnational law and governance and therefore was an appropriate model for thinking about the globalization of human rights more generally. Since legal pluralism had furnished a valuable framework for studying colonial legal settings, it might be reoriented to provide insights into newer transnational legal processes such as human rights, cultural rights, and indigenous rights. Merry noted several criticisms of the idea of legal pluralism, but she appealed to newer formulations of legal pluralism that conceived of customary and colonial legal systems as "mutually constitutive," rather than as isolated and distinct. Finally, Merry identified cognate theories in the form of Foucauldian discourse theory and Geertzian theories of "law as culture." She also noted that some of these approaches had recently been combined in innovative ways by post-modernist legal theorists such as Santos (1987, 1995: 116), who employed ideas of legal pluralism and "interlegality" to destabilize and decenter the liberal idea of a formal, unified legal order. This seems to be the approach preferred in this book's Introduction by Mark Goodale, which adheres to the premise of a "transnational normative pluralism" where human rights have become "decentered."

While Merry opened up a whole new area for anthropologists to study using the tools developed for studying colonial law, it was debatable how much colonialism actually resembled present-day "transnational" legal processes. In fact, there was little that was "transnational" about colonial law, since colonized peoples by definition did not enjoy their own sovereignty within separate nation-states and therefore their legal systems were, in formal terms, entirely encompassed by that of the colonial power. True, both colonial and modern transnational legal systems are characterized by legal action at a great distance, but ultimately colonized populations were under the indirect rule (if they behaved well) or the direct rule (if they didn't) of colonial rulers in London, Paris, or Madrid.

France, in particular, operated a more unified and centralized legal structure and colonial subjects had significant judicial status before French courts, and so there is an argument for saying that colonial law was "intra"-national rather than "trans"-national. Colonial law was most unlike the modern system of, say, international human rights conventions or the European Court of Human Rights. In addition, as Merry recognized in her essay, the formulation that legal systems are "mutually constitutive" does not really tell us a great deal about them or how they interact, other than that they are intimately related to one another in some indeterminate way. The actual substance of that relationship remains elusive and necessitates a multitude of questions about specific social and legal practices.

Despite these remarks, Merry's essay was inventive and wide-ranging enough to facilitate the entry of anthropologists into a whole new terrain of human rights and international legal processes. It was theoretically ecumenical enough to allow researchers to plunder the available array of theories in the anthropology of law at that time, from Geertzian culture theory to a Foucauldian discourse approach, to tried-and-tested theories of legal pluralism. The next section backtracks into the history of the anthropology of law and examines the historical development of legal pluralism and evaluates its usefulness for thinking about international legal processes in the present day.

Goodale notes in his Introduction that one of the first problems faced by anthropologists of human rights law is what he calls "normative pluralism," or how to define the socio-legal concepts that originate simultaneously in international, national, and local settings and how to understand the relationship between them. Goodale's discussion critically evaluates a number of spatially-oriented analytical models including the global/local distinction prevalent in globalization theory (which he finds wanting), and the "transnational" domain located beyond the scope of the nation-state (deemed a significant improvement). Both editors encourage anthropologists to focus more attention on the "in-between" space positioned between global centers of human rights norms and laws and the local contexts which resist, appropriate or transform them.

In the past, this has conjured up a number of spatial models that have both clarified and obscured important aspects of the operation of law and rights. Existing theories of legal pluralism provide a template for modeling the relationship between different legal structures, as legal pluralism had developed as a way to think first about the relationship between customary law and colonial law and then later the relationship between local courts and those of the post-colonial nation-state. Understanding the relevance of legal pluralism for the anthropology of human rights requires an intellectual history that takes us into the history of legal anthropology and, in particular, into the legal history of colonial Africa.

FROM LEGAL PLURALISM TO SOCIAL PROCESS

Stated briefly, legal pluralism is an analytical concept that addresses the existence of more than one mechanism for generating rules and adjudicating disputes within a single political unit.[2] Legal pluralism originated in anti-positivist legal philosophy in the early twentieth century, as a reaction to the established view in law schools (known as "legal centralism") which only regarded state law as "proper law."[3] In reality, argued pluralists, state law was far from absolute, and in many colonial

[2] I thank Franz von Benda-Beckmann for his gracious and insightful comments on this section and for encouraging me to clarify my position.
[3] For a discussion of legal pluralism in legal philosophy and sociology, see Santos (1995, Part II).

or recently post-colonial contexts, it was not particularly central in the normative ordering of society. This line of argument has deep roots in anthropology, as Bronislav Malinowski was asserting in 1926 that social norms in non-state societies perform the same regulatory functions as legal norms, thus non-codified social rules should be raised to the status of "law." Over time, this became the conventional view in legal anthropology.

In the 1970s and 1980s, legal anthropologists such as Jane Collier (1975) and Sally Engle Merry (1988) continued to conceptualize legal and social norms as equivalent and mutually constitutive. However, legal pluralism came increasingly under criticism as a result of its emphasis on the autonomy of social norms produced in non-state contexts. Pluralists by definition saw non-state law as a sphere of semi-autonomous authority and adjudication, which employed distinctive procedures embedded in a morality distinct to state law.

Marxist legal historians took particular exception to this understanding when applied to colonial legal systems and argued that in colonial Africa there was only "a single, interactive colonial legal system."[4] South African historian Martin Chanock (1985, 1991) asserted that colonial and customary law were unified into a single instrument of dispossession and were part of a wider administrative policy of creating and maintaining a particular type of peasantry.[5] Rather than being the product of immutable native tradition, "custom" was manufactured by colonists to reinforce the position of chiefs who were colonialism's agents at the local level.

For some, this undermined the premise of legal pluralism completely – it became a colonial fiction, an integral part of the ideology of British and Dutch colonial rule in Africa and Asian colonial territories. For others, the colonial state's influence on local law was nothing new. It had long been understood that customary law was profoundly shaped by the colonial experience but that the social norms and practices of customary law (both during and after colonialism) were not reducible to the logic of the colonial state.

Legal pluralism was challenged further in the mid-1980s onwards by "legal centralist" critiques. The centralists identified a logical contradiction: when the domains of the legal and non-legal are fused, the category of law becomes meaningless, as it includes everything from table manners to liability law to international covenants of human

---

[4] Mann and Roberts (1991: 9).   [5] Chanock (1991: 71).

rights. This makes defining law impossible since every social norm is defined as "legal," but common sense tells us that not every social convention has the status or authority of established "law." Legal pluralism, Brian Tamanaha (1993) argued, neglects how the rules of state law are created by specialists within state bureaucratic structures and backed by a state apparatus of coercion including the military and the criminal justice system. Moreover, Tamanaha points out that legal anthropologists never formulated a cross-cultural definition of law that did not somehow rely upon the state as its model. Since the state is the primary institution in society making and enforcing social norms, we had might as well make it the center of our theory of law.[6]

Legal anthropologists were turning more to the study of international law in the early 1990s just at a time when there was significantly more criticism of their intellectual tools for understanding law and its relationship to non-state rule systems. Anthropologists were slow to move away from legal pluralism and it took a while for the various critiques to filter their way into anthropological theorizations of law. This was not just a matter of inertia – there were even some good intellectual reasons to maintain a commitment to legal pluralism. Legal pluralism provides a fairly accurate model of society as made up of a diversity of modes of conflict resolution (from marriage counseling to industrial relations arbitration) and it undermines the conventional law school myth that law's empire is unchallenged. In many African countries, local political leaders often adjudicate local disputes rather than magistrates and there are large swathes of the world where as Sally Falk Moore puts it, the power and authority of state law is often "nominal rather than operational" (1986: 150).

Many of the new anthropological studies of international law and human rights in the 1990s tried to revise and reformulate legal pluralism in various ways. Some attempted to revive legal pluralism by combining it with legal processes that cut across and connect the various legal and social fields – processes such as the globalization and the "vernacularization" of international legal language. Sally Engle Merry's (1997) chapter on "Legal Pluralism and Transnational Culture" documented the use of international human rights law by the Hawaiian sovereignty movement. Merry asserted that, although human rights were originally part of a western legal regime, closer examination

---

[6] It should be noted that Tamanaha (2000) later recanted his position and opted instead for a "non-essentialist version of legal pluralism."

reveals that the Hawaiian indigenous rights movement combines three legal levels simultaneously: global human rights law, national law, and local Kanaka Maoli law.

Operating at three legal levels involves the deployment and refiguring of western law in more plural terms, and Merry uses legal pluralism as one model to think about the relationship between the global and local. The Tribunal's legally plural framework expressed the claims of an emergent nationalism, in that it drew together claims based upon notions of descent, culture, and tradition, but also used the language of sovereignty, citizenship, and constitutionalism. Cultural appropriations of western law by local groups are fundamentally creative and represent a pluralistic form of resistance to global homogenization (and, read, legal centralism).

Despite the chapter's title and the formal adherence to legal pluralism, the concept is used fairly sparingly in Merry's chapter, and the weight of the theoretical discussion of transnational law tips towards new conceptual terms such as vernacularization. Legal vernacularization is part of a process of the emergence of new national identities and Merry's study details the appropriation and reinterpretation of international law by the Hawaiian Sovereignty Movement at the People's International Tribunal of Native Hawaiians in 1993. The Tribunal was constituted as a criminal trial, with the US government indicted on nine charges, and drew upon the symbolic power of law to recommend the return of Kanaka Maoli land and water rights, and political sovereignty for the Kanaka Maoli people. Merry concludes that law is a site of contestation, where the hegemony of formal law is undermined by vernacularization and the redefining of the legal subject.

In my own work on the South African Truth and Reconciliation Commission (Wilson 2001), I also employed legal pluralism to think about how popular conceptions of justice interacted with human rights enshrined in the national constitution and international treaties. In some ways, my own efforts paralleled those of Sally Merry's, insofar as I attached a number of cross-cutting processes to the model of pluralism. I chose to focus not on the vernacularization of rights language, but the active centralization and pluralization of state institutional power over the course of the twentieth century. I argued that we needed to replace the stark dualism of legal pluralism vs. legal centralism by a redefinition of the subject matter. Instead of adopting over-systematizing theories which construct the "legal" and "societal" as two total and coherent cultural systems with distinct logics,[7] we need to analyze how non-state adjudicative contexts such as local courts are transformed over time by the social actions of individuals and collectivities, within a wider context of state regulation. Local township courts, magistrates' courts and human rights commissions were therefore simultaneously subjected to *centralizing* and *pluralizing* discourses and strategies.

In this revised view, legal pluralism addresses questions of how social actors (including both individuals and collectivities) contest the direction of rapid social change in the area of justice, and what the effects of this are for the legitimization of new forms of nation-state authority. The struggle over defining justice in the first years of post-apartheid South Africa presented itself as a struggle over how to deal with the political crimes of the apartheid past, and, in so doing, to reconfigure legal authority in the present. If this were a theory of legal pluralism at all, it was a legal pluralism of action, movement, and close interaction between legal orders in the context of state hegemonic projects. In the post-apartheid South Africa, this involved looking at how state officials, township court officers, and Anglican ministers combined transnational human rights talk, religious notions of reconciliation, and popular ideas of punishment in an effort to control the direction of social change (or "historicity," in the formulation of Alain Touraine 1995: 219, 368).

In the years since this work was published, my views have changed somewhat, in part due to the expansion (some would say rampant inflation) of the concept of human rights, both in the academy and in the world. This has sewn a great deal of confusion and seldom are we entirely certain what people are referring to when they refer to "human rights" or "a human rights movement." Human rights institutions can now include agencies of the United Nations, national government human rights commissions, private philanthropic foundations (e.g., the Macarthur Foundation), multinational corporation foundations (e.g., the Reebok Human Rights Foundation), as well as grassroots citizens' organizations. Human rights are articulated in (usually non-binding) international human rights treaties (usually binding), national legal codes, alternative dispute resolution mechanisms and in the discourses of a plethora of non-state actors. Human rights have gone from a general list of what governments should not do to their citizens in the 1940s to a full blown moral-theological-political vision of the good life.

---

[7] An approach found also within the postmodernist legal theory of Santos (1995: 116).

Human rights cover issues as disparate as the maltreatment of prisoners in US military jails, access to anti-retrovirals to treat HIV/AIDS and instruction in one's mother tongue in schools. New rights are added all the time, thus expanding the rights framework into areas for which it was not originally designed or intended.

Scholars of human rights have not always clarified this complex scenario, and oftentimes have exacerbated the sloppiness and over-generality of the usage. In anthropology, this derives in part from over-extending the Geertzian premise that law is a distinct form of imagining the social. The tendency has been exacerbated by Foucauldian think-ing which treats human rights as a discourse, often including all the discourses which inspire or jostle alongside it. Human rights have been applied to any normative discourse that draws legitimacy in some way from universal concepts of humanity or humanness or human dignity, regardless of whether the said discourse has any legal sanction or close association with human rights charters. We might remember here that religious fundamentalists also have a universal discourse on human dignity, and Stalinism had an elaborate ideology of universal and common humanity.

How might we start to clarify what we are speaking about, without engaging in tiresome definitional debates or gatekeeping? The legal centralist response would be to refer only to those rights enforceable in a court of law as human rights, but this is probably too restrictive and loses sight of how legal institutions and concepts can be shaped by societal moralities and social movements. Legal pluralists would want to include all of it as human rights, but this loses sight of the legal character of rights and the primacy of states and intergovernmental organizations in formulating and enforcing them. Perhaps the best way to proceed is to try to be more precise in our use of terms and to distinguish between "human rights law" and "human rights talk," where the former refers to positivised rules in national or international law and the latter refers to how people speak about those norms, or aspire to expand or interpret them in new ways. Perhaps most importantly, this allows us distinguish between written codes that have the backing of a coercive bureaucratic apparatus and those which may well not.

FOUR PROCESSES OF LAW AND RIGHTS

The argument so far has assessed the usefulness of the theory of legal pluralism and the uses made of it by anthropologists studying transnational human rights law and discourse in the 1990s. We have arrived at the point where we might question more the usefulness of spatial models, without discarding the pertinent questions they raise about the relationship between state law and non-state rules and norms. How then might we theorize the impact of transnational law or the international language of rights upon specific social contexts? I would argue that we need to identify a number of processes which interconnect the various social and legal fields that anthropologists study and examine their socially transformative nature. Below I identify four such processes that have become visible in recent anthropological studies of human rights social movements, including those contained in this edited volume.

The legalization of rights, or politics by other means

Legalization refers to the way in which moral claims become positivized in law, be it that of the nation-state or an international body. There has been a long-term trend for human rights activists to seek the formal legal recognition of certain liberties, immunities and privileges, a strategy which Goodale terms, in his characteristically pithy style "the legal positivism of human rights instrumentalists." To state it in legal terms, human rights organizations seek to make an ever-widening set of claims "justiciable." Since the early 1960s, human rights activists have sought to channel moral indignation into legally enforceable mechanisms at the national and international level. The main thrust of their work has been to create new international conventions that positivize certain norms and standards so they have legal sanction. While individuals and groups may articulate social norms and moral claims in a number of different ways, human rights activists perceive that in the rough-and-tumble of national and international politics such articulations must be enforceable in a court of law if they are to endure.

With the relative success of this strategy, especially in the 1990s, many more local moral claims have been reformulated in the language of human rights and this has exacerbated the tendency to channel societal discord into the legal process, and thereby to channel political contention into the legal process. A variety of social and material conflicts, from land titling to the language of instruction in schools, are now expressed by local political actors in such a way that the law can hear them; that is, they seek to conform to legal convention and precedent. What are the consequences of this? A number of

351

anthropologists have argued that the legalization of social conflicts is "depoliticizing" insofar as its turns political problems into technical, legal problems (Speed and Leyva 2008; Wilson 1997: 148–149).

The legalization of rights is mystifying (in the historical materialist sense) insofar as it raises false expectations that the state can solve social and economic problems, and normalizing, insofar as it employs the legal/bureaucratic system but does not challenge it. We can hear echoes of the debate over customary and colonial law between legal pluralists and centralists – is customary law/human rights law a site for autonomy, or part of a grand global scheme of subjugation? Mahmood Mamdani's (2001) analysis of the Rwandan genocide in *When Victims Become Killers* illustrates this line of argument, since Mamdani (2001: 270–276) opposes a legalized, Nuremberg-style model of identifying individual perpetrators and holding them accountable at the international criminal tribunal in Arusha, Tanzania, on the grounds that this only gives a semblance of "justice." Mamdani writes (2001: 273): "The prime requirement of political reconciliation is neither criminal justice nor social justice but *political justice*."[8] The reality of the genocide is to be found not in individual actions, but in the "logic of colonialism" (2001: 9).

Shannon Speed in chapter 4 in this book, on the Zapatista Autonomous regions of Chiapas develops a critique of the legalization of rights notions. While Speed cautions first, that indigenous rights and human rights discourses may seduce social movements into participating in a "legal system where legal process is an empty signifier," she is careful to recognize that struggles to enforce legal rights can lead to important achievements for marginalized groups. Second, Speed offers an intriguing ethnographic example of what a non-legal vision of human rights might look like. Since establishing human rights *qua* rights through the formal legal system may reinforce the authority of the neo-liberal state, the Zapatistas have bypassed the Mexican state and sought to anchor human rights in their exercise and concrete practice. Here, human rights seem to serve as a language of governance (thus as human rights *talk*), insofar as they articulate a collectivist vision of popular sovereignty expressed in the Zapatista leaders' statement that they "lead by obeying" (*mandar obediciendo*). There are strong echoes here of Jean-Jacques Rousseau's *Social Contract*, in which he writes: "Now, as the sovereign is formed entirely of the individuals who

---

[8] Emphasis in original.

compose it, it has not, nor could it have, any interest contrary to theirs."[9] The question then becomes – is this best described as system of rule by human rights legal *rights*, or as a form of human rights talk that might actually refer to something else entirely (a system of popular sovereignty)?

Looking at another group of papers, we see that the legalization of human rights is not always to be decried, since access to justice matters for accountability, for admittance to state legal and political institutions and as a way to legally restrain corporate exploitation.[10] Since state institutions are a significant source of material resources, some claims are going to have to be legalized in order to make them durable and enforceable. In her discussion of efforts to control the sex trade, Kay Warren in chapter 6 above, examines the process of drafting of a UN protocol against human trafficking. Feminist movements and governments sought together to control sex trafficking by developing international laws regulating this activity. Governmental and non-governmental organizations (NGOs) brought competing frames of reference to the table based on radically different ways of understanding both sex work and the nature of human trafficking. They debate whether to focus on the human rights of victims or the identification of international criminal organizations, and about whether prostitution should be abolished, or the conditions of sexual labor improved. Nevertheless, these groups eventually forged a single legal text. Clearly, converting demands to control human trafficking into a UN protocol was a contested project, and the ultimate document contains contradictory ideas as well as ambiguity. Warren argues that, since the completion of the protocol in 2000, various actors have continued to develop their own interpretations of the meanings of the legal text. Yet, the legal text remains a central element of the anti-trafficking movement.

In chapter 5 Jean Jackson provides evidence as to how indigenous rights activists in Colombia have insisted upon a "right to culture" and thereby managed to pry open new legal avenues and make courts more accessible to indigenous communities. In demanding the recognition of diversity and countering the exclusionary character of the legal process, indigenous activists have constructed a framework which integrates a

---

[9] Rousseau (1968 [1762]: 63).
[10] For an expansion of this argument in the context of the Guatemalan Historical Clarification Commission, see Wilson 2005.

number of different areas including bilingual education, land titling, customary health practices, and greater autonomy in local and regional government. These points apply more widely in Latin America. For instance, in Guatemala, activists have pressed for the right to simultaneous translation in the courtroom into Mayan languages as part of a wider set of claims for linguistic and cultural rights in education and government. This provides one insight into why the global human rights framework appeals to groups seeking greater self-determination; human rights talk is broad enough to serve as an umbrella for a broad array of different kinds of claims, and it also stops short of a demand for full sovereignty and self-determination, a rather pragmatic strategy given the history of state violence against indigenous groups in Latin American history. At first glance, this may seem rather reformist and tame, but if a robust indigenous rights legal framework is implemented then this could lead to a thorough-going decentralization of state institutions and provide a considerable challenge to the political and legal unity of the liberal state.

In his discussion of a case brought in the US courts by Burmese individuals, in chapter 7 John Dale presents us with another example of the value of being able to formulate and enforce certain types of claims in law. In 2004, a dozen Burmese invoked an over 200-year-old statute – the 1789 US Alien Tort Claims Act (ACTA) – won a case against a US corporation, Unocal, for violating their human rights in international law during the building of a natural gas pipeline in Burma. The remarkable legal precedent in this case is how violations against non-US citizens, outside of the United States, by a multinational company, were made "justiciable" in a US court. Unocal had violated an international treaty to which the United States was a signatory, namely the Convention Against Torture and Other Cruel, Inhuman or Degrading Treatment or Punishment (signed in 1988), as well as the US domestic legal code, the 1991 Torture Victim Protection Act. Dale then goes on to document how in recent years a number of other cases have been brought against oil companies by Nigerian and Indonesian plaintiffs in US courts under ACTA. Once again, then, we get a clear sense that, while the legalization of human rights is *ex post facto* and cannot prevent abuses from occurring, it can in certain cases provide accountability for some of the more egregious forms of exploitation carried out by multinational corporations.

The process of legalization of rights may indeed be an indication of the reign of technocratic legal elites but, in the three cases above, we can also see their potential as a mode of political engagement. Borrowing from Clausewitz,[11] we might recognize the potential for human rights law to be a form of "politics by other means," rather than as wholly "depoliticizing."

Human rights and the verticalization of conflict

A number of writers have drawn our attention to how international law often "verticalizes" local conflicts; that is, it lifts questions of conflict resolution out of a local or regional context and raises it to a higher level, usually that of the nation-state or international court or commission. Verticalization is built into the structure of international human rights law, which has "*jus cogens*" status (literally "higher law") raising it above all other legal norms and formally granting jurisdiction to international courts hearing human rights cases. In such scenarios, local actors enlist the power and authority of the United Nations or a regional court of human rights (the Inter-American Court in Washington DC, or the European Court in Strasbourg) on their behalf. This has occurred in a number of cases in Latin America where indigenous peoples have sought to connect with international actors in their struggles with corporations or their own nation-state.

As we have seen in John Dale's chapter, the International Labor Organization has been one of the more successful intergovernmental bodies, and has promulgated a set of international labor standards that local actors can appeal to in an attempt to constrain the more exploitative activities of multinational corporations. The legalization of a dispute not only verticalizes a conflict, taking it out of the hands of local political actors, but can also internationalize the conflict by circumventing the nation-state. Appealing for the involvement of international actors also means bypassing municipal and nation-state institutions and forging alliances with a number of non-legal and non-state actors such as international NGOs and powerful private foundations such as the Ford Foundation.

On the one hand, this may allow local actors to realize goals that they have been struggling to achieve for centuries, such as titling land, or gaining revenue from mining sources in their territories. However, the verticalization of disputes is also a double-edged sword. While it can offer international aid to beleaguered local actors, and it can also

---

[11] And from Rick Abel (1995) who wrote a book about South African law under apartheid called *Politics by Other Means*.

pit one group of poor people against another, and ratchet up the stakes and the potential for violent conflict between them. David Stoll's (1997, 2007) accounts of the changing economic relations in post-conflict highland Guatemala are highly informative in this regard. In the Maya-Ixil area of Quiché, non-indigenous landowners have steadily sold off their holdings to Ixils as a result of the armed conflict. This has allowed a new elite of Ixil professionals to exercise significantly more local political and economic authority than before the armed conflict. These transformations have coincided with a kind of ethnic détente between Ixils and Ladinos (non-Ixils) which Stoll says is jeopardized by interfering international human rights organizations. Where there is an ongoing transfer of property and political power from Ladinos to Ixils at the municipal and regional level, the verti-calization of land conflicts and the involvement of international actors may be counterproductive.

Paying attention to the verticalization of conflict is a palliative to approaches which conceptualize the social and legal fields as consti-tuted by horizontal networks of voluntaristic actors. It bears restating that the different levels of law are constituted in different kinds of bureaucratic and institutional frameworks; for instance a local village court in Botswana may have only the most meager of institutional resources, but these would increase significantly as one moved to magistrates' courts of the nation-state, and then, at the transnational level, one would see how an international tribunal is embedded in the idiosyncratic bureaucracy of the United Nations, or the European Union. These different kinds of legal bodies also have access to coer-cive apparatuses of a qualitatively different order – while an individual flouting a community court decision may be fined or beaten, signifi-cantly greater forms of retribution await those in national domestic courts and, moving to the international level, the picture changes once again. Bringing the internal, domestic, conflict in Kosovo in 1999 to the United Nations' Security Council ultimately led to NATO strike aircraft bombing Serb positions. Network theory and other approaches which focus upon purely horizontal relations have trouble coping with the asymmetry of power and the hierarchy of jurisdictions in the international legal order. Despite the criticisms made of the verticality of the global/local model, problems of scale remain, and it's unclear that simply decentering law and human rights talk into competing normative discourses or human rights institutions into horizontal net-works resolves them in an adequate manner.

The vernacularization of human rights and legal discourse

The two categories above refer to primarily to political processes but legal anthropologists have sought ways of talking about the cultural dimensions of international law (the Geertzian "law as culture") as well as international law's interaction with local cultural forms, without reproducing static ideas of "local culture." This is necessary in order to point out the blindness of black letter law to socio-cultural context and the unbridled universalism characteristic of some versions of international human rights law.

Human rights law does not play out the same way everywhere, and we need to comprehend why translation between international law and local cultural norms is often a partial, unpredictable, and haphazard process. As Sally Merry (2006) points out, anthropologists are uniquely situated to study the translation of a global discourse into specific cultural contexts and she has recently elaborated upon and updated her ideas, presented previously in this chapter, regarding the vernacularization of human rights talk. Vernacularization as an idea originally sought to explain how national languages developed and changed in nineteenth century Europe, as elites moved from Latin to colloquial Castilian or everyday Danish. Merry sees a similar process going on with transnational human rights talk as it is exported from its sites of production in the chambers and committee rooms of Manhattan and Geneva to a nongovernmental office in a shantytown in Mumbai. Merry focuses in particular on the intermediaries (e.g., local activists, lawyers, and NGO leaders), those individual "knowledge brokers" who translate human rights talk both downwards into local argot as well as upwards, for instance, when they turn local grievances into funding proposals for international donors.

Merry (*ibid.*) breaks vernacularization down into two subcategories or subprocesses which she calls *replication* and *hybridity*. Replication refers to the process where a human rights discursive concept is implanted in a cultural context with very little attempt at contextualization or modification according to local needs. Merry gives us a detailed example of replication when she discusses the fate of a US program to end domestic violence when it was brought to Hong Kong. This program operated with a criminal justice model that woman were rights-bearers who could take their partners to court if they abused them and also a therapeutic intervention model which set up therapy groups for batterers.

Hybridity refers to a much deeper engagement with the local context and occurs "when institutions and symbolic structures created elsewhere merge with those in a new locality, sometimes uneasily" (2006: 46–48). Here, Merry provides empirical material on women's courts that emerged in India to deal with domestic violence cases and other family law issues. These courts were more able to combine local social norms with ideas of justice and here human rights talk became more enmeshed in the values and institutions of local Indian society. Merry's academic study has clear policy implications for realizing women's human rights under law, and she clearly thinks that hybrid structures are more likely to prosper in non-western contexts in the long run. At the same time, she is aware of the paradoxes of human rights talk, one being the tension between the universalizing of rights within a western individualist framework (supported by donors with deep pockets) and the need to make rights meaningful to local actors who may have very little experience of either liberal democracy or the rule of law.

Aspects of this vernacularization argument can also be found in some of the chapters in this volume. In documenting the use of human rights talk by Nepalese Buddhists, Leve, in chapter 2, is in part describing a process of vernacularization, insofar as Buddhists activists claim their freedom to practice their religion in terms of a human right. Yet Leve's account illustrates a much more partial and paradoxical process than that encountered by Merry. There are such profound contradictions between Theravada Buddhism's understanding of the place of the self in the world and the individualism and secularism of human rights talk, that combining them is an act of "epistemic violence" that forces the Buddhist activists into a "double-bind".

The concept of vernacularization may need some further recalibration to take into account such partial effects and in his chapter on Bolivia, Goodale proposes some useful conceptual refinements. He notes first of all that vernacularization does not imply that transnational human rights networks are compressed or reduced in the process of translation, but remain trans-local and connect up local actors to an extensive network of human rights institutional nodes at the regional, national, and international levels. He also makes a distinction between connotative and denotative power, where the latter refers to the way in which actors reference specific human rights laws and treaties and the former refers to the much more widespread phenomenon where actors gesture towards aspects of human rights talk with very little specificity, or actual content. Goodale's distinction assists ethnographers of rights talk to distinguish between vernacularization where meaningful translation is occurring, and where local political actors overlay other distinctive political projects with the legitimating mantle of rights, but to which they may have only a fleeting and expedient commitment.

Likewise, in chapter 8, Wastell introduces the concept of "cycling" to refer to the way in which human rights provisions in the new Swazi constitution are refracted through the lens of Swazi divine kingship and Swazi customary law. From reading Wastell's chapter one gets a sense that this is in part a process of vernacularization – where human rights are colloquialized when embedded in a specific African monarchical polity – and partly something else altogether. When Wastell refers to the introduction of constitutional protections for human rights (however weakly defined in relation to the unaccountable power of the king) as a possible reproduction of a colonial scale and logic, one sees how the ambivalence that she reports for Swazis is also present in her own work. Her use of Luhmann's social systems theory and its functionalist model of hermetically sealed and incommensurable systems leaves little room for constitutionalism and customary authority to recognize one another and bend to the other's will. Since Wastell frames this interaction as a potential conflict over essences, it is not clear on what terms cycling is meant to occur. This takes us back to the debates about legal pluralism and the critiques of separate and autonomous spheres of customary and state law and morality.

There are bound to be some instances where the vernacularization of human rights talk occurs in the most limited of ways, if at all. In chapter 1, by Daniel Goldstein, we can discern an even greater disjuncture between human rights talk and local ideas of security than among the Nepali Buddhists. Goldstein reminds us of the limits of vernacularization and the possibility that human rights talk may be utterly rejected in favor of other, less procedural and more punitive models of justice. In a crime-ridden Bolivia, characterized by chronic physical insecurity, human rights discourse is seen by poor urban residents as "protecting the criminals" and giving them undeserved protections from retributive justice. While Goldstein invokes philosopher Giorgio Agamben to suggest that authoritarian justice lies at the heart of every liberal democratic state, his findings are more applicable to countries where neo-liberal states have essentially privatized citizens' security (as in much of Latin America), or where societies have experienced long-term political violence, as in South Africa, much of Central America, and certain parts of Eastern Europe.

In these cases, human rights talk is the most popularly recognizable feature of a non-existent, or at least severely compromised, system of the rule of law. When the rule of law remains so imaginary and elusive, citizens will often reject the principles of liberal justice, and may seek other more immediate and severe solutions to their problems of physical security. What Goldstein's chapter offers is a compelling ethnographic insight into the reasons for growing popular support for authoritarian rule in Latin America. As in Weimar Germany, democracy becomes the scapegoat for the radical insecurity in Bolivian citizens' lives, and authoritarian justice promises an alternative route to the stability and order that democracy and legal rights cannot seem to deliver.

Of course, human rights law and security do not always have to be contraposed in this way, and political philosophers such as Fernando Tesón (2005: 59) have asserted that the security of the person is *the* primary human right and that security measures are justified not by Hobbesian conservative notions of social order and stability, but precisely in order to protect human freedoms, human rights, and democratic principles of justice. In this regard, Goldstein seems to have acceded too much ground to the view of human rights which portrays them as antithetical to security, rather than as another way of achieving citizens' security (albeit one which may take a little longer than "immediate justice"). Nonetheless, it is worth being reminded that in some situations of radical insecurity, the scope for the vernacularization of human rights is very circumscribed indeed.

Law's epistemology: the construction of knowledge and power

We have seen how anthropologists have attempted to comprehend the political and cultural dimensions of international law, but recently a new area of discussion has been opened up around law's epistemological processes and how law is simultaneously a form of knowledge production and a form of power. Since this is a recent and lively area of discussion, and one which is alluded to in various chapters in this volume but not fully explored, I will spend rather longer on it that the previous three categories.

What is law's "will to truth" and how might its truth-finding methods selectively include and exclude various types of knowledge about social reality? We know that law establishes truth to render judgment but what exactly do we know about international law's theory of knowledge and its concrete truth-finding practices? How do international legal research practices construct knowledge about society that facilitates and legitimizes the operation of state and intergovernmental power? If Geertz (1983) is right that law is a "model for" society, then which society is international law a model for? What consequences does international legal knowledge have in far-flung settings such as Bosnia or Sierra Leone or East Timor?

The insights of prior legal anthropologists regarding law's epistemology have surfaced in anthropological studies of courts, human rights commissions, and truth commissions. In particular, researchers have drawn our attention to courts' and commissions' over-reliance upon positivist (that is, statistical and forensic) methods to producing and evaluating evidence, and knowledge creation more generally. Annelise Riles (2006) notes an anthropological skepticism towards the legalistic, instrumental and technocratic inclinations of international legal practitioners. Riles (2000, 2006) has criticized spatial and foundational models of human rights law and instead she conceives of human rights as embedded in deracinated and virtual networks, and constituted entirely by legal knowledge practices.[12]

A recent and influential approach to legal epistemology comes from Bruno Latour (2004) who carried out ethnography in both a French neuroscience laboratory and the *Conseil d'Etat* – the pinnacle of French administrative law. On the face of it, law and science seem to construct knowledge in a similar positivist, forensic, logical, and empirically-minded way. Indeed, lawyers and scientists conspire to gain from the social standing of the other: "judges appropriate the scientist's white coat in order to represent their role, while, on the other [hand], scientists borrow the judge's robes of purple and ermine in order to establish their authority" (Latour 2004: 106).

Yet if one looks deeper at everyday practices, there are profound differences in the knowledge making practices of each group, according to Latour. First, scientists are passionate about their research, which has a raw and immediate quality about it, as they make haphazard and hesitant utterances about what they see before them in the electron

---

[12] Some anthropologists have criticized the over-reliance of human rights institutions on positivist approaches to knowledge, on the grounds that such methods often exclude the subjectivity of victims, perpetrators and bystanders. In their studies of the South African Truth and Reconciliation Commission (TRC), a number of anthropologists argued that a positivist approach to documenting the apartheid era failed to address fully questions of meaning and intentionality. See Lars Buur (2001), Fiona Ross (2002), and Richard Wilson (2001). On the silencing of victims in courtrooms, see Dembour and Haslam 2004.

microscope. Scientific articles convey this passion. A concern with innovation leads scientists to demonstrate how their results transform all knowledge about the subject as it is presently conceived. While they make the best case they can for their results, ultimately scientific articles retain an openness to further questioning. They are always to an extent in doubt until they have been subjected to extensive peer review and testing over a period of time. Ultimately, scientific knowledge has a direct relationship with reality. Its truths are tested by the very objects to which they refer – the morphology of the rat's brain, the neuron, or the neuropeptide. Admittedly these are mediated though real scientists who are often embroiled in controversies in peer reviewed journals, but the facticity of the objects they study hangs over the scientific endeavor "like the sword of Damocles" (Latour 2004: 107).

The legal officials at the *Conseil d'Etat* have a completely different emotional approach to their subject – one which is dispassionate, smooth, unhurried, and calm. Their writing is correspondingly detached as legal officials write with an utter indifference to the facts of the case. Their only concern is with exegesis and identifying the relevant point of law. There is a calculated lack of innovation and they seek to demonstrate how their present approach is continuous with previous legal precedent. A final judgment is a seamless and unchallengeable official decree. It is formal state policy which holds once and for all, or until it is overturned in a future decision, but this is never presaged.

The contrast between law's approach to knowledge and that of science is starkest in its handling of evidence. *Conseillers* move from one text to another; from case files to legal case law books to memoranda, but "always remaining in the world of texts" (2004: 75). Latour asserts that an "incontrovertible" legal fact is really not a fact at all; it is merely a statement lodged in the file which has not been challenged by any party to the proceedings. For the law, it does not matter whether there is any link between the unchallenged statement in the file and the reality outside the court. This is precisely a point that any researching scientist would want to question and empirically test. *Conseillers*, on the other hand, are content to remain within their rigorously regulated textual universe.

Latour claims that there is no truth to law in a scientific sense, since law only establishes truth through its own legal rhetoric and textual exegesis. His (2004: 107) view is summarized in the phrase: "The strange thing about legal objectivity is that it quite literally is *object-less*, and is sustained entirely by the production of a mental state, a bodily *hexis*, but is still quite unable to resign its faculty of judgment by appealing to incontrovertible facts" (emphasis in original). In sum, legal epistemology is a scientist's nightmare, "a mode of unfettered arbitrariness" (2004: 109). What lesson does Latour draw from his comparison of law and science? "It is now essential that science should not be asked to judge and that law should not be asked to pronounce truth" (2004: 113).

While Latour's ethnographies of science and law are rich and pathbreaking and his writing style is highly engaging, we ought to approach his deductions and conclusions with a degree of circumspection. Saying that law ought to be more like science in its approach to truth is all very well, but there are problems with this also, as anthropological critiques of positivism above have shown. The idea that law should not pronounce truth is illogical and self-contradictory. That is law's function and, without it, the law ceases to be the law and becomes something else; perhaps a talking shop, a community bulletin board, or a cabaret bar. Legal institutions cannot do anything – judge, convict, acquit, or sentence – without pronouncing somehow upon truth.

In the context of mass human rights violations, Latour's conclusion is a recipe for silence, denial, and impunity since the pronouncing of certain baseline truths is essential to challenging lies about the past. There is a uniquely pressing impulse that is simultaneously political, ethical and historical, to establish "who did what to whom" in conditions of great epistemological uncertainty. Of course, this must be done in the most careful manner possible, ensuring that the deductions do not exceed the evidence, and ensuring that evidence is derived from defensible techniques and an array of qualitative and scientific methods. For those who living and working in places like Argentina, Chile, or South Africa, verification and accountability are not to be dismissed lightly, and a number of anthropologists have argued for writing a historical account of events and thereby establishing accountability and the rule of law.[13]

At a deeper level, Latour misconceives the anti-realism of law and its detachment from fact and investigation. This happens in part because it appears that he never got "behind the scenes" in the *Conseil d'Etat* in the same way he did in the neuroscience laboratory and because he takes the practice of French administrative law to be indicative of all law, when it is only really indicative of, well, French

---

[13] See John Borneman 1997 and Richard Wilson 2001.

CONCLUSION: THE ANTHROPOLOGY OF HUMAN RIGHTS

administrative law.[14] The neuroscience laboratory is similarly only one
example of how scientists create knowledge. If Latour had compared
other kinds of legal and scientific sites, say, criminal law with theoretical physics, he would have come up with the opposite set of results,
where law passionately confronted reality head on, and science coolly
remained with a world of textual abstractions.

Finally, Latour does not reflect suffiently upon the wider context of
the French judicial system and the place of the *Conseil d'Etat* within it.
If Latour had ventured into any lower criminal court in France he
would have seen investigative judges who actually go beyond their
textual universe and investigate in a manner comparable to the scientist. They walk around crime sites and measure distances and photograph persons, buildings, and other objects and request batteries of
forensic tests. These features are even more pronounced in an adversa-
rial Anglo-American context where defense and prosecutorial teams
carry out investigations independently and where there are juries that
perhaps provides Latour's "object that speaks back" that French administrative legal officials so patently lack. In the Anthony Sawoniuk case,
tried in Britain, the judge and entire jury flew to Domachevo, Belarus
to examine the physical sites where Sawoniuk had murdered his Jewish
victims in 1942 and to corroborate one eyewitness's testimony.[15] After
the 2004 Outreau affair, the French judicial system has been thrown
into crisis and there are now significant pressures to move towards a
more accusatorial Anglo-American model of law. The top French
judge and advocate of judicial reform Jean-François Burgelin declared
to *Le Figaro*: "The Napoleonic system has had its day."[16]

If we turn now to international criminal law as practiced at International Criminal Tribunals (ICTs), this point about the greater realism
of criminal law is made all the more forcefully and it furnishes us with a
clear demonstration of what studying international law can bring to
more national legal processes. At the ICTs for the former Yugoslavia and
for Rwanda, real research investigation takes place, thus lifting courts

---

[14] Latour reveals his parochial standpoint when he apportions blame for the present parlous state
of affairs whereby law cloaks itself in the mantle of science but respects none of its conventions.
He (2004: 89) points the finger at British empiricist philosophers from the seventeenth century
such as John Locke (died 1704) and David Hume (died 1776) and the reader is left amazed at
the power of two philosophers to so effectively determine the operation of state legal authority
in another country, hundreds of years after their deaths.
[15] R. v. *Sawoniuk* (2001) Cr App R 220, Court of Appeal (Criminal Division) of the United
Kingdom.
[16] "The French Judicial System: Exit Napoleon." *The Economist* February 11, 2006, p. 48.

out of the hermetically sealed textual space Latour has put them in. Prosecutors break out of the world of exegesis and rules to confront the messiness of evidence produced from a variety of different methods including interviews, satellite intercepts, seized archival evidence, and the grisly evidence exhumed by forensic anthropologists at mass murder sites. In short the prosecutor's office does conduct rigorous inquiry, more or less of the kind that Latour has seen in his neuroscience laboratory. Finally, if we examine ICT Yugoslav judgments closely, we see that they are not characterized by the kind of closure identified by La Tour in a *Conseil arrêt*. They admit reasonable disagreement and indicate where some points of fact are not as robust as others, thus recognizing that the process of documenting violence in the former Yugoslavia is a work in progress that no one judgment entirely completes.

CONCLUSIONS

In this concluding chapter I have reviewed some of the leading developments and debates in the anthropology of human rights and law since 1992. I have taken the position that colonial law is not a fully adequate model for thinking about the operation of international human rights law. The main anthropological theory of colonial law, legal pluralism, might be complemented by a concern with the cross-cutting sociolegal processes at work across the globe. We should investigate those processes directly and follow the connections across domains or fields of law such as customary courts, magistrates' courts, the preparatory committees of international human rights conventions, etc. The processes identified include, *inter alia*, the legalization of human rights talk, the verticalization of conflict, the vernacularization of human rights talk, and finally the legal construction of knowledge and power.

Where do we go next with this framework? As in this volume, the weight of anthropological discussion of human rights talk has been on the impact of human rights discourse on local social and political contexts. There is now a great deal of information on how indigenous groups mobilize around the idea of indigenous rights, locally, nationally, and to an extent internationally (see Jackson, chapter 5, and Speed, chapter 4, in the volume). Anthropologists have furnished insights into how local social actors experience fear and insecurity (see Goldstein, chapter 1 in this volume) and how, afterwards, they formulate ideas of reconciliation and retribution and how they discuss memory and forgetting.

What still needs to be done is for anthropologists to venture into the sites of production of international human rights laws and norms and to gain access to international criminal tribunals and examine their knowledge construction practices. Researchers need to document and analyze how the verticalization of a national conflict occurs at the United Nations, or how legal and political experts who author minority rights treaties respond to the hybridization of the terms they have sought to define. There are a small number of anthropologists doing just this work, including, among others: Anders 2005 on the United Nations' Special Court for Sierra Leone; Clarke 2008 on the International Criminal Court; Dembour and Haslam 2004 on the International Criminal Tribunal for the Former Yugoslavia; and Eltringham 2004 on the International Criminal Tribunal for Rwanda. We look to them for still deeper ethnographic insights into the internal discourses, procedures, and epistemologies of international human rights law.

REFERENCES

Abel, Richard. 1995. *Politics by Other Means: Law in the Struggle against Apartheid, 1980–1994*. London: Routledge.

Anders, Gerhard. 2005. "The New Global Legal Order as Local Phenomenon: The Special Court for Sierra Leone." Paper presented at conference on "Developing Anthropology of Law in a Transnational World" held at Edinburgh University, June 9–11, 2005.

Borneman, John. 1997. *Settling Accounts: Violence, Justice, and Accountability in Postsocialist Europe*. Princeton, NJ: Princeton University Press.

Buur, Lars. 2001. "The South African Truth and Reconciliation Commission: a Technique of Nation-state Formation." In T. B. Hansen, and F. Stepputat, eds., *States of Imagination:Ethnographic Explorations of the Postcolonial State*. Durham and London: Duke University Press.

Chanock, Martin. 1985. *Law, Custom and Social Order: The Colonial Experience in Malawi and Zambia*. Cambridge: Cambridge University Press.

Chanock, Martin. 1991. "Paradigms, Policies and Property: a Review of the customary law of land tenure." In K. Mann, and R. Roberts, eds. *Law in Colonial Africa*. London: James Currey.

Clarke, Kamari. 2008. *Transformations in Sovereignty: the Cultural Politics of Transnational Justice* (forthcoming).

Collier, Jane. 1975. "Legal Processes." *Annual Review of Anthropology* 4: 121–144.

Dembour, Marie-Bénédicte, and Emily Haslam. 2004. "Silencing Hearings? Victim-Witnesses at War Crimes Trials." *European Journal of International Law* 15: 151–177.

Ehrlich, E. 1975 [1936]. *Fundamental Principles of the Sociology of Law*. Trans. W. L. Moll. New York: Arno Press.

Eltringham, Nigel. 2004. *Accounting for Horror: Post-genocide Debates in Rwanda*. London: Pluto Press.

Geertz, Clifford. 1983. "Fact and Law in Comparative Perspective." In *Local Knowledge: Further Essays in Interpretative Anthropology*. New York: Basic Books.

Latour, Bruno. 2004. "Scientific Objects and Legal Objectivity." In Alain Pottage, and Martha Mundy, eds. *Law, Anthropology and the Constitution of the Social: Making Persons and Things*. Cambridge: Cambridge University Press, pp. 73–114.

Malinowski, Bronislav. 1926. *Crime and Custom in Savage Society*. London: Kegan Paul.

Mamdani, M. 2001. *When Victims Become Killers: Colonialism, Nativism and Genocide in Rwanda*. Princeton: Princeton University Press.

Mann, Kristin, and Richard Roberts, eds. 1991. *Law in Colonial Africa*. London: James Currey.

Merry, Sally Engle. 1988. "Legal Pluralism." *Law and Society Review* 22(5): 869–901.

Merry, Sally Engle. 1992. "Anthropology, Law and Transnational Processes" *Annual Review of Anthropology* 21: 357–379.

Merry, Sally Engle. 1997. "Legal Pluralism and Transnational Culture". In Richard A. Wilson. *Human Rights, Culture and Context: Anthropological Perspectives*. London: Pluto Press.

Merry, Sally Engle. 2003. "Rights Talk and the Experience of the Law: Implementing Women's Human Rights to Protection from Violence." *Human Rights Quarterly* 25(2): 343–381.

Merry, Sally Engle. 2006. "Transnational Human Rights and Local Activism: Mapping the Middle," *American Anthropologist* 108(1): 38–51.

Moore, Sally Falk. 1978. *Law as Process: An Anthropological Approach*. London: Routledge.

Moore, Sally Falk. 1986. *Social Facts and Fabrications: "Customary" Law on Kilimanjaro, 1880–1980*. Cambridge: Cambridge University Press.

Moore, Sally Falk. 1991. "From Giving and Lending to Selling: Property Transactions Reflecting Historical Changes on Kilimanjaro." In K. Mann, and R. Roberts, eds. *Law in Colonial Africa*. London: James Currey.

Moore, Sally Falk. 2001. "Certainties Undone: Fifty Turbulent Years of Legal Anthropology, 1949–1999." *Journal of the Royal Anthropological Institute*, 7(1): 95–116.

Moore, Sally Falk. 2005., ed. *Law and Anthropology: a Reader*. Oxford: Blackwell.

Riles, Annelise. 2000. *The Network Inside Out*. Ann Arbor: University of Michigan Press.

Riles, Annelise. 2006. "Anthropology, Human Rights, and Legal Knowledge: Culture in the Iron Cage." *American Anthropologist* 108(1): 52–65.

Ross, Fiona C. 2001 "Speech and Silence: Women's Testimony in the First Five Weeks of Public Hearings of the South African Truth and Reconciliation Commission." In V. Das, Arthur Kleinman, Margaret Lock,Mamphela Ramphele, and Pamela Reynolds, eds, *Remaking a World: Violence, Suffering and Recovery*. Berkeley: University of California Press.

Ross, Fiona C. 2002. *Bearing Witness: Women and the Truth and Reconciliation Commission in South Africa*. London: Pluto Press.

Rousseau, Jean-Jacques. 1968 [1762]. *The Social Contract*, trans. Maurice Cranston. London: Penguin.

Santos, B. de Sousa. 1987. "Law: a Map of Misreading; Toward a Postmodern Conception of Law.' *Journal of Law and Society* 14: 279–302.

Santos, B. de Sousa. 1995. *Toward a New Common Sense: Law, Science and Politics in the Paradigmatic Transition*. New York: Routledge.

Schapera, Isaac. 1938. *A Handbook of Tswana Law and Custom*. London: Oxford University Press.

Speed, Shannon, and Xochitl Leyva. 2008. "Human Rights in Chiapas: Global Discourses, Moral Grammars and Local Meanings." In Pedro Pitarch, Shannon Speed, and Xochitl Leyva, eds. *Human Rights in the Maya Region: Global Politics, Cultural Contentions, and Moral Engagements*. Durham, NC: Duke University Press (forthcoming).

Starr, June, and Mark Goodale, eds., 2002. *Practicing Ethnography in Law: New Dialogues, Enduring Methods*. New York: Palgrave St. Martin's Press.

Stoll, David. 1997. "To Whom Should We Listen? Human Rights Activism in Two Guatemalan Land Disputes.' In Richard A. Wilson, ed. *Human Rights, Culture and Context: Anthropological Perspectives*. London: Pluto Press.

Stoll, David. 2008. "Human Rights, Land Conflict, and Memories of the Violence in Ixil Country of Northern Quiché." In Pedro Pitarch, Shannon Speed, and Xochitl Leyva, eds., *Human Rights in the Maya Region: Global Politics, Cultural Contentions, and Moral Engagements*. Durham, NC: Duke University Press (forthcoming).

Tamanaha, Brian. 1993. "The Folly of the 'Social Scientific' Concept of Legal Pluralism." *Journal of Law and Society*, 20(2), pp. 192–217.

Tamanaha, Brian. 2000. "A Non-Essentialist Version of Legal Pluralism." *Journal of Law and Society*, 27, pp. 296–321.

Tesón, Fernando. 2005. "Liberal Security." In Richard Ashby Wilson, ed. *Human Rights in the "War on Terror"*. Cambridge: Cambridge University Press.

Touraine, Alain. 1995. *Critique of Modernity*. Oxford: Blackwell.

von Clausewitz, Carl. 1982 [1968]. *On War* (Penguin Classics. Abridged edn.). Harmondsworth: Penguin.

Wilson, Richard Ashby. 1997. *Human Rights, Culture and Context: Anthropological Perspectives*. London: Pluto Press.

Wilson, Richard Ashby. 2001. *The Politics of Truth and Reconciliation in South Africa: Legitimizing the Post-apartheid State*. Cambridge: Cambridge University Press.

Wilson, Richard Ashby. 2005. "Judging History: the Historical Record of the International Criminal Tribunal for the Former Yugoslavia" *Human Rights Quarterly*, 27(3), pp. 908–942.

INDEX

caracoles, Zapatistas, 163, 169, 181, 182
Catholic Relief Services, 33
CATW (Coalition against Trafficking in Women), 257
CEDAW (Convention on the Elimination of All Forms of Discrimination Against Women), 1–2, 260
Celerina (Zapatista), 181
Center for Constitutional Rights, 297
centralism, legal, 345, 346, 350
Chandler, David, 163
Chaney (California State Superior Court Judge), 311
Chanock, Martin, 346
Chaves, Margarita, 226–231
Cheney, Dick, 310
Chevron/Chevron-Texaco, 308, 309
Chiapas region, Mexico. *See also* Zapatista *Juntas de Buen Gobierno*
 resource wars, 120
 tourism and rights violations in, 119
children
 Bolivian security concerns regarding young people, 71
 Committee on the Rights of the Child, trafficking protocol overlap with, 253
 UN trafficking protocol and. *See under* United Nations Human Trafficking Protocol
 US reservations on ICCPR death penalty provisions, 279
 vulnerability, stress on, 196
China
 Burmese gas pipeline project and, 291
 prisoners' rights in, 119
 Tiananmen Square, 286
 Tibet, religious rights in, 29
Christian iconography of suffering, 198
"citizen security" (*seguridad ciudadana*), 59–60
Clarke, Kamari, 366
Cleveland, Sarah, 300
Coalition against Trafficking in Women (CATW), 257
COCOPA, 168, 183
collective decision making in Zapatista *Juntas*, 184–187
collective rights. *See also* indigenous peoples, rights of
 individual rights *vs.*, 118, 177
 Western jurisprudence, conflicting with, 208
Collier, Jane, 346
Colombia
 human trafficking in, 244, 266
 rights to indigenous culture in, 31, 198, 204–205
 cabildos (local governing and juridical authorities), 213–214, 226–231

constitution of Colombia, 211, 213–214
contested indigenous status of *colonos* (Putamayo case), 226–231
customary law, application of, 213–214, 215–226
drug trade and, 207
economic aid packages, 207–208
global/local betweenness in human rights and, 209–211
highly politicized contexts, application of traditional law in (Piñacué case), 221–226
historical background to mobilization of indigenes in Colombia, 205–209
interplay of indigenous law and authority with Western political concepts, 208, 231–235
legalization of human rights, 353
multiculturalism, effects of, 206, 211, 232
ongoing conflict, context of, 207, 213, 214, 220, 227, 235
otherness of indigenous custom, need to assert, 215
participation in political process, 212
"repugnance," concept of, 225, 232
serious crimes, ability of indigenous jurisdictions to deal with (Gembuel case), 215–221
shift from minority rights to rights as autonomous peoples, 206
state recognition, absence or dismissal of, 206
strategies for claiming, 210
use of human rights discourse, 211–214
vulnerability issues, 31, 198, 209
rubber tappers in, 44
colonialism
 bifurcation, 329–331
 exceptionalist doctrine arising from, 54
 human rights discourse, relationship to, 274, 275, 276
 legal pluralism and, 343–344, 346, 365
 mental, 125
 Spanish Crown and Mexican colonists, 121
 as violence, 43, 44
colonos in Patamayo, Colombia, contested indigenous status of, 226–231
Commission on Human Rights, UN, 3, 153
Committee on the Rights of the Child, trafficking protocol overlap with, 253
conceptual approach to human rights, 7
Confucius, 117
connotative and denotative power of rights in Bolivia, 134, 146–151
consensus decision-making evidenced in UN Human Trafficking Protocol, 250–251

372

ATCA (Alien Tort Claims Act), 296–297
corporate personhood, 302
international human rights regime, development of, 300–302
international law (law of nations) and, 296–300
jus cogens norms, 300–302, 305
post-Unocal suits brought under, 309–310
reform efforts, 308–309, 314
background to, 285–287
creation of transnational legal space for, 293–295
discursive ambivalence, 302–311
corporations creating, 303–304
states creating, 305–311
forced labor, 285–287, 305
foreign policy and foreign investment issues, 290–293
global/local betweenness in human rights, 315
globalization discourse and transnational discourse distinguished, 288–289
implications for transnational movements' relationship to human rights, 311–316
legalization of human rights, 354
neoliberal ideas, as challenge to, 291, 295
pro-democracy movement, 286–287, 289–290, 291–292
slaves, peasants treated as, 286, 287, 305
transition from national to transnational discourse, 289–293
TVPA (Torture Victim Protection Act), 298–299, 354

Valentine, David, 44
vernacularization, 280–281, 347, 348, 357–360
verticalization of conflicts, 355–356
victims and victimhood. *See* vulnerability
Vienna Convention on the Law of Treaties (1969), 301
violence, 27–29
Bolivian concepts of, 28, 46–47. *See also* "security and human rights tensions," under Bolivia
Colombian indigenous traditional law as, 215–221
Colombian *pueblos'* response to, 214
cultural factors, 42, 45
emotional, psychological, and financial dimensions, 42, 44
global/local betweenness, 47
invisible and made visible, 242, 263–266
legitimate and illegitimate, 42
narratives of, 44, 45

Nepali Buddhists' secularist claims, epistemic violence of, 28, 45–46, 81, 106, 107. *See also* Nepali Buddhists, use of human rights discourse by
perpetual threat of, 44
as physical injury or death, 41–42
practice of human rights and, 41, 45
problem of defining, 41–48
structural, 43–44
vulnerability, 30–32, 195–203
agency and, 195–197, 202
Christian iconography of, 198
Colombian indigenes and, 31, 198, 209. *See also* Colombia, rights to indigenous culture in
definition of human rights victims in terms of, 199
human trafficking and, 32, 195, 197, 200–203, 244, 247. *See also* United Nations human trafficking protocol
humanitarian *vs.* human rights concerns, 197–198
media representation of, 198
political neutrality, effects of, 198
refugees, depoliticized portrayal of, 196–197
of women and children, 196

war metaphor for political undertakings, 54
"War on Terror," 54, 310–311
Warren, Kay, ix, 32, 197, 200–203, 242, 353
Washington consensus, 50
Wastell, Sari, ix, 33, 196, 274, 280, 320, 359
Weber, Max, 97
wedding regime of Montesinos/SLI in Bolivia, 147–149, 159
Weimar Germany, 360
Western domination of rights movement, 118–120, 126–128, 233, 274
whipping as punishment under Colombian indigenous law, 215–221, 223
Wilson, Richard A., ix, 34–35, 233, 342, 348–349
Wilson, Rob, 15
Wiwa v. Royal Dutch Petroleum Co., 310
WLSA (Women and Law in Southern Africa Research Trust), 327
Wolf, Eric, 121
Women and Law in Southern Africa Research Trust (WLSA), 327
women's rights
in Arab countries, 281
CEDAW, 1–2, 260
domestic violence, 44, 46, 195, 357, 358
feminism
human trafficking protocol, different perspectives on, 258, 262

383

9 780521 683784